ERNEST FLAGG

American Monograph Series

General Editor: David G. De Long

Bertram Grosvenor Goodhue, Richard Oliver. 1983

The Almighty Wall, The Architecture of Henry Vaughan, William Morgan. 1983

On the Edge of the World, Four Architects in San Francisco at the Turn of the Century, Richard Longstreth. 1983

Mizner's Florida, American Resort Architecture, Donald W. Curl. 1984

Charles A. Platt, The Artist as Architect, Keith N. Morgan. 1985

Ernest Flagg, Beaux-Arts Architect and Urban Reformer, Mardges Bacon. 1986

Ernest Flagg at about the age of forty
(*King's Notable New Yorkers,* 1899, p. 391).

ERNEST FLAGG

Beaux-Arts Architect and Urban Reformer

MARDGES BACON

THE ARCHITECTURAL HISTORY FOUNDATION,
NEW YORK, NEW YORK
*THE MIT PRESS, CAMBRIDGE, MASSACHUSETTS,
and LONDON, ENGLAND*

Mardges Bacon is Associate Professor of Fine Arts and American Studies at Trinity College.

Library of Congress Cataloging in Publication Data

Bacon, Mardges.
    Ernest Flagg: beaux-arts architect and urban reformer.

    (American monograph series)
    Includes bibliographic references.
    1. Flagg, Ernest, 1857–1947. 2. Eclecticism in architecture—United States. I. Title. II. Series: American monograph series (Architectural History Foundation (New York, N.Y.))
NA737.F52B32   1986   720'.92'4   85-80
ISBN 0-262-02222-2
All photographs are by the author unless otherwise credited

This book is made possible, in part, with public funds from the New York State Council on the Arts.
Additionally, the foundation gratefully acknowledges Lila Acheson Wallace's contribution to *Ernest Flagg, Beaux-Arts Architect and Urban Reformer.*

Designed by Gilbert Etheredge

Contents

TO R.E.B.

Acknowledgments

This book was based on my dissertation, completed in 1978 for Brown University. I owe a special debt of gratitude to William H. Jordy, who shaped each chapter with his insights; my appreciation for his interest in and commitment to this study can never adequately be expressed. Kermit Champa and Howard Chudacoff were especially helpful in the formative stages of the research. I am indebted also to the late Alan Burnham whose work on Ernest Flagg preceded mine, and to Adolf K. Placzek for his enduring support of this project. I am extremely grateful to Neil Levine for his incisive criticism of my dissertation, particularly with respect to French developments. I owe special thanks to Thomas Fisher whose many observations helped to shape the final manuscript. I am indebted also to Henry-Russell Hitchcock who read the manuscript and offered several important suggestions. Two individuals who read portions of the manuscript, Samuel Haber and Sarah Bradford Landau, deserve my warmest thanks and appreciation.

Many members of the Flagg family gave their support and encouragement, besides contributing to the research. I wish to thank the late Mrs. Ernest Flagg for making the Flagg Family Papers available for my study and for sharing with me many recollections of her husband's architectural career and their family life. Ernest Flagg's daughter, Mrs. John Melcher, also was especially generous and helpful. Mrs. Anthony Szápáry, a distant cousin, assisted me with research. A special note of thanks is reserved for George McKay Schieffelin, a grandnephew of Ernest Flagg, who shared with me his knowledge of the family history and of the Scribner commissions, and for Charles Scribner III for his continuing interest in this study.

Without aid from the staffs of a number of libraries, archives, institutions, and companies, this book would not have been possible. I am indebted to Angela Giral, Janet Parks, and Herbert Mitchell of Avery Library, Columbia University, to Mary Ison of the Library of Congress, to Christopher Hail of the Frances Loeb Library, Harvard University, and to Ralph Emerick, Peter

Knapp, Patricia Bunker, and Stephen Wolff of Trinity College Library, Hartford. Arthur Breton of the Archives of American Art and Steven Miller of the Museum of the City of New York were especially helpful. Among the many individuals who assisted me with historical research on various Flagg commissions, I am most grateful to Katherine M. Kovacs, Archivist, The Corcoran Gallery of Art; Emmanuel Mesagna of the Fire Department of the City of New York; Brother Roger Chingas, F.S.C., La Salle Military Academy; William W. Jeffries, Director, and James W. Cheevers, Senior Curator, The Museum, United States Naval Academy; Shirley Zavin, Marjorie Pearson, and James T. Dillon of the New York City Landmarks Preservation Commission; Herbert S. Bailey, Jr., of Princeton University Press; Andrew McGowan of St. Luke's Hospital; and Betty Hope and William L. Brunner of The Singer Company.

I am much indebted to a number of individuals who have contributed their advice and expertise: Stanford Anderson, Wayne Andrews, Curtis Channing Blake, the late René de Blonay, Mosette Glaser Broderick, Robert Bruegmann, Richard Chafee, John A. Chewning, Robert B. Davies, Arthur Cort Holden, the late Kenneth Kaiser, Peter Kemble, Carol Herselle Krinsky, François LeCoeur, Roy Lubove, Robert U. Massey, Helen D. Perkins, Jason L. Potek, Catha Grace Rambusch, J. Ronald Spencer, Albert Homer Swanke, Richard C. Tilton, Richard Trenner, David Van Zanten, Michel Vernes, James L. West, and Rudolf Winkes. I would also like to express my gratitude to David G. De Long, general editor of the American Monograph Series, and to Victoria Newhouse, Julianne Griffin, Karen Banks, and Jo Ellen Ackerman of the Architectural History Foundation for their editorial assistance.

Research for and preparation of this manuscript were made possible by a travel grant from Brown University and two grants from Trinity College: a Junior Faculty Research grant (1979) and a Mellon Fund for the Eighties grant (1982–83). Research in New York, Washington, and Paris was made possible also by the generous assistance of Simon and Ursula Hemans, Melanie Tarkenton, William H. Williams, and Colette M. and Marie-Pierre Landry. I am especially grateful to Paniporn Phiansunthon and Nancy Sowa who assisted in the preparation of the manuscript, and David Bohl who printed many of the photographs.

A final expression of gratitude is extended warmly to the many colleagues, friends, and family members who have followed the progress of this book. I would especially like to thank Ruth E. Bacon, Ruth Anne Argento, William H. Bacon III, and the late Rear Admiral Alexander C. Husband.

Foreword

Prior to the appearance of this study, those who had known anything at all about Ernest Flagg tended to identify him only with his Singer Tower in the downtown financial district of New York City. When completed in 1908, its vaguely mansarded pinnacle briefly existed as the tallest skyscraper in the world. But its glory lasted a mere eighteen months before Napoleon Le Brun's tower for the Metropolitan Life Insurance Company, modeled on Venice's Campanile, went higher. Shortly thereafter, Cass Gilbert's Gothicized Woolworth Building eclipsed them both when completed in 1913, and held the record for height for better than a decade. These three towers were the most prominent pre-World War I progenitors of the towered skyline that came to characterize Manhattan in the 1920s and 1930s.

As other towers rose around it, however, the Singer rather faded from public consciousness — more so, it would seem, than the other towers, which were more vivid as tower images. It may have been that the bulbous quality intrinsic to the mansard form was sufficiently incongruous as a tower climax that it eventually came to seem quaint; the more so because of the varied puncture of its curved, sloping, copper skin with bull's-eye, arched, and pedimented openings, all framed with knobby moldings and topped by an equally encrusted cupola. Then, too, this ornamented mansard was so Parisian in quality that it may have appeared somewhat alien to New York.

Not that the Singer Tower was exactly ignored or forgotten. Rather, with time, it became one of those monuments that was simply *there,* perhaps reassuringly so. It was an extraordinarily slender tower, in a proportion of width to height of one to seven. Its masonry-walled corners in red brick (concealing structural cross bracing), bound round with widely spaced bands of white stone, enframed tall metal arches filled with windows on all four faces of the tower. One might imagine it as a proudly corseted female image — for if the Singer Tower could be identified with either gender, it was surely female —

topped by the climactic Edwardian bonnet. For those who took the trouble to look at it, it was a tower of decided character.

Then, in 1967, the original record was inverted. The Singer Tower became the tallest building, up to that time, ever to be demolished. It and a neighbor went down to make room for Skidmore, Owings & Merrill's metal and glass box-with-plaza for U.S. Steel. At the time of its destruction there was the inevitable flurry of regretful publicity, especially for its rediscovered lobby with a double row of low domes, originally glazed, which marked each of the structural bays of the building. Still, on the whole, the tower disappeared with surprisingly little fuss.

Just before its demise, Flagg's work began to be rediscovered in other ways. In the late fifties, a group of architects scouting lower Broadway when this was still virgin territory for architectural discovery came across Flagg's precursor for the Singer Tower just below Prince Street, his twelve-story Singer Loft Building (1902–4). In 1957, *Architectural Forum* recorded the expedition for posterity. Here was a comparable elevational format: an enframed central arch, filled with windows, and rising the full height of the building, but handled far more boldly than the similar motif in the Tower. Panels of red terra cotta infilling an exposed metal lattice comprised the frame for the arch, which was filled with tiers of recessed floor-to-ceiling metal doors, each of which opened onto long narrow metal balconies bridging the width of this center-piece. The mix of terra cotta and glass with the elegantly ornamented open-work of the metal frame was, once more, Parisian, recalling that city's turn-of-the-century storefronts and exposition buildings. This discovery, in turn, encouraged the reexamination of Scribner's Book Store (1912–13) on Fifth Avenue, a little down from Rockefeller Center.

Then, when the revival of interest in the Ecole des Beaux-Arts occurred, especially with the exhibition of Ecole drawings at the Museum of Modern Art in 1975, Flagg came to the fore yet again. This time it was the rediscovery of a series of three articles by him in *Architectural Record* in 1894, which are probably the best early accounts we have of the nature of training at the Ecole des Beaux-Arts by an American architect who attended the school at a time when it represented the pinnacle in preparation for anyone ambitious for success in the profession. The revival of interest in the training and ideals of the Ecole des Beaux-Arts also brought renewed attention to Flagg's monumental buildings, the best-known of which are probably his Corcoran Gallery in Washington, D.C. (1892–97), and most of the campus for the Naval Academy in Annapolis (1898–1908).

Clearly, here was an architect whose work exemplified, to a degree matched perhaps by that of no other American, the full range of what the Ecole des Beaux-Arts had to teach. On the one hand, Flagg had absorbed the rationalistic side of nineteenth-century Ecole education, as exemplified in the work of Henri Labrouste and the architects of the so-called *Néo-Grec* movement of which he was a part, together with that of Eugène Viollet-le-Duc. On the other hand, he embraced its monumental side as this was most conspicuously epitomized for the late nineteenth century in Charles Garnier's Opera. Of all the Americans from his generation for whom study at the Ecole des Beaux-Arts marked the mecca of architectural training, Ernest Flagg would seem to be the paradigm.

Hence the importance of this groundbreaking study. It opens with an account of the architectural situation in Paris around 1890, when Flagg attended the Ecole des Beaux-Arts, and goes on to demonstrate how Flagg extended and adapted his French training in his American practice. But Flagg's career has the additional interest of unexpected venturesomeness. Most readers coming to Flagg for the first time will be surprised to learn of his importance in the movement for low-cost housing during the first decades of the twentieth century. He advocated a pioneering scheme to counteract the deleterious effects of the crowding skyscraper towers, which were already apparent before the completion of the Singer Tower. He developed novel designs for suburban houses that combined plainness of detail with a harmonic geometric system. He realized the first automobile parking garage of architectural consequence in New York — and possibly in the United States. All of these projects had a French connection.

Hence the fascination of his career. There is an idiosyncratic originality about his work that dots it with unexpected episodes. But there is the paradigmatic quality about it, too, that marks it as a (possibly *the*) consummate exemplar of the full range of Ecole des Beaux-Arts training and ideals in the United States.

William H. Jordy

Introduction

During the Progressive Era from 1890 to 1917, Ernest Flagg addressed many central issues in architecture. The application of French Beaux-Arts theory and design to American building, the planning of large institutions, the design of skyscrapers, and the reform of tenement house building in New York City were all within the wide scope of his accomplishments. Flagg saw himself as a rugged individualist in this era of invention and reform. "If Progress is to be made," he wrote in 1922, "some one must blaze the way."[1]

With no formal architectural training in America, Flagg studied at the Ecole des Beaux-Arts in Paris. When he returned in the 1890s to advance the cause of Beaux-Arts architecture in America, he was criticized for his Francophilic attitude toward architecture. "We are certainly ourselves very far from that humble attitude toward our French 'betters' which Mr. Flagg recommends, and we trust such unworthy humility will not be cultivated among us," wrote the editors of *Architectural Review* (Boston) in 1894.[2] Although many leading architects, including Charles F. McKim, John M. Carrère, Thomas Hastings, William Boring, and George B. Post, privately appreciated Flagg's talents, they spoke of him cautiously in public. Such critics as Montgomery Schuyler and Russell Sturgis virtually ignored Flagg's work with the exception of his Singer commissions. Only Harry Desmond, editor of *Architectural Record* and author of the introduction to his journal's retrospective of 1902, "The Works of Ernest Flagg," was a committed supporter. H. Van Buren Magonigle's extensive historical survey of American architecture in 1934, "A Half Century of Architecture," makes only one brief allusion to Flagg.[3] Fiske Kimball's *American Architecture* of 1928 overlooks him altogether. By contrast, Flagg was honored in France early in his career with a silver medal at the Universal Exposition of 1900.[4]

In spite of his efforts to establish new directions in architecture, Flagg remained an outsider to the New York establishment. He was excluded from and even punished by the profession for what McKim called his "bad manners."[5] Flagg was fiercely competitive, shrewd, and reclusive — factors not likely to encourage personal and professional rapport with clients and colleagues. He advocated his strong convictions on Beaux-Arts architecture and on the need for urban reform, promoting them through family patronage, extensive writings, and sheer will. Not until the end of a long career did Flagg finally achieve the professional status and recognition he had long sought.

Flagg's diversified architectural career spanned more than forty years. To convey the broad dimensions of this career, the present study is organized into two parts. The first part is devoted to Flagg's early career and his Beaux-Arts education, the theory and practice of French architecture during the early Third Republic — essential in understanding the "Frenchness" of Flagg's personal style — his leadership in the Beaux-Arts movement in America, and the turbulent aspects of his patronage and practice. The second part addresses discrete architectural problems: traditional Beaux-Arts institutions and building types, domestic architecture, commercial and utilitarian building, skyscraper imagery and reform, model tenements and other forms of urban housing, and modular design applied to small stone houses. To each building type, Flagg brought fresh insight.

Part 1

CHAPTER ONE

Early Career

IN THE WINTER and early spring of 1945, during the closing months of the Second World War, New York architects paid a long-overdue tribute to Ernest Flagg. He was eighty-eight years old and had suffered a heart attack at his office the previous July. On February 14, the New York Chapter of the American Institute of Architects (A.I.A.) held a dinner in his honor at the Architectural League of New York and gave him a citation.[1] Now in the closing years of his life and long forgotten by such organizations, Flagg was suddenly brought out of the shadow and formally recognized by the profession. Flagg's house and office at 109 and 111 East 40th Street were adjacent to the headquarters of both the Architectural League and the New York Chapter of the A.I.A. According to Arthur Holden, then Chapter president, "We unearthed that he was just down the street and I went to call on him. He was working at the drawing board."[2] Flagg had outlived all of his close rivals. A younger generation of A.I.A. members, not threatened by his success or his personality, wished to honor him.

When Flagg appeared at the A.I.A. dinner that February, no one had seen him in years. Younger architects marveled at his activity and vigor.[3] "He cut a very graceful figure," said Holden. "Everyone was very taken with him."[4] Regarding Flagg as an example to follow, rather than as a contentious figure to exclude or ignore, the A.I.A. recognized his contributions to the profession: "He has met every problem of his long career with courage, imagination and energy."[5] Ralph Walker, another A.I.A. member, later insisted that they ought to have nominated Flagg for a gold medal.[6] Flagg generated so much enthusiasm that Hugh Ferriss and Chester Price, the current and past presidents respectively of the Architectural League, arranged for an exhibition of his work at the League headquarters in March and April.

The League also honored Flagg with a luncheon that spring. There

Ferriss and George Licht, first winner of the Paris Prize, gave talks and Flagg read his paper, "A Fish Story: An Autobiographical Sketch of the Education of an Architect."[7] Most people assumed that it would be about his years of study at the Ecole des Beaux-Arts in Paris. However, Flagg chose to discuss not his formal education but his experience. It is from Flagg's paper that we learn much about his family, his childhood, and his early career.

Flagg's father, Jared Bradley Flagg (1820–99), was a clergyman, a portrait painter, and an academician; he is best remembered today for a biography of his father's half brother, Washington Allston, *The Life and Letters of Washington Allston* (1892).[8] But Jared Bradley's youth, like that of his son Ernest, was nomadic, entrepreneurial, and lacking in formal education. At the age of eleven he left school to become a shop clerk.[9] A year later, in 1832, he "took up the serious study of art" in New Haven with his older brother George Whiting Flagg, a genre painter who had studied with Washington Allston.[10] As a teenager, Jared Bradley began to exhibit portraits at the National Academy of Design in New York. In 1837 he showed a portrait of Captain Leonidas Polk, a Protestant Episcopal clergyman and soldier, and the following year exhibited one of his father, Henry Collins Flagg, who was then mayor of New Haven.[11] Determined to make a living through portrait painting and to pay off "many and pressing" small debts, Jared Bradley began his career as an itinerant.[12] In the space of four years, he moved consecutively to Bridgeport, New York City, Newark, Hartford, Cincinnati, Boston, and back to Hartford.[13] During this time he was aided greatly by the patronage of relatives better situated than his immediate family. His sister, Rachel Moore Gwynne, of Cincinnati, provided useful introductions. His brother Henry, a lieutenant in the Navy stationed in Boston, secured for him portrait commissions from officers there. While in Boston, Jared Bradley consulted Washington Allston on the problem of studio lighting but never studied formally with him.[14] In 1839 he settled in Hartford and two years later married an orphan girl of eighteen, Sarah Montague.[15] But their marriage was brief. In 1844, two years after the birth of their son, Montague, Sarah died.[16]

According to Jared Bradley, an artist during the mid-nineteenth century might earn professional success from an early age, but his personal life was still suspect. "Immorality and dissipated habits were associated in the public mind with the life of an artist," he later recalled in his autobiography. Even though during his brief marriage Jared Bradley had "conducted himself as to disappoint the public apprehension," he felt that his career as a painter was a social liability. Jared Bradley wished to remarry. He also wished his professional career to keep pace with his ambition. "Contact with cultivated people," he wrote in his autobiography, "quickened in me a desire to supply my lack of education." Associations with clergymen "encourage[d] in me noble purposes, and a desire for intellectual improvement," he continued. All this led him to a remedial course of study at Trinity College, Hartford, and later with private tutors of theology in preparation for the ministry.[17]

In 1846, during this period of study, Jared Bradley married Louisa Hart who, like his first wife at the time of their marriage, was only eighteen. She was the daughter of Dr. Samuel Hart, a physician from New Britain, Connecticut. Their first child, Charles Noel Flagg, was born in 1848. That year Jared Bradley established a residence in New York. He pursued his painting career there, was elected to the National Academy of Design, and continued to prepare for the ministry.[18] In 1854 he was ordained to the Episcopal Church and was subsequently called to parishes in Stamford and Birmingham, Connecticut.[19] The following year he began an eight-year tenure as rector of the fashionable Grace Church in Brooklyn Heights, New York.[20] In 1857 he was awarded an M.A. degree from Trinity College and in 1863 an S.T.D. (Doctor of Sacred Theology) degree from Columbia University.[21] His two degrees, however, were both honorary. During eight years of residence in Brooklyn Heights, Louisa Hart Flagg gave birth to four of their six children: Jared (1853), Ernest (1857), Washington Allston (1860), and Louisa (1862).

Despite his social and professional status at Grace Church, Jared Bradley felt compromised and in 1863 — ironically the same year he received his honorary divinity degree from Columbia — he resigned his parish. But there are two versions of his resignation. By his own account some years later, Jared Bradley maintained that as rector he was forced to ingratiate himself to his wealthy parishioners, and he particularly resented the conservative bias of a parish that eschewed any liberal views on religion. During his tenure at Grace Church, he later confessed, "I did not find . . . courage to investigate upon lines leading outside the walls and defences of the Church. . . . A man to be free in the pulpit should be, as Saint Paul was, pecuniarily independent of those to whom he preaches."[22] Thus, as Jared Bradley later recollected, "enfeebled in health and oppressed with Parochial burdens, I resigned my Parish and fell back on my art for the support of my family."[23] He was now willing to accept the career that he had once branded a "social liability."

But Jared Bradley's letter of resignation, the Vestry Minutes of Grace Church, and published accounts differ considerably from his later recollection. They document a second version in which his wife's ill health, rather than his own, caused him to resign and move his family in the late fall of 1863 to the purer climate of Minnesota. The break was amicable.[24] The family remained at least six months in Saint Paul where Jared Bradley continued to preach, and then they returned to New York. Apparently, the climate of Minnesota was not sufficiently restorative to Jared Bradley's wife, for Louisa Hart Flagg died on January 18, 1867, only a few months after giving birth to their sixth child, Rosalie. Two years later Jared Bradley entered into another marriage, his third, to Josephine Bond of Cincinnati.[25]

To support his family Jared Bradley Flagg devoted the remaining thirty years of his life to painting, scholarship, and speculative businesses with family members in which his son, Ernest, took an increasingly active role. In public, he combined art and business, the spiritual and the material, with Protestant and capitalist vigor that late-nineteenth-century America applauded. In private, he became an atheist, which may account for his later explanation of his resignation from Grace Church. He exhibited regularly at the National Academy of Design and was widely recognized in New York and New England for his portraiture.[26] At the Philadelphia Centennial in 1876 Jared Bradley exhibited a painting of Commodore Cornelius Vanderbilt.[27] He was also a painter of narrative works and "ideal pieces"; his painting "Hester Prynne" was exhibited at the National Academy of Design in 1895 and placed on sale for the heady sum of $2,000.[28] In spite of his largely self-taught background in art, Jared Bradley continued a family tradition. Other artists in the Flagg family were his older brothers, Henry Collins (1811–62) and George Whiting (1816–98), his first son, Montague, (1842–1915), and most successful of all, his second son, the Hartford painter, Charles Noel Flagg (1848–1916).[29]

Thus, from the sacred to the profane, Jared Bradley transferred his allegiance from the institution of the Church to the life of art, gradually establishing a strong axis between New England and New York in the worlds of religion and art. His son Ernest, who grew up in New York and Connecticut, thus learned to view his family as one inextricably bound to the history and culture of New England but tied also to the promise of New York. In 1926 Ernest Flagg culminated a genealogical study of his family with a scholarly publication entitled somewhat pretentiously *Genealogical Notes on the Founding of New England: My Ancestors Part in that Undertaking.* There Ernest meticulously traced his family roots to Thomas Flegg (the earlier spelling) who had immigrated to America from Norfolk, England, in 1637 and settled in Watertown, Massachusetts.[30] By documenting his family's genealogical history, Ernest wished to establish the preeminence of his ancestry within the intellectual, religious, merchant, and governing elite of New England. To suggest a continuum between that distinguished lineage and Flagg's own generation, he included in the book photographs of his six brothers and sisters.

With ancestors among the gentry of New England, Ernest perceived the Flagg family as American aristocracy. Even if their immediate circumstances were limited, the Flaggs were ambitious. They were linked by marriage to two prominent New York families, the Vanderbilts and the Scribners.[31] Ernest's first cousin, Alice Moore Gwynne, married Cornelius Vanderbilt II (1843–99) in 1867. During his childhood, Ernest overheard family discussions of the match. At first Alice "would not have him," Ernest later recalled of Cornelius Vanderbilt. But family pressure helped to change her mind. Alice's mother was "much in favor of the match, for although the Vanderbilts might not be in our social sphere," Flagg was later to recollect of the discussions, "they were very rich and their position would doubtless improve."[32] A more socially prestigious liaison at the time was the marriage in 1882 of Flagg's sister, Louisa, to Charles Scribner (1854–1930). Ernest's well-established relatives eventually became his patrons: the Vanderbilts with their large fortune and influence, and the Scribners with their publishing house and position in New York society. The enduring support of the Vanderbilts and Scribners was central to Flagg's education and architectural career, since most of his commissions were the result of patronage rather than competitions. Like other architects of his generation and social background, Ernest might have confined himself exclusively to commissions of a lavish nature, were it not for an extraordinary turn of events which marked his young career.

Ernest was born in Brooklyn on February 6, 1857, two years after his father began his rectorship at Grace Church. When Ernest was nine, his mother died. Under his stepmother's influence, he and the older Flagg children were sent away to school or left to their own resources while the younger ones were farmed out to relatives. Although Ernest was privileged to attend a number of private schools, among them the Episcopal Academy of Connecticut in Cheshire, Hopkins Grammar School of New Haven, and the Columbia Grammar School in New York City, he admitted that his formal education lacked both continuity and discipline. In his words, "we had moved about so much that, at different times, I had attended ten different schools and never learned much in any of them."[33] In effect, Ernest's early years, like those of his father, were unstable and uprooted.

"A Fish Story" is a picturesque account of the circumstances that led young Ernest to embark on a series of businesses when, according to him, "times were hard for the family."[34] But what is "fishy" about Ernest's story is that his poverty may have been more mythical than actual. Even though his father's painting career in the 1870s and 1880s may not have been lucrative, it supplied his sons with sufficient capital to invest in a succession of small businesses.[35] Written when he was eighty-eight years old, Ernest's "Fish Story" may have been intended to identify its author with the contemporaneous fictional hero, Horatio Alger.

In 1872 at the age of fifteen Ernest, like his older brother Jared before him, became an office boy on Wall Street. The Flagg brothers thus left behind the paternalism of private boys' schools with their methods of forced study. Two years later, and with the backing of their father's capital, Ernest and Jared engaged in what they believed was a promising business selling salt codfish at the Fulton Fish Market. Ernest kept the account books. In 1876 they rented commercial space in a building at the corner of Washington and Warren streets.[36] During their years in the codfish business, the Flagg brothers moved to several locations on the Lower West Side. Until they could afford to rent rooms uptown, they also lived in this commercial and tenement district, often sleeping on the top floor of the building in which their business was located. During these years the two young merchants encountered many difficulties. Nonetheless, Ernest eventually bought out his brother's share in the equity, parlayed his assets, and began a new career as an oleomargarine entrepreneur. In the days when butter was the only acceptable spread and the sale of oleomargarine was illegal in America, Ernest found a market for his product in England. But in March 1881, according to a report in the *New York Times,* the business failed and Ernest was in debt to his creditors.[37]

Ernest's efforts to reverse his financial upset, combined with a desire to rise socially as well as economically, resulted in a series of events that would be crucial to his future career as an architect. He entered the arena of land and apartment building speculation at a time when New York was experiencing dynamic change. It was a family operation, undertaken by Ernest, his brother Jared, and his father, who financed the venture. Continuing a tradition established by his father, who retained his clerical title, Ernest pursued a life of free enterprise encouraged by the Protestant ethic and the forces of capitalism that permeated late-nineteenth-century America.[38]

During the early 1880s New York real estate developed an entirely new pattern of urban housing, coupled with land distribution and expanding boundaries of residential districts. The apartment house, long a solution to high-density living in Europe, had only recently been introduced by building speculators into New York City.[39] The need for larger tracts of land on which to build caused promoters to buy vacant lots, especially in the West Side blocks adjacent to Central Park, then considered the upper reaches of Manhattan. They also purchased parcels of land in the already established mid-town residential areas where existing single-family houses were demolished to make way for new construction. In the early 1880s, architects and builders specialized in the design of new apartment blocks, some of which reached the height of ten or twelve stories. Furthermore, with the introduction of elevators and fireproofing, the advantages of high-rise apartment dwelling had become attractive to the affluent. "Living at the top of an absolutely fire-proof building," suggested the editors of *Record and Guide* in 1883, "is as safe as living at the bottom; the air is better; the prospect is wider."[40]

The scale of these apartment houses impressed New Yorkers who were accustomed to single-family dwellings or to the so-called French flats, modest apartment houses of four or five stories that Richard Morris Hunt had introduced in Manhattan with his diminutive Stuyvesant apartments at 142 East 18th Street (1869–70; demolished). As the scale of new apartment houses increased, so did the speculator's risk. The cost of both ground and building for a major apartment project might easily exceed $1 million.[41] Thus, to facilitate the financing of these operations, a method of cooperative ownership by joint stock companies was devised. The system owed its origins to Philip G. Hubert (1830–1911), a Frenchman who had come to America in 1849 and devoted the latter part of his career to solving the problems associated with multiple dwellings.[42] In 1879 Hubert organized the first land and building improvement society based on cooperative principles, which he called "The Hubert Home Association" or "Home Club."[43] But according to Ernest Flagg, Hubert's cooperative plan worked successfully for the first time when in 1880–81 Jared Bradley Flagg and several of his friends helped to back the Rembrandt apartment house at 154 West 57th Street (demolished), located next to Carnegie Hall.[44]

During the 1880s, long after his resignation from the ministry, Jared Bradley Flagg promoted cooperative apartments designed by Hubert's firm, Hubert, Pirsson & Co.[45] The firm's largest apartment complex, financed by cooperative arrangement, was the Central Park apartments or Navarro buildings (1881–85; demolished), named after their codeveloper, Jose F. de Navarro. Consisting of eight semidetached buildings, the Navarro was located on Seventh Avenue between 58th and 59th streets.[46] The Navarro's amenities were innovative. "These houses are very much in advance, in size, construction, ventilation, light and convenience, of anything built in this city," proclaimed the editors of *Building* in 1883.[47] Following the principles of the Home Club, the speculators formed an independent company or "Club" for each of the eight apartment houses. Similar to present arrangements for cooperative apartment houses, ownership was "subject only to such restrictions and charges for service, heating, and other contingent expenses, as are necessary for the comfort and convenience of all."[48]

The immediate success of the Navarro proved that cooperative financing held clear advantages for speculator and apartment owner.[49] The speculator preferred joint ownership because it distributed the risk and gave an immediate return on his investment. Owner-occupants favored the cooperative scheme because it gave them a share in the equity. Furthermore, in the 1880s the social acceptability of occupant ownership rested upon the distinction between a tenement and an apartment. Owner-occupancy was possible only for apartments.[50]

Influenced by French example, Hubert introduced to New York with the Rembrandt and the Navarro not only the cooperative dwelling but also the "duplex" plan.[51] Hubert's duplex plan divided apartment units into two sections: the front, containing the main rooms (drawing room, dining room, library, and principal bedrooms), had high ceilings; the rear, "duplexed" into two stories for kitchens and servants' quarters, had low ceilings.[52] The Rembrandt duplex apartment house and studios contained six stories in front and nine stories at the rear.[53]

Given his father's involvement in the Rembrandt's Home Club scheme, Ernest had the opportunity to observe the development closely. He saw defects in Hubert's duplex system, especially its lack of economy and difficulty of circulation. Ernest devised a modified plan whereby each unit might function as an autonomous two-story apartment with its own interior staircase similar to a small house. The lower story was slightly higher than the bedroom floor above it.[54] The building employed a skip-stop elevator system with a landing on every other floor. This simplified the circulation and reduced the number of corridors. In 1891 the editors of *American Architect* recognized the merits of the improved duplex and praised Ernest Flagg, "an amateur of remarkable talent," for his "ingenuity."[55]

Ernest promoted his duplex plan, acting as developer for two eleven-story fireproof apartment houses organized on the cooperative principles of the Home Club.[56] Convinced of the advantages of this double-story arrangement,

12

Hubert, Pirsson & Co. became the architects of the first building to use the improved duplex, a Home Club-financed apartment house at 121 Madison Avenue (1882–83).[57] It contained only five duplex apartments, each one occupying two floors.[58] Yet the editors of *Record and Guide* proclaimed this apartment house the tallest such structure ever built.[59] Hubert, Pirsson & Co.

1. Charles W. Clinton. The Knickerbocker (demolished), 245 Fifth Avenue, New York City, 1882–83 (New York Public Library).

had been swift to adopt Ernest Flagg's duplex scheme and to claim it as their own.[60]

The second of the two apartment houses, which Ernest Flagg developed and the Home Club financed, was the Knickerbocker at 245 Fifth Avenue (1882–83; demolished). Considerably more elegant than 121 Madison Avenue, it was designed by the New York architect, Charles W. Clinton (Fig. 1).[61] Clinton accommodated Flagg's duplex plan to a brick elevation of stone and terra cotta, with ornamental iron including one of the earliest metal and glass marquees in New York. The Knickerbocker's high quality of workmanship was due to its builder, David H. King, Jr., also known for his construction of George B. Post's Mills Building. The Flaggs financed the project through the formation of a joint stock company, the Knickerbocker Apartment Company.[62] The cost, including both ground and building, was reported at nearly $1 million.

Attracted by the quality of the workmanship, fireproof construction, flexible plan, and financial incentives, distinguished buyers took up residence at the Knickerbocker. They included the merchant-politician Isaac Bell and the banker James T. Woodward.[63] New Yorkers in the 1880s were quick to recognize the manifest advantages of cooperative ownership. To Ernest Flagg, the economy, efficiency, and luxury of the duplex cooperative apartment seemed obvious.

"A Fish Story" does not account for one ambitious but aborted project which Ernest, Jared, and their father hoped would prove as successful, both architecturally and financially, as their previous efforts with 121 Madison Avenue and the Knickerbocker. If two cooperative duplex apartments of modest dimensions were immediate successes in the area just north of Madison Square, how much more promising would be a truly large-scale venture, similar to the Central Park apartments, developed on the newly fashionable Fifth Avenue Plaza. In December 1882, Jared Bradley Flagg paid $850,000 cash for a large parcel of land on the site of the present-day Plaza Hotel in the vicinity of the Central Park apartments then under construction.[64] The parcel containing twelve city lots extended 200 feet on the west side of the Fifth Avenue Plaza, 125 feet on West 58th Street, and 175 feet on West 59th Street. Identified in a prospectus of the Plaza scheme as "Promoter," Ernest Flagg developed the project through subscriptions to a joint stock company, the Fifth Avenue Plaza House Club. The prospectus of the Fifth Avenue Plaza Apartments, as they were to be called, also indicated that while William A. Potter served as architect, he received assistance with "interior plans prepared by Ernest Flagg," presumably because some units were to be duplex apartments.[65] Special amenities for the Fifth Avenue Plaza Apartments included fireproof construction and a restaurant. Although the prospectus specified an "open court," it contained no plan.[66] Critical of the Flaggs as promoters, the editors of *Record and Guide* explained that "a clergyman and his sons . . . had made a great deal of money in previous schemes, especially in two well-known apartment houses, one on Fifth Avenue and another on Madison. They would have succeeded in the Plaza enterprise in all probability, but their own share of the benefits was to be so extravagant that the would-be investors with them couldn't see it."[67] The demise of the Fifth Avenue Plaza House Club due to financial collapse was only symptomatic of a whole range of social and legal issues — including "keeping out the undesirables," as one account later put it — which doomed the further development of the duplex cooperative apartment house from the mid-1880s until the first decade of the twentieth century when duplexes became popular again.[68] In any event, the majority of New Yorkers who could afford first-class apartments in the mid-1880s still preferred single-family houses.[69] Even Ernest Flagg, who lived in the Knickerbocker from the 1890s until about 1905, was later to eschew the purchase of cooperative apartments.[70]

Very little is known of Flagg's career during the five years that intervened between the failure of the Fifth Avenue Plaza House Club in 1883 and his departure for Paris in 1888. In "A Fish Story," however, Ernest states that his two successful apartment house schemes had earned him "some reputation as a planner."[71] This, in turn, led his cousin by marriage, Cornelius Vanderbilt, to seek his advice regarding possible future alterations to Vanderbilt's then recently completed residence on Fifth Avenue between West 57th and 58th streets (1880–82; demolished), designed by George B. Post.[72]

According to Flagg, Vanderbilt had been "very much dissatisfied with the plan of his house . . . what he really wanted was more and larger rooms."[73] At his cousin's request, Flagg drew up plans which consolidated several existing small rooms into larger ones and proposed alterations calling for the annexation of space occupied by the adjacent houses along Fifth Avenue up to 58th Street. That idea seemed most satisfactory to Vanderbilt. But it was not until the early 1890s that he acquired the adjoining property and commissioned George B. Post to undertake extensive remodeling, with Post's former teacher, Richard Morris Hunt, assisting in the design of the tower to crown the Fifth Avenue front (1892–94).[74] Although Flagg's plans for the addition never were executed, Vanderbilt saw promise in his young cousin's architectural abilities. As a result, so Flagg later recalled, Vanderbilt "told me that I ought to become an architect and that if I would go to Paris and enter the Ecole des Beaux-Arts, he would pay the cost."[75]

Apart from his general awareness of the reputation which the Ecole des Beaux-Arts enjoyed in America in the 1880s, Cornelius Vanderbilt had personal reasons for specifying the Ecole. By the 1880s, the greatest recipient of Vanderbilt patronage (primarily from his brother, William Kissam Vanderbilt) was Richard Morris Hunt who in 1846 was the first American to attend the Ecole.[76] Furthermore, when Cornelius Vanderbilt later remodeled his Fifth Avenue house, he asked Hunt to assist Post, and when he sought an architect to design The Breakers at Newport, he again looked to Hunt. Anticipating Flagg's need for both formal architectural training and professional credentials, Cornelius Vanderbilt would logically have regarded study at the Ecole as expedient.

Given the unsettled nature of Ernest Flagg's education and early career, it is not surprising that his later architectural practice should have been unorthodox. Unlike his American contemporaries who studied at the Ecole, Flagg lacked preparation at a technical school or a prestigious college. He relied, instead, upon Yankee ingenuity and family connections.

Thus, as Flagg set off for the Ecole at thirty-one years of age, he was already armed with experience in speculative building. Although he had received no formal architectural training up to this time, he had been closely associated with several architects and builders. Moreover, he had demonstrated original thinking in his plans for the duplex apartment and the alterations for the Fifth Avenue house of Cornelius Vanderbilt. In short, Flagg had had some experience as a developer and planner, but he lacked formal study. The education in architectural principles that awaited him at the Ecole des Beaux-Arts would allow him to develop his personal talents and open the way to a career as one of America's most inventive turn-of-the-century architects.

CHAPTER TWO

The French School

"THE FRENCH SCHOOL" was a term that Flagg used in two senses: first, to describe the theory and practice of French architecture; and second, to identify the school where he studied, the Ecole des Beaux-Arts. Flagg used the term principally in the first sense; in doing so, he grouped together diverse tendencies as a means of distinguishing French from American developments. The two uses of the term, "the French school," help reveal how Flagg acquired knowledge of the theory and practice of architecture.

Reconciling in Architecture the Polarities of Art and Science

When Flagg arrived in Paris in the spring of 1888, he was inevitably drawn into the current debate of "the French school": how to reconcile in architecture the polarities of art and science which had been in conflict throughout the century. This debate touched on all aspects of culture and society. At mid-century, two related patterns of social thought — rationalism and romanticism — opposed one another, but their relationship with respect to architecture was especially complex and sometimes paradoxical. Broadly stated, the prevailing social philosophy in France at mid-century was positivism, a pastiche of the eighteenth-century Enlightenment beliefs in science and reason. Comptian positivism was most often coupled with materialism, or the belief in material progress. The cult of positivism stood in reaction to the idealism of the first decades of the century. By the 1890s, social theorists in Europe were attempting to counterbalance positivism with a new form of idealism. They included Bergson and Durkheim (in his later years) in France, and Weber and perhaps Freud in central Europe. But only Weber was successful in mediating the two persuasions by fusing the scientific objectivity of positivism with the powers of intuition. Although the polarities of art and

17

science permeated intellectual life and affected all disciplines, the conflict in architecture was unique among the arts and professions because architecture was a practical art which dealt with both aesthetic judgment and problems of construction. Flagg's arrival in France coincided with the first inkling of a "revolt against positivism," a phenomenon that conditioned architectural theory and practice in the decade of the 1890s.[1]

Flagg came to France also at a point when many architects, including his teacher, Paul Blondel (1841–97), followed the teachings of an earlier generation, the so-called Romantic Rationalists of the second quarter of the nineteenth century. Together with the ideas of this group, there was active interest in two architect-theorists who had opposed one another in the 1850s and 1860s: Charles Garnier (1825–98) and Eugène-Emmanuel Viollet-le-Duc (1814–79). Like their counterparts in social philosophy, these two men had grappled with the polarities of art and science.

The Romantic Rationalists of the 1830s and 1840s were bound by the common goal of correcting the idealism of earlier French neoclassicism through rationalism — that is, a reasoned approach to architecture as decorated structure. By the late 1860s these architects were identified with the *Néo-Grec* movement, led by Louis Duc (1802–79), Henri Labrouste (1801–75), Félix Duban (1797–1870), and Léon Vaudoyer (1803–72). Under the strong guidance of Labrouste, *Néo-Grec* architects sought first to refine and rationalize architectural form by effecting a reciprocity between structure and decoration, and between interior planning and exterior design. Second, they wished to inculcate meaning in architecture through symbolic expression and an abstract language of expressive ornament, using motifs incised or carved in low relief onto planar masonry surfaces. Labrouste's Bibliothèque Sainte-Geneviève in Paris of 1838–50, illustrated a union of rationalist principles thought common to both Greek and medieval architecture (Fig. 2).[2] In other celebrated monuments by this group — Duc's Palais de Justice (1852–69), Duban's Ecole des Beaux-Arts (1832–64), and Vaudoyer's Marseilles Cathedral (1845–93) — structural and aesthetic concerns were also interdependent.[3]

But the revolutionary interlude of *Néo-Grec* achievement which successfully reconciled art and science in architecture did not preclude a debate in the 1850s and 1860s between opposing camps: idealized classicism and structural rationalism. This debate became a battle of wills between Charles Garnier, the partisan of academic or conservative classicism, and Viollet-le-Duc, the partisan of Gothic or structural rationalism. It paralleled the struggle and subsequent failure to reform the Ecole des Beaux-Arts, initiated in 1863

18

2.   Henri Labrouste. Bibliothèque Sainte-Geneviève, Paris, 1838–50.

by Henri Labrouste and continued by Viollet-le-Duc.[4] Although Garnier had once studied with Viollet-le-Duc and later joined his office, he came to eschew the rationalist's theory of architecture.[5]

In 1861 Garnier achieved sudden prominence by winning the competition for the Paris Opera over other entrants, including Viollet-le-Duc (Fig. 3). The submissions of Garnier and Viollet-le-Duc characterized the debate in the 1860s. Garnier's entry stressed brilliant composition and scenography.[6] By contrast, Viollet-le-Duc's entry, a fine perspective drawing, emphasized structural principles over composition. Garnier's robust elevations and well-articulated spatial organization reflected the Opera's social activity; he pursued a formal and pictorial architecture that came to be associated with idealism and aesthetic concerns.[7] Viollet-le-Duc advocated building that embraced a unified and rational expression of structure and decoration fulfilling moral requirements, rather than social organization. Throughout the early Third Republic, it was Garnier's approach, rather than Viollet-le-Duc's, that was to condition the mainstream of architectural theory and practice, as well as the curriculum of the Ecole des Beaux-Arts in which *dessin géométral* (planimetric drawing emphasizing exterior contour) triumphed over *dessin perspectif* (perspective drawing).[8] In the end, Garnier's impact remained dominant.

19

3.   Charles Garnier. Opera, Paris, 1861–75 (author's collection).

Architectural Theory and Practice During the Early Third Republic, 1871–1900

During the third quarter of the century, when Flagg was a student at the Ecole des Beaux-Arts, a new generation of architects had taken up the Garnier–Viollet-le-Duc debate. Yet there were no longer the clear demarcations that formerly had existed between three camps of architecture: classical, *Néo-Grec,* and Gothic. Architects practicing during the early Third Republic came to regard the question of historical style in a more abstract manner. Like Garnier and Viollet-le-Duc, they adopted a formalist approach to style, recognizing an architect's personal style and artistic genius as transcending the strict parameters of historical style. The formalist approach to style became the underlying factor in an architect's work, permitting him a wide range of choice. Students, like Flagg, learned the theoretical underpinning for this approach at the Ecole and absorbed its lessons in their later practice.

Flagg was influenced greatly by the legacies of Viollet-le-Duc, Garnier, and their respective followers. Viollet-le-Duc's closest supporters were especially zealous in their desire to promote the structural properties of Gothic precedents. They were largely guided by their mentor's visionary designs for an architecture of the future suggested in plates from the second volume of his *Entretiens sur l'architecture,* published in 1872.[9] From these designs they extrapolated a set of principles for a new architecture celebrating rationalism of structure and materials, rather than emphasizing planning or composition. They, like Flagg, came to experiment with new combinations of masonry, metal, terra cotta, and glass in order to encourage structural revelation, planar wall surfaces, and decoration intrinsic to materials. In this respect, the followers of Viollet-le-Duc also looked to *Néo-Grec* architecture when they synthesized modern materials and modern equivalents to past structural systems to explore new avenues of design.[10] In large measure, *Néo-Grec* architects advanced rationalism in practice farther than did the structural rationalists themselves; for, despite the far-reaching implications of Viollet-le-Duc's theory for a future architecture which he envisioned in the *Entretiens,* his executed works, by comparison, were timid and avoided the bold design which the plates otherwise might have predicted.[11]

Viollet-le-Duc's followers—notably the architect-critics Anatole de Baudot (1834–1915) and Paul Gout (1852–?)—realized many of their mentor's experimental designs in structural revelation and new effects of

4. Viollet-le-Duc. *Hôtel* or Town House (*Entretiens sur l'architecture,* vol. 2, pl. XXXIII).

21

coloration in mixed materials. De Baudot adapted the rational principles of Gothic architecture to modern methods of construction for his Saint-Jean de Montmartre, Paris (1897–1905). The church was built of reinforced concrete and covered with a revetment of brick and terra-cotta tiles, a method of construction similar to the one that Flagg subsequently employed in his Automobile Club of America (see Fig. 92).[12] Viollet-le-Duc's followers also specialized in building types, such as schools, whose utilitarian nature warranted "rational" treatment. Both de Baudot's Lycée Lakanal at Sceaux (1886–96) and Paul Gout's Lycée Racine in Paris (1888) illustrated efforts to rationalize masonry wall surfaces.[13] Particularly influential to Flagg, their use of brick and stone in a gridded organization reflected Viollet-le-Duc's similar treatment for an *Hôtel* project which he praised for its economy and illustrated in the second volume of the *Entretiens* (Fig. 4).[14] The *Hôtel* or Town House had brick walls detailed with stone quoins and window surrounds. The project was undoubtedly inspired by the masonry architecture built during the reigns of Henry IV (1589–1610) and Louis XIII (1610–43), which Viollet-le-Duc admired. The architecture of this period, he argued, "became reasonable, chastened, and modest in its ornamentation, and in structure severe and studied; . . . employing only the means and forms necessary to the expression of its practical requirements. . . . Construction was the main element of design, it was emphasized and honored."[15]

In spite of the efforts of a few followers to retain the spirit of Viollet-le-Duc's rationalist theory during the closing decades of the nineteenth century, the prevailing trend was toward academic classicism, idealism, and aesthetic concerns—in short, the fulfillment of the Garnier tradition. Charles Garnier became the hero and his Opera, the unqualified *beau idéal* to a generation of architects practicing during the early Third Republic. Many of them, including Paul-Henri Nénot (1853–1934), Julien Guadet (1834–1908), and J. L. Pascal (1837–1920), had worked in the Garnier office at the time of the Paris Opera commission.[16] As these architects mastered the compositional principles of Garnier's Opera, their works affirmed a loyalty to Garnier's brand of academic classicism. Notable among them was Nénot's new Sorbonne, one of the great institutions of the nineteenth century which was nearing completion at the time of Flagg's arrival in Paris. Strongly reminiscent of Garnier's Opera (see Fig. 3), the Sorbonne's principal elevation on the rue des Ecoles (1884–89) employed a similar composition: an arcade below and an engaged colonnade above, flanked by dominant end pavilions (Fig. 5).[17] But the Sorbonne's hipped roofs, punctuated with *oeils-de-boeuf,* also reflected Ludovico Visconti's

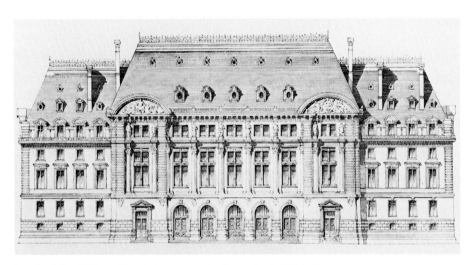

5.   Paul-Henri Nénot. New Sorbonne, rue des Ecoles, Paris, 1884–89
(*La Construction Moderne* IV, August 10, 1889, p. 520).

6.   Ludovico Visconti and Hector Lefuel. New Louvre, Paris,
1852–57 (Library of Congress).

and Hector Lefuel's earlier use of profile and ornament for the mansarded pavilions of the new Louvre of 1852–57 (Fig. 6). Like the Opera, the new Sorbonne stressed composition, yet it rejected Garnier's and Lefuel's sculptural and baroque tendencies (responding to the scholastic character of a university) in favor of more planar treatments, a general trend in architectural practice during the early Third Republic to which Flagg's work also adhered. This design approach was characteristic of Guadet's Hôtel des Postes in Paris (1880–87) and Pascal's Faculté de Médecine et de Pharmacie in Bordeaux (1880–88).[18]

Although the prevailing current in Beaux-Arts theory and practice was academic classicism, architects increasingly accepted "rationalism" to meet modern building requirements and programs. Thus, except for the most parochial followers of Garnier and Viollet-le-Duc, most French Beaux-Arts architects of Flagg's generation were inclined to regard academic classicism or structural rationalism as design options or available "styles." They selected these according to building type or program. Within a given architect's oeuvre, they came to assume, one building might strictly reflect a conservatively classical or idealist persuasion, while another might explicitly convey the rationalist emphasis on structure and materials. P. R. Léon Ginain (1825–

7. Léon Ginain. Musée Galliera, Paris, 1879–94.

8.   Léon Ginain. Bibliothèque de la Faculté de Médecine, Paris, begun in 1878 (*Encyclopaedia Britannica*, 11th ed., vol. 2, fig. 110).

98), for example, used academic classicism for his Musée Galliera in Paris of 1879–94 (Fig. 7). By contrast, his Bibliothèque de la Faculté de Médecine in Paris, begun in 1878 (Fig. 8), was a planar and restrained evocation of the *Néo-Grec* spirit that informed Labrouste's Bibliothèque Sainte-Geneviève.[19] As Flagg was later to learn, Ginain clearly viewed *Néo-Grec* as one of several available styles, rather than as a governing design principle. A similar diversity among the buildings of Emile Vaudremer (1829–1914) is apparent in the dramatic contrast between the classicism of his Notre Dame d'Auteuil in Paris (1876) and the rationalism of his Lycée Buffon on the avenue Pasteur in Paris (1887–89).[20] Even within the same building type, the railroad stations of Juste Lisch (1828–1910) illustrated such diverging tendencies. His Gare Saint-Lazare (1886–89), a masonry structure, revived a seventeenth-century classicism well integrated to its Parisian environment.[21] By contrast, his Gare du Havre (1888–89), which combined an exposed cast- and wrought-iron skeleton with polychromed terra-cotta and brick infill, strongly suggested two projects by Viollet-de-Duc, illustrated in the second volume of the *Entretiens:* the composition of the *Hôtel de Ville* or Town Hall, and the structure and materials of the French Town House and tiled shopfront (Figs. 9, 10).[22] Lisch's and Viollet-le-Duc's similar methods of construction and decoration were both informed by Jules Saulnier's Menier Chocolate Mill at Noisiel-sur-Marne (1871–72).[23]

The synthesis of classical idealism and rationalism within one building or building complex, depending on programmatic requirements or architec-

9. Viollet-le-Duc. *Hôtel de Ville* or Town Hall (*Entretiens sur l'architecture,* vol. 2, pl. XXIV).

10. Viollet-le-Duc. Town House and tiled shopfront (*Entretiens sur l'architecture,* vol. 2, pl. XXXVI).

11.   Paul-Henri Nénot. New Sorbonne, rue Cujas, Paris, 1884–89.

tural character, became an increasingly standard practice during the early Third
Republic which was conveyed to Flagg during his school years in Paris. At the
new Sorbonne, for example, Nénot prescribed formal classicism for the grand
entrance on the rue des Ecoles (see Fig. 5), but articulated the school laborato-
ries on the rue Cujas with a rational treatment in brick that economized wall
surfaces (Fig. 11).[24] Similarly, Jacques Hermant (1855 – 1930), Vaudremer's
student and Flagg's contemporary at the Ecole, employed academic classicism
for his Caserne des Célestins (quarters for the Garde républicaine) on the
boulevard Henri-IV in Paris (1890 – 96), its details resembling a fifteenth-century Florentine Renaissance palace (Fig. 12). But the Caserne's heavily rusticated basement and monumental arched entrance displayed a fortified character expressive of military housing and a scale associated with the work of such
French Revolutionary Classicists as Claude-Nicolas Ledoux.[25] Hermant articulated the brick walls of the Caserne with stone quoins and *chaînes* above the
ground floor, which resulted in a legible use of materials rationally related to
structure that was similar to Nénot's facade on the rue Cujas. Like the school
designs of de Baudot, Gout, and Emile Vaudremer, this treatment was common to late-nineteenth century utilitarian building. As with Hermant, Ed-

27

12. Jacques Hermant. Caserne des Célestins (quarters for the Garde républicaine), boulevard Henri-IV, Paris, 1890–96 (*AABN* LXIII, March 25, 1899, p. 95).

mond Guillaume (1826–94) also synthesized these approaches in his *maison commerciale* of 1880 at 3 (now 5) rue d'Uzès, Paris (Fig. 13).[26] Guillaume anticipated the conviction of Paul Sédille (1836–1900), his fellow classicist, that by the mid-1880s, all architects had become "more or less rationalists."[27] Guillaume's loft building employed masonry bearing walls with articulated corners to allow the center to be opened up by the use of cast-iron Corinthian columns. A metal-and-glass opening both monumentalized the facade and facilitated the passage of light to the interior. Flagg was later to use this compositional format in many of his most significant commercial buildings. These examples thus illustrated the tendency among French Beaux-Arts architects during the late nineteenth century to "think" at once in both modes or "styles": academic classicism and structural rationalism. Carried to America, this practice distinguished the work of Flagg, Thomas Hastings, and other architects who shared their Beaux-Arts training and persuasion.

The fusion of classical idealism and rationalism was a prominent characteristic of the architecture of the 1889 Universal Exposition. Flagg arrived in Paris on the eve of that international fair when the Champ de Mars was the scene of assembly line construction. In his praise of the Paris fair as a reflection of the rational and aesthetic concerns of "the French school," its methods and principles, Flagg demonstrated his understanding of this synthesis. In an essay of 1894, "Influence of the French School on Architecture in the United States," Flagg spoke of the merits of the Paris exposition to an

13. Edmond Guillaume. Maison commerciale, 3 rue d'Uzès, Paris, 1880 (*Revue Générale de l'Architecture et des Travaux Publics* XXXVII, 1880, pl. 30).

14.   Jean-Camille Formigé. *Palais des arts libéraux, Porche centrale,*
1889 Exposition Universelle, Paris (*La Construction Moderne*
IV, July 13, 1889, pl. 91).

American public which was then hosting its own world's fair in Chicago. Flagg
admired the Paris fair buildings for their application of "the discoveries and
resources which modern science has placed at the disposal of the architect . . . to the fine art architecture." They were, he explained, "strictly
modern in design and construction," and "honestly what they pretended to be,
buildings for a fair in the last years of the nineteenth century."[28] Flagg's
approbation was not exclusively directed to those displays of structural prowess
by engineer-architect teams (the Tower by Eiffel and Sauvestre, or the *Galerie
des Machines* by Contamin and Dutert) in which metal had been treated
fundamentally as a frank expression of engineering. Rather, like the French
rationalist critic, Paul Gout, Flagg embaced the fair architecture as a whole.[29]

   From references to the exposition's architecture in his own work, it is
clear that Flagg viewed with special interest the buildings of Jean-Camille
Formigé (1845 – 1926) who had trained at the Ecole during Paul Blondel's
student days. Employing new materials and technology, Formigé strove for,
but did not always attain, decorated structure. His buildings combined in
discrete parts a masonry and metal structure infilled with polychromed terra
cotta and glass. Flagg was particularly impressed by the example of Formigé's

twin buildings, the *Palais des arts libéraux* and the *Palais des beaux-arts*. Each exhibition hall contained an open shed-like space organized into a series of bays. Three elements dramatized each hall: a pair of monumental entrances in masonry terminating two branches of a T-plan, a metal dome with tile infill, and a central entrance *(porche centrale)* giving access to a rotunda beneath the dome (Fig. 14). The central entrance with its three monumental arches approached the scale and treatment of eighteenth-century Revolutionary Classicism. But Formigé's articulation of each bay, identical in its metal structure but

15. Jean-Camille Formigé. *Palais des arts libéraux,* Bay, 1889 Exposition Universelle, Paris (*Encyclopédie d'architecture,* IV.1, 1888–89, pl. 23).

31

subtly varied in its polychrome decoration, was recognized by rationalist observers as the architectural *tour de force* of these festival sheds (Fig. 15).[30] This system of ornamented construction, combining iron and terra cotta in legible parts, looked back to Viollet-le-Duc's celebrated project for a Town House and tiled shopfront (see Fig. 10), and to Saulnier's Menier Chocolate Mill, and directly influenced Flagg's approach to materials in his Singer Loft Building and Automobile Club of America more than a decade later (see Figs. 91, 92).

Flagg considered the buildings of the 1889 Paris fair, including the domed *Palais des industries diverses* by Joseph-Antoine Bouvard (1840–1920) in collaboration with the engineer, Victor Contamin, an ensemble which celebrated the fusion of science and art.[31] Their program—a series of vast display rooms—encouraged a frank expression of metal framing, whether opulently decorated or actually revealed. Such self-evident construction of largely prefabricated parts enabled the observer to comprehend the modern process of assemblage and eventual disposability. With the exception of the controversial Tower by Eiffel and Sauvestre, the fair buildings illustrated the consummate fusion of conservative classicism with structural rationalism. The fair thus symbolized the collective enjoyment of a country embracing its material wealth, it culture, and its progress in technology a century after the revolution. But all this was to be short-lived. By the turn of the century the newly attained equilibrium between art and science, which Flagg continued to uphold in America, broke down as conservative classicism enjoyed a resurgence in the structures for the Paris exposition of 1900.

Flagg undoubtedly knew firsthand most of the Parisian buildings previously cited. But his own experience at the Ecole des Beaux-Arts explains the degree to which he, unlike most American students, understood "the French school" in all its complexities, and why his own work illustrated the rich synthesis of approaches so conspicuous during the early Third Republic in France.

The Ecole des Beaux-Arts

Like most American students who entered the Ecole des Beaux-Arts in the late 1880s, Flagg remained just long enough to master the technique and principles taught at "the French school," as he also called it. Although Flagg lived in Paris nearly two-and-a-half years, he spent over a year in preparation for the Ecole's entrance exams. In June 1888, not long after his arrival, Flagg presented his credentials, including a required letter from the U.S. Legation, to school officials.[32] In return he was granted the right, according to a school document dated June 13, 1888, "to attend lectures and study temporarily in the galleries of the Ecole des Beaux-Arts" in preparation for the exams which were then given twice a year, in March and July.[33] Rather than proceed with all the entrance exams at one time and thereby risk failing several of them for lack of preparation (H. H. Richardson, among other architects, had failed some for that reason), Flagg took the exams in three rounds.[34] In July 1888, "at the first examination after my arrival," Flagg later recounted, "I could only take what were known as the admissables, that is to say, examination in architectural design, drawing from a cast, and modeling in clay; for these required no French."[35] Flagg spent the following academic year in the preparatory atelier of M.A.G. Guicestre, learning French and studying for the exams. He passed the remainder of the exams, both oral and written, in March and July 1889. "At the next examination," Flagg remembered, "I took the other things: descriptive and solid geometry, history, algebra, arithmetic, etc."[36] On August 2, 1889, Flagg was admitted to the second class.[37] He placed sixth among the thirty-six entrants in his class and ranked ahead of all other Americans.[38] Typical of most students preparing for the exams, Flagg lived only a few blocks from the Ecole des Beaux-Arts, at 63 rue de Seine. By the time he entered the school in August 1889, Flagg had moved to 18 rue Séguier, a street nearby.[39]

Evidently Flagg's acceptance into the Ecole des Beaux-Arts, which necessitated a long and arduous preparation for the entrance examinations, was reward enough, for he made a calculating statement to that effect more than a decade after his return to New York: "The important thing is to get into the Beaux-Arts just for the prestige it gives one in this city."[40] As was true of foreigners before him, Flagg never intended to finish the Ecole course that culminated in a diploma. This required an average of between six and ten years of study and Flagg was already too old.[41] In fact, no American had received a diploma from the time it was instituted at the Ecole des Beaux-Arts in 1867 through Flagg's tenure there.[42] In an effort to garner some of the school's prestige, and also to identify themselves as graduates of the French school, American students during the 1890s began to seek the diploma. (The Grand Prix was not open to foreigners.) These objectives inspired Flagg's American classmate, Herbert Dudley Hale (1866–1909). A slow starter at the Ecole — Hale stood near the bottom of his entering class — he was honored in 1895, along with Joseph H. Freedlander (1870–1943) and John Vredenburgh Van Pelt (1874–1962), as the first three American *diplomés*.[43]

16. Ernest Flagg at the Château of Blois, summer 1888 (Flagg Family Papers).

These three American graduates of the Ecole des Beaux-Arts initiated a trend. By the turn of the century, over a dozen more diplomas had been granted to American students. But Flagg held to the prevailing point of view that American students should restrict their study to the first few years of the program. He realized that the basic technique and principles of design were taught during these years. Unlike French nationals anxious to secure prizes, Americans were not concerned with the rigid paternalism of the atelier or Ecole politics. Flagg and most of his American classmates were eager to learn the fundamentals, either more intensively or at least more hastily than their French counterparts, in order to speed their return to America to pursue architectural practice or teaching.

34

17. Ernest Flagg. Drawing of the staircase at the Cathedral of Sens, summer 1888 (Flagg Family Papers).

Flagg was also too old to embark on an extended period of study, a fact he carefully concealed from authorities. Entrance to the Ecole des Beaux-Arts and the right to remain there were restricted to those under thirty years of age.[44] In 1889, when Flagg passed the entrance exams and entered the second class, he was actually thirty-two. Yet in his letter of reference from the U.S. Legation, his *carte d'élève,* and in all Ecole documents, Flagg gave his date of birth as 1860, instead of 1857.[45] By falsifying his age, Flagg was able to remain in the Ecole program until his alleged thirtieth birthday, February 6, 1890; although like other students he could retain his atelier affiliation indefinitely.[46] In fact, Flagg remained enrolled beyond that date. His record of *concours* (competitions) indicates that he had received a total of two credits, or *valeurs,* for

35

obtaining a *deuxième mention* in two separate *éléments analytiques* (analyzed elements) of November 7, 1889, and January 3, 1890.[47] Supplementary certificates further document that Flagg was enrolled in four competitions or *concours d'émulation* — three *projets rendus* (rendered projects) and one *esquisse* (sketch) — from November 8, 1889 to April 2, 1890, without, however, securing any additional *valeurs* or *mentions*.[48] Flagg's recorded career at the Ecole proper lasted scarcely six months. We may only speculate that he left the Ecole sometime between April 2, 1890, when he enrolled in his last *concours,* an *esquisse,* and August 13, 1890, when a diary of his European travels notes that he left Paris for Chartres en route to Italy.[49]

American students at the Ecole des Beaux-Arts formed strong friendships during their school years. In the summer of 1888, when Flagg was still preparing for the entrance exams, he and Albert Brockway (1864–1933), a fellow American student in the Atelier Guicestre, bicycled on a thousand-mile sketching tour of the Ile-de-France.[50] Their excursion included visits to Reims, Mont-Saint-Michel, Nantes, the Loire Valley, Sens, and Chartres. Flagg, then bearded, posed confidently for a photograph in front of the celebrated staircase at the château of Blois (Fig. 16). Even at this time his architectural drawings were distinguished, as the sketch he made of a staircase at the Cathedral of Sens illustrates (Fig. 17). The subject matter of his art, however, formed part of a standard repertory for American Ecole students.

In addition to Albert Brockway, Flagg formed a close friendship with Walter B. Chambers (1866–1945), another American student in Guicestre's preparatory atelier.[51] Nine years younger than Flagg, Chambers's youth was offset by his strong academic background as a Yale student in the class of 1887. Unlike Brockway, who had selected Léon Ginain as his *patron* on entering the Ecole, both Flagg and Chambers had chosen the atelier of Paul Blondel.[52] During the summer of 1890, Flagg's last as a student in Europe, the friendship of these two atelier *camarades* grew as they traveled within France to the areas south and west of Paris including the towns of Poitiers, Angoulême, and Périgueux, as well as to the regions of Provence and the Auvergne. Flagg continued to travel on his own that summer, reaching Italy toward the end of September.

Flagg's record of these travels contains enthusiastic observations on a wide range of architectural monuments. Those in Rome impressed him most forcefully. "I have come to the conclusion," he wrote, "that there is more of interest to be seen in Rome than in any other city in the world."[53] Flagg recorded his visits to Renaissance buildings, and like many architects trained at the Ecole des Beaux-Arts, he praised ancient Roman buildings and criticized baroque works. Despite Flagg's deep admiration for Roman and Renaissance architecture, direct Italian influence was to appear sparingly in his work, so committed was he to "the French school." Flagg approached Italian architecture as fundamental to a classical French education, much as a student of Romance languages would be grounded in Latin. Yet his firsthand knowledge of buildings in Rome was limited. In the study of details, he preferred to consult Letarouilly's *Edifices de Rome Moderne*.[54] During his years in Paris, Flagg acquired an impressive collection of architectural books. In this endeavor, he may have been assisted by his sister and brother-in-law, Louisa and Charles Scribner, whom he visited in London in August 1889. Because of his contacts with book publishers and dealers, Scribner was in a likely position to help Flagg amass a library. Flagg's collection contained works by French authors including J. F. Blondel, Durand, Reynaud, Blanc, Viollet-le-Duc, and Choisy, as well as those by such English architects and theorists as Stuart and Revett, Robert Adam, Chambers, Nash, Pugin, and Garbett.[55]

During the last quarter of the nineteenth century, so great were the numbers of American students to gain entrance to the Ecole that they comprised the largest group of its foreign students.[56] Our knowledge of their experiences has been greatly informed by Flagg's three-part article of 1894, "The Ecole des Beaux-Arts."[57] Written largely for the benefit of prospective American students, Flagg's series provided a physical description of the school and a summary of its resources. It also presented his personal account of the competitive admissions procedure, the curriculum (including a survey of teaching methods), and the role of the atelier, or studio, and of its director, or *patron*. In addition, Flagg's article described general student camaraderie and pranks, and concluded with a brief summary of Beaux-Arts theory. Both the format and treatment of Ecole curriculum in Flagg's article were modeled largely after Alexis Lemaistre's anecdotal account, *L'Ecole des Beaux-Arts dessinée et racontée par un élève*, published the year of Flagg's entrance in 1889.[58] While the description of the buildings followed Eugène Müntz's more objective survey of the same year, *Guide de l'école nationale des beaux-arts*, the American perspective and personal experiences were uniquely Flagg's.[59] His work stands as one of the earliest and most detailed discussions of the Ecole des Beaux-Arts by an American alumnus.[60]

Flagg recognized that although a student at the Ecole des Beaux-Arts would participate in courses ranging from ornamental design, mathematics, and stereotomy, to the theory of architecture, the real vehicle for learning architecture was the atelier.[61] The atelier functioned as a unique institution within the school structure. To the atelier, and specifically to its *patron,* the Ecole delegated the responsibility of instructing the student. Thus, in a sense, the *patron* became the advisor to his students. He was, in Flagg's words, "the master from whom one learns the great, fine art Architecture."[62] During the two afternoons a week in which he visited his atelier, according to Flagg's experience, the *patron* criticized the work of each student, and thereby largely determined his progress.[63]

Among the dozen or so ateliers from which students during the last quarter of the nineteenth century could make their selection, three in particular attracted Americans who subsequently enjoyed prominent careers.[64] Yet none of these affiliations emulated the association of the first American alumnus, Richard Morris Hunt, with the atelier of Hector Lefuel.[65] The first succession of American students favored the independent atelier of Honoré Daumet. In the late 1860s three Boston-educated men became students of Daumet: Francis Ward Chandler (1867–69), Robert Swain Peabody (1868–69), and Charles Follen McKim (1868–69).[66] Later in the 1880s and 1890s, a number of architectural students from New York joined the Atelier Daumet.[67] This group was led by Richard Howland Hunt who entered in 1885; it included Hunt's brother, Joseph Howland Hunt (1895), Whitney Warren (1887), Lloyd Warren (1892), Samuel Breck P. Trowbridge (1888), Joseph McGuire (1889), and Joseph H. Freedlander (1889).[68] Richard Howland Hunt's selection of the Atelier Daumet may have been due in part to his admiration for Daumet's château of Chantilly (1875–82).[69] (However, no student formerly in the McKim office chose his employer's *patron,* for McKim had had an unhappy association in the Atelier Daumet and would have preferred to study with Viollet-le-Duc, if he had taken students.)[70]

Another independent atelier, directed by Emile Vaudremer, attracted a second group of American students after one of its leading alumni, Eugène Letang, was appointed in 1872 to head the design studio in the newly established School of Architecture at the Massachusetts Institute of Technology by its founder, William Robert Ware. Letang influenced a succession of M.I.T. students (as well as those within the Boston community) to join the atelier of his admired former *patron.* Letang's influence extended to one of M.I.T.'s greatest alumni, Louis Sullivan, who wrote (of himself) that "As Eugène Letang had come from the Atelier Vaudremer, it seemed but natural that Louis should feel at home there."[71] Admitted to the Ecole in 1874, Sullivan was joined in Vaudremer's atelier by two fellow M.I.T. students, Arthur Rotch who came the same year and William Rotch Ware, the nephew of William Robert Ware, who arrived in 1875. Other students in the Atelier Vaudremer included Alexander Wadsworth Longfellow, another M.I.T. graduate and a former draftsman in H. H. Richardson's office, who entered in 1880, and Walter Cook, a Harvard graduate who joined in 1874.[72]

It was not until the 1880s and 1890s that a number of American students followed Richardson's lead in selecting the conservative official atelier of Jules André and his de facto successor, Victor Laloux (1850–1937). (Unlike the independent or free ateliers of Daumet and Vaudremer, the official atelier of André was controlled by the Ecole des Beaux-Arts.)[73] These students thus comprised a third line of atelier affiliation. Two New Yorkers, Thomas Hastings and Bernard Maybeck, entered André's atelier in 1880 and 1882 respectively.[74] During the last decade of the century, as the numbers of Americans accepted to the Ecole mounted steadily, American students showed an increasing preference for the Atelier Laloux. Among the many American students to join this atelier in the 1890s were Californians John Galen Howard, who had worked in Richardson's office before 1885, and Arthur Brown, Jr., the only American to win the prestigious Prix Godeboeuf (1900), as well as Edward Casey and William Delano.[75] In the first decades of the twentieth century, the general admission of American students to the Ecole was significantly increased, due in large measure to the training these entrants had acquired in architectural schools in the United States. At this time, the Atelier Laloux was most favored by Americans, ultimately schooling the greatest number of alumni, approximately one hundred.[76]

Too self-reliant to follow the lead of his compatriots, Ernest Flagg chose none of these ateliers. At a time when most students were entering official ateliers, Flagg preferred to join an independent one.[77] In commenting later on his selection, Flagg admitted his elitist bias: "The company in the outside [independent] *ateliers* is somewhat more *chic* than in the others and the student receives more attention from the *patron,* as there are generally fewer pupils."[78] Sometime after August 1889, Flagg joined the independent atelier of Paul Blondel because there were no Americans in it.[79] Flagg was especially impressed that even though this atelier had only been established in 1881, "it had secured much more than its share of honors."[80] Flagg's choice was based also on Blondel's paternalism, for he "had the well-deserved reputation of taking more pains with his pupils than any other *patron* in Paris."[81] Thus Flagg, soon joined by Walter Chambers and Herbert Dudley Hale, launched a new line of American atelier affiliation. During the sixteen years in which Blondel was its

18. Paul Blondel. *Palais des arts,* 1876 Premier Grand Prix de Rome
(*Grands Prix de Rome, d'Architecture de 1850 à 1900,* vol. 2, pls. 270–72).

patron (1881–97), the Atelier Blondel trained a number of American students
who were later to enjoy distinguished architectural careers.[82] These included
Grosvenor Atterbury (1869–1956), Donn Barber (1871–1925), Benjamin
Wistar Morris (1870–1944), and James Gamble Rogers (1867–1947).[83]

Paul Blondel was a follower of Louis Duc and represented to Flagg a
vital link with the earlier generation of *Néo-Grec* architects.[84] Officially, however, he had been a student of Honoré Daumet. In the Atelier Daumet,
Blondel had been a *camarade* of the Americans Chandler, Peabody, and
McKim. During his twelve years at the Ecole, most of the prestigious laurels
had been his.[85] In 1876 he won the Premier Grand Prix de Rome for a *Palais
des arts,* culminating an educational marathon (1864–76) which spanned the
turbulent reforms of 1863, their subsequent reactions, and the upheavals
created by the Franco-Prussian War. Following the traditional five-year tenure
in Rome, Blondel returned to Paris in 1881 to found his atelier and begin
professional practice.[86] Later he assumed various government posts, including
inspecteur des bâtiments civils.[87]

Paul Blondel's work represented little real innovation, but rather a
continuation of the principles, however weakened, of *Néo-Grec* architecture.
He remained especially attached to the legacy of Louis Duc, the most esteemed
architect of the preceding generation. In Flagg's words, Blondel's "work was
stamped with that character, manly refinement and elegant originality which
one sees in the works of Duc, whose friend and ardent admirer he was."[88]
Blondel's debt to Louis Duc was implicit in his prize-winning entry for a *Palais
de justice* in 1875, and in his Grand Prix design of 1876 for a *Palais des arts*
(Fig. 18).[89] Blondel's best-known building in Paris, a medical clinic called the
dispensaire Furtado-Heine of 1884, with a crèche (nursery) and atelier
d'aveugles (workshop for the blind), broadly conveyed his affinities to *Néo-
Grec* architecture and to structural rationalism (Fig. 19).[90] Its pavilioned plan

and elevations, combining brick and limestone to form a gridded composition, reflect other utilitarian buildings of the 1870s and 1880s, especially schools. But its *Néo-Grec* detailing and sober Doric columns strongly recall Louis Duc. Blondel's work also illustrated the prevailing tendency in the 1880s to consider rationalism and classicism as available styles, principally depending on building type. While the design for his Furtado-Heine clinic might be considered "rational," his entry for the Opéra-Comique competition of 1893 was appropriately "classical."[91]

In spite of his brilliant student career and his acquisition of several government posts and commissions, Blondel's work remained largely unpub-

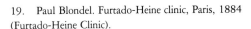

19.   Paul Blondel. Furtado-Heine clinic, Paris, 1884
(Furtado-Heine Clinic).

lished and uncelebrated. Only his medical clinics such as Furtado-Heine achieved recognition. Even Flagg was not familiar with many of Blondel's major buildings, for they were located in the city of Mulhouse which Flagg most likely never visited.[92] Nonetheless, Paul Blondel's use of eclecticism, whether applied to a utilitarian building or to an opera house, made a deep impression on Flagg during his formative years.

Parti *and a Theory of Choice*

Through the influence of Paul Blondel and the Beaux-Arts system, Flagg formulated a theory of knowledge applied to architectural design. In identifying the dichotomies of intuition and reason, art and construction, Flagg's ideas paralleled those of the social theorists of the 1890s. To reconcile these polarities in architecture, Flagg employed the notion of *parti* as a kind of creative force, similar to nineteenth-century notions of creativity and intuition.[93]

For Flagg there were two paths to a knowledge of architecture: one which could be taught, and one which could not. The first path, according to Flagg, comprised those fundamental laws of the human intellect and human form which rationally govern architectural design. "The principles taught there," Flagg observed of the Ecole des Beaux-Arts, "can be applied as well to the cottage as to the palace, for they are the principles of good taste."[94] The student's *patron* was responsible for transmitting these principles of good taste. Through Paul Blondel, Flagg undoubtedly was guided along this path to Charles Blanc, an architectural theorist whose principles of composition supported *dessin géométral*.[95] "The evidence of the intellect of man in architectural design," Flagg maintained, "lies in the symmetry and logical disposition of the parts as shown principally upon the plan."[96] On the application of the human form to architectural design, Flagg cited Blanc's academic treatise of 1867, *Grammaire des arts du dessin:* "The lesson of the human form as applied to such design is perfect symmetry to the right and left of the central axis and diversity from head to foot."[97] The second path to a knowledge of architecture was also conceptual. The measure of a student's success, Flagg maintained, was "his ability to seize the *parti*."[98] The term *parti* was derived from *prendre parti,* literally to take a side or make a choice.[99] In 1825 the theorist Antoine-Chrysostome Quatremère de Quincy defined *parti* as "choice" in his dictionary, *Architecture*.[100] But by the 1940s Georges Gromort used *parti* to mean "inspiration."[101]

Flagg's definition of *parti* stands within a late-nineteenth-century context, reflecting earlier uses but anticipating its modern definition.

This word *parti,* as used at the school, means the logical solution of the problem, and as every true architect must have two natures, the practical and the artistic, the *parti* must be the logical solution of the problem from his dual standpoint as constructor and artist.

      The ability to grasp the right *parti* is a gift of nature, it can be acquired only to a limited degree. It is the characteristic of genius in architecture.[102]

Flagg's definition of *parti* thus joined together the rational and the intuitive, the pragmatic and the ideal. The process of arriving at *parti* was an act of reason, but the ability to "grasp" it was an act of intuition, a "gift of nature." The architect was a problem solver, reconciling through choice the demands of form and structure. Significantly, this approach to architecture allowed the architect to develop his own style and produce custom design, a practice which Flagg observed of "the French school."

      To Flagg *parti* was not synonymous with, but was revealed by, the plan. In school *projets,* students, like Flagg, were especially concerned with such objective and expedient components as plan.

As the *parti* is most clearly shown on the plan, the plan becomes the chief consideration . . . of the jury; it is scarcely an exaggeration to say that in making awards the plan counts for nine points out of ten.[103]

Flagg's understanding of *parti* flowed directly from Charles Blanc, who gave discrete identities to art and science through his definition of architecture as "the art of construction according to the principles of beauty."[104]

Within every true architect there are two men, an artist and a builder. These two men are reunited in one as they must be, one practicing what the other has conceived, and both agreeing to unite use with beauty. But that which, in architecture, concerns science, must be clearly distinguished from that which is art.

      As a builder, the architect is concerned with what is necessary and useful [*commode*]: he tests materials, he calculates resistance and load. . . . As an artist, the architect invents combinations of lines and planes, solids and voids, which might arouse in the soul of the observer impressions of surprise or grandeur, terror or pleasure, power or grace . . . his art, in escaping the laws of utility and control of the necessary, elevates itself to ideas which sentiment alone must judge . . . and which are superior to calculation.[105]

Blanc's clear separation of the artist from the builder, and the supremacy of art and sentiment over practical concerns were modes of thought cradled in the spirit of the 1860s. Flagg's use of *parti* three decades later was intended to reconcile the two.

In effect, Flagg's concept of *parti,* formulated in the 1890s, meant a theory of eclecticism—literally a theory of choice—which synthesized and simplified the various positions of his predecessors and contemporaries. Where Flagg called for *parti,* Blanc called for "fitness," "solidity," "beauty," and "character"; Guadet called for "composition" and "character." Garnier and Viollet-le-Duc, by contrast, summoned the notion of a formalist interpretation of style to define their own paths to architectural design.

Charles Blanc called for a reaffirmation of traditional Vitruvian criteria—*utilitas, firmitas, venustas*—by substituting for them the French equivalents of *convenance, solidité, beauté.* These were conveyed in a plan, section, and elevation respectively. Beauty in the elevation was the direct result of fitness [*convenance*], shown in the plan, and strength, shown in the section drawing.[106] Fitness, Blanc maintained, "is the ability to adapt a work to its purpose [*destination*]," thereby determining one aspect of beauty called "character."[107] "Fitness," Blanc further argued, "always engenders the type of beauty which is called character, that is, the general expression of the monument, the first thought which arises in the mind of the spectator. From as far away as you perceive it, a building must tell you: I am a temple, a law court, a custom house."[108] The architect as builder is principally concerned with strength, as revealed in the section drawing.[109] But it is in the elevation, Blanc continued, that "the builder becomes an artist, it is there that monuments worthy of this name bear the mark of the sublime or that of the beautiful."[110] He concluded that "the genius of the architecture" is revealed in the elevations.[111] Loyal to the mid-century ideals of the Ecole des Beaux-Arts, Blanc reaffirmed the superiority of the architect as artist.

By the turn of the century the central themes of Beaux-Arts teaching which Flagg had discussed in his writings had been systematically formulated by Julien Guadet, the French theorist.[112] In his *Eléments et théorie de l'architecture* (1901–4), Guadet reaffirmed, elaborated, and codified the theory that Blanc had previously proposed. While Blanc had stressed the development of architectural design through fitness, beauty, and character, Flagg had emphasized *parti.* Guadet, on the other hand, relied upon composition and character. Composition was, for Guadet, "the solution to the program," the fundamental organization of spaces according to certain architectural principles or *grandes règles.*[113] It was also the coordination of "elements" — a wall or an order — whose respective expressions of architectural character were acquired by the sure knowledge of and "analogy with the most beautiful models."[114] Guadet's *Eléments et théorie de l'architecture* assumed an eclectic language of architecture, selected from diverse periods and places, in which the three grammatical divisions of ancient architecture were reconfirmed: composition, proportion, and construction operated as method, solution, and *raison d'être,* respectively. Proceeding from the mind to the body, Guadet observed, architecture might be that which "conceives, then studies, then constructs."[115] Guadet's notion of composition closely paralleled Flagg's concept of *parti* because both joined together reason and intuition. The process of composition for Guadet, like that of *parti* for Flagg, was rational and scientific. Guadet declared: "As method, I will always endeavor to go from the simple to the compound, from known to unknown. I aim to show that in architecture all proceeds from deduction."[116] But Guadet believed that composition itself could not be taught and, like Flagg's notion of *parti,* could only be acquired to a limited degree by experience, since both depended on intuition.[117]

In addition to composition, Guadet sought a knowledge of architecture through a broader search for character which might supersede historical styles. Guadet's definition of character, which in effect justified eclecticism, largely followed Blanc's two interpretations. The first adopted the poetic (but not the sentimental) meaning of character as architectural impression or appearance. Through the proportions of various "elements of architecture," Guadet attributed the character of "monumental effect" to a wall, or "grace and refined elegance" to an Ionic order.[118] The second interpretation distilled Blanc's notion of character as "general expression" — that intrinsic character which might distinguish a palace from a prison. To buttress his preference for eclecticism and, at the same time, rationalize the picturesque, Guadet called for "variety," as an expression of character in building types or "elements of composition." "Variety," according to Guadet, would mediate between "the architectural impression and the moral impression of the program."[119] But, Guadet believed, it was still the pursuit of individual character, according to building type or program, that would support eclecticism and rescue modern architecture from aesthetic banality, cultural indifference, and monotony.[120] Only the recognition of variety or character in modern architecture, as opposed to an indifference to character in ancient architecture, could adequately express the complexities of a modern civilization.[121]

Guadet's treatise has been justifiably criticized for its reliance upon architectural models removed from their historical and cultural contexts. "Affirming ideas of stylistic reminiscence, but indisposed to attribute a compulsive urgency to style," Colin Rowe has argued, "Guadet's method ends by destroying the logic of the historical process, while insisting on the value of the historical precept."[122] To the twentieth-century mind, the analogy between the diversity in modern life and the need to express that diversity through variety and character in architecture seems a shallow justification for assuming eclecticism. But Guadet defended it with the historicist argument that modern architecture reflected modern life, and that "the most beautiful periods of art are those where tradition was most respected, where progress was continued perfection, evolution, and not revolution."[123] Earlier this historicist argument was defended by Viollet-le-Duc in his "reply to all those who are asking for *a style belonging to our time:* 'When *our time* shall be something else besides a composition of pagan, Christian, and mediaeval traditions . . . when . . . we shall have obliterated memory, — then, and not till then, can we have what has never yet been seen, a *new style.*' "[124] In their defense of eclecticism, Guadet, Viollet-le-Duc, and Blanc in France, as well as Flagg and others in America, were inextricably tied to the nineteenth-century belief in historicism and the perpetuation of cultural values.[125]

Whether initiated by intuition or reason, the architect's personal notion of style justified and encouraged a theory of choice, to which Flagg subscribed. This formalist approach to design was articulated in the 1860s by Garnier and Viollet-le-Duc who differentiated between the roles of intuitive and rational causation. Garnier admitted the idea of a personal style: "The style I employ is my own; it is that of my own will and my own inspiration; it is the style of my times . . . it is my personality."[126] In Garnier's experience, the artist must be guided first by intuition or "feelings alone," rather than "trying to reason."[127] But Viollet-le-Duc advocated both the notion of a personal style, comparing an architect to "the writer in any language [who] has his peculiar style," and the concept of a universal style as "inspiration . . . which has been rigorously analyzed by reason before it has been expressed."[128]

For Flagg, his personal use of *parti* brought into harmony the intuitive bias of Garnier and the rational bias of Viollet-le-Duc. Flagg's understanding of *parti* as a "logical solution," or a problem-solving concept, illustrated his scientific and rational approach to design, so like that of Viollet-le-Duc. Yet the "ability to grasp the right *parti,*" was still, in Flagg's words, "a gift of nature," flowing from Garnier's intuited approach. Thus the thrust of Flagg's definition of *parti,* both reasoned and intuited, reflected his peculiar vantage of

46

the 1890s. In Flagg's use of *parti,* ends were as important as means; "choice" as important as the problem-solving process. Moreover, it was Flagg's intuited *parti,* or that which was "characteristic of genius in architecture," that enabled him to subscribe to a formalist approach to style. Flagg's tribute to Garnier makes this explicit.

A great work of architecture, like any other great work of art is chiefly valuable for the seal of personality which it receives from its author. . . . Take the Paris Opera House as a case in point. The work is stamped all over with the personality of Charles Garnier, and although opinions may differ in regard to matters of detail, all will agree that its author is a man of genius; his production will always rank as a work of art.[129]

The formalist approach to style successfully linked architectural theory and practice during the early Third Republic. Whether initiated by reason or intuition, the artist's personality or style distinguished architecture as both an art and a science. This theory of choice promoted design that appropriated a particular style for a building type or program. Thus by the late nineteenth century, the idealism of the academic classicists and the logic of the structural rationalists coexisted. As we have seen in France, structural rationalism was no longer categorically accepted by some architects and rejected by others. Rather, it had become an available style suitable for commercial and utilitarian buildings, especially schools and hospitals. Structural rationalism was not principally suited to civic buildings or to those with formal or ceremonial functions. These works required the idealized character of academic classicism. Thus an architect might at once employ traditional masonry construction and a correspondingly conservative design for a civic building, while selecting new materials with ornament rationally related to structure for a commercial building.

To reconcile the dichotomy between reason and intuition, construction and art, architects during the closing decades of the nineteenth century came to recognize their unique place in history. If they commanded the rich repository of historical styles, so they also commanded modern structural capabilities. This freedom of choice produced *fin-de-siècle* optimism for an architecture of the future. Charles Blanc's prophesy of the late 1860s for France seemed relevant again when Ernest Flagg cited it in the 1890s for America.

How can one despair of our architecture now, when we remember that the knowledge of these beautiful models is entirely recent and that the true Renaissance does not date beyond thirty years. Guided by an intelligent study and luminous criticism armed at all points, our school has before her the most illustrious career. She can henceforth,

47

reconciling the rivalries, cover the most immense voids, sustain vaults at prodigious heights, employ for the future needs of an advancing humanity either the sublime effects of the Egyptian art, the expressions of strength, grace and magnificence invented by the Grecians, the richness of the Arabian fantasy, the gravity of the Roman style, or the pathetic eloquence of the Gothic. But her regeneration can only be accomplished upon one condition, that she will not be led by the way of archaeology into the pure imitation, but on the contrary seize the spirit of things, separating from such a mass of relics the many and grand ideas which can be disengaged from them.[130]

Emerging from the polarities of art and science between 1830 and 1850 had come the creative forces of *Néo-Grec* expression. The legacy of *Néo-Grec* architecture, although ultimately weakened to an available style, was transmitted to Flagg in the last decades of the century through his teacher, Paul Blondel, and the writings of Charles Blanc. Given the prevailing theory of choice, the regeneration of architecture in the late nineteenth century would be possible not by way of "archaeology" or "imitation," but by the ability to "seize the spirit of things." Blanc's fervent message was also Blondel's instruction to Flagg when criticizing his work as "a compilation, not architecture but archaeology."[131] The best French buildings of the early Third Republic were to fulfill these "architectural" expectations; but the promise of "the French school" in America was not yet a reality when Flagg returned there in 1891. "The French school," Flagg insisted, "desires of her pupils that they know everything, then forget all and be themselves."[132] Their efforts would result in the right *parti*. By following this logical process, Flagg argued, American architects would soon develop "the *parti* for America."[133] That *parti* would be based on formalist approaches to style combining reason and intuition; on judicious choice, not determinism; and finally, on "architecture," not "archaeology." To Flagg this was an end-of-the-century search for a final reconciliation between art and science.

CHAPTER THREE

The French School Comes to America

THE ARCHITECTURAL climate of America, and especially of New York, during the last quarter of the nineteenth century changed from an English to a French persuasion. Until the 1880s, England was the dominant influence on American architecture, even though few American architects studied in that country. By contrast, France offered the unparalleled advantage of professional training in architecture, planning, and building technology to any American student who qualified for entrance to the Ecole des Beaux-Arts. One indication of this trend is the shift of interest in the 1870s from the English moral-ethical tradition of John Ruskin to the French structural-rationalist theories of Viollet-le-Duc. The latter became increasingly celebrated after William Robert Ware translated for American audiences the first volume of Viollet-le-Duc's *Entretiens sur l'architecture*. This and succeeding editions of the *Entretiens* in English helped to spread Viollet-le-Duc's doctrine in America. This shift of influence in effect signaled a more fundamental change. America's appreciation of the English emphasis on moral progress and a genteel tradition gave way to a new awareness of the glorification of science and technology, so esteemed in France.[1] At the same time, the introduction of French culture to America in the 1890s, popularly symbolized by the Chicago fair, was consistent with two articles of American faith: idealism and progress.[2]

When Ernest Flagg returned to New York early in 1891, he brought with him French artistic values as well as a firm grounding in French architectural training.[3] One brief year of study at the Ecole, preceded by a year and a half in preparation for the entrance exams, entitled him to be known as an *ancien élève*. Thus equipped, Flagg proceeded to launch a successful practice in New York and to further the principles and aesthetics of the Ecole des Beaux-Arts.

Flagg's return to America and his zealous promotion of "the French

49

school" coincided with a rise in the number of Americans to study in Paris. Over 350 of them were enrolled at the Ecole between 1890 and 1910.[4] Earlier, from 1852 to 1880, there were more than eighty American students at the school, the largest concentration of them coming from Boston.[5] After 1880, as New York replaced Boston as the financial and commercial capital of the United States, it soon became the cultural mecca as well, a fact signified for many by William Dean Howells's move from Boston to New York in 1888. Thus, after 1880, many alumni of the Ecole des Beaux-Arts were predominantly drawn to the greater New York area.[6]

The Society of Beaux-Arts Architects

Impetus to found "a French school" in America occurred in the spring of 1893 when a group of Ecole alumni gathered in New York to discuss the permanent organization of an association. This movement grew directly out of the Paris atelier experience of these American students in the 1880s.[7] Not only did they intend to promote French methods and principles, but they also wished to reconstitute in America the *esprit de corps* that they had enjoyed in their French ateliers. At their first meeting on April 3, 1893, Ernest Flagg summarized the objectives of the proposed association in his report on behalf of the Committee on Permanent Organization. Its goals, Flagg declared, were to preserve "the principles of taste acquired at the Ecole des Beaux-Arts," to oppose "the vagaries and abuses of architecture as it is too generally practised in the United States," to recruit "young men who have had the advantages of such an education," and to join forces toward the "ultimate formation of an American school of architecture, modeled after the Ecole des Beaux-Arts."[8] The movement continued to gain momentum and in January 1894, Articles of Incorporation were filed for "The Beaux-Arts Society of Architects." Officers for the first term were William A. Boring, president; Charles Follen McKim, vice-president; Walter B. Chambers, secretary; and Ernest Flagg, treasurer.[9] Within a year the organization came to be known as the Society of Beaux-Arts Architects.[10] Increasingly the new society promoted its educational role, for this would clearly distinguish it from a number of ostensibly professional but primarily social clubs in New York, the most prominent of which was the Architectural League of New York, founded in 1881.[11]

In advancing the superiority of their French training, the society's members saw themselves as a professional elite. Although there was no equal in America to the Ecole des Beaux-Arts, two events had moved architectural education and practice toward professionalization: the establishment in 1857 of the organizational body, the American Institute of Architects; and the formation in 1865 of the school of architecture at M.I.T. where William Robert Ware had emulated the curriculum of the Ecole des Beaux-Arts.[12] By 1890, six American schools of architecture had been established based upon Ware's example. These included the school of architecture at Columbia which Ware himself established in 1881, after Richard Morris Hunt had refused an offer to organize a program there.[13] The number of architectural schools stood at thirteen by 1900.[14]

During the formative months of the Society of Beaux-Arts Architects, the need for such an organization was challenged by a guarded architectural community in New York. An editorial in the *American Architect* on February 3, 1894, suggested that the new society was redundant, "as New York already possesses a school of architecture of the highest class [Columbia], modelled, so far as its teaching of design is concerned, on the Paris Ecole des Beaux-Arts, besides a beautiful exhibition-hall, and an admirable library of architecture, to say nothing of the [Architectural] League rooms, which form as pleasant a club-house."[15] To mitigate such criticism, the society shifted its efforts away from establishing a school of architecture, toward organizing a system of ateliers. This central element of Beaux-Arts education had been absent from the society's early objectives until it responded to Flagg's address of October 1894, which urged the organization "to establish ateliers where students can work by themselves."[16] "We can transform ourselves into a veritable academy," Flagg argued, "not necessarily by the founding of schools ourselves, but by bringing our influence to bear upon schools already in existence."[17] In his capacity as treasurer and trustee of the society, as well as an officer of the Committee on Education, Flagg did more than any other member to shape the ultimate character of the society's mission. His appeal for a system of ateliers defined the society's organizational structure.

The atelier was to become the society's principal vehicle for a Beaux-Arts education in America, as it had been in France. Several forerunners of the atelier system had existed in the United States during the nineteenth century. Those of Richard Morris Hunt, held at his Tenth Street Studio Building in New York in the 1860s, and of H. H. Richardson, who combined an office and atelier at his home-studio in Brookline, Massachusetts, in the 1870s and 1880s are the most well known.[18] But the first American atelier, modeled expressly on the French prototype and organized independently from any office (in which students were received for instruction only), was established in New York in 1893 by two Ecole alumni, E. L. Masqueray and Walter B.

Chambers.[19] The Atelier Masqueray-Chambers, as it was called, was located at 123 East 23rd Street. In spite of the subsequent formation of other ateliers in New York, the architectural community still recognized the Atelier Masqueray-Chambers as "the most important and successful one in this country."[20] Like its French counterpart, this atelier charged a small operational fee. The widespread formation of both independent and office ateliers in New York soon followed. The office atelier, however, was less successful, and some architects, like Flagg, abandoned theirs in favor of independent ateliers.[21]

The Society of Beaux-Arts Architects continued to be the focal point of a debate over who should assume the guardianship of architectural education in America, professional educators or practicing architects.[22] The atelier system of the society had attempted to bypass formal architectural education. In an effort to reclaim their authority, schools such as Columbia, after 1895, established ateliers under the direction of prominent Beaux-Arts men, notably Charles McKim and Thomas Hastings.[23] Practicing architects, on the other hand, justified their own ateliers on the grounds that they provided their draftsmen with the only means of instruction in Beaux-Arts principles of design, since architectural schools were only open to fully enrolled students.[24]

Despite the adoption in the 1890s of the Beaux-Arts program by architectural schools, the society continued to increase the scope of its own teaching program during the following decades. To deal with this expanding educational role, a new organization, the Beaux-Arts Institute of Design, was formed in 1916. It coexisted with the society which concerned itself with social activities.[25] The Beaux-Arts Institute of Design established a formidable program of architectural training and a network of ateliers, and circulated competitive projects nationwide to both students and office draftsmen.[26] Its teaching program reached a peak in the early years of the Depression, then lapsed into a steady decline following the rise of the Modern Movement.[27]

The "Parti" for America

Flagg's efforts to found a national school of architecture within the Society of Beaux-Arts Architects were directed toward two central objectives: to shape a national style of architecture and to promote the influence of "the French school" in America. Flagg thought that a new national style of architecture — one responding to modern civilization — would be scientific because it would not imitate French architecture but follow "the principles and spirit of the French school."[28] In his article of 1894, "Influence of the French School on Architecture in the United States," Flagg claimed that this French school in America would not study the *parti* for France, but encourage a national style, or *"parti* for America."[29]

    Style, in America as in France, had two meanings. Russell Sturgis discussed both of these in the third volume of his *Dictionary of Architecture and Building* of 1902. The first defined *style* in formalist terms as "character," or "individuality," whereby "such a building has style."[30] The second considered style in its historical context. "For a style to exist," wrote Sturgis, "there must be a recognized artistic treatment common to all the buildings of an epoch, or of a group, while those buildings have also their individual peculiarities."[31] A national style, according to Flagg, would join together the two definitions. On the one hand, Flagg equated genius in architecture with personal genius — the genius of a Garnier or a Richardson. On the other hand, Flagg called for architects trained in Beaux-Arts principles of design to work in unison toward a national style so that "the school herself and her methods will be felt rather than the personality of the individual who has been trained there."[32] In Flagg's view, the *parti* for America would embrace diverse historical and cultural aspects of Renaissance classicism, including French, English, Spanish, Italian, and American. But the formation of a national style, this *parti* for America, could only be obtained by the cumulative force of a nation of architects committed to the same principles — the principles taught at the Ecole des Beaux-Arts.

    In his search for a national style, Flagg was joined by another Beaux-Arts-trained architect, Thomas Hastings (1860–1929). As fellow supporters of the Society of Beaux-Arts Architects, Flagg and Hastings were kindred spirits. Working independently, they proposed a scientific explanation to justify Renaissance classicism — whether "modern Renaissance," "modern French," or "modern French Renaissance" — as a national style based on evolution. "All the so-called 'styles' of the past," wrote Flagg in 1900, "have been created by a slow system of evolution from what has gone before, accomplished by the combined effort of all the minds engaged, working along the same lines."[33] Similarly, Hastings observed, "Style, in its growth, has always been governed by the universal law of development." The evolution of style, he continued, "has made itself felt unconsciously in the architect's designs, under the imperatives of new practical problems, and of new requirements and conditions imposed upon him."[34] In defining that evolution, Hastings argued from an overtly Darwinian position: "The laws of natural selection and of the survival of the fittest have shaped the history of architectural style just as truly as they have the different successive forms of life."[35]

Thus modern architecture, as heir to the Italian Renaissance—first in France, then in England and America—evolved directly from the Renaissance: "With the revival of learning . . . with the birth of modern science and literature . . . with this modern world there was evolved what we should now recognize as the modern architecture, the Renaissance."[36]

Yet the "Darwinian" evolution of Renaissance classicism was interrupted in the early nineteenth century by the revival styles: Greek, Gothic, Romanesque, and Queen Anne. Flagg and Hastings recognized two defects of the revival styles. First, they encouraged an architecture of imitation, rather than evolution. Flagg deplored the consequences of such revivals, which they regarded as having originated in England and continued in America when Greek and, later, Gothic Revival replaced colonial architecture, when "invention gave way to copying" and architects "abandoned their national style."[37] He also regretted the break in France where "the style of Louis XVI was replaced by the horrors of the Empire and Paris became endowed with such buildings as the Madeleine, the Bourse, the Odeon and the Vendome column."[38] But unlike England or America, France suffered only a brief interlude of revivalism. Flagg attributed its swift recovery to French logic; Hastings credited it to the survival of classicism in France where architects "work on a common principle."[39]

The second defect of the revival styles, according to Flagg and Hastings, was their failure to reflect their own age. According to Hastings, the Gothic Revival was not suited to life in the late nineteenth century, but only to life in the Middle Ages.[40] By retrieving the lost thread of Renaissance architecture, he and Flagg hoped to propel its evolution toward a national style appropriate to modern times.[41] In the process Flagg and Hastings posed, but did not resolve, a conflict central to architecture during the decade of the 1890s: its requirement to be both Renaissance and modern. This union was as paradoxical and anachronistic as Gothic architecture was to late-nineteenth-century life. But Flagg and Hastings did not regard it so. They looked to science and evolution as forces distinguishing "modern Renaissance" from what they considered to be the revival styles. In an article of 1900, "American Architecture as Opposed to Architecture in America," Flagg declared that "a revolution is in full progress among us."[42] "Let no one mistake," he wrote, "the introduction of what appears to be modern French architecture as only a passing fancy to go the way of the 'Richardsonian Romanesque,' 'Queen Anne' and 'Italian Renaissance.' "[43] By the application of "logical reasoning," Flagg concluded, "the whole body of American architects are to work together along the same lines — to think in the same style," and thereby "make possible the evolution of a national style of our own."[44]

In contrast to his aspirations for a national style, Flagg saw the architectural profession split by factionalism. Around 1900 American architecture was divided into three identifiable movements. The first was led by Louis Sullivan (1856–1924) and the architects of the Chicago school. The second movement, in opposition to the first, was dominated by the Eastern architects of the World's Columbian Exposition in Chicago of 1893, who were primarily trained at the Ecole des Beaux-Arts in Paris but who strayed from its principles. The third movement was led by a group of architects, including Flagg, who also were trained at the Ecole des Beaux-Arts but who, unlike the group associated with the second movement, remained committed to the fundamental principles of Beaux-Arts theory and design as they understood them.

Most critics and historians from the 1890s to the Depression made no distinction between the last two movements. They labeled that architecture collectively as "classic revival" or "Beaux-Arts," in opposition to the architecture of the Chicago school. They assumed erroneously that the architecture of the Chicago fair reflected the theory and design taught at the Ecole des Beaux-Arts. In 1894 Flagg tried unsuccessfully to combat this view, arguing that "the French school" was not responsible "for the buildings of the late Chicago Exhibition, nor can it be denied that they were due in a great measure to her influence, yet these buildings were as far as possible removed from her principles, and it was in France that they were most vigorously denounced."[45] Thus Flagg's hopes for "a French school in America" were challenged by critics who dismissed the architecture of the Chicago fair (misrepresenting the work of *all* Beaux-Arts architects) as just another revival style doomed to failure. Among the most articulate of these critics was Montgomery Schuyler. In an essay of 1898, he promoted this misunderstanding of the Chicago fair buildings as products of "the Paris school." Schuyler predicted the failure of the "present classical revival" because the French sense of order and logic was too foreign to the American mind which had long been conditioned by the "British or Teutonic predilection for the romantic and the picturesque," to the point of being an "inveterate racial trait."[46] He further charged that this style was too "pompous and formal" and would fail like "all our 'styles' . . . because they have been remote from our vernacular building language" or "Anglo-Saxon temperament."[47] Schuyler determined that the attempt to "domesticate" Parisian architecture in America "by a band of zealous propagandists . . . has the air of a concerted endeavor to 'expel nature.' "[48] Schuyler concluded that a "classic revival" and an American "vernacular" (as represented by Sullivan and his followers—proponents of the first movement), were two opposing sensibilities. Schuyler preferred such a vernacular building tradition.

Flagg publicly responded to Schuyler with a defense of "the French school" in America. He did not, however, praise the buildings of the Chicago fair which he felt merely imitated French architecture without reflecting its principles. Flagg's criticism applied especially to Charles B. Atwood's Fine Arts Building because it closely copied Emile Bénard's Premier Grand Prix design of a Palace for an Exhibition of Fine Arts of 1867.[49] Using the evolutionary argument, Flagg challenged Schuyler's assumption that the history of American architecture was inherently antithetical to the precepts of order and logic. Flagg cited eighteenth-century American architecture, before the succession of revival styles, which demonstrated "logical symmetry and order in design."[50] Yet while Flagg conceded a recent American love for "disorder, irregularity, affectation, lack of applied logic," and the "picturesque," he refused to attribute it to "an inveterate racial trait," but rather to a lack of architectural education.[51]

Earlier in the decade, Henry Van Brunt (1832–1903), the architect and writer, recognized similar polarities. Van Brunt hoped that a modern style might result from a hybrid of a vocabulary of "classic" form and a new technology, for which "romantic lines" were appropriate. Thus, unlike Schuyler, Van Brunt saw possibilities for a new classicism, "independent of precedent," if it employed "the science of construction."[52] Flagg would largely have agreed with Van Brunt's assessment.

In an essay of 1928, "The Poles of Modernism: Function and Form," the historian Fiske Kimball identified the first two movements as a polarization of science and art in architecture.[53] Kimball saw the decade of the 1890s as a watershed between the two opposing forces, symbolized by the buildings of the Chicago fair and their architects: "five from the West" (or Midwest) and "five from the East."[54] The first movement, the pole of "function" (dominated by architects from Chicago and the Midwest), embraced truth to nature, now allied with science, technology, and structural expression. Its exponents had been John Ruskin, Viollet-le-Duc, Gottfried Semper, and their followers in America: Sullivan, Van Brunt, and John Root (1850–91). The second movement, or pole of classic "form" (dominated by architects from the East), stressed the independence of beauty and art from nature and science. Kimball saw this "classic" movement preoccupied with abstract form in which mass and space were preeminent. Like Schuyler, Kimball associated erroneously the work of the "classic" persuasion with the principles taught at the Ecole des Beaux-Arts, where "there was indifference to structural suggestions, but the keenest striving to express arrangement [composition] and 'character.' "[55] Kimball's association was incorrect, for even though a disregard for structural rationalism described much of the work of the "classic" camp and particularly the Chicago fair buildings by Eastern architects, it did not accurately reflect the principles of Beaux-Arts theory and design, as did the work of Flagg and others of his persuasion. Among those proponents of the "classic" movement Kimball identified the Chicago fair's master planner, Daniel H. Burnham (1846– 1912) and a number of architects who had trained at the Ecole des Beaux-Arts, including Charles McKim of McKim, Mead & White, John Russell Pope (1874–1937), Guy Lowell (1870–1927), and Henry Bacon (1866–1924). Kimball cited Burnham's and McKim's plan, the Senate Park Commission Plan for Washington, D.C. (1901), Pope's Temple of the Scottish Rite, Washington, D.C. (1910), Lowell's New York (County) Court House (1912–27), and Bacon's Lincoln Memorial, Washington, D.C. (1911– 22).[56] These American architects maintained a laissez-faire attitude and a freedom from the canons of Beaux-Arts theory and design, in contrast to Flagg and Hastings who were more doctrinaire.[57] With the success of the Chicago fair, American architecture came to be dominated by its classical vocabulary and revivalism, its sweeping facades, large scale, and uniform vision. In spite of his Ecole background and role as a founding member of the Society of Beaux-Arts Architects, McKim and his firm frequently departed from Beaux-Arts principles. In its use of a plaster veneer for walls, which imitated solid masonry and masked structural supports, McKim, Mead & White's Agriculture Building within the fair's Court of Honor may have shown an "indifference to structural suggestions" (as did Richard Morris Hunt's Administration Building), but it affirmed the fair's ideal of classical form and unity.[58] Moreover, some architects trained at the Ecole charged that McKim even ignored Beaux-Arts principles of composition by abusing precedent. They cited works other than Chicago fair buildings. For example, McKim defined the Boston Public Library (1888–95) as a massive block in which its uniform exterior did not articulate interior spaces in the orthodox Beaux-Arts manner. The library's obvious use of a prototype, Labrouste's Bibliothèque Sainte-Geneviève (see Fig. 2), smacked of imitation and revivalism because the use of an arcade along its sides (from the French model) did not correspond to its interior disposition of spaces.[59]

Mediating Schuyler's poles of "vernacular" and "classic revival," Van Brunt's "romantic" and "classic," and Kimball's "function" and "form" was the third movement led by a group of Beaux-Arts architects who were expressly loyal to the precepts of their French education. Like French architects of the early Third Republic, these American architects of "the French school," a generation younger than Richard Morris Hunt, considered academic classicism and structural rationalism to be available styles, even mixing them in varying degrees. They assimilated the weakened legacy of the *Néo-Grec* tradition and the ideals of Garnier when they adopted the principles of Guadet's teaching at the Ecole and his *Eléments et théorie*. They promoted "character" or symbolic expression in architecture. They subscribed to the principles of composition which valued the rational correspondence between a plan and an elevation so that exteriors might articulate legible volumes of interior space. Flagg was the most doctrinaire member of this group; others included Thomas Hastings, John M. Carrère (1858–1911), William A. Boring (1858–1937), Edward T. Tilton (1861–1933), and Whitney Warren (1864–1943)—all of whom were officers of the Society of Beaux-Arts Architects during its formative years. Collectively, they assumed a posture more consistent with Beaux-Arts teaching than did those Eastern architects associated with the Chicago fair and the "classic revival."

In an effort to distinguish the objectives of the "classic revival" from those of "the French school," Flagg identified two opposing currents in American building: the first, "archaeological"; the second, "architectural." The "archaeological" force stood for the "unreasoning imitation of foreign buildings and ancient styles which were out of date and abandoned by the people who produced them centuries ago, which have nothing to do with modern ideas."[60] The architecture of the Chicago fair represented the "archaeological" current. By contrast, the "architectural" force stood for "the introduction of modern ideas, modern forms, modern methods adapted to the life, habits, modes of thought, resources and appliances of the day," making "use of modern inventions and all the resources which modern science has placed at the disposal of the architect, which, if used logically that is, with the aid of reason, will call for new, fresh forms."[61] Of the two persuasions that Flagg identified, only the "architectural" would produce a "national style."

In addressing the issue of a national style in 1899, Flagg formed a temporary alliance with the Architectural League of America, a newly founded consortium of thirteen architectural clubs, geographically concentrated in the Midwest, but which included eastern groups, among them the Society of

Beaux-Arts Architects.[62] Members of the Architectural League of America sought to reform American architecture by stemming the tide of reactionary developments evident at the Chicago fair. The League also served as an antidote to the professional establishment, the American Institute of Architects, then under the leadership of the architects who dominated the Chicago fair, Robert S. Peabody (president), Daniel H. Burnham, and George B. Post.[63]

In a letter of 1899 to Albert Kelsey, future president of the Architectural League of America, Flagg stated, "We have no such thing as American architecture, though we have architecture in America."[64] That year Kelsey addressed the League's first annual convention in Cleveland by appropriating Flagg's theme and vigorously counseling delegates to reform the practice of "servile copying" and to choose "progress" before "precedent."[65] The delegates also heard the contents of a letter from Louis Sullivan who urged architects to reject "a fraudulent and surreptitious use of historical documents, however suavely presented, however cleverly plagiarized."[66] At the League's second convention, held in Chicago the following year, the delegates heard a continuation of the same theme in Flagg's paper, "American Architecture as Opposed to Architecture in America."[67] Elaborating on his letter of 1899, Flagg's paper, in turn, dramatized and popularized Kelsey's arguments. It was embraced by the organization and widely disseminated through the architectural press.[68]

In a dramatic interpretation of the events a half-century later, William Gray Purcell, a Prairie-school architect who had worked in Sullivan's office, described the era around 1900 as "a deadly battle — a battle for life — Sullivan and Wright were the spear points that struck fire against McKim, Mead and White's roman holidays, York and Sawyer's burdened orders, Carrère and Hastings' cynical sophistries, Cope and Stewardson's tudor college buildings."[69] Purcell regarded Flagg as a dissenter to what he called the "New York Renaissance."[70] "The old bozart and Architectural School crowd came to despise him," Purcell recalled in 1950, "because after doing a brilliant job in Paris and here with the French Renaissance system, he walked out on it just as they began to dimly see that a new world really was coming and they feared it. That to them was unforgiveable."[71] If Kelsey and the Architectural League of America embraced Flagg because he was an outsider to the "classic revival" movement and the A.I.A., Purcell, a generation or more later, admired Flagg for the same reasons. In general, Flagg sided briefly with Louis Sullivan and his followers, adherents of the first movement, because he admired their understanding of structural rationalism, derived in part from French models. Specifically, Flagg joined forces with the Architectural League of America and the Chicago school for two reasons: first, he believed in a national style that would eliminate "archaeology"; second, he began to use the skeletal frame around 1900. Inspired by the writings of Louis Sullivan and particularly by Sullivan's Bayard (Condict) Building in New York (1897–98), Flagg abandoned masonry bearing walls for skeletal construction in his Bourne Building (1898–99) and Singer Loft Building (1902–4), both in New York. Now praising the tall building with its steel frame as one of the truly "American ways of building," Flagg also sought an American form of decoration using new materials.[72] But Flagg's association with the Chicago school was tangential and short-lived. After 1904 he employed a masonry veneer on each of the skeletal structures of his next commercial buildings (see Chapter VI). Moreover, at the same time that Flagg designed the Singer Loft Building, he continued to use the "modern French Renaissance" style, as in his buildings for the United States Naval Academy (see Chapter IV). Flagg would have called the Naval Academy buildings "architectural"; Purcell, "bozart." Flagg was neither a dissenter from the French Renaissance nor a follower of the "classic revival" movement of McKim, Mead & White.

Despite Purcell's interpretation, Thomas Hastings's position was closest to Flagg's. In effect, Hastings would have supported the League's platform when he denounced the architecture of the Chicago fair and its revival of classical models. His biographer, David Gray, recalled that Hastings "recognized the epoch-making character of the Chicago Exposition, but regretted what he deemed its archaeological flavor and was offended by the unhappy violations of scale which appeared in some of the buildings."[73] Where Flagg relied on French models, Hastings employed many variants of academic classicism: Spanish Renaissance for the Ponce de Leon Hotel in St. Augustine (1885–87); Italian Renaissance for the Jefferson Hotel, Richmond, Virginia (1893–94); and Georgian-Federal for the Elihu Root House, New York (1903). The firm of Carrère & Hastings articulated the spatial functions of its New York Public Library (1897-1911) in the Beaux-Arts manner, employing Perrault-like classicism for the library's monumental stone entrance on Fifth Avenue, in contrast to the tall banks of metal and glass openings on its Bryant Park elevation which served to light the stack spaces within.[74] Like Nénot's Sorbonne, Carrère & Hastings' library demonstrated the use of academic classicism for a ceremonial function and structural rationalism for a utilitarian one. The firm's Blair Building, New York (1902–3; demolished), also enclosed its metal frame in a masonry revetment, but employed a similar fenestration to suggest its skeletal structure.[75]

Even so, Hastings strayed from French expressions of structural rationalism in a way that Flagg did not. Unlike Hastings, Flagg based his preference for rationalism and planarity on the legacy of Viollet-le-Duc and the issue of nationalism. Viollet-le-Duc, whose admiration for French architecture of the early seventeenth century was based on its apparent rationalism, disliked French architecture of the fifteenth century and the period of Louis XIV because it was dominated by Italian influence. By contrast, Viollet-le-Duc regarded the architecture of the early seventeenth century, during the reigns of Henry IV and Louis XIII, to be free from foreign influence and, therefore, genuinely French.[76] Viollet-le-Duc and his followers praised this architecture for its articulation of construction, rational application of ornament, and surface planarity. Much of Flagg's architecture reflected the same French chauvinism and rationalism as the seventeenth-century architecture of Salomon de Brosse, Jacques Lemercier, and François Mansart. Hastings, on the other hand, often used sources other than French ones and was freer in his articulation of surfaces. Where Flagg invariably chose planar surfaces reflecting early seventeenth- and eighteenth-century models, Hastings often preferred the sculptural robustness associated with the period of Louis XIV. Carrère & Hastings' H. T. Sloane House at 9 East 72nd Street of 1894–96 illustrated well the firm's taste for sculptural surfaces and columnar treatment (see Fig. 65). Moreover, Hastings was often indifferent to rational decoration. Preferring to emphasize the pictorial, rather than the structural aspects of classicism, Hastings maintained, "We need not fear to build attics or to decorate with pilasters and pediments, if they look well."[77]

Nonetheless, in addition to much of Hastings's architecture, the work of Flagg's contemporaries who shared his "architectural" persuasion was faithful to the canons of Beaux-Arts theory and design. Boring & Tilton's Administration Building, United States Immigrant Station on Ellis Island (1895–1902), and Warren & Wetmore's Grand Central Terminal (1903–13; with Reed and Stem) illustrate imaginative efforts to adapt Beaux-Arts principles to unprecedented building programs.[78] The facades of both buildings demonstrate a masterful articulation of their vaulted interior spaces. Like the Paris Opera (see Fig. 3) and other works on a civic scale, the monumentality of these buildings derives from and expresses their function of containing large crowds.

Flagg's concept of a national style or *parti* for America envisioned

French principles of architecture adapted to native conditions. It embraced the application of science to architecture and an evolutionary concept of style. The perfection of Renaissance classicism through rational methods of design and a reasoned approach to architecture as decorated structure would, Flagg thought, ensure its evolution and transformation from France to America. Science and evolution would thereby distinguish modern Renaissance classicism from the nineteenth-century revival styles, including the "classic revival" which Flagg considered equally imitative and archaeological. In reviving eighteenth-century classicism, Flagg sought forms common to both America and France which he admired for the same reasons that Viollet-le-Duc admired the French architecture of the early seventeenth century: its nationalism, articulation of construction, rational application of ornament, and surface planarity. Hybrid forms of American and French classicism resulted from his efforts. For example, his YMCA at Cooperstown, New York (1897–98), reflected the colonial architecture of the region and the *Néo-Grec* architecture he admired (see Fig. 40).[79]

To Flagg, "Beaux-Arts" was synonymous with the teachings of the Ecole des Beaux-Arts, "the French school," and the "architectural" force. But to most others, "Beaux-Arts" signified any association with or influence of the Ecole des Beaux-Arts, whether or not consistent with the precepts of Beaux-Arts theory and design. In the search for a national style of architecture, or "*parti* for America," Renaissance classicism in all its modes (modern French, Spanish, Italian, and Colonial or Federal Revival) enjoyed nearly a half-century of reign.[80] Like the nineteenth-century revival styles that preceded it, Renaissance classicism eventually lost its preeminence with the impact of the Modern Movement of the 1930s, but many of the rational principles of "the French school" — Beaux-Arts principles — survived.

Patronage and Practice

Although Flagg would prove to be an innovative figure in American architecture, his career was marred by a series of events resulting from his personal relations with patrons and fellow practitioners. Irrespective of factors governing architectural design, these events played a critical role in many of Flagg's earliest and most important commissions. The complexities of Flagg's personal relations, therefore, require that matters of patronage precede a discussion of his work.

Ernest Flagg was nearly thirty-four when he returned to New York in 1891 to begin his architectural career; and while he was equipped to design the large-scale commissions for which his Beaux-Arts training prepared him, such commissions proved more difficult to obtain than he had imagined. Competition in New York was fierce for both the experienced and the unseasoned architect. Flagg's family connections increased his chances for patronage; yet his personal temperament often worked against him. Among professionals, Flagg was outspoken and often arrogant. Socially, he was reclusive. For the first eighteen months after his return from Paris, Flagg was later to recall, his only project was the design of a tombstone for Samuel Tilden in New Lebanon, New York.[81] Then family connections helped to launch his career with two important commissions: St. Luke's Hospital and the Corcoran Gallery of Art. But Flagg's behavior helped to cause difficult relations with these and future clients.

Flagg's first patron was Cornelius Vanderbilt II. After having financed Flagg's architectural education at the Ecole des Beaux-Arts and his European travel, Vanderbilt helped to secure for Flagg the commission for St. Luke's Hospital in New York City. On April 25, 1892, St. Luke's officials announced an invitational competition for a new hospital on Morningside Heights. To augment the five architects selected — James Renwick, Heins & La Farge, James Brown Lord, George E. Harney, and Charles W. Clinton — a general invitation was extended to other architects.[82] Vanderbilt, then chairman of the Executive Committee of the Board of Managers, was an ex-officio member of the Building Committee.[83] In May of that year, Vanderbilt's oldest son, William Henry, died of typhoid fever.[84]

Little more than two months later, on August 1, 1892, plans for the new hospital, both solicited and unsolicited, were submitted by ten architects including Ernest Flagg.[85] The following month the Building Committee announced the preliminary results of the competition. Of the ten entries, those of Lord, Harney, Flagg, and Heins & La Farge were judged "best worthy of careful comparison and study" and placed on exhibition at St. Luke's.[86] Of the plans submitted by seven architects who responded to a general invitation, only those of Ernest Flagg were still under consideration in late September 1892. Apart from the merits of his plans, Flagg's good fortune was most certainly due to his unique relationship with Vanderbilt. Ever since the late 1880s, when he had first received the patronage of his Vanderbilt cousin, Flagg had been more than just a poor relation. He had become a surrogate son. The members of the Board of Managers and Building Committee, no doubt swayed by their compassion for Vanderbilt, were especially receptive to Flagg's plan. But it is not surprising to learn that a charge of favoritism reached the daily press. In a letter to the *New York Times,* one New Yorker criticized the management of St. Luke's Hospital for its premature public exhibition of competition drawings which, he charged, were preferentially hung; the writer also attacked the press for its own bias.[87] In addition, an article exceedingly favorable to Flagg's entry appeared in the New York paper *The Mail & Express* on September 7, 1892. The article promised "words of criticism by an expert," but its author was Flagg's friend, Walter Chambers.[88] At twenty-six years of age and only recently returned from the Ecole des Beaux-Arts, Chambers could hardly qualify as an "expert." Chambers's article was calculated boosterism, written expressly for the purpose of advancing Flagg's position, and perhaps at Flagg's request.

On November 28, 1892, the Building Committee announced that Ernest Flagg had won the St. Luke's Hospital competition. The decision to appoint Flagg as architect was unanimous, provided that Charles W. Clinton, one of the five architects originally invited to compete, would be appointed associate architect.[89] A decade before, Clinton had been associated with Flagg as the architect of the Knickerbocker apartment house. Since St. Luke's was Flagg's first building commission, a collaboration with a more experienced architect such as Clinton was considered essential.

To a fiercely competitive architectural community, the hospital commission made Flagg the object of considerable jealousy and mistrust. While the press praised Flagg's scheme, architectural critics were reluctant to commit themselves. The disparity between the architectural merits of Flagg's design and the opportunism of the building commission was alluded to even by Harry Desmond in his Introduction to "The Works of Ernest Flagg": "Rarely has an architect been so fortunate," Desmond observed, "as to make his debut upon so monumental a stage, and a student of architectural history might be piqued to inquire whether this unusual opportunity was not merely a gift of chance, were he not estopped by the architectural worth of the building itself, and by the rapid professional successes that followed it."[90] Desmond concluded that aside from "the 'personal factor,' the explanation of both the initial opportunity and the subsequent success is to be found in the fact that Mr. Flagg brought to his task a very thorough preparation obtained at the Ecole des Beaux Arts."[91]

Although Vanderbilt may have helped to launch his cousin's architectural career, he did not commission Flagg to design a building for himself.[92] Instead, other members of Flagg's extended family and his friends provided direct patronage. Among them were relatives, such as the Scribner family and

Vanderbilt's widow (the former Alice Gwynne), and friends, who included the Clark family, heirs to the Singer Manufacturing Company; Frederick G. Bourne, president of the Singer Company; Darius Ogden Mills, the philanthropist and reformer; and Edwin Ginn, the Boston publisher. From these relationships, Flagg was to receive the bulk of all future commissions. Such patronage played a large role in maintaining his office as a leading architectural firm until the First World War, in spite of the turbulent events which followed the St. Luke's competition.

In October 1891, nearly a year before Flagg had submitted plans for St. Luke's Hospital, he had received an introduction to the trustees of the Corcoran Gallery of Art through John Quincy Adams Ward, the eminent American sculptor and academician who was undoubtedly a friend of Flagg's father, Jared Bradley.[93] On April 9, 1892, Flagg and John M. Carrère each presented his own plans for the new Corcoran to the chairman of the Building Committee, Edward Clark (former architect of the Capitol), and other trustees.[94] Remaining uncommitted to either architect, the Building Committee decided to hold a limited competition among eight architects, including Flagg and Carrère & Hastings, who submitted plans on January 31, 1893.[95] In spite of the competition, however, Flagg was given preferential treatment probably due to his family connections to the world of art. While no commitment was made to Flagg from April 1892 through January 1893, he had received more assistance, criticism, and paternalistic good will from Clark and the Corcoran curator, F. Sinclair Barbarin, than any other competitor. But Flagg had worked at his own expense, dutifully responding to Barbarin's continual requests for changes to his drawings.[96] A somewhat irregular architect-client relationship, therefore, had already been established by January 31, 1893, when a trustee committee decided that "all plans except those of Mr. Flagg be not approved, and the Committee express a preference for those of that gentleman, but defer action."[97] It was not until Flagg submitted a number of alternative designs for the main elevation and after several more months of negotiations that he was informed in a letter of April 18, 1893, of his appointment as architect. Three days later his drawings were published in the Washington paper, the *Evening Star*.[98]

Once again, cries of favoritism toward Flagg issued from the press and the profession. The editors of *American Architect* took exception to the irregularities of the "competition, if it may be called one," charging that Flagg held an unfair advantage over the other entrants since he alone "had full knowledge of the desires of the committee and a long time to study the problem."[99] From

Flagg's point of view, however, the competition was an obstacle and an unnecessary delay in receiving the Corcoran commission.

Corcoran trustees continued to maintain an unorthodox architect-client relationship, especially when Charles Glover — soon to become president of the Riggs National Bank in Washington — took charge of the project.[100] Even before the contractors' bids were received, Glover departed from common practice by selecting John S. Larcombe as clerk of the works.[101] It was customary for the architect to engage a clerk of the works of his own choice, although the client was responsible for the clerk's fee. The clerk of the works would oversee construction operations, looking out for the best interests of both architect and client. Clerks of the works were usually older men with much building experience and a knowledge of the building trades. But Larcombe was young. Flagg claimed that "he had no experience whatever in work of this kind, . . . was ignorant of the ordinary methods employed in construction of this nature; he had no knowledge of engineering either as regards steel construction . . . or plumbing."[102] His only experience, Flagg later alleged, was "obtained in attending to odd jobs" and as "sort of a runner" for the Riggs Bank.[103]

On June 23, 1894, the firm of Norcross Brothers of Worcester was awarded the building contract, since they were the lowest bidders.[104] From that time until the completion of the Corcoran Gallery on January 8, 1897, more than a year after the contract deadline of December 1895, numerous difficulties impeded the progress of the building. The most burdensome of these, Norcross insisted, was the incompetence and interference of Larcombe and his assistant. Norcross Brothers charged that the clerk's inspection was "a source of unnecessary expense and a hindrance to the prosecution of our contract."[105] Although Flagg's contract gave him full control over the clerk of the works, his desire to maintain cordial relations with the trustees kept him from any extreme action. With both Norcross's superintendent and Flagg's representative continually at odds with Larcombe and his staff, Norcross finally took a stand.[106] On October 7, 1896, Norcross, backed by thirty years of experience and a considerable reputation — the firm was H. H. Richardson's favorite builder — refused to allow Larcombe on the building site.[107] This action prompted Corcoran trustees and their lawyers, Carlisle & Johnson, to threaten both Norcross and Flagg with the termination of their contracts.[108] Flagg acquiesced to Corcoran demands, ordering Norcross to admit Larcombe and his assistant on the condition that "they do not represent me in any way."[109] Flagg defended himself in his letter of October 16, 1896, which listed grievances against the clerk.[110] In their reply, Corcoran lawyers informed Flagg that they chose to ignore his grievances and took their course of action because the Building Committee could not "rely upon your firmness and fairness in any matter involving the contractors Messers Norcross."[111] They took this position not only because Flagg had sided with Norcross in the clerk-of-the-works dispute, but also because he had defended Norcross's claim on the ticklish matter of cost overruns. Flagg felt that Norcross was justified in claiming extra compensation for extensive alterations to the plans and extra structural, mechanical, and finishing work that the trustees had approved, as well as for delays which both Flagg and Norcross insisted were caused by the continual interference of the clerk of the works.[112] The trustees, however, blamed Flagg and Norcross for the year of delays and substantial cost overruns.[113] Long after the completion of the Corcoran, Norcross continued to press its claim through offers of compromise in an effort to avoid litigation. The claim was finally settled out of court on April 8, 1899, although Norcross still sustained considerable losses.[114]

The Corcoran experience was a particularly sobering one for Flagg, and its damaging effects reverberated well into his professional career. Flagg had matched the arrogance of the Corcoran trustees and lawyers with his own. But in the end, he paid for it. Years later, Flagg continued to justify his position to Charles Glover: "You must see that in taking the stand which I did, and incurring the enmity of so prominent and honorable body, as the trustees of the Corcoran Gallery, I had nothing to gain and much to lose in a material way. You yourself on several occasions have taken the trouble to remind me of the various important commissions which I lost through that stand, but I fail to see how I could have acted otherwise than I did and maintain my self respect."[115]

While Flagg was engaged in the St. Luke's Hospital and Corcoran commissions, he also prepared designs for two large projects, the New York Public Library and the Cathedral of Saint Peter and Saint Paul in Washington, which were widely published. Officials of both institutions solicited designs from Flagg, but later chose to disregard them. In the case of the Episcopal cathedral, the commission was even publicly announced as going to Flagg prior to the events of October 1896 at the Corcoran. After that date, however, the commitments to Flagg for both the library and the cathedral were withdrawn.

In September 1892, a few months after he had first submitted his plans for the Corcoran to Edward Clark, and just two months before winning the St. Luke's competition, Flagg published a design for the Tilden Trust Library in *Scribner's Magazine* and elsewhere.[116] Sponsored by John Bigelow, editor, diplomat, and Tilden trustee, Flagg's scheme had originated as a plan for a National Library (Library of Congress). Even Samuel Tilden had approved the plan a year or so before his death in 1886.[117] (Evidently Flagg had received John Bigelow's support before he left for the Ecole des Beaux-Arts.) Flagg's design, which specified the elevated Croton Reservoir site in Manhattan, seemed to satisfy what Bigelow called "the two primary requisites of a dwelling-place for books — light and air."[118] In spite of the link with Tilden, Flagg's design was put aside and subsequently replaced by another Flagg proposal to relocate City Hall on the reservoir site and adapt it for use as the Tilden Library.[119] But this scheme, like the previous one, was short-lived.[120] In 1895 the Astor and Lenox libraries merged with the Tilden Trust to form the New York Public Library. When the state legislature passed a bill on May 19, 1897, authorizing the City of New York to erect a new fireproof building on that site, John Bigelow's concept of the library had already survived more than a decade of trustee debate over efforts at consolidation.[121] A year before legislative approval, Dr. John Shaw Billings became the first director of the New York Public Library. A celebrated physician and the planner of Johns Hopkins Hospital, Billings formulated a library plan with the assistance of Columbia University professor William Robert Ware.[122] It was also Billings who suggested to the Executive Committee the idea of a competition with strong programmatic requirements that reflected his own library plan.[123] But John Bigelow, sharing Flagg's concern that architects be given more artistic freedom, was able to modify Billings's restrictive program with more flexible guidelines.[124]

Following legislative action, the Executive Committee acted precipitously to select an architect, not by appointing Flagg, but by holding two competitions: an open competition in line with the public nature of the library, and an invitational competition of six leading architects chosen by the Executive Committee.[125] In November 1897, Carrère & Hastings, one of the architectural firms invited by the trustees, was selected.[126]

When the Board of Trustees polled its choices for the six architects to invite, Flagg appeared in fifth place. But Flagg was excluded from the invitational competition, despite the vote and the steadfast efforts of his supporter, John Bigelow.[127] Rumors had reached New York that Flagg's professional standing had been compromised by the Corcoran affair. In an effort to confirm these charges, New York Public Library trustee G. L. Rives wrote directly to Corcoran lawyer Calderon Carlisle on May 8, 1897: "I understand that you have some decided views in regard to Mr. Flagg's capacity and conduct," wrote

Rives, "and I shall be very much obliged if you will furnish me *in confidence* with your . . . opinion on the subject."[128] Carlisle referred the letter to the Corcoran Board of Trustees which drafted guidelines for its official response to the effect that "while the Board considered Mr. Flagg an able man, so far as the designing of the building was concerned, its experience with him in carrying out these designs had been full of annoying difficulties."[129] Although Carlisle's reply to Rives is no longer extant, its contents were conveyed to John Bigelow by a New York Public Library trustee, Lewis Ledyard. According to Bigelow, "he [Ledyard] said their reports current unfavorable to his [Flagg's] professional character while his professional merits were not contested. At last, he [Ledyard] said in confidence that the Trustees of the Corcoran . . . had dismissed him [Flagg] for conspiring with his contractors so that the Trustees found themselves entirely at the contractor's mercy."[130] Nonetheless, Bigelow only confirmed his enduring support for Flagg. His diary contains the thrust of his reply to Ledyard, "that we have no right to pay any attention to the allegation that they had dismissed Flagg, whatever the cause if they dared not let the public know that he was dismissed. It was like condoning a felony and disqualified them as witnesses."[131] Ledyard's account of the events, as Bigelow recorded it, was erroneous. Corcoran trustees had only threatened to dismiss Flagg and Norcross; they had not actually done so. Moreover, the allegation against Flagg for "conspiring with his contractors" was sufficiently misleading so that it was easily interpreted as a charge of collusion.

If the influence of the Corcoran trustees and lawyer could extend as far as New York, it could more easily reach the short distance to Mount St. Alban, site of the future Washington Cathedral. On January 6, 1893, Congress approved the incorporation of the Protestant Episcopal Cathedral Foundation of the District of Columbia. It had originally been the idea of Charles Glover who, along with Calderon Carlisle, had been among its incorporators and first trustees.[132] In 1895, when relations between Corcoran trustees and their architect were still cordial, cathedral incorporators and trustees asked Flagg's advice on the question of style, inviting him to prepare two sets of plans: one a Renaissance design, the other Gothic.[133] After considering both sets, the Building Committee chose Flagg's Renaissance design.[134] There was initial enthusiasm for and a public exhibition of his cathedral drawings at the Pennsylvania Academy of Fine Arts and National Academy of Design in New York early in 1896. Yet the Building Committee's commitment to Flagg's "modern French Renaissance" design was subsequently tacitly ignored.[135] Flagg also lost a commission for the proposed Hearst School for Girls, adjoining the cathedral site.[136] None of the contemporary literature deals with Flagg or his design after 1896. Henry Y. Satterlee, then Bishop of Washington, omitted any reference to Flagg in his book, *The Building of a Cathedral* of 1901. It was not until 1906 when land was secured and funds obtained that cathedral trustees could again make preparations. Yet Flagg was not consulted. Even though the question of style remained undecided, an advisory committee, consisting of Daniel H. Burnham, Charles F. McKim, Charles Moore, and others, was formed that year and the Board of Trustees resolved the issue when it voted unanimously in favor of Gothic.[137] At the request of Bishop Satterlee, the English architect, George Frederick Bodley, in collaboration with Henry Vaughan of Boston, submitted Gothic designs for the cathedral which were accepted in 1907.[138] Evidently Carlisle and Glover had exercised as much influence with cathedral trustees — they had been in an even better position to do so — as they had with New York Public Library trustees.

Flagg's troubles were not over. His large talent and meteoric success, as well as his competitiveness and opportunism, caused him to be both envied and mistrusted in professional circles. Moreover, an underground circuit of slander and libel continued to pursue him. But Flagg's conduct only exacerbated the already strained relations with potential clients and fellow architects. In the midst of his difficulties with New York Public Library trustees and lawyers during the spring and summer of 1897, Flagg took on the leading member of the architectural establishment, Charles F. McKim, and became embroiled in another controversy, this one over the competition for a new National Academy of Design building. Six months earlier, McKim and other members of the profession had sided with tenement house architect James E. Ware in his dispute with Flagg over the authorship of a plan.[139] In an effort to assign blame for his professional troubles, Flagg wrote an accusatory letter to McKim. On May 26, 1897, McKim replied to Flagg "regarding reports which you state have reached you as coming from this office, and reflecting upon your character."[140] McKim vigorously denied the charges. Flagg's motive in writing must have been to dissuade McKim from serving as a juror in the National Academy of Design competition, for McKim replied that he had no knowledge that he had been selected for the jury and would decline the invitation if asked.[141] The same day, McKim forwarded a copy of Flagg's letter and his reply to another New York architect, Walter Cook. "From what I hear," McKim wrote to Cook, "he [Flagg] seems to live a life of contention and general hot water. As I have not the slightest possible acquaintance with him, I have no means of knowing anything about him, except by hearsay."[142] But as events unfolded, McKim changed his mind and accepted the invitation to serve as a juror, thus breaking his word to Flagg. The National Academy of Design, like the Corcoran Gallery of Art, was an invitational competition, but limited to six entrants: George B. Post; Henry J. Hardenbergh; Babb, [Walter] Cook & Willard; Carrère & Hastings; E. P. Casey; and Ernest Flagg.[143] Undoubtedly wary of Flagg's reputation and his family connections to the National Academy of Design — Flagg's father and brother were prominent academicians — the five other competitors wrote collectively to McKim on June 14, 1897.[144] McKim responded to their "united and urgent request" of him to serve as a member of the jury.[145] In effect, McKim and the other competitors raised personal, rather than artistic, objections to Flagg. In November of that year, it was announced that Carrère & Hastings had won both the New York Public Library and the National Academy of Design competitions.[146]

Thus Flagg's early architectural career was marked by a recurring pattern of conflict with patrons and suspect competitions. His troubles reached a climax around 1900 with his work on the United States Naval Academy. Both Flagg's master plan and his commission as architect for the Naval Academy became controversial because neither had received Congressional approval; nor had even a projected cost for the new Naval Academy been fully tabulated. Naval Academy officials may have been troubled by the implementation in 1897 of the Tarsney Act which encouraged competitions for federal buildings and established guidelines for them.[147] During the spring of 1900, when Congressional appropriation for new construction seemed probable and the first phase of Flagg's plan (armory, boathouse, and powerhouse) was already in progress, there was still doubt among some officials in the Department of the Navy as to the future course of rebuilding the Naval Academy, since no formal procedure had been established to direct the building campaign. This uncertainty was due in part to "grumblings among rival architects [who] threatened to hinder the work," observed the *Washington Times*.[148] There was also pressure from the A.I.A. and its secretary-treasurer, Glenn Brown, who wrote to Secretary of the Navy, John D. Long, in March 1900, asking to know "the proposed cost of the new buildings at Annapolis and whether they were given to Mr. Ernest Flagg, without competition."[149] In response, the Department of the Navy secured the advice of several prominent architects including George B. Post, Charles F. McKim, and John M. Carrère to determine "the best method of procedure in carrying out the plans for the new buildings prepared at the Naval Academy."[150] Reporting on a meeting of the three New York architects on July 10, 1900, F. W. Hackett, Assistant Secretary of the Navy, conveyed both their endorsement of Flagg's plan and their vote of confidence in his ability. Hackett reported the "unanimous sense of these gentlemen that in as much as the general plan had been started by Mr. Flagg, and as that architect had already proceeded some ways in working out that plan, it would not in their opinion now be advisable to throw open the construction of these buildings to competition." The Assistant Secretary added that "the New York architects spoke highly of the capacity and talent of Mr. Flagg."[151]

Understandably, Flagg's commission for the Naval Academy was the object of professional scrutiny by the A.I.A. and members of the architectural community, who supported the Tarsney Act. But like many architects, including Frank Lloyd Wright, Flagg mocked the results of most competitions, even though he chose to enter many of them.[152] Even in the competitions Flagg won, including St. Luke's Hospital and the Corcoran Gallery of Art, patronage was still a contributing factor. In another competition, Flagg used his connections with Mrs. Alfred Corning Clark to persuade the sponsoring organization, the City and Suburban Homes Company, to select his plan for the Clark tenements.[153] Flagg's actions aroused the jealousies of his fellow architects who recognized favoritism. Moreover, two public commissions in which Flagg initially was associated as architect, the New York Public Library and the United States Naval Academy, should have been awarded on the basis of an open, or at least a limited, competition. The trustees of the New York Public Library came to realize this only after they became aware of Flagg's difficulties in Washington. Aside from their personal reservations about Flagg, the trustees belatedly realized the importance of an orthodox procedure in selecting an architect.

There is little doubt that the architectural community, especially in New York, mistrusted Flagg, however much they admired his "capacity and talent." From the time that Flagg, his father, and brother were engaged in speculative building in New York during the 1880s, they were decidedly controversial. Then, in the midst of the Corcoran affair in 1896, family difficulties added to Flagg's own. Jared, his favorite brother, was arrested for running a house of prostitution by renting what were euphemistically called "furnished flats." But Jared's term of thirty days in the Tombs did not dissuade him from future brushes with the law in which he vehemently proclaimed his innocence.[154] On the one hand, Flagg's early business association with Jared undoubtedly encouraged his shrewdness. On the other hand, Jared's troubles may have injured further Flagg's reputation.

Dismayed by Flagg's conduct as an architect, the professional establishment took its revenge. Even though Flagg's closest colleagues were elected to membership in the A.I.A. early in their careers, Flagg was excluded until he was in his mid-fifties. Flagg was denied membership in the New York Chapter of the A.I.A. until 1911 and in the national Institute until the following year. Flagg's case had become a *cause célèbre* in New York. On April 12, 1911, Flagg noted in his diary that he was finally elected to membership in the New York Chapter of the A.I.A. "after having been kept out of it for nearly twenty years through the energies of S[tanford] White and others."[155] Prior to that time, certain applicants were continually blackballed by the "secret letter-ballot." In 1909, Flagg had failed once again to be elected to the A.I.A. due to this election procedure.[156] Two years later Flagg received word from John Carrère, who "had fought out my case with the Institute, with the result that the whole system of election had been changed," and asked Flagg's "permission to nominate me again." Mead had consented to second the nomination.[157] In truth, by the time he was finally elected to the A.I.A., Flagg's practice had fallen off so much that he was no longer a threat to the architectural community in New York. Moreover, many A.I.A. members whom Flagg had perceived as adversaries, including Stanford White and Charles F. McKim, were then dead. On November 21, 1911, six months after his election to the A.I.A., Flagg was further welcomed by the profession when the Society of Beaux-Arts Architects elected him president for the first of two terms.[158] In 1926 he was made a Fellow of the A.I.A.

If Flagg preferred to cultivate patrons rather than enter competitions, logically he should have formed a business partnership. But Flagg's independent nature and cantankerousness turned him away from such arrangements, with some notable exceptions. In the early 1890s Flagg shared his practice with fellow classmates at the Ecole des Beaux-Arts. The first was John P. Benson who became associated with Flagg as early as October 1891 when they formed an office located at 64 Cedar Street.[159] In 1892 they were joined by Albert L. Brockway.[160] Both Benson and Brockway assisted with the Corcoran project, but as draftsmen, not as designers.[161] The office moved to Broad Street the following year. Benson and Brockway remained with Flagg until 1894 when they were replaced by Walter Chambers.[162] In 1897 Flagg and Chambers moved into the Mills Building at 35 Wall Street where they remained until 1919 when they moved to an office at 111 East 40th Street, next to Flagg's town house.[163] Yet the two men's practices were independent. Francis Swales, an architect trained at the Ecole des Beaux-Arts, described the extent of the partnership in which each was "absorbed in his individual work," although "they continued to share the expenses of their offices—an amicable arrangement that has gone on during more than thirty years."[164] Swales concluded that "the separate work of the members of the original firm is still often thought of as by Flagg and Chambers, though the style of each is very different and individual, Mr. Flagg's work being based upon the modern French school, while that of Mr. Chambers has had its inspiration in old English and early American models."[165] Chambers, however, assumed much of the joint office management until 1907 when Arthur T. Sutcliffe took over that responsibility.[166] A graduate of Yale University and a member of many New York clubs, Chambers was considerably at ease with clients and could have mitigated Flagg's abrupt nature and lack of rapport with some of them.[167] However, each went his own way. Flagg's sense of the importance of complete design control and his contentiousness required independence from any traditional partnership. Thus, while most of the American Beaux-Arts architects of Flagg's generation formed partnerships (Carrère & Hastings, Boring & Tilton, Trowbridge & Livingston, Warren & Wetmore), Flagg, remaining true to French practice, preferred to work alone.

In the final analysis, Flagg's loss of these important commissions was not due to any lack of ability since his clients and fellow architects freely applauded his design acumen. Rather, Flagg failed to gain many commissions he sought because his personal and professional conduct was questioned and his views on the importance of French architecture and theory were at variance with those of the professional establishment. Flagg did not lose his reputation with clients until the Corcoran affair in 1896. But fellow architects had questioned his professional ethics as early as the 1880s, when Flagg was engaged with his father and brother in land and building speculation. The St. Luke's Hospital and Corcoran commissions renewed the suspicions of these architects about his integrity. Moreover, his close relationship with Jared, a convicted felon, further injured Flagg's reputation. Some architects opposed Flagg for personal and political reasons. Charles McKim and others had found him arrogant and self-righteous. Furthermore, Stanford White and McKim differed with Flagg on matters of architectural politics, for they were in different camps. White and McKim also supported professional guidelines (for example, A.I.A.-supported standards and the Tarsney Act) while, according to one New York architect, Flagg existed "a little outside the usual channels of the profession."[168] Moreover, when Flagg courageously promoted "the French school" in America and criticized the buildings of the Chicago fair as misrepresentations of French theory and practice, he took an unpopular stand but remained true to his Beaux-Arts education. Flagg's talent and energy allowed him to overcome such difficulties and maintain an active office practice for forty years.

Part 2

CHAPTER FOUR

Beaux-Arts Works

IN DESIGNING institutions and traditional building types with formal or ceremonial programs, Flagg, like French architects of the early Third Republic and American architects of "the French school," demonstrated his ability to synthesize diverse styles. He stressed academic classicism and ceremonial planning, but also regarded the legacies of the *Néo-Grec* movement and structural rationalism as design options or available styles appropriate to certain building types and programs. For traditional building types, Flagg applied the Beaux-Arts method of studying composition and character. Flagg's concept of *parti* —his theory of choice—allowed him to consult historical precedents in a way that he considered "architectural" and not "archaeological." He designed each work according to the special needs of its building type and program. A church or a tomb, for example, was given an especially formal and monumental character, while an armory might be given a utilitarian treatment. Although building types and programs required different expressions of character, they were linked together through Flagg's own personal sense of style. The two uses of style—the historical and the personal—by architects of "the French school" would, for Flagg, result in a national style, or *"parti* for America." Flagg's Beaux-Arts institutions confirmed a belief in material progress and the cultural values of what George Santayana called a genteel tradition.[1] At the same time, they did not ignore structural or programmatic innovations.

Corcoran Gallery of Art

Flagg's *parti* for the Corcoran Gallery of Art (Fig. 20) evolved from an earlier project for the National Academy of Design. While still a student in the Atelier Blondel, Flagg had developed a scheme for an art gallery on a site occupying the block bordered by Madison and Vanderbilt avenues, and 43rd

20.   Ernest Flagg. Corcoran Gallery of Art, Washington, D.C.,
1892–97 (Library of Congress).

and 45th streets in Manhattan. He hoped to interest the National Academy of
Design in his scheme.[2] Perhaps through his father, Flagg learned of the
National Academy's need for expanded school facilities and exhibition areas.[3]
By the mid-1880s, the National Academy had outgrown Peter B. Wight's
Venetian Gothic building (1863–65) at 23rd Street and Fourth Avenue.[4]
The Academy would either have to move or enlarge its present building. But in
1891, when Flagg proposed his plans for a new building, the academicians saw
no way to obtain the adequate funds for such a structure. That fall, John
Quincy Adams Ward, a former president of the National Academy, intervened on Flagg's behalf suggesting to the Corcoran trustees that Flagg's plans
for an art gallery and art school might suit their more immediate needs.[5]

     The first Corcoran Gallery of Art by James Renwick, located nearby
on Pennsylvania Avenue at 17th Street, was designed in 1859. It opened to the
public in 1874.[6] The school was housed in a building annex which it soon
outgrew. When the gallery's founder, William Wilson Corcoran, died in
1888, he left a bequest of $100,000 for a school fund. This encouraged the
trustees to reassess their entire facilities. Consequently, at the time that Ward
first approached the Corcoran trustees in 1891, a site had already been pur-

chased for a new gallery only a few blocks south of the Renwick structure.[7] The new site also was located on 17th Street, diagonally across from Alfred B. Mullett's State, War, and Navy Building (1871; now the Executive Office Building), bordered by E Street to the south and New York Avenue to the north, with which it formed an acute angle.

From the time that he first showed his plans for the Corcoran to Edward Clark and other trustees on April 9, 1892, until the final plans were approved a year later, Flagg continued to evolve his original *parti*. No documents exist, however, to suggest that Flagg presented the drawings he had prepared in France to the Corcoran trustees. Flagg's competition drawings (January 31, 1893) of the front elevation on 17th Street show a block-like loggia above three entrances with a hemicycle to the northeast. Here the frontispiece, with its paired columns and straight lintels, reflects the colonnaded east front of the Louvre (1667–70) by Louis Le Vau and Claude Perrault, and the pavilions of Visconti's and Lefuel's new Louvre (see Fig. 6). To nineteenth-century architects like Flagg, the Louvre represented the quintessential model for a museum, even though it had not become one until 1793. In a letter of May 28, 1892, to the Corcoran curator, F. Sinclair Barbarin, Flagg expressed his concern for the architectural character of the facade: "I have tried to make it simple and monumental and above all to give it the appearance of an art building."[8]

A subsequent project, Flagg's entry in a competition of 1897 for a new National Academy of Design, reflects the massing and specific details of the

21.   Ernest Flagg. Project for a National Academy of Design, 1897
(*Arch Rev* V, January 1898, pl. VIII).

Corcoran's projected elevation (Fig. 21). It was planned for a new site on 109th Street, near the future Cathedral of St. John the Divine in upper Manhattan, which the Academy had purchased.[9] The winning entry by Carrère & Hastings, however, was not executed and a new National Academy of Design building was never constructed. The Academy relocated to other quarters after the Wight structure was sold to the Metropolitan Life Insurance Company. It was demolished in 1901.[10]

Many features of Flagg's entry compare favorably with the Corcoran elevation of January 1893. There is a tripartite massing associated with "modern French Renaissance" design, a rusticated ground floor with three entrances, a monumental *étage noble* containing a loggia with paired columns, and pitched roofs with skylights. Both projects also show a profusion of ornamental details, including sculptural relief, a *chéneau* or ornamental gutter, and wrought-iron cresting, all of which reflect *Néo-Grec* models.[11] The National Academy of Design plan with its light court, hemicycle, and galleries recombines the spatial elements of the Corcoran design into a more hierarchical and scenographic sequence.[12]

Both the Corcoran and National Academy projects show the strong influence of Paul Blondel. A wash drawing of Blondel's 1876 Grand Prix for a *Palais des arts* (see Fig. 18), for example, indicates the essential elements of Flagg's Corcoran entry: a pavilion arrangement strung together with each part containing a separate function, a metal and glass shed for the sculpture court, and elegant ornament in low relief rationally related to the structure. These elements are identifiable in a section drawing by Flagg (Fig. 22). Executed with the meticulous craft of an Ecole student project, this rare and particularly distinguished wash drawing was among those Flagg presented in January 1893. The section drawing indicates the spatial sequence: vestibule, sculpture court, staircase, painting gallery. It indicates works in the Corcoran collection such as the Bayre sculpture, *Theseus Slaying the Centaur*. But it also takes liberties with the actual collection, illustrating a number of casts or copies including Michelangelo's *David* and Bologna's *Rape of the Sabine Women*. In the main picture gallery Flagg depicted an imaginary collection of works by or in the manner of Michelangelo, Guido Reni, Poussin, and other celebrated painters—all skied on the exhibition wall. Flagg perceived the future Corcoran to be the American Louvre.

The gallery's corner site posed a difficult problem for a Beaux-Arts architect dealing with a noncommercial structure. Flagg solved it by placing at the corner an auditorium, instead of an entrance which the trustees preferred.[13]

22. Ernest Flagg. Project for the Corcoran Gallery of Art.
Section, wash drawing, 1893 (Corcoran Gallery of Art Archives).

The use of cylindrical elements to express corner sites was a logical solution for
urban planners since the mid-nineteenth century when Baron Georges Haussmann, Prefect of the Seine (1853–70) during the reign of Napoleon III,
reorganized Paris. Haussmann's plan called for the creation of boulevards,
celebrating their intersections with corner pavilions. When the Corcoran was
completed, it faced a park (today the Ellipse) whose then uninterrupted vista
extended to the Capitol.[14]

    The Corcoran plan (Fig. 23) constituted the most unchanged aspect of
the scheme, even though the trustees did not adopt its proposed second
phase.[15] The plan was the Corcoran's greatest strength, for this was from the
beginning the principal thrust of the collaboration between Flagg and the

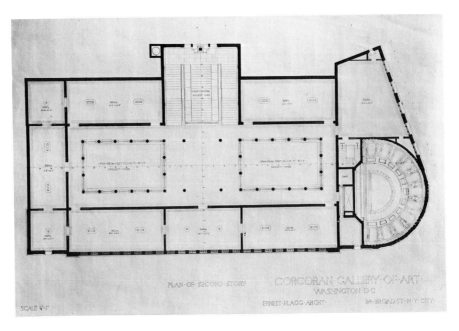

23. Ernest Flagg. Corcoran Gallery of Art.
Plan (Corcoran Gallery of Art Archives).

trustees.[16] It was characterized by a simplicity of composition, eliminating rigid axiality and hierarchy of parts. There was, however, a sequence of rooms, each rendered autonomous by natural and artificial light sources, provided by skylights modeled after those on the 1889 Paris exposition buildings and a blaze of incandescent lights totaling nearly 4,000 bulbs.[17] The *tour de force* of the interior was the so-called Atrium or double light-court onto which open nearly all the rooms that surround it (Fig. 24). The Atrium, the largest space, consisted of two levels and two wells around which a wide circulation corridor was provided. Picture galleries banked the perimeter of the second floor of the Atrium. The use of the orders for the Atrium was classically correct: Greek Doric below, Greek Ionic above. While the two-level balcony arrangement of the Corcoran Atrium derived from the historical precedent of the Roman basilica, the most striking comparison was with a *Néo-Grec* example, Louis Duc's diminutive Atrium Court of the Palais de Justice.[18] Duc's Atrium Court, consisting of only four columns on each of its long sides, employed a similar use of two light wells, the same disposition of Doric and Ionic orders, as well as a railing of similar Greek-inspired design as Flagg's Atrium. The image of Duc's Atrium Court, if not its exact vocabulary of forms, may have inspired the Corcoran Atrium.

Although the Corcoran trustees had effectively selected Flagg as architect on January 31, 1893, they were dissatisfied with his presentation drawing for the front elevation on 17th Street and asked him to modify it. By April of that year, when Flagg had submitted three additional versions, the trustees chose one which eliminated the central loggia on 17th Street and added a wing to the E Street corner (Fig. 25).[19] As built, the Corcoran Gallery of Art consists of three discrete parts: the gallery occupying the main block on 17th Street, the art school on New York Avenue, and a convex auditorium or hemicycle which links them together at the corner and serves both. The main block is emphasized, slightly projecting from the flanking end pieces. The curved auditorium expresses the urban vitality and vehicular movement occurring at this prominent intersection.[20]

24.   Ernest Flagg. Corcoran Gallery of Art.
Atrium (Corcoran Gallery of Art Archives).

83

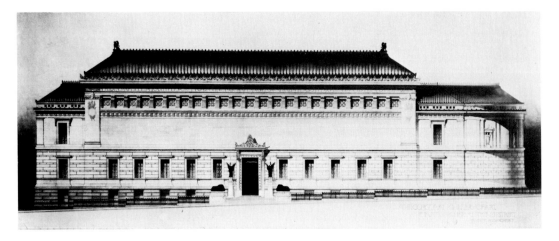

25. Ernest Flagg. Corcoran Gallery of Art.
Wash drawing, 1893 (Corcoran Gallery of Art Archives).

The Corcoran Gallery of Art synthesized a composition and massing appropriate to the palace-museum building type and displayed a style that was identified as *Néo-Grec*.[21] Inspired by examples of sixteenth-century French Renaissance châteaux such as Chambord, Flagg employed a *fossé*, or ditch, to accommodate the building to its sloping urban site.[22] Further, the *fossé* justified a heavily rusticated basement of pink Milford granite which rooted the building to the ground while reinforcing a monumentality similar to the Corcoran's French Renaissance models. Above the granite basement, the channeling of Georgia marble for each of two stories became progressively finer. Through its massing, its composition, and its use of materials, the Corcoran conveyed the image of the building's bearing-wall construction.

Moreover, the Corcoran successfully grappled with the character and image, as well as the composition and program, of the art building as both repository and school. Flagg reached into the history of French classicism to solve the Corcoran *parti*. From the first, he perceived the essence of the Corcoran as "simple," "monumental," and having "the appearance of an art building." Thus to convey the building as a museum — the main event of the program — was to symbolize that fact on the principal 17th Street facade, for the identity of the picture galleries on the building's exterior was explicit. Flagg had already been persuaded by the trustees to abandon the traditional Louvre-like frontispiece. Moreover, with few French precedents for this building type — and virtually no classical examples of American museums — Flagg was left to cast about for an appropriate image among related building types.[23] So he folded into the final design of the 17th Street facade an already fixed composition from a related building type in France, the library. The museum was programmatically allied to a library, for, instead of being a repository of books, it was a repository of paintings. This allusion is further supported by the nineteenth-century convention of stacking paintings vertically in an exhibition gallery. Both the method of stacking and the allusion were forcefully illustrated in Flagg's section drawing for the Corcoran competition (see Fig. 22).

The gallery wall thus became the dominant element of the Corcoran *parti*. Its identity and expressive power were recognized by the architectural press. The editors of *Architectural Review* observed that "in the Corcoran Art Gallery at Washington Mr. Ernest Flagg has frankly admitted the necessity of the blank wall, and used it without any effort to cut it up with the many devices and disguises so often used, and the result justifies him."[24] The composition of this gallery wall is ultimately derived from and analogous to *Néo-Grec* library models. The Corcoran's main block, or *corps de logis,* is secured by an entablature which establishes a scale for the whole and justifies the presence of corner piers which enframe the blank wall of the *étage noble* and extend downward to the rusticated ground floor and basement. Above the *étage noble,* a continuous unrelieved band of ventilators, or claustra, in a Greek-inspired star pattern, is punctuated at regular intervals by small-scale Doric piers and executed in the same Georgia marble. A metal and glass hipped roof crowns the block.

The Corcoran facade has its strongest affinities to Ginain's Bibliothèque de la Faculté de Médecine (begun in 1878), both in terms of the massing and the composition (see Fig. 8). Like the Corcoran, Ginain's library has a two-part elevation with corner piers enframing the reading-room level. The ornament is *Néo-Grec*: large- and small-scale friezes with triglyphs and metopes expressed as shields. The imagery of the library's corner piers, each with a large shield containing the initials "RF" (République Française) pressed onto a fern, was common among *Néo-Grec* works.[25] Flagg quoted Ginain's motif precisely with the substitution of the initial "C" (Corcoran).[26]

But a more significant transformation of French library models was Flagg's adaptation of the *parti* in Labrouste's Bibliothèque Sainte-Geneviève to serve a museum function (see Fig. 2). The Corcoran illustrates that Flagg understood the way in which Labrouste expressed the meaning of a library, for the Bibliothèque Sainte-Geneviève employed a roster of celebrated authors, carved on the facade and corresponding to those books which were located literally on the inner face of the stack wall.[27] Observing this use of language in architecture, Flagg chose a less literal conception. The Corcoran's gallery wall was left blank with a banner of artists' names inscribed in the frieze above: PHIDIAS . GIOTTO . DVRER . MICHAELANGELO . RAPHAEL . VELASQUEZ . REMBRANDT . RVBENS . REYNOLDS . ALLSTON . INGRES (see Fig. 20). With the exception of Dürer, the list was Flagg's own; many were those whose paintings and sculptures Flagg had imagined in the section drawing (see Fig. 22). Representing American art was Washington Allston, the painter whom Flagg believed best represented the academic tradition in American painting.[28] Allston had been both a mentor and close relative of Flagg's father. Corcoran trustees approved the selection.[29]

A clear desire to associate his name with Allston's prompted Flagg to "sign" the Corcoran facade: . ERNEST . FLAGG. INV . MDCCCXCIII. The Flagg inscription received the trustees' unanimous support.[30] The practice of signing buildings in France during the 1880s and 1890s was common for commercial structures and apartment houses, but not for government buildings or prestigious commissions such as libraries and museums. Neither Labrouste nor Ginain, for example, signed his library.[31] The practice of signing buildings in America during the 1890s was not without controversy. When McKim, Mead & White disguised their initials within the roster of authors which appeared on the facade of the Boston Public Library, they were accused of self-advertising and severely criticized for it.[32] However, American architectural journals, such as *American Architect,* and professional organizations supported the practice.[33] Moreover, the Corcoran was identified as a particularly good example of a signed building. The inscription was legibly carved and discreetly placed in the lower right-hand corner of the front elevation, in much the same place a painter's name would appear on a canvas.[34] Flagg continued this practice in later years.[35]

But the source of drama in the facade — the taut surface tension of the blank gallery wall, charged by the seemingly endless band of ventilators — was not due to any *Néo-Grec* or "modern French Renaissance" composition. What might account for this prismatic quality is the influence of the visionary projects of the French Revolutionary Classicist, Etienne-Louis Boullée. His project for a library invites an interesting comparison. Like the pedimented entrance portico that relieves the tension in the facade of Boullée's Royal Library, the Corcoran's entrance sharply punctuates its planar elevation.[36]

The Corcoran school wing on New York Avenue followed another celebrated and equally appropriate *Néo-Grec* model. It was directly inspired by Duban's Quai Malaquais front of the Ecole des Beaux-Arts (1858–62).[37] In both cases the north elevation permitted the use of a generous expanse of windows. Flagg's example, however, relied specifically on Duban's elevation for its scale, its segmental arch windows separated by Doric pilasters, and its ornament in low relief.

In reviving the *Néo-Grec* style of architecture in 1893, Flagg did so a full generation after it had ceased to evolve in France and at a time when it was considered one of many available styles, both in France and America. For his models, Flagg chose the French Renaissance châteaux of the fifteenth and sixteenth centuries in order to identify the Corcoran as a palace-museum of "the French school." He also chose *Néo-Grec* in order to pay homage to Duc, Duban, Labrouste, and their follower, Paul Blondel. The Corcoran could thereby attempt to emulate the structural expression, logical planning, rationalism, and ornamental scheme of its *Néo-Grec* prototypes. Like them, the Corcoran employed masonry construction with no disguised metal bearing supports. Exposed steel beams, which spanned the light court and supported the glazing above, comprised the only structural metal present. However, Flagg's functional use of iron attempted to approximate Greek methods of construction in which blocks of stone were joined by bronze crampons, thus eliminating the need for mortar. In his specifications for the Corcoran's granite work, Flagg called for the masonry to be secured by "iron strap spear anchors" in which each "end of strap is to be turned down 2 inches and let into stone work."[38] Flagg's use of iron served an ancillary role permitting him to specify only "a thin bed of mortar."[39] Although Flagg's approach was far from Greek methods and the *Néo-Grec* ideal, the Corcoran still achieved an image of its masonry bearing-wall construction. Moreover, logical planning produced an explicit reciprocity between the Corcoran's interior and exterior. Three separate functions — gallery, hemicycle, and school — were identified in plan and correspondingly demarcated on the exterior as distinct volumes. The whole composition was concerned with the geometry of architectural form. The main block, articulated in large-scale parts, interlocked with the end block and hemicycle in small-scale parts. The hemicycle charged the elevation with movement as it wrapped around the New York Avenue corner and terminated in the art school block. This interlocking of parts was a celebrated attribute of *Néo-Grec* architecture and another attempt to abstract and rationalize French classicism.

Néo-Grec ornament in stone, which was used by the followers of Labrouste and Duc to convey meaning, symbolism, poetry, and expression, was transformed by Flagg into a more objectified statement. The metamorphosis of the library *parti* to express the gallery wall and the corresponding role of ornament was an attempt to transplant *Néo-Grec* ideals in America. Further, two contrasting experiences, both flowing from a *Néo-Grec* interpretation of the stone medium, engaged the observer. The first experience of the Corcoran was gravity — the gravity of its rusticated granite base supporting marble walls above it. This was most apparent through the sensitive scaling of the masonry at each level and the relationship of the building to its site. The second experience of the Corcoran, enhanced by the role of ornament, was one of supreme elegance, lightness, and linear rhythms. This effect, concentrated at the level of the entablature on the 17th Street facade, served as a counterpoint to the gravity of the base.

Masonry carving animated the Corcoran's facade with Greek-inspired motifs, emphasizing the lithic quality of the stone. Basement windows, similar to those on Richard Morris Hunt's Lenox Library, New York (1869–77; demolished), contained prop supports articulated by Greek-derived relief.[40] Ornamental cast and wrought iron affirmed the spanning and supporting potential of iron. Metal prop supports and a claustra filled the windows of the art school and the end block on E Street. They emulated the serene Greek-inspired designs of similar details on Duban's Seine front of the Ecole des Beaux-Arts.

Flagg chose such models for the Corcoran because they illustrated the ideals of French classicism. But when Charles Follen McKim designed the Boston Public Library (1887–95), a building similar in character and program (both were repositories), he did not share all of Flagg's concern for Beaux-Arts principles. When McKim borrowed specific models, including Richardson's Marshall Field Wholesale Store, Labrouste's Bibliothèque Sainte-Geneviève (see Fig. 2), and Alberti's side elevation of San Francesco (Tempio Malatestiano) in Rimini, he did so for merely pictorial reasons.[41]

Flagg's revival of *Néo-Grec* looked back to earlier uses in America as well as in France. Richard Morris Hunt, who introduced *Néo-Grec* to America, had abandoned it for nearly twenty years. Although Hunt employed *Néo-Grec* detailing for the Main Building of the United States Naval Observatory, Washington, D.C. (1892), and for the pedestal of the Statue of Liberty (1884–86), his last important building to revive *Néo-Grec* was the Lenox Library.[42] Thus when Flagg's *Néo-Grec* scheme for the Corcoran was published in April 1893, its classicism recalled Hunt's earlier work. In the same year a slightly revised version of Henry Van Brunt's earlier essay, "Greek Lines," appeared in book form.[43] Its publication must have helped to initiate the resurgence of *Néo-Grec* in America. The next year, Hunt published his design for the Fogg Art Museum (later Hunt Hall).[44] Both Corcoran and Fogg designs convey close interpretations of *Néo-Grec*. Hunt may have consulted the Corcoran design, published the previous year. Both expressed their two separate functions in which the gallery block was united with an auditorium. They employed a planar elevation maintaining the identity of the wall with sparse Greek-derived ornament and exploited the possibilities of large- and small-scale elements working together to break down the sense of monumentality by relating the whole to human scale. This reflected the principles and aesthetics of *Néo-Grec* architecture.

The Corcoran Gallery of Art remains a unique achievement and one of Flagg's most elegant and eloquent works. Flagg's design and Norcross's execution account for the bold, yet refined, articulation of stone. In spite of the traumatic events surrounding the Corcoran's construction and the consequences for Flagg's professional standing, the building was admired by the architecturally sophisticated public. When the readers of the *Brochure Series* were asked to vote on "The Ten Most Beautiful Buildings in the United States" in 1899, the Corcoran just missed the list, placing first on a supplementary list of the next ten in popularity.[45] Yet due to the politics of the commission, the architectural press tacitly ignored Flagg's achievement, preferring instead to reproduce photographs of the gallery.

St. Luke's and Other Hospitals

In spite of the events surrounding the St. Luke's Hospital competition, the Board of Managers, critics, and the public were drawn as much to the new aesthetic sensibilities of Flagg's design as to its functional and utilitarian considerations (Fig. 26). St. Luke's Hospital demonstrated to the Board of Managers Flagg's ability to combine "the best internal arrangement" with "the greatest architectural beauty."[46] His design also satisfied the board's requirements to provide fireproof construction, regulated heating and ventilation, "materials thoroughly impervious to disease germs," and maximum southern exposure to the wards.[47] *Harper's Weekly* typified the new awareness and appreciation of both the formal and functional qualities of the design; the editors praised Flagg's plans for their "symmetrical perfectness so loyal to the French Renaissance," and their "harmonious beauty in the rendering of detail." Flagg, they concluded, "has omitted nothing that modern ingenuity could suggest in the way of modern improvements and conveniences to render the institution a model after which other hospitals will be designed."[48]

26. Ernest Flagg. St. Luke's Hospital, New York City.
Perspective, 1892–93 (EFP, AL, CU).

Although different in historical style from the Corcoran Gallery of Art, the design of St. Luke's Hospital also presented the image of a palace: the palace hospital. With its pavilions, block-tower, and dome, St. Luke's reflected the classical palace hospitals of the seventeenth century: Libéral Bruant and Jules Hardouin Mansart's Hôtel des Invalides, Paris, founded in 1670, and Sir Christopher Wren's Royal Naval Hospital, Greenwich, founded in 1694. More directly, Flagg folded a number of historical quotations into an inventive scheme which fulfilled the need to find an expressive language of form appropriate to the character of a modern hospital and to specific planning conditions.

Commanding the promontory of Morningside Heights, or "New York's Acropolis," as an observer described it in 1900, St. Luke's Hospital had been joined by a complement of neighboring institutions: Low Library and the other new buildings of Columbia University, and the future Cathedral of St. John the Divine.[49] Together, these three institutions, as that commentator indicated, cared for "body," "mind," and "souls."[50] These buildings, publicly

90

accessible from the heart of Manhattan by the Amsterdam Avenue trolley, also brought a new scale to the Upper West Side. All three shared a common objective: the search for character and a corresponding style ("modern French Renaissance" for St. Luke's, Roman for Low Library, and Gothic for the Cathedral of St. John the Divine). Flagg designed St. Luke's in what he called "the renaissance style of the modern French school."[51] The style, unique among the competition entries, was controversial. Most of the architects, including James Brown Lord, attempted to harmonize their elevations with the future Gothic cathedral.[52] But when Walter Chambers praised those qualities in St. Luke's which produced order and clarity, as opposed to those which only produced homogenity of style (currently in vogue at the Chicago fair), his criticism was surprisingly well received. "The other architects have evidently thought it desirable to make their designs harmonize in style with the cathedral of St. John the Divine, near which the hospital is to stand," Chambers wrote. "Such an attempt at harmonious ensemble seems to us entirely uncalled for. The Hotel Dieu at Paris stands side by side with Notre Dame. There is no attempt at harmony, and both buildings gain by the contrast," Chambers concluded.[53] The equation between the two churches and the two hospitals served Flagg well.

St. Luke's departed from the predominant use of red brick and the High Victorian design that prevailed in the then most recent American hospitals, including Richard Morris Hunt's administration building of the Presbyterian Hospital in New York, George B. Post's New York Hospital, and Johns Hopkins Hospital in Baltimore. Instead, Flagg's St. Luke's employed limestone and light-colored brick to produce a new image: part hospital, part church, and part palace. Gone was the castellated look of the old St. Luke's Hospital by John Warren Ritch on West 54th Street and Fifth Avenue (begun in 1854; demolished in 1896), described in *King's Handbook of New York City* in 1893 as "constructed of brick, painted a modest drab."[54]

The religious character of St. Luke's Hospital was plainly recognized by both critics and the public. Yet the press, observing that "the architect has taken pains to make his plans so that any one may see that St. Luke's is a church institution," was misguided by its assumption that the image was as straightforward as it seemed.[55] While the character of this Episcopal-affiliated hospital was identified by the chapel, the latter was not celebrated by the hospital's dome. Rather, the dome served an entirely different function. Like the Ether Dome of Charles Bulfinch's Massachusetts General Hospital (1818–23), the drama of the hospital was the amphitheater.[56] At St. Luke's a vaulted operat-

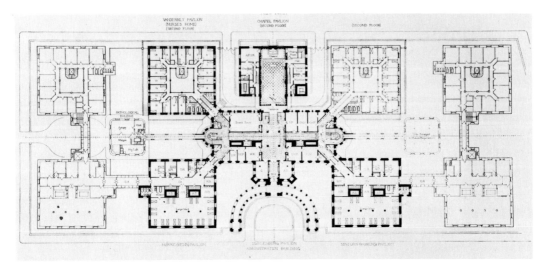

27. Ernest Flagg. St. Luke's Hospital. First floor plan
(indicating second floor plans for rear pavilions)
(*Brickbuilder* V, February 1896, pl. 7).

ing theater, 40 feet high, was embraced within the drum of the dome. The
dome itself concealed the hospital's water tank, a utilitarian necessity, if a
symbolic anticlimax.[57] There, Flagg summoned seventeenth-century French
sources in François Mansart's dome of the Val-de-Grâce, Paris, and Jules
Hardouin Mansart's dome of the Invalides, Paris, for a sufficiently commanding architectural crown. In parallel efforts, both the operating theater and water
tank had been accommodated to appropriate historical motifs, as the pavilion
arrangement had similarly found expression in the *parti* of a seventeenth-
century French palace. Both in plan and elevation, Salomon de Brosse's
Luxembourg Palace, a building which Flagg had frequently visited, was the
acknowledged source for St. Luke's.[58]

Five pavilions, forming the core of the St. Luke's plan, comprised the
first stage of the hospital, completed in 1897 (Fig. 27). They were: an
administration building or pavilion (Muhlenberg); a chapel pavilion (Chapel)
linked by passages to two pavilion dependencies principally containing wards
for men (Norrie) and women (Minturn); and a nurses' residence (Vanderbilt).[59] A smaller independent structure housed the pathology department and
ambulance services. Five additional pavilions were planned for future development, although only three of the Flagg designs were executed.[60] Flagg's plan,
proposing ten pavilions in all, was unique. Although the program had called
for a hospital accommodating 350 patients, Flagg had anticipated a future

patient capacity of 600, virtually doubling the size and services of St. Luke's through an extendable scheme.[61]

St. Luke's frankly recalls the Luxembourg Palace plan, with its *corps de logis* serving as the model for the hospital's administration pavilion.[62] Moreover, St. Luke's derives its image principally from the south or garden facade of the Luxembourg Palace, with its mansarded pavilions and three-story projecting frontispiece (Fig. 28). The south (garden) facade of the Luxembourg was actually the work of Alphonse de Gisors, who rebuilt the facade from 1836 to 1841, largely according to de Brosse's original conception.[63] Likewise, both the white colonnaded vestibule and the chapel of St. Luke's were inspired by the Luxembourg Palace's reception room and chapel, which were added in the nineteenth century. The vaulted interior of St. Luke's chapel and the motif used in the chancel window are derived from Gisors's new Luxembourg Palace chapel in the east wing of the forecourt, formerly occupied by a gallery.[64]

To suit the character of a hospital, Flagg eliminated much of the sculptural effects of the Luxembourg Palace. He also substituted buff-colored brick on the upper stories of the St. Luke's facade. Only the ground floor is rusticated, employing a *fossé,* or ditch (like that of the Corcoran Gallery of Art), which lends monumentality to the building. Banal and utilitarian elements are expressed ceremonially through the use of historical motifs. The ventilating flues of the hospital, for example, resemble those of the Luxembourg Palace. Even the articulation of separate towers, containing staircases and water closets,

28.   Salomon de Brosse and Alphonse de Gisors. Luxembourg Palace, Paris. South (garden) facade.

is similar to the expression of towers on the fifteenth-century Ducal Palace at Urbino, if also common to nineteenth-century hospital design.

Although the Building Committee did not specify a pavilion plan, all entries submitted in the St. Luke's competition employed it. Among them, Flagg's plan was the most literal interpretation.[65] Since the mid-eighteenth century, the pavilion plan had been the preferred type because it responded to the prevailing explanation of disease. Before the discoveries of Louis Pasteur in the 1860s and Robert Koch in the 1870s and 1880s, disease was commonly attributed to "miasmas," or currents of contaminated air. In short, environmental factors were believed to be the only cause of disease.[66] At a time when outside air was considered superior to inside air, hospital planners thus favored a pavilion plan to stimulate a maximum circulation of fresh air, thereby dissipating diseased inside air through natural ventilation.[67] Particularly after the Crimean War when Florence Nightingale advocated its use, the pavilion plan became universally adopted in England and America, as well as in France.[68]

By the 1870s and 1880s, as scientists identified the bacterial or causative agents for a wide range of diseases and Joseph Lister developed antiseptics, physicians may have understood or accepted the germ theory of disease, but they were still cautious about disease prevention within a hospital.[69] Edmund Parkes, a British physician and author of a comprehensive, authoritative, and frequently reissued medical handbook, *A Manual of Practical Hygiene,* stated that "the risk of transference or aggravation of disease is least in the best-ventilated hospitals." Even if the use of antiseptics assured a measure of protection, a maximum degree of ventilation, preferably natural, would provide a fail-safe method of disease prevention.[70]

The acceptance of the germ theory of disease was not accompanied by any radical alteration in the prevailing pavilion arrangement. On the contrary, European and American physicians, public health officials, and hospital planners during the last quarter of the nineteenth century used the fail-safe argument of disease prevention to justify and even perfect the pavilion plan. Although the technology of artificial ventilation was available to them and hospitals employed it, they still relied upon the security of natural ventilation. (One significant and early exception was George B. Post's precocious design of New York Hospital [1869–77], with its prominent ventilating towers.)[71] Flagg's pavilion arrangement at St. Luke's, therefore, was no more than a perfection of a long-established plan, still generally regarded in the 1890s as the safest and most hygienic type.

94

Flagg loosely modeled his scheme for St. Luke's after the celebrated plan for Johns Hopkins Hospital, designed in 1876 by Dr. John S. Billings. Even though Billings supported the new germ theory, he favored the pavilion plan because of its ability to provide maximum natural ventilation and isolation. Each ward at Johns Hopkins Hospital was housed in a separate pavilion.[72] Like Billings, Flagg also chose the pavilion plan for its capacity to isolate, to ventilate, and to provide natural light. Replacing the linear, U-shaped arrangement of Johns Hopkins in which pavilions were distantly strung together, the St. Luke's plan was centralized and bilaterally symmetrical. The extended corridors of the Billings plan, which Flagg thought to be potential germ conduits, were eliminated at St. Luke's.[73] The essence of Flagg's scheme lay in the autonomy of each pavilion, even greater than in the Billings plan. At St. Luke's, each semidetached pavilion was, in effect, isolated from every other one, connected only by means of diagonal passages (at all levels) containing fenestrated arcades. Flagg called these devices "fresh-air cut-offs." There each passage was cross-ventilated, prohibiting the circulation of air horizontally from one pavilion to the next. With no staircases in the ward pavilions, air could not pass vertically from one ward to another above it.[74] Departing from the established pattern of siting, the ward pavilions were now oriented toward a southern exposure, increasing the accessibility of light to them, though patients received only indirect light.[75] The pavilions on the north side, those facing 114th Street, were characterized by 30-foot-square light courts, glazed above and similar to the courts in Flagg's subsequent housing project, the Mills Hotel No. 1 (see Fig. 129). For these reasons St. Luke's was regarded in the popular press as an improvement over the Billings plan at Johns Hopkins Hospital.[76]

Flagg may have had several reasons for employing the pavilion plan long after the advantages of natural ventilation ceased to justify it. The scheme responded to an ongoing fear of contagion—confirmed by New York's cholera epidemic of 1893. Planners believed that the St. Luke's pavilion plan, with its possibilities for isolation and its "fresh-air cut-offs," was best equipped to combat contagion. This implied a preference for natural ventilation, a major concern of St. Luke's Board of Managers when they had chosen the Morningside Heights location for the new hospital.[77] Flagg, like most other hospital planners of the period, considered St. Luke's mechanical ventilation system (provided by mammoth fans and an extensive flue system), as well as its electric lighting, to be supplemental to natural air and light. The ingenuity of the St. Luke's plan lay in Flagg's adaptation of the pavilion scheme to the restrictions imposed by its costly urban site. To conform to the New York City street

29.   Ernest Flagg. St. Luke's Hospital. Section (*Brickbuilder* V,
February 1896, pl. 11).

pattern, with its long east – west and short north – south blocks, Flagg devised a
series of pavilions, square in plan, grouped around the periphery of the
Morningside Heights block, and linked to the central administration pavilion
through diagonal passages.

The plan of St. Luke's strongly adhered to Beaux-Arts principles of
separately articulated spaces and functions. Wards and patient areas were kept
independent from service functions including mechanical and utility areas as
well as circulatory spaces. Staircases and elevators were independent; none were
given direct access to any ward. Even water closets were stacked in separate
towers, appended to the sides of the pavilions, for purposes of isolation and
sanitation.

Aside from the increased isolation of each ward, the most progressive aspect of the St. Luke's plan was its economy of design whereby all identical services and facilities — wards, dining rooms, corridors — were stacked vertically within a skyscraper format. The first floor varied little from the fourth. Only in section were both the complexity and economy of the parts, as well as the split-level relationship between the pavilions on 113th Street and those on 114th Street, apparent (Fig. 29). No space was wasted in any of these pavilions, which ranged from five to nine stories. The general kitchen, for example, was relegated to the space above the chapel. Children's wards were housed above the main vestibule, and isolating rooms were contained within the mansarded roofs above the wards.

With his penchant for invention, Flagg increased the efficiency of both the pavilion plan and the amenities of the fireproof hospital, while providing it with full services. The omission of moldings, cornices, sharp edges, and corners in the interior was strictly observed. Even such amenities as porcelain-lined bathtubs which fitted into the wall replaced the earlier hospital's free-standing tubs on legs. Flagg maintained that he invented this new design and used it for the first time at St. Luke's.[78]

Flagg looked for guidance to French pavilion hospitals because they had successfully combined the art and science of hospital planning. The St. Luke's plan may have appeared strictly utilitarian, but, in fact, it also reflected the architect's aesthetic bias. Flagg maintained that the clarity and symmetry of its discrete parts made the St. Luke's pavilion plan beautiful.[79] He further argued that a plan which combined "beauty of arrangement" with "practical common sense and convenience" could achieve hygienic results, whereas a faulty plan such as a block plan had to "rely upon aseptic solutions and artificial ventilation."[80] Even though Flagg may have consulted authoritative medical judgment in promoting the pavilion plan, he was still relying as much on art, intuition, and nature as on science and technology. These reasons ultimately determined the St. Luke's *parti*. The success of St. Luke's Hospital contributed to the survival of the pavilion plan into the twentieth century.[81]

Along with efficiency, economy, and utility, St. Luke's Hospital sought comforts for the privileged patients who occupied it. In an effort to provide spiritual comfort, the Reverend William Muhlenberg, founder of the first St. Luke's Hospital, believed that patients should be treated as "guests of the church."[82] As the church furnished spiritual comfort, Flagg sought to assure physical comfort. While taking advantage of the fresh air and light that Morningside Heights provided naturally, St. Luke's, so Flagg maintained, also ensured privacy and a congenial atmosphere. If hospital conditions at the new

St. Luke's were sterile (by nineteenth-century standards), the mood was not. Each private room and suite was to be equipped with its own fireplace.[83] Moreover, each of the beds in the women's wards, which like the men's wards were limited to twenty, was provided with a white cloth screen to allow for the patient's privacy.[84] These amenities were, in effect, modern versions of those found in such French medieval hospitals as Tonnerre, which Flagg knew from the writings of Viollet-le-Duc and the French engineer, Casimir Tollet.[85]

The design of St. Luke's, which Flagg generalized into principles in his article, "The Planning of Hospitals," earned him a considerable reputation as a hospital planner.[86] Following St. Luke's, he designed three hospitals, all of which have common ancestry in the New York model. The largest of these was St. Margaret Memorial Hospital in Pittsburgh (1894–98).[87]

In the bequest of Pittsburgh iron and steel industrialist John H. Shoenberger, who died in 1889, funds were allocated for a "Protestant Episcopal Church Hospital" to be a memorial to his deceased wife, Margaret.[88] Shoenberger, who had spent his last years in New York City, had admired the old St. Luke's Hospital, a familiar image on Fifth Avenue. His will stipulated that the design and plan of the memorial hospital scrupulously follow the New York model, allowing for "all such modern improvements and conveniences as the sound judgments of the trustees thereof may suggest."[89]

By 1894 when the newly formed Board of Trustees of St. Margaret Memorial Hospital was finally able to act on the provisions of the Shoenberger will, old St. Luke's had already been declared obsolete. It faced imminent demolition upon the completion of the new hospital in the next few years. In an effort to carry out the spirit of the Shoenberger will, therefore, the Board of Trustees for the Pittsburgh hospital selected Ernest Flagg as architect.[90] While Flagg agreed to "follow the general character of the old St. Luke's building," as an article in the *Philadelphia Press* of January 1896 reported, he maintained that "it would be necessary to make some changes to introduce modern improvements."[91] Flagg, however, had no desire to have his design conform to the block plan of Ritch's hospital of 1854. By the late 1870s St. Luke's had acquired a fearful reputation among progressive hospital planners, even though the New York elite still considered it *the* place to be hospitalized. One writer of the period denounced the lack of hygienic conditions in the old St. Luke's: "At the time of our visit," he reported, "not a window in it was open, and we considered it a receptacle for foul air."[92]

Flagg's design for St. Margaret Memorial Hospital skillfully evoked the profile and composition of Ritch's St. Luke's elevations (Fig. 30). Trans-

30. Ernest Flagg. St. Margaret Memorial Hospital, 265 46th Street, Pittsburgh, 1894–98 (St. Margaret Memorial Hospital).

31. Ernest Flagg. St. Margaret Memorial Hospital. Plan (*Works,* fig. 20).

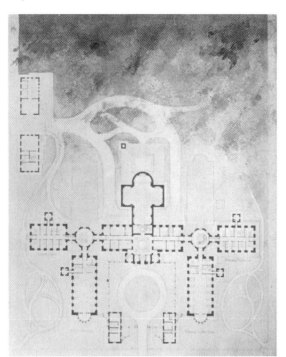

posing Ritch's Italianate design into one decidedly informed by French classicism, Flagg retained the twin towers and side wings, as well as the general symmetry present in old St. Luke's. The substitution of red brick and sandstone trim for painted brick was still a substantial departure. Yet, Flagg was careful not to employ a specific historical style, but a mixture of French sources. Flagg's design for St. Margaret's with a two-story pedimented frontispiece and towers, recalled early eighteenth-century French models, even though the gravity and sculptural treatment of its facade evoked sixteenth-century French models and its red brick reflected northern baroque churches.[93] Furthermore, the chapel at St. Margaret's, cruciform in plan with domical vaulting, reflected the French classicism of the St. Luke's chapel.[94]

Where high land values, a constricted site, and street grid had determined a tightly organized pavilion arrangement at St. Luke's, the acquisition of a large plot of open and "comparatively inexpensive" land in Pittsburgh permitted a more intricate and decentralized pavilion plan for St. Margaret's (Fig. 31). However, those principles which inform the St. Luke's plan are again operable at St. Margaret's. Even though the chapel at St. Margaret's dominates the plan, the towers which actually express the hospital's religious character (like the dome at St. Luke's) are separate elements. A division of the plan into five pavilions, and the functions the pavilions contain, are similar to the *parti* at St. Luke's.[95] But at St. Margaret's, the pavilions are interconnected by octago-

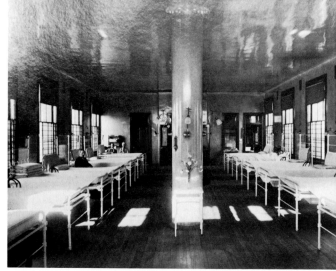

32. Ernest Flagg. St. Margaret Memorial Hospital. Men's ward (St. Margaret Memorial Hospital).

33. Ernest Flagg. Naval Hospital, Annapolis, Maryland, 1904–7
(Naval Hospital, Annapolis).

nal towers which function as "fresh-air cut-offs" and contain staircases. Wards
permit the benefits of isolation, ventilation, and light (Fig. 32). Men's and
women's wards each contain a glazed hemicycle solarium in their narrower
south end. Flagg followed the St. Luke's pattern of stacked wards and services,
the separation of functions, and the use of innovative fixtures. He also introduced an important construction innovation for the domical vault of the
chapel. Completed in 1898, the chapel vault employed an early use of reinforced concrete, a material consistent with Flagg's interest in wider applications
of new technology.[96]

The concept of the pavilion plan and many of the essential components
of Flagg's design for St. Luke's and St. Margaret's were again brought together
in two naval hospitals: one in Washington, D.C., of 1903-6; the other in
Annapolis, Maryland, of 1904-7 (Fig. 33).[97] Both were built when most of the
new buildings at the Naval Academy by Flagg were still under construction.[98]
The significance of these two hospitals, which follow the pavilion plan, lies in
Flagg's accommodation of their style to Tidewater regionalism. They relate
particularly well to Flagg's domestic architecture. In fact, in their plan, composition, scale, materials, ornament, and functional details, these small-scale

34. Ernest Flagg. Naval Hospital, Annapolis, Maryland. Ward pavilions
(Naval Hospital, Annapolis).

hospitals are most similar to examples of domestic building of the colonial
period in the Tidewater region. The Naval Hospital at Annapolis, with its
central administration building and double pavilion wings linked at right
angles to it, reconstitutes the plans of many colonial buildings and their
dependencies in Annapolis, particularly the mid-eighteenth-century houses by
William Buckland.[99] The plan of each hospital, so similar to St. Luke's and St.
Margaret's, is not the only eighteenth-century reference. Apart from the use of
buff-colored brick — substituted for red brick, which was less suitable for a
hospital than for domestic architecture and more compatible with the other
new buildings of the Academy — a number of elements evoke the image of the
southern colonial house. For the administration building Flagg employed a
hipped roof, a classical entrance portico in wood, and quoins. Each of the
pavilion wings displayed a parapet gable containing stepped patterns of brickwork and punctuated with an oculus to accommodate an exhaust fan (Fig. 34).
Such gables of elaborately patterned brick with *oeils-de-boeuf* for utilitarian
construction are lavishly illustrated in the French publication by Pierre Chabat,
La Brique et la terre cuite of 1881.[100] The Naval Hospital in Washington
shares the essential features of its counterpart at Annapolis. Each hospital
illustrates Flagg's concern to rationalize and beautify utilitarian buildings, both
in terms of plan and materials.

35.   Ernest Flagg. Project for the New York Public Library. Perspective by
V. Perard, 1892 (*Arch Rev* I, September 12, 1892, p. 69).

36.   Ernest Flagg. Project for the New York Public Library. Plan, 1892
(*Arch Rev* I, September 12, 1892, p. 71).

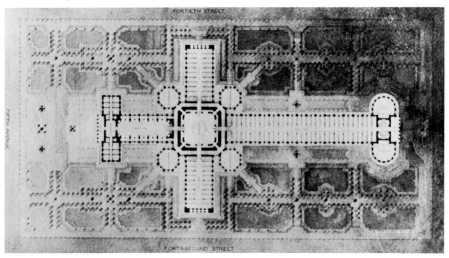

Libraries and Churches

In his project for the Tilden Trust Library of 1892 (Fig. 35) and in
three small rural libraries, Flagg applied the architectural principles he had
learned at the Ecole des Beaux-Arts. The Tilden Library plan (Fig. 36), a Latin
cross, contained a central rotunda modeled after the one at the British Museum.[101] The parts of Flagg's Tilden plan — central rotunda with octagonal
reading rooms clustered around it and long wings for stack areas — were all

37. Ernest Flagg. Sheldon Library, St. Paul's School, Concord,
New Hampshire, 1900–1901 (EFP, AL, CU).

38. Ernest Flagg. Lawrence Library, Pepperell, Massachusetts, 1899–1901.

separately expressed; each space was provided with its own light source. The
elevation, therefore, reflected the plan. Critics labeled its style *Néo-Grec* and
compared it favorably to Louis Duc's Palais de Justice. For reasons of efficiency
and surveillance, however, its dispersed plan with long wings undoubtedly
failed to inspire the confidence of librarians.

In two subsequent works — the Sheldon Library at St. Paul's School, Concord, New Hampshire, of 1900–1901 (Fig. 37), and the Lawrence Library, Pepperell, Massachusetts, of 1899–1901 (Fig. 38), Flagg consolidated his evolving library plan. Here similar programs called for similar solutions. Like the Corcoran Gallery of Art plan, these library plans showed a clarity of parts defined on the exterior as separately expressed volumes. The Lawrence Library plan, like the Sheldon Library, was dominated by a central hall containing reference services and a circulation desk (Fig. 39). Ancillary spaces — reading room, stacks, and stairhall — were well articulated spatial components. Like the Tilden Library, each space was defined by an independent light source. Thermal windows lighted the higher parts of the Sheldon Library, while louvered windows brought light and ventilation to the upper reaches of the Lawrence Library. The stacks of both libraries were lighted by vertical windows.

Like Peter Harrison and H. H. Richardson before him, Flagg's task was to identify the architectural character of the rural New England library. Flagg's Lawrence and Sheldon libraries were particularly sensitive to the domestic scale that had characterized small libraries in America since Harrison's Redwood Library, Newport (1748–50). The Lawrence Library combined red brick with limestone trim, an association with Colonial Revival architecture of the period.[102] The triple-arched portal with its emphasized corners reflected a

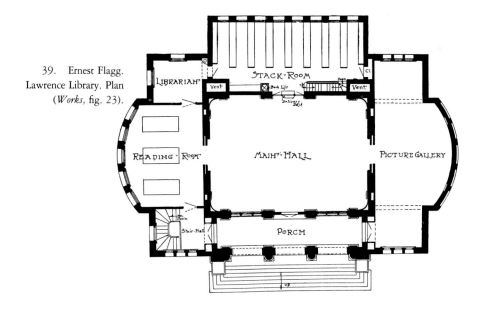

39. Ernest Flagg. Lawrence Library. Plan (*Works,* fig. 23).

40.   Ernest Flagg. YMCA Building, Cooperstown, New York, 1897–98
(*Arch Rec* X, October 1900, p. 184).

similar treatment at Carrère & Hastings' New York Public Library, Jean-Camille Formigé's twin Palais at the 1889 Paris fair (see Fig. 14), and Ginain's
more sculptural Musée Galliera, Paris (see Fig. 7).[103] Lawrence Library is
especially distinguished for its use of ornamental iron cornices, brackets, and
louvered windows. Such ironwork was Flagg's trademark, used not for structural reasons, but for aesthetic ones in order to identify the library as a product
of "the French school."

Dramatically different from the Lawrence Library in its architectural
imagery, the Sheldon Library employed an obvious conceit. It bore a strong
resemblance to John H. Duncan's "Grant's Tomb" (The Grant Monument),
a structure that had been completed only recently along Riverside Drive, New
York (1890–97).[104] Flagg may have wished to realize the librarian's dream:
"quiet as a tomb." If so, his model was persuasive. The elegiac character of the
library—a memorial to St. Paul's School trustee William Crawford Sheldon,
Jr.—combined with its isolated pond site and a structure of Concord granite,
all suggest a comparison with monumental tomb sculpture.[105] But both Flagg
and Duncan may have drawn their *partis* from a common French source which
employed a solid base and drum: Ledoux's Barrière de la Villette, Paris
(1784–89).[106]

A third rural building combined a YMCA, a library, and a museum at
Cooperstown, New York (1897–98).[107] Club functions dominated the program for the YMCA Building (Fig. 40). As before, Flagg consulted regional

characteristics without forgetting his French training. A wooden entrance porch with paneled piers stretched across the entire facade, in the way that Louis-Pierre Baltard, on a more monumental scale, had screened his Palais de Justice, Lyons (1832–42), or American architects had defined the temple fronts of their modest domestic buildings.[108] Like the Corcoran Gallery of Art, the frieze contained such *Néo-Grec* detailing as metopes expressed as shields. The YMCA Building suggested an accommodation to vernacular regionalism. Its domestic scale, plain facade of local gray stone, and porch with ornamental trim of wood, were general characteristics of the architecture and use of materials that had prevailed in Cooperstown since the eighteenth century. In this way it differed from urban YMCAs of the period.

During the late nineteenth century the town was dominated by the philanthropic and social activities of Mrs. Alfred Corning Clark who, widowed in 1896, had become an heir to the Singer Manufacturing Company fortune.[109] Mrs. Clark was one of Ernest Flagg's earliest and most influential patrons and the client for this new institution, also known as the Clark Building.[110] Celebrated for its colonial architecture in the eighteenth century, its Greek Revival architecture in the nineteenth century, and the literary heritage created by its favorite son, James Fenimore Cooper, Cooperstown was a traditional town with a strong sense of its past. Flagg's clever design for the YMCA Building—recalling American architecture of the late Federal and Early National periods and French *Néo-Grec* ornament—was compatible with the town's self-image.

Whether a project for a national cathedral, a suburban church, or a chapel for a hospital or a school, Flagg's *parti* for a church was invariably an auditorium. For Protestant church architecture, Flagg consistently designed a centralized auditorium, the acoustics of which would be favorable for preaching and singing. Flagg expounded these views in 1895 when he submitted both a "Gothic" and a "Renaissance" design for the Cathedral of Saint Peter and Saint Paul (Washington Cathedral).[111] Flagg clearly favored his Renaissance design (Fig. 41). In an effort to persuade cathedral trustees to select it, Flagg also submitted an essay in which he argued for the superiority of Renaissance over Gothic architecture on the basis of functionalism. Gothic design, Flagg maintained, was anachronistic to modern church building because of its "multiplicity of supports," long and narrow nave with obstructed views from side aisles, its limited visibility and acoustics, and its inability to accommodate the modern technology of fireproof construction.[112] By contrast, a Renaissance design with its centralized plan and domical vaulting fulfilled these modern requirements. Although there were pre-Renaissance precedents for the use of centralized plans and domical vaulting, Flagg chose to ignore them.[113] Flagg may have argued for the functional advantages of a Renaissance design, but he was equally motivated by an aesthetic preference. Gothic did not fit easily into his world view. With support in the architectural press for the practical benefits of Flagg's choice, cathedral trustees accepted his "modern French Renaissance" design by January 1896.[114]

Flagg's design set a precedent for American church building because it attempted to promote the requirements of assembly over those of liturgy. Although Flagg considered the new scale appropriate for a national cathedral, it was unduly large. The domical structure of white marble, which Flagg envisioned, would have been the most monumental church of Renaissance design in America, as New York's Cathedral of St. John the Divine was conceived as the largest church of Gothic design. Cruciform in plan (interior dimensions: 224 × 176 feet) with a rotunda in the center (interior height: 208

41. Ernest Flagg. Project for the Cathedral of Saint Peter and Saint Paul (Washington Cathedral), Washington, D.C., 1895–96 (*Harper's Weekly* XL, January 25, 1896).

42. Ernest Flagg
(George M. Bartlett,
associate architect).
Farmington Avenue Church
(now Immanuel Congregational
Church), Hartford, 1897–99.

feet), Flagg's design was to be a national church auditorium in which, the *New York Herald* reported, "3500 people will be able to see and hear the Bishop from under the great roof."[115] The church dome recalled the dome of the Invalides, while the gargantuan arched entrance, which spanned a clear 80 feet, reflected the portals of the 1889 Paris fair.[116]

A decade later, after Flagg had been dropped from the Washington Cathedral project and his Renaissance design abandoned, the question of style arose again. In 1906 cathedral trustees formally voted in favor of Gothic.[117] Due to the efforts of Bishop Henry Satterlee who urged "a *genuine* Gothic Cathedral on this side of the Atlantic," George Frederick Bodley, a British architect specializing in Gothic design, was selected.[118] Bishop Satterlee's desire to plant a "genuine" Gothic cathedral had overpowered Flagg's earlier objective to plant a "genuine" Renaissance cathedral in America.[119]

In his design for the Farmington Avenue Church, Hartford (1897–99; now Immanuel Congregational Church), Flagg (with George M. Bartlett as associate architect) further explored the church as auditorium (Fig. 42).[120] At the same time, he revived early medieval architectural forms, a popular practice in Germany, America, and elsewhere at mid-century known as *Rundbogenstil* (round-arched style).[121]

This red brick church, commanding a hill site directly across from Mark Twain's High Victorian residence at Nook Farm (1873–74) by E. T.

Potter and A. H. Thorp, was considered an architectural aberration when completed in 1899.[122] The use of plain red brick — then the ubiquitous building material of factories and mills — and exotic tile ornament for a church in Hartford's residential West End, was the object of considerable local ridicule.[123]

When the church's pastor, the Reverend W.D.L. Love, and its trustees decided to move the congregation from the center of Hartford to the affluent West End in 1897, they abandoned and subsequently demolished their own Pearl Street Church (1851 – 52).[124] The trustees wished for a new image, altogether different from Minard Lafever's stone and spired church, a hybrid of "colonial" and "Romanesque" forms common to New England churches in the 1850s and 1860s. Not only had conditions in downtown Hartford become unmanageably congested, but the old structure was no longer adequate to meet the new programmatic requirements of the modern church.[125] Flagg's design thus responded to the Building Committee's efforts to satisfy a new program and to realize a new architectural form reflecting "the most modern ideas of church architecture."[126] *The Congregationalist,* literary vehicle of the national church organization, reported that "for an exterior a departure was desired from the old Puritan style, and also the cathedral and Gothic ideas were laid aside." The journal concluded that the resulting design is "thought to be utterly unlike anything in the country, suggestive perhaps of the mosque or synagogue."[127] The dramatic change in architectural form signaled a break from the traditional Congregational meetinghouse form in favor of a centralized plan with a rotunda. Earlier, Carrère & Hastings had used the rotunda for its Central Congregational Church, Providence (1891).[128]

Flagg recalled Early Christian, Byzantine, and Romanesque architecture for the plan, massing, style, and composition of the Farmington Avenue Church. He modeled the cruciform plan of the church, its use of brick, its pediments on each arm of the cross, and its Byzantine-influenced tile ornament after the Merovingian Baptistère Saint-Jean at Poitiers.[129] Flagg had been intrigued particularly with the baptistry during a visit to Poitiers in the summer of 1890. In it, he saw the promise of "a very peculiar plan which might be used with success."[130] Flagg's design for the Farmington Avenue Church reconstituted the volumes of the Poitiers structure, its cross arms and its apse, so that they would radiate from a central rotunda. To fulfill other programmatic requirements, including bell tower, entrance porch, and porte cochere, Flagg looked to Roman basilicas and Northern Italian round arch churches. The massing of the Hartford church, for example, is similar to the eighth-century

Roman basilica of S. Giorgio in Velabro.[131] Flagg undoubtedly found the Roman basilica as adaptable as McKim, Mead & White did in its design for the Judson Memorial Church, New York, of 1893.

Aside from any specific sources that Flagg used, the massing and composition reflected his personal style and Beaux-Arts education. Symmetry and axial organization of parts predominated. The massing of the rotunda, projecting above the main block, and the placement of subordinate parts were common to the Tilden, Sheldon, and Lawrence libraries (see Figs. 35, 37, and 38). Yet there was also an abstract relationship among the parts, separately expressed as volumes. The controlled tension among these forms and the differences in their basically similar elements (viz., a porte cochere on one side corresponding to a vestibule and staircase leading to a gallery on the other) were characteristic of late-nineteenth-century American and English architecture (for example, McKim, Mead & White houses in Newport, particularly the Commodore William Edgar House of 1885 – 86) and the domestic architecture of Richard Norman Shaw and Edwin Lutyens in England.[132] This freedom of composition and massing within the parameters of Beaux-Arts design was also an essential component of Flagg's domestic architecture.

Also characteristic of his style, Flagg monumentalized each projecting arm of the Hartford church with a pediment and round-arch window below, similar to the monumental entrance of his Washington Cathedral design and examples of French architecture during the early Third Republic. In contrast to the plainness of the red brick, each pediment contained yellow and green tiles adapted from the Poitiers baptistry.[133] Like the brickwork, the glazed tile ornament was controversial.[134]

In spite of the criticism the brickwork received in the popular press — red brick was considered too ordinary for ecclesiastical architecture — it was the *tour de force* of Flagg's design. The Farmington Avenue Church demonstrated Flagg's theories on the bonding of brickwork which he published in *Brickbuilder*.[135] Here brick construction followed methods which, Flagg believed, affirmed the logic of the material: bricks were laid up in regular bonds with relieving arches and flat arches. Moreover, Flagg believed that such methods of construction ensured the aesthetic potential intrinsic to the medium, realizing "all sorts of interesting patterns and endless varieties of beautiful wall surfaces by the use of brick of the standard size regularly bonded to and forming an integral part of the body of the wall."[136] Flagg designed his brickwork to illustrate the rational principles of decorated structure, yet his insistence on recessed mortar joints was not completely functional.[137]

111

The interior of the Farmington Avenue Church has a spare, almost secular, quality. Its plain walls and plaster vault, ornamented in eighteenth-century relief painted white, convey the residual mood of the New England meetinghouse.[138] Originally, an imposing organ occupied the central position in the chancel.[139] Together the pulpit and organ served the church's two primary functions: preaching and singing. By day, natural light flooded the interior on all sides through arched openings and reinforced the centrality of the space. Copper tracery, modeled after that which Alphonse de Gisors had used in the Luxembourg Palace chapel and which Flagg had designed earlier for the St. Luke's chapel, secured a large expanse of clear glass. Panels of red Bohemian glass, etched with a floral motif, formed a thin border to each window and provided the only color in an otherwise white interior. By night, garlands of electric light, composed of hundreds of bare bulbs punctuating the cornice and moldings, unified the interior space. This simple and direct lighting was undoubtedly inspired by the use of incandescent lights at the 1889 Paris fair. Flagg often adopted this method because of its variety of effects.

In defining the church as auditorium, Flagg emphasized the centrality of the rotunda and the subordination of the ancillary functions. Exteriors corresponded to interior volumes so that constituent parts were legible. In so doing, Flagg brought into sympathetic alliance the Beaux-Arts principles of composition, the French structural rationalism of the early Third Republic, the structural expression inherent in the *Rundbogenstil,* and the traditional planarity of American church architecture.

Schools: The United States Naval Academy, Annapolis

Of all Flagg's designs for institutions, the United States Naval Academy at Annapolis is his most monumental — some fifteen or so major buildings replacing thirty or more older structures of the Academy. Flagg rightfully regarded the Naval Academy work as his most important and prestigious commission.[140] Designed from 1896, just three years after the Chicago fair, the new Naval Academy shared its scale and plan with American and French exposition architecture. The Naval Academy also approached the formal qualities and academic classicism of an Ecole *projet*. But the diverse buildings within the Naval Academy complex equally illustrated Flagg's facility with structural rationalism.

While the U.S. Navy had experienced a renewal during the 1870s and 1880s, it was not until the last decade of the century that two events caused a new assessment of the navy's viability and future. The first was a series of publications by Captain Alfred Thayer Mahan, a professor of military history at Newport's Naval War College. Defining a new ideological basis for an aggressive navy, Mahan advocated a policy of tactical defense combined with a program of mercantilistic and territorial imperialism. He first articulated the historical premise for this doctrine in a publication of 1890, *The Influence of Sea Power Upon History, 1660–1783*.[141] Mahan's writings strongly influenced a number of key American political and military leaders, including Theodore Roosevelt who became Assistant Secretary of the Navy in 1897.[142] The second event was the Spanish-American War. Fought and won largely on the seas (April to August 1898), it affirmed the viability of Mahan's theories and permanently shaped a new policy of naval supremacy. Thus a strong navy for control of the seas was an economic and political imperative, as well as a military objective.

These events forced a fresh appraisal of the navy, its training, facilities, and institutions. Consequently, the architecture of the existing Naval Academy became the object of sharp journalistic criticism: "a motley assemblage of buildings," wrote *Scientific American* in 1898, "which are now inadequate and out of date, so that they tend to militate against the success of the modern courses of instruction."[143]

In the spring of 1895, President Cleveland appointed a Board of Visitors "to examine and report upon the condition of the grounds and buildings, and sanitary condition of [the] Academy."[144] The Board consisted of a dozen members including several army and naval officers, a clergyman, congressmen, and university professors.[145] Among them a New York industrialist, Robert M. Thompson, who had graduated from the Academy in 1868, inspected the institution and submitted a report to Secretary of the Navy, Commodore H. A. Herbert, on June 7, 1895. The 1895 Board of Visitors recommended that a second board, consisting of five naval officers, be appointed to repeat the inspection of all Naval Academy buildings and submit a detailed report of their findings, along with plans indicating both existing buildings and proposed new structures.[146]

The new board, headed by Commodore Edmund O. Matthews, Chief of the Bureau of Yards and Docks, met on July 16, 1895, to fulfill the mandate of the Board of Visitors. Their report, submitted to the Secretary of the Navy on January 16, 1896, outlined the "very bad condition" of the present buildings — some thirty-five single buildings and building complexes — and recommended that land be filled in and a seawall constructed to accommodate a plan for "the erection of substantial fireproof buildings of indestructible material, properly arranged and situated, to be convenient, healthy, and thoroughly adapted to the requirements of an institution that is to last for all time."[147] Accompanying the recommendations were two plans: one indicating the location of present buildings, another illustrating a master plan with new structures.

To formulate the new plan, Robert M. Thompson played an instrumental role. President of the Orford Copper Company in New York, Thompson had been an active alumnus who from the late 1880s had promoted a rigorous athletic program.[148] It was Thompson who engaged Flagg.[149] Although only a plan accompanied the Matthews Board report of 1896, Flagg evidently had developed a comprehensive scheme which is no longer extant. Still surviving, however, is a photograph of a perspective of 1898 by H. Dole (Fig. 43) that corresponds to the Flagg plan of 1896.

Flagg's early scheme received the enthusiastic support of navy spokesmen, especially Theodore Roosevelt who, as Assistant Secretary of the Navy, endorsed it in a letter of December 27, 1897, to his superior, Commodore Herbert. While Roosevelt proceeded cautiously, he did urge new construction

43. Ernest Flagg. United States Naval Academy, Annapolis, Maryland.
Perspective by H. Dole, 1898 (U.S. Naval Academy Museum).

for an armory, a boathouse, and a powerhouse, plus "the dredging and building of a sea wall so as to provide for the basin in which the training ship and torpedo boats should lie."[150] More importantly, Roosevelt supported the future implementation of Flagg's plan. The Assistant Secretary sent his endorsement: "I heartily commend it for its simplicity, dignity, and adaptation to the practical needs of the institution."[151] In spite of Roosevelt's obvious appreciation of the very qualities in the scheme which Flagg too considered most significant, the architect mistrusted the politician's hawkish motives and, ironically, his attitude toward government spending. In recalling an incident years later, Flagg expressed his displeasure with Roosevelt's peremptory reception of him and his Naval Academy drawings: "I had hardly begun to explain them when he stopped me and said, with his usual impulsiveness, 'I see it all, I see it all, we must not consider cost.' With that we were dismissed."[152]

To implement Flagg's monumental plan, more land needed to be obtained through the annexation of an area adjacent to the Academy grounds and by dredging to reclaim land. Congress authorized the expansion of the Naval Academy along its southwest border "by purchase or by condemnation for public use" of private property, as early as June 10, 1896.[153] The acquisition of this property met no opposition by the City Council of Annapolis which, on February 4, 1898, approved the purchase of a first parcel of land comprising sixty-nine lots of private property.[154] Navy officials also urged self-righteously, that two additional waterfront blocks be condemned for their potentially deleterious effect upon young naval cadets and officers. In advocating the annexation of the second parcel, Lieutenant-Commander E. K. Moore, "In Charge of Buildings and Grounds," submitted his evaluation of the area to the Naval Academy Superintendent, Captain P. H. Cooper. In these two blocks, Moore reported, were "noisy rum shops" and "one large oyster packing house" which "employs a number of people of both sexes, not of the highest character, whose language is loud, boisterous, and very unsavory, and can be heard over that part of the Academy where the new Cadet Quarters are to be located."[155] In effect, navy officials regarded the situation as potentially dangerous. Should the waterfront blocks remain intact, Naval Academy officials feared the corruption of its cadets by female factory workers (much as Mérimée's Carmen corrupted the soldier, Don José). They hoped, instead, that the "old Colonial town," as one Naval Academy professor wrote in 1899, might produce a purified environment in which "opportunities for intercourse with its refined and cultured society, all aid in forming from the embryonic naval cadet a courteous gentleman and a healthy, polished, efficient naval officer."[156] To this end, the entire area "between the Academy grounds and King George Street, and extending from Governor Street to the water front," was purchased by Congressional appropriation on March 3, 1899.[157]

Conforming to the wishes of the Matthews Board of 1896, Flagg's original plan called for the wholesale destruction of the Naval Academy's existing buildings, barring only a few exceptions. Two historic buildings were initially exempt from demolition: the colonial Government House of Maryland, an eighteenth-century red brick structure used as a library which Flagg hoped to restore to a superintendent's residence; and Fort Severn, which was built in 1808, manned during the War of 1812, and provisionally saved because of its historic association as the site chosen by George Bancroft when he founded the Naval Academy in 1845.[158] But by 1901, even the intention to preserve the colonial structure was abandoned by navy officials and all of the old Naval Academy buildings, except Fort Severn, were slated for demolition "in the march of academic improvement," observed the *New York Times* in 1904.[159] Furthermore, despite the initial good intentions reserved for the venerable Fort Severn, even this landmark was demolished in 1909.[160] Thus, no sooner had the new Naval Academy opened than it sundered a long historical association with colonial Annapolis and, in the process, virtually eradicated all trace of its own ancestry.

It was not until May 4, 1898, when Recitation Hall, a red brick Victorian structure of the existing campus, was declared unsafe that initial Congressional appropriations of $1 million were made for the erection of an armory, boathouse, powerhouse, and a portion of the seawall.[161] Later that month, Flagg entered into a contract with Naval Academy Superintendent, Philip H. Cooper, to design these three structures. Flagg would receive a fee of 5 percent of their total cost.[162] Yet from the first, the recommendations of the Matthews Board and the substance of Flagg's plan did not go unchallenged by Congress or by the press. Early in 1899, as construction on new buildings was under way, the *New York Times* reported that Congress had never approved the Naval Academy plan. The press also disclosed the demolition of the Academy's existing buildings, declaring some of them — contrary to the thrust of the Matthews Board report — to be in "very good condition."[163] Spearheading Congressional approval and appropriation was I. E. Mudd, Representative from Maryland; in opposition was Charles A. Boutelle, Representative from Maine who was also a retired naval officer and chairman of the Committee on Naval Affairs.[164] After vigorous debate, funds totaling $8 million were finally appropriated by a Congressional Act, approved June 7, 1900, for the "re-

44.   Ernest Flagg. United States Naval Academy. Perspective by Hughson Hawley,
1899 (*Architectural Annual 1900,* p. 188).

building of the Naval Academy."[165] In addition to the difficulties surrounding
the appropriation, Flagg's plan and commission had also been the subject of
some controversy because neither had received Congressional approval; nor
had a projected cost for the new Naval Academy been fully tabulated. That
same year both his plan and his commission as architect were subjected to
Congressional and peer review, eventually receiving the navy's endorsement.[166]

During the course of the Congressional review, most of Flagg's original *parti* for the Naval Academy was retained. However, the strong harbor
image was gradually eroded as the plan neared execution. A perspective by
Hughson Hawley of 1899 (Fig. 44) illustrated the waterfront orientation of
Flagg's plan which projected the image of such Imperial Roman ports as Lepcis
Magna in North Africa during the time of Septimius Severus. Combining the
elements of the Roman port city, including a harbor, a lighthouse, and an
amphitheater, with the functions of aquatic sports and naval training, Flagg's
design called for a basin on the Severn River at Annapolis with beacons
bracketing its entrance and an amphitheater overlooking it. Within the basin,
torpedo boats, launches, and sailing vessels would be moored and accessible
from the boathouse. Hawley's perspective also indicated the Chapel at a higher
elevation, on axis with the amphitheater and bandstand. Although the basin
was dredged, construction of either of the two stone lighthouses or the amphitheater, "upon which," remarked Flagg, "so much of the beauty of the plan
depends," never took place.[167]

117

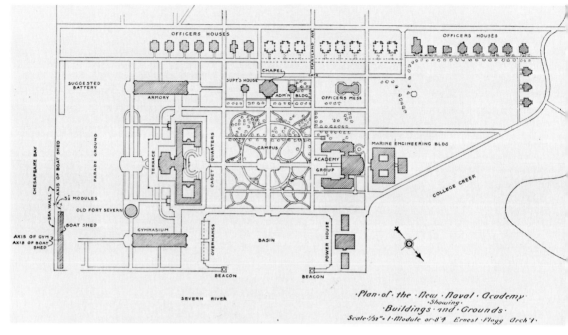

45.   Ernest Flagg. United States Naval Academy. Plan (*AABN* XCIV,
July 1, 1908, fig. 2).

46.   Ernest Flagg. United States Naval Academy, Annapolis, Maryland. Aerial
photograph taken in 1922 (U.S. Naval Academy Museum).

Flagg's plan as executed involved three major building complexes, each facing the Yard, as seen in an aerial photograph of 1922 (Figs. 45, 46). Although most of the Victorian buildings of the Academy were demolished, Flagg's plan did preserve, at least, the picturesque landscaping and circuitous paths of the old campus, onto which he superimposed a cross axis of paved arteries on the existing green space. Thus the new campus was at once scaled to and designed for individuals and couples strolling, as well as for battalions marching.

The final plan indicated a balance of parts and a studied asymmetry characteristic of late-nineteenth-century Ecole *projets*. The Bancroft Hall group consisted of Bancroft Hall (the cadet quarters) facing the Yard, and Memorial Hall facing Chesapeake Bay, with Dahlgren Hall (the former armory now used as a student center) and Macdonough Hall (the boathouse-gymnasium) on either side. Balancing this complex across the yard was the so-called Academic group. There, Mahan Hall (a library-auditorium building) stood in the center, flanked by Maury Hall (an academic building) and Sampson Hall (a physics and chemistry building). Isherwood Hall (a marine-engineering building) was located behind them.[168] Commanding the entire Yard and the main axis to the Severn, the Chapel formed the focus of a third group of buildings that included the Superintendent's House on one side and the Administration Building on the other. The Officers' Mess and a row of Officers' Houses were removed to the northwest boundary of the Academy grounds.[169]

The first two structures of Flagg's plan to be placed under construction, on March 28, 1899, were Macdonough Hall and Dahlgren Hall (Fig. 47). Because of their utilitarian nature, Flagg synthesized in their design elements of French classical idealism and structural rationalism. Each of the two nearly identical granite structures was part fortified gate, part arsenal, part warehouse. Massive battered towers faced Chesapeake Bay and the Yard. These monumental triumphal gates led to a shed-like space spanned with exposed metal trusses and a glazed skylight. The heavily rusticated tower walls, symbols of the invincibility embodied in Mahan's thesis, bore the Naval Academy seal and motto, *Ex Scientia Tridens* (From Knowledge, Sea Power).[170] Flagg thus envisioned the twin structures to be symbolic as well as functional: "the Boat House on one side of the quarters, typifying the nautical side of the midshipman's training, and the Armory on the other, typifying the military side."[171] Unfortunately Flagg's scheme was compromised in 1906 when the Department of the Navy decided that the structure first intended as a boathouse could better serve as a gymnasium.[172] This decision removed any

47.   Ernest Flagg. Dahlgren Hall. View from northwest, 1896–1903
(U.S. Naval Academy Museum).

48.   Léon Chifflot. *Porte d'entrée d'une Capitale* (*Croquis d'Architecture*,
Intime Club, XXIII, December 1896, no. XII, f. 6).

compelling need for the navy to complete Dewey Basin according to Flagg's original plan.

The fortified gate had been a common image of French classicism. Boullée, for example, had used it for his project for a City Gate.[173] Likewise, when an Ecole *projet* called for a building type with a military function and corresponding character, the fortified gate was inevitably the preferred image. In 1896 Léon Chifflot had undoubtedly taken Boullée's project as the model for his *Porte d'entrée d'une Capitale* (Fig. 48). Winner of the Concours Achille Leclère of 1896, Chifflot's Ecole *projet* served as a fortified gate and military post for twenty-five men.[174] Flagg would have known this widely published design. A less specific image of the fortified gate, also adapted to military housing, was Jacques Hermant's Caserne des Célestins, Paris, of 1896 (see Fig. 12). However, its particular significance with respect to the Naval Academy is more apparent in Bancroft Hall.

The designs for the armory and boathouse-gymnasium symbolized their military and naval functions and achieved structural expression. Flagg enclosed a monumental arched opening between the granite piers of each tower gate, while exploiting the decorative possibilities of combining masonry, metal, and glass. Spanning each vast arch was a metal grill painted green with ornamental terra-cotta tiles as infill.[175] This screen, although unique in America at this time, was not Flagg's invention, for it had formerly been the structural and decorative system widely employed by Formigé and others in the buildings of the 1889 Paris fair (see Fig. 15). The shed-like appearance of these structures also recalled the French railway station.[176] In designing these structures, Flagg adapted a French system of decoration, which he considered rational, to an American building type, the armory. He followed that procedure a few years later with another uniquely American building type, the skyscraper. These two Academy structures conveyed further elements of Flagg's style including emphasized corners with a large-scale central arch, so like Flagg's churches and chapels.

Although critics generally ignored Flagg's design for the armory and boathouse-gymnasium, American architects did not. While a student at the Ecole des Beaux-Arts (Atelier Blondel), Donn Barber (1871–1925) adopted Flagg's *parti* in a decidedly literal way in his project for a Railroad Station, which helped him to secure a diploma in 1898.[177] The Saint Louis firm of Eames & Young, similarly influenced, recombined the elements of Flagg's *parti* in their competition drawings of 1903 for the Riding Hall of the Military Academy at West Point.[178]

49. Ernest Flagg. Bancroft Hall (cadet quarters). View from the Yard
1899–1906 (U.S. Naval Academy Museum).

50. Ernest Flagg. Bancroft Hall group. Executed plan (*AABN* XCIV,
July 1, 1908, fig. 4).

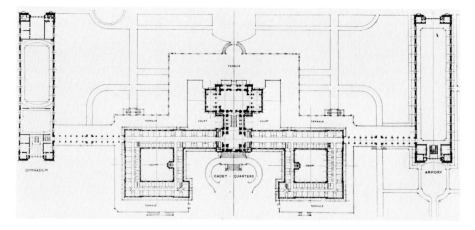

Bancroft Hall, the cadet quarters where midshipmen were billeted, was the focus of the Bancroft Hall group (Fig. 49). It had direct access to the armory and boathouse-gymnasium through a colonnade. As executed, the plan of Bancroft Hall (Fig. 50) — said to be the largest dormitory in the world — called for a deep forecourt formed by a *corps de logis* and projecting side wings, each with a central light court indebted to the plan of Ange-Jacques Gabriel's Ecole Militaire.[179] When Flagg was directed to widen the corridors of his plan for Bancroft Hall to enable the formation of battalions indoors, he was forced to change his original conception of a monumental triumphal arch whose entablature was emblazoned with John Paul Jones's heroic motto, *Don't give up the ship!*[180] The new principal facade was thus transformed into a planar entrance gate suggesting a variation of Philibert de l'Orme's entry gate to the Château d'Anet in Dreux (1549–55). Flagg's use of an arcuated lintel motif is especially consistent with de l'Orme's conception of the entrance gate, even though Flagg incorporated it within a straight entablature and textured wall surface with channeled joints. As in his libraries and first scheme for the Corcoran, the entrance gate reflected Flagg's personal style as much as French academic classicism. However, the naval imagery of Bancroft Hall, with the Naval Academy arms over the main entrance and trophies commensurate with the memorial function of the building mounting each of the flanking piers, follows the decorative theme common to French military architecture.

The elevation of Bancroft Hall represents a curious architectural acculturation of French form and American materials. Flagg's original design of the entire Naval Academy specified red brick with limestone trim, apparently to complement the regional character of colonial Annapolis. Flagg may have envisioned it in the manner of Jacques Hermant's widely published Caserne des Célestins (see Fig. 12), or the brick school architecture of the late nineteenth century, reflecting the style of architecture during the reigns of Henry IV and Louis XIII which Viollet-le-Duc and others considered rational.[181] Outside forces, however, were to militate against Flagg's concept. During the fall of 1898 a number of New England granite companies, including one from Auburn, Maine, which were supported by E. C. Burleigh, Representative from Maine, lobbied Congress to recognize the merits of Maine and New Hampshire granite "as being eminently suitable for the proposed new building in Annapolis."[182] The granite lobby was successful. When supplementary Congressional appropriations for the armory and boathouse-gymnasium were enacted on March 3, 1899, monies were allocated for the substitution of Maine granite in place of brick and limestone. Maine granite was also specified for the

123

51. Ernest Flagg. Memorial Hall, Bancroft Hall group, Chesapeake Bay front, 1899–1906 (*AABN* XCIV, July 8, 1908, pl. 19).

entire Bancroft Hall group, under contracts dated January 15, 1902.[183] Flagg was bitterly disappointed with the substitution.[184]

The principal entrance facing the Yard was planned with a monumental horseshoe ramp to accommodate battalions marching in formation (see Fig. 49). The ramp, a large-scale version of those used since the Renaissance for vehicular circulation, was ideal for the passage of marching cadets. The relationship between program and scale was no better exemplified than in the juxtaposition of a cadet battalion and the exterior of Bancroft Hall. It was the marching battalion that gave an accurate scale to the monumental elements of the Bancroft Hall elevation. (During the first academic year of the new Naval Academy, 1907–8, Bancroft Hall quartered 854 midshipmen.) The Beaux-Arts attitude toward monumental scale was most cogently stated by Guadet in speaking of St. Peter's Basilica "when an entire people circulating between its walls and under its vaults give their true scale to these colossal elements!"[185] The same could be said of an audience in procession which gives scale to the staircase of Garnier's Opera, or a marching regiment of troops which gives scale to the boulevards of Haussmann's plan of Paris.

The architectural *tour de force* of Bancroft Hall, however, is apparent not from the Yard, but rather from Chesapeake Bay (see Fig. 46). Its projecting pavilion served the dual functions of a Memorial Hall above and Recreation Hall below in which the Academy's mess hall was situated (Fig. 51).[186] Bold massing and heavily rusticated granite served as a foil to the pomp of naval maneuvers and military marching. Cadets gained access to the parade ground and waterfront from this pavilion with its horseshoe ramp and terracing below in the spirit of Vignola's Palazzo Farnese at Caprarola (1559–73). It too had changed from its earlier conception which had featured a mansarded pavilion (see Fig. 43) more like A. J. Gabriel's frontispiece to the Ecole Militaire. But despite its superficially Italian quality, the design was still very French. Its orientation toward the water and its general design also bear a striking resemblance to a number of entries in an Ecole *concours* of 1888 for a Naval School with which Flagg, then studying for the entrance exams, would have been familiar.[187] The horseshoe ramp and staircase was also a widely used architectural element in France where it appears in Jean Androuet Du Cerceau's Cour du Cheval Blanc at Fontainebleau (1632), Lefuel's Cour du Manège at the Louvre, and the entrance that Garnier designed for Napoleon III at the Paris Opera. Additionally, the opulence and ceremonial functions of Flagg's mansarded pavilion reveal affinities to French theater architecture, such as Louis Bernier's Opéra-Comique, Paris (1892–98).[188]

Equally opulent is the interior of Memorial Hall, with its limestone walls and coved ceilings decorated with stucco.[189] Both the method of concrete vault construction as well as the ornamental designs of the plaster surfaces are similar to the spans of the Grand Palais and Petit Palais at the 1900 Paris exposition. There François Hennebique designed the floors and cantilevered stairs of reinforced concrete. For the exposition's temporary buildings, Hennebique also designed reinforced concrete frames which were ideally (and economically) suited to their stucco veneers.[190] In his first specifications for the Naval Academy of 1899, Flagg called for a similar system of concrete fireproofing for floors, partitions, and vaulting. Of the three methods then in use, Flagg preferred the French system of *béton armé* (a method of reinforced concrete that Hennebique had patented in 1892), to either the heavy and expensive hollow-tile construction of most American fireproof buildings, or the tile vaulting system invented by Guastavino which many other Beaux-Arts architects preferred. But because concrete construction was so relatively new in America, Flagg had to justify his reasons for specifying it exclusively. In response to criticism by congressmen and competing tile contractors, Flagg

52.   Ernest Flagg. Mahan Hall, Academic group, 1896–1907
(U.S. Naval Academy Museum).

53.   Ernest Flagg. Dolphin lamp,
Mahan Hall (U.S. Naval Academy).

maintained that ferro-concrete was lighter and, therefore, a more economical system of fireproofing than hollow-tile construction. Moreover, he asserted, concrete construction was not an "untried system," as its critics maintained, but rather one already used extensively in Europe, particularly in France.[191] Memorial Hall was thus a good example of Flagg's notion of *parti* where the values of academic classicism, and their appropriate expressions of character, were fused with a new European technology.

Memorial Hall commands the highest position within the hierarchy of the Bancroft Hall building complex. Its dominant placement illustrates the essence of Beaux-Arts planning principles. Approaching from the Yard entrance, the visitor proceeds through an ornate, compartmentalized vestibule, up a steep flight of stairs to a richly decorated climactic space within Memorial Hall. In reaching this destination, the spatial sequence is prescribed along the main axis of the complex, front to rear, bottom to top. In terms of its plan as well as its expression of character, Memorial Hall and the entire Bancroft Hall

54.   Ernest Flagg. Mahan Hall. Vestibule.

127

group typify the Beaux-Arts spatial experience and consequently represent some of Flagg's most academic statements.

Directly opposite Bancroft Hall stands the library portion of Mahan Hall, the central focus of Flagg's Academic group (Fig. 52).[192] Executed later than the Bancroft Hall group, the Academic group is the result of an effort by the Department of the Navy to cut expenditures, even after Congress had raised the limit of its appropriation to $10 million.[193] Construction of the exterior of the Academic group was forcibly economized by the substitution of gray face bricks for an all-granite facade. Brick was integrated with granite in a manner similar to French school architecture, including Nénot's rue Cujas facade of the new Sorbonne (see Fig. 11), that was considered rational. Some of the maritime imagery was also omitted in the executed building, though a pair of cast-iron dolphin lamps flanking the entrance gives some indication of the intended decoration (Fig. 53). The clock tower of Mahan Hall resembles

55. Ernest Flagg. Mahan Hall. Staircase (*AABN* XCIV, July 1, 1908, pl. 8).

French models and symbolizes the clock tower on the red brick academic building of the former campus.[194] The *étage noble* is dominated by an arcuated lintel forming the monumental arch of the centerpiece with pairs of columns punctuating a large window expanse and flanking paneled piers which help to maintain the identity of the wall plane. Like Bancroft Hall, the exterior of Mahan Hall is relatively unimaginative by comparison with the interior. Flagg's creativity is expressed not in the static spaces but in the dynamic ones. He conceived the ground floor vestibule as a barrel-vaulted nave with side aisles finished in Caen stone. Alcoves were planned for displaying such colorful naval memorabilia as captured flags in the bays of transverse intersecting vaults (Fig. 54). The variety and complexity of this hall reflects such French achievements as the vestibules of Duc's Palais de Justice, or Nénot's Sorbonne.

The central staircase is even more theatrical (Fig. 55). Above the second of two flights of stairs (the plan is modeled after Labrouste's Bibliothè-

56. Ernest Flagg. Chapel, 1896; 1904–8. Photograph taken c. 1920 (U.S. Naval Academy Museum).

que Sainte-Geneviève), leading to the library, a series of domical vaults containing skylights charges the spatial experience of the visitor ascending or descending. Earlier Garnier had used similar skylight vaults for the ground floor vestibule of the Paris Opera. Later Flagg employed this same device in the lobby of the Singer Tower (see Fig. 109).

The Chapel forms the apex of the Naval Academy plan, commanding the architectural ensemble through image and function (Fig. 56). The Naval Academy Chapel — part memorial, part auditorium — was inspired by J. Hardouin Mansart's military chapel, Dôme des Invalides (1679–91). The Chapel's Greek-cross plan and interior, surfaced with heraldic ornament, were also modeled directly after the Invalides; the crypt was strongly suggestive of Visconti's Tomb of Napoleon which was later added to the Invalides (1841 – 53).[195] Flagg originally had conceived of the Chapel as a "Pantheon of the Navy" containing catacombs for naval heroes.[196] In his initial plan of 1896, he had intended that a domical vaulted crypt be included to receive the body of John Paul Jones, in the event that his grave should eventually be found.[197]

It was not until 1905 when an extended search in Paris led by General Horace Porter, Ambassador to France, was at last successful, that Jones's body was exhumed for identification and his remains subsequently transported to Annapolis.[198] Despite the initial fanfare accompanying the recovery of John Paul Jones's body (commemorative services were held at Annapolis on April 24, 1906), Congress was slow to appropriate funds necessary for completing the Chapel crypt to receive his sarcophagus. When Congress eventually appropriated $75,000 for this purpose, Flagg dashed off several letters in the spring of 1911 to the Secretary of the Navy inquiring about a possible commission.[199] However, that same spring, Flagg became a source of embarrassment to the navy when his lawyers filed a petition claiming fees due for architectural services.[200] Even earlier, Flagg had antagonized navy officials when he maintained that he had suggested a search for the body of John Paul Jones and should, therefore, "share in the honor."[201] Although Flagg had envisioned the Chapel crypt with this purpose in mind, he had not voiced his intention to Secretary Long until 1900, a year after the Porter search had begun.[202] Flagg was denied the commission for the Chapel crypt; it was given to Whitney Warren, whose less imaginative design was executed in time for the reception of John Paul Jones's sarcophagus on January 26, 1913.[203]

Flagg's Chapel interior (above the crypt) was planned as a centralized space, dominated by an organ, that served, like the Farmington Avenue Church, as an auditorium for preaching and singing. The Chapel was designed to serve secular as well as ecclesiastical needs. In his article of 1902, Commander Richard Wainwright, Superintendent of the Naval Academy, referred to the structure's dual function as "Auditorium and Chapel."[204] In 1939–40 the Chapel was enlarged according to Paul Cret's design of 1938 which violated Flagg's centralized plan but was nonetheless a successful addition. Cret's alteration extended the Chapel's entrance toward the Yard, resulting in a Latin-cross plan and a space to accommodate 2,000 midshipmen.[205]

The Chapel was the most structurally advanced of the Naval Academy buildings because its skeletal frame and dome employed the new technology of concrete construction. Yet Flagg originally had planned for the Chapel to be constructed entirely of granite, made possible by a $400,000 appropriation in 1900.[206] By 1903, however, the allocation proved inadequate as construction costs rose substantially (Flagg estimated a 30 percent increase in cost and the expected enrollment dictated an increased seating capacity of 25 percent).[207] Due to the Chapel's dominant role in the ensemble, its design, Flagg maintained, could not be "recast in a lower key."[208] Still Flagg was forced to keep within the $400,000 figure. To resolve the financial constraints, he later confessed, "I was put to my wits' ends."[209] But in effect, he did "recast" the Chapel, not "in a lower key," but in higher technology. His new solution abandoned bearing-wall masonry construction. In place of the massive walls used for the Bancroft Hall group, he chose a daring and economical substitution: a reinforced concrete frame infilled with masonry (Fig. 57).[210] The integrated use of concrete, granite, brick, and terra cotta in legible parts approached the ideals of structural rationalism. Now both the domical vault and the structural supports were constructed according to the same ferro-concrete process (Fig. 58). Flagg employed the patented Hennebique system which he had used, along with the Kahn system, for the fireproofed vaults of the other Naval Academy structures.[211] The system, still considered experimental, was so new in America that Flagg's Chapel received enthusiastic notices in engineering and popular scientific journals. In 1905 *Scientific American* reported that the Naval Academy Chapel "represents the most elaborate form of framework of this kind which has yet been attempted in the United States."[212] But there were precedents in Flagg's own designs. As early as 1892, he had specified concrete construction for the rotunda of his New York Public Library project.[213] In actual construction, though on a much smaller scale, the chapel of St. Margaret Memorial Hospital, Pittsburgh, was executed in ferro-concrete.

The buildings surrounding the Academy Chapel, including the Super-

57. Ernest Flagg. Chapel.
Ferro-concrete frame (*AABN*
XCIV, July 1, 1908, fig. 6).

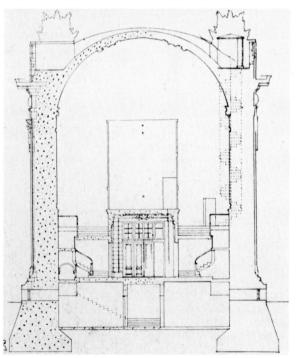

58. Ernest Flagg. Chapel.
Ferro-concrete frame.
Section (*AABN* XCIV, July 1,
1908, pl. 4).

intendent's House, Administration Building, Officers' Mess, and Officers' Houses, form an effective transition from the large-scale granite buildings of the Academy to the colonial architecture of Annapolis. Like the naval hospitals, they are domestic in scale and inspired by the region's examples of American Palladianism, even though they are executed in gray brick.

Expanded enrollments in the Naval Academy after 1908 led to alterations in Flagg's plan. A program, begun in 1957, to reclaim fifty-three acres of land, led to the filling in of Dewey Basin.[214] The following decade, a new mathematics and science building, designed by John Carl Warnecke, was initially planned so that it threatened to obscure the Severn riverfront and the reciprocal vista between the Chapel and the Severn. Realizing the consequence of this scheme, the navy and Warnecke resolved the problem to their satisfaction with an altered scheme in which two structures of lesser density (Michelson and Chauvenet halls) were separated by a low terrace on axis with the Chapel.[215] However, this new arrangement preserved only a token aspect of the intended Naval Academy plan, which Flagg had once envisioned as an amphitheater overlooking a beaconed harbor.

With the completion of the new Naval Academy in 1908, many architectural critics praised Flagg's design, even though some analysts, such as Montgomery Schuyler, ignored it and preferred the Gothic buildings of Cram, Goodhue & Ferguson's Military Academy, West Point.[216] The editors of *Architectural Review,* commenting on the retrospective collection of Flagg's buildings published in *Architectural Record* (April 1902), proclaimed the design of the Naval Academy "in every respect the finest work that Mr. Flagg has thus far produced."[217] Albert Kelsey, editor of the *Architectural Annual* 1900, was even more generous when he predicted that the future implementation of the Naval Academy plan would surpass all previous government building: "We are aware of no more scientific, comprehensive, modern or businesslike scheme and we are gratified to find the Government availing itself of the private initiative made toward the construction of this group of buildings."[218] In effect, the Naval Academy plan was the first instance in which Beaux-Arts planning was methodically applied to a large-scale government complex. Flagg's general scheme of 1896 indeed set a precedent for federal planning. In particular, the Senate Park Commission Plan for Washington, D.C., of 1901, and Ralph Adams Cram's general scheme for West Point of 1902–3 followed Flagg's lead.[219]

During the building of the new Naval Academy from 1899 to 1908, work proceeded with relatively little friction until Flagg was unable to collect

59.   Ernest Flagg. Pomfret School. Aerial view (James H. Goodwin).

supplemental fees for his architectural services and eventually filed a suit
against the government for $104,104.06. At roughly the same time, Cram
suffered a similar fate as architect for several buildings at West Point. In the
end Flagg fared better than Cram. Unwilling to file a suit in the Court of
Claims, Cram was never able to collect damages; nor was he able to execute his
master plan for West Point. Yet, unlike Flagg, Cram eventually received
another West Point building commission.[220] Flagg, with his general scheme
completed, risked only the Chapel crypt commission by his action, but it did
not help his contentious reputation. At the end of a protracted court case, Flagg
was finally awarded damages of $49,100 in 1916.[221]

Pomfret School

Construction of the Naval Academy was already well advanced by
1906 when Flagg received the commission to design a complex of new

buildings for Pomfret School, a private Episcopal school in rural Connecticut. In a period of expansion during the first decade of the twentieth century, Pomfret School changed from a collection of vernacular buildings — most were colonial and Colonial Revival frame structures adapted to school use — to a planned institution. The building campaign was financed principally by two patrons: Edward Walker Clark, one of three sons of the Singer heir, Alfred Corning Clark, and Frederick G. Bourne, Singer Manufacturing Company president and Flagg's patron of long-standing.

Pomfret School lies on the ridge of a windy bluff, recessed from the town's main road. Facing the venerable First Congregational Church of Pomfret, the school was intimately associated with the town from its establishment in 1894. Its first Main House had been the former Charles Grosvenor Inn (burned in 1900). By 1906 Flagg had designed for the school a master plan which had transformed the casual relationship among the buildings of the existing campus into a formal institutional complex.[222] Flagg's master plan reinforced the enduring colonial image of the New England village green (Fig. 59). Defining the ridge of the Pomfret hillside, the scheme called for a School

60. Ernest Flagg. Pomfret School. Arcade, 1906–11 (*Pomfret School,* Pomfret, Connecticut, ATSP, AL, CU).

61. Ernest Flagg. Clark Chapel, Pomfret School. 1907–9 (Pomfret School).

Building anchored at right angles to a series of semidetached pavilion dormitories with an open arcade connecting them on the downhill (west) side. The Chapel to the south was appropriately visible from the main road, while a gymnasium and infirmary were dispersed along the slope of the hill. Flagg's pavilion arrangement suggested the influence of Thomas Jefferson's design for the University of Virginia.[223] The dynamic focus of the scheme was the arcade. It acted as both spine and artery, linking the dormitories together while providing covered access to classrooms in the School Building (Fig. 60). This concept was frankly Jeffersonian, one which appeared at both Monticello and the University of Virginia. For the Pomfret School arcade, Flagg converted the topographical refinements of Jefferson's multilevel planning to northern requirements. Its virtues tragically unrecognized, the functioning arcade was obliterated in 1957 when dormitory remodeling caused it to be walled in.

In his search for an appropriate expression of character, Flagg had to consider both the domestic and the ecclesiastical sides of this Episcopal-affiliated boarding school. The School Building with its belfry and white appliqué ornament, similar to the Colonial Revival structures of the former campus, as well as the dormitories and infirmary maintained such a domestic scale and architectural character. Flagg showed no less sensitivity to historicism in treating the Chapel commissioned by Edward Clark in 1907 as a memorial to his son George Newhall Clark (1885–1906), a Pomfret alumnus (Fig. 61).[224] He chose Norman architecture as an appropriate model for this school chapel, and deemed it compatible with the Colonial Revival campus. The Clark Chapel emulated the rich textures of Norman architecture and eliminated the dry, machine-like finish of the stone work typical of buildings by Flagg's contemporaries, especially Ralph Adams Cram.

Flagg himself compared the relative merits of the Naval Academy and Pomfret School campuses, following a visit to Pomfret in November 1910 when work there was nearing completion. "These [buildings]" he maintained, "are certainly among the best things I have done. This school is better architecturally than Annapolis."[225] Flagg's assessment was undoubtedly due to the fact that Pomfret School was executed as he planned it; the Naval Academy was not. With such liberal patrons as Bourne and Edward Clark, Flagg had greater freedom of action at Pomfret School than under the bureaucratic supervision of the Naval Academy. His Naval Academy scheme had been subjected to a succession of changes over roughly a ten-year interval between design and construction. At Pomfret School, while the building program proceeded in stages, execution scrupulously followed design. Flagg was free to integrate the Pomfret School campus into the town, but with the Naval Academy, he had had to settle for half measures. Flagg had used Colonial and Federal Revival forms for the peripheral buildings of the Academy, including the Superintendent's House, the Administration Building, the Officers' Mess and Houses, and the Hospital — all of which were more domestic in scale and character — in an effort to make the connections with the town which he had originally intended for all the buildings. By contrast, the campus plan of Pomfret School overtly reflected that of the village green. Its style, however, looked more to Flagg's architecture than to regional examples. Flagg's use of Colonial and Federal Revival forms for the New England school, small naval hospitals, and town houses (including his own), affirmed his personal sense of style and, like Hastings, his conviction that American architects should return to eighteenth-century forms, both American and French, in order to pick up the lost thread of Renaissance classicism. Flagg saw Pomfret School as part of the process of evolution that would contribute to the creation of a national style of architecture.

Other Commissions

As with the Naval Academy and the Pomfret School, Flagg's two concerns — to express architectural character and to integrate a new structure

137

62.   Ernest Flagg. Princeton University Press Building, Princeton,
New Jersey, 1910–11 (Princeton University Press).

within an existing town fabric—dominated his design for the Princeton
University Press building (1910–11; now Scribner Building) in Princeton,
New Jersey (Fig. 62). The idea for the new Press building originated with
Flagg's brother-in-law, Charles Scribner, who suggested in a letter to Whitney
Darrow, director of the Press, that it "might possibly be built around a court
like the Plantin Museum." In the course of his travels during the summer of
1910, Scribner sent Darrow a postcard of the Plantin Museum in Antwerp. Its
message read simply "Regards. C.S."[226] The Plantin Museum formerly
housed the celebrated press founded in 1579 by Christopher Plantin. Flagg did
not know the Flemish museum firsthand, but he had access to a historical study
of it by the British architect and historian R. Phené Spiers, which included
photographs and watercolor drawings.[227] In his design, Flagg respected the
wishes of his client, even though he avoided any conspicuous resemblance to
the Plantin model. He substituted a quadrangle plan, open at the street, for the
Plantin's enclosed court. Details, such as the open timber-trussed roof of the
pressroom, recalled the spirit rather than the form of the sixteenth- and early-
seventeenth-century model.[228] Moreover, Flagg disregarded the red brick
facade of the Plantin Museum, which would not have harmonized with Princeton

138

University's newest stone structures. Flagg also eschewed the dry archaeology of Walter Cope's and John Stewardson's "Tudor Gothic" buildings which anticipated the "Collegiate Gothic" structures designed by Cram, Goodhue & Ferguson.[229]

Flagg marked the transition between the Princeton University Press building and the street with a Tudor gateway. Characteristic of his small houses of the period, Flagg exploited the picturesque effects of a slate roof and belfry, and of Princeton's traditional building material, a local gray stone, while cleverly integrating such utilitarian features as common factory windows and large dormers equipped with exhaust fans. Thus Flagg successfully adapted the Press building to the character and regionalism of Princeton architecture, while reflecting the venerable Plantin model in its plan and pressroom interior.

There is perhaps no better illustration of the quintessential elements of Flagg's Beaux-Arts classicism than those present in the Frederick G. Bourne

63.   Ernest Flagg. Frederick G. Bourne Tomb, Greenwood Cemetery, Brooklyn, New York, 1902 (*Works,* fig. 9).

Tomb, Greenwood Cemetery, Brooklyn (c. 1902; Fig. 63). Like Flagg's churches and utilitarian architecture, the tomb is dominated by a round arch which gives it monumentality. The arch was both a motif in Flagg's personal style and common to the architecture of the early Third Republic. Dramatically isolated from the arch by a beveled archivolt, the cartouche signifies the hallmark of Beaux-Arts architecture in America. Sparsely ornamented in *Néo-Grec* detailing, the cornice circumscribes and effectively secures the block. Flagg also designed the Samuel J. Tilden Tomb (1892), in New Lebanon, New York, a cumbrous work, as well as monumental sculpture including the Soldiers' and Sailors' Monument, New Britain, Connecticut (1899), and projects in New York City for the William Cullen Bryant Monument, Central Park (1893), and a Naval Arch (1901).[230] These tombs and monumental sculpture have one thing in common: they are remarkably "French." No one could mistake the Bourne Tomb for the work of an architect trained outside the Beaux-Arts system. In tombs, as in large Beaux-Arts works, the *partis* were informed by Flagg's loyalty to the French school, its principles and aesthetics. Yet in domestic architecture and such related building types as hospitals and schools, Flagg's search for character led him to consult a broader range of national traditions.

CHAPTER FIVE

Town and Country Houses

Ernest FLAGG'S domestic architecture before World War I comprised a relatively small body of work, particularly with respect to country houses. His clients tended to be a few loyal patrons, mostly the new breed of American millionaire and the philanthropist-reformer, some of whom were his own relatives.

When it came to the question of historical style, Flagg treated his domestic buildings with more freedom than he did his institutions. His country houses especially were marked by a strong sense of regionalism and picturesqueness combining English, American, and French influences. They demonstrated the condition which Paul Cret described in 1908: "At the same time the United States was importing formal architecture from France, they were borrowing domestic architecture from England."[1] For his first two house commissions, the R. Fulton Cutting House, New York, and the Edwin Ginn House, Winchester, Massachusetts, Flagg designed in "modern French Renaissance" for the former, and in a Colonial or Federal Revival style for the latter. One in the city, the other in the country, together they confirmed Flagg's objective to return to French and Anglo-American classicism in order to evolve a national style of architecture, or "*parti* for America." Some town and country houses, such as his own Manhattan residence, were hybrids: Colonial or Federal Revival forms for the exterior, "modern French Renaissance" design for the interior. In still others, such as the Clark House, New York, Flagg designed both exteriors and interiors as hybrids of Anglo-American and French classicism. In this case, as with Hastings's "Blairsden," the country house of C. Ledyard Blair in Peapack, New Jersey (1898–1903), Flagg designed planar walls in red brick with marble quoins, mixing American colonial or federal forms with French architecture of the late sixteenth, early seventeenth, or eighteenth centuries.[2]

While Flagg's few country houses were dispersed throughout New York and New England, his town houses were built principally on New York's Upper East Side. Most conformed to the Manhattan block and lot pattern, rather than being diminutive versions of civic or commercial palaces, or even urban châteaux. In his town houses Flagg demonstrated American equivalents to the illustrations of Parisian domestic architecture which accompanied his article of 1894, "Influence of the French School on Architecture in the United States."[3] In effect, his Manhattan town houses attempted to bring about academic clarity, organization, and uniformity. In them Flagg sought to eschew the eccentricities of Richardsonian Romanesque, Queen Anne, and other cognate styles that dominated New York domestic architecture in the 1880s and 1890s and were particularly evident in the West Side row house.[4] The planar treatment of Flagg's wall surfaces lacked the robust sculptural elements advocated by many of his fellow Beaux-Arts architects, as in the case of the Senator William A. Clark House on Fifth Avenue at 77th Street (1903–4), a "French" design by the American firm of Lord, Hewlitt & Hull, with Kenneth Murchison (and his Ecole patron, Henri Deglane, as consulting architect). Like the French examples in his article of 1894 — those works by Pascal, Mewès, and others — Flagg's town houses reflected a restrained and economical approach to design that was considered rational.[5]

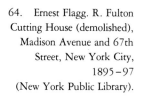

64. Ernest Flagg. R. Fulton Cutting House (demolished), Madison Avenue and 67th Street, New York City, 1895–97 (New York Public Library).

142

Flagg's first town house was commissioned in 1895 by Robert Fulton Cutting, a philanthropist-reformer who would eventually become president of the City and Suburban Homes Company, a tenement house building company.[6] The Cutting House which stood on the southwest corner of Madison Avenue and 67th Street (demolished) employed an elegant "modern French Renaissance" design (Fig. 64). Its limestone and buff-colored brick facade was regularly punctuated with large-scale window elements, each stamped with the ubiquitous "Beaux-Arts" cartouche, and ornamented with a roof crest. An iron and glass marquee sheltered the 67th Street entrance. The plan was both American and French. It exemplified the American basement house (where the entrance was on the street level or elevated a few steps from the ground and the dining room was one story above), introduced to New York in 1880.[7] The ground level contained an entrance hall, billiard room, and staircase leading to the principal floor above, where the drawing room, dining room, and library were located; the upper two floors contained bedrooms. The décor signaled a new lightness illustrated by the drawing room which, according to a report in the *New York Tribune,* was paneled in "oak to the ceiling and the wood is enameled and sculptured in the French style."[8] There Flagg followed a contemporary French vogue for reviving eighteenth-century classicism.

The O. G. Jennings House, 7 East 72nd Street (1898–99; now Lycée Français de New York) was the result of a collaboration with Walter Chambers, a Yale classmate of Oliver Gould Jennings (Fig. 65).[9] Chambers may in fact have secured the commission, although Flagg was unquestionably responsible for its design. On a narrow lot, 28 × 100 feet, next to Carrère & Hastings' recently completed H. T. Sloane House of 1894–96 (9 East 72nd Street; now also Lycée Français de New York) the Jennings House was built in the same Indiana limestone as a complement to the earlier house. Yet at the Jennings House, Flagg deliberately strove for a planar treatment of wall surfaces, in opposition to the sculpturally effusive Sloane House. In a comparison of the elevations of both houses, the point-counterpoint intent of Flagg's design emerges. Thus, where the Sloane House had a planar ground floor elevation, robust *étage noble* (the main living area above the ground floor), and relatively simplified attic story, the Jennings House asserted a planar but textured ground floor with channeled and vermiculated stone, restrained *étage noble,* and attic story which burst into a decorous roof crest with cartouche ornament. This elegant town house was at once a complement to its neighbor and the frontispiece that commanded the whole ensemble. In plan, the Jennings House followed the English basement model with an entrance and dining

65.   Ernest Flagg and Walter B. Chambers. O. G. Jennings House (now Lycée
Français de New York), 7 East 72nd Street, New York City, 1898–99; Carrère &
Hastings designed the H. T. Sloane House at No. 9 (right), 1894–96
(Wayne Andrews).

room on the ground floor and a library, gallery, and drawing room on the main
(first) floor above it.[10] In style, however, the Jennings House resembled a
Parisian *maison privée* of the late nineteenth century, similar to César Daly's

examples in his *L'architecture privée,* but accommodated to the vertical format necessitated by New York's peculiarly narrow lot.[11]

Two additional town houses displayed the "modern French Renaissance" style: the Arthur Scribner House at 39 East 67th Street (1903–4), and the Courtlandt F. Bishop House at 15 East 67th Street (1903–4; now Regency Whist Club).[12] Although less opulent than the Jennings House, these town houses were composed of five stories instead of four, and continued to assert the planarity of their street facades.

In his design for the Alfred Corning Clark House on the northeast corner of Riverside Drive and 89th Street, Flagg synthesized late-eighteenth-century American federal forms with French architecture of the late sixteenth and early seventeenth centuries (Fig. 66; demolished). In describing the Clark House, the editors of *Architecture* called it "a good illustration of French Renaissance adapted to American conditions."[13] Unlike Flagg's other town houses, this freestanding house which commanded a view of the Hudson River was reminiscent of many large Manhattan residences of the 1880s and 1890s popularly called châteaux. When first completed, the Clark House was invariably referred to as the "Clark Estate," so strongly was it associated with the real estate holdings of the Clark family.[14]

The Clark House, with its block-like mass of red brick with white trim, exemplified Federal Revival architecture, recalling the town houses of Charles Bulfinch and Samuel McIntire. Its proportions, classical ornament, and manipulation of materials suggested the influence of American Georgian-federal, Queen Anne, and especially the English domestic architecture of Richard Norman Shaw (compare Shaw's 170 Queen's Gate, London, of 1888–90).[15]

But even though the house adhered to an Anglo-American tradition, there were strong inflections for which only French influence could account. Its scale and siting, along a bend in Riverside Drive, its plan and composition reflected the principles of Beaux-Arts design and recalled Viollet-le-Duc's project for a Modern French Town Mansion, or *Hôtel* (see Fig. 4).[16] Both the Clark House and Viollet-le-Duc's project for a Town House incorporated an ancillary wing and a porte cochere. The Clark House ell (unlike wings of Shingle Style houses which functioned as servants' quarters) contained a conservatory and bowling alley, both features more common to late-nineteenth-century country estates than to town houses. Flagg's plan, with its recreational wing defining one edge of an irregular lot, also suggested the "butterfly" plans of Viollet-le-Duc's *Hôtel* as well as Edwardian houses.[17] In addition to the ell, the most expressive feature of the Clark House facade was its entrance. There an exotic metal and glass marquee was partially supported by brackets and partially cantilevered from the entrance portico, dramatizing both the aesthetics of ornament and the science of construction (Fig. 67). The curvilinear lines and fan-like projection of this wrought-iron structure approached Art Nouveau design. Moreover, the facade of the Clark House was organized by its windows, linked principally vertically but also horizontally through white marble banding. The use of stone quoins and banding against patterned red brick emphasized planarity and suggested constructional polychromy (the use of a variety of colorful materials in the facing or construction of a building, fulfilling a need for truthfulness). As in Viollet-le-Duc's *Hôtel*, the Clark House indicated an adaptation of the brick and stone architecture built during the reigns of Henry IV and Louis XIII, such as the Place des Vosges in Paris (begun in 1605). Viollet-le-Duc, Flagg, and many French architects of the early Third Republic admired this late-sixteenth- and early-seventeenth-century architecture for its structural rationalism and Gallic qualities. In his design for the Clark House Flagg thus demonstrated a rational effort to classicize

66. Ernest Flagg. Alfred Corning Clark House (demolished), Riverside Drive and 89th Street, New York City, 1898–1900 (*Architecture* II, July 15, 1900, p. 252).

67. Ernest Flagg. Alfred Corning Clark House (demolished). Portico (*Works,* fig. 49).

further the picturesque New York château, continuing in the tradition of Richard Morris Hunt's Elbridge T. Gerry House, Fifth Avenue at 61st Street (1891–94; demolished) and George B. Post's Cornelius Vanderbilt House, Fifth Avenue, between 57th and 58th streets (1880–82) including a tower addition of 1892–94 by Hunt (demolished), with which Flagg had had a close association earlier in his career.[18] In this Beaux-Arts interpretation of the Federal Revival, Flagg's Clark House marked an advance in nineteenth-century America's search for a national style that would evolve logically from historical precedents.[19]

When Flagg designed his own town house at 109 East 40th Street (1905–7; demolished), he departed from the strict use of "modern French

147

Renaissance'' (Fig. 68). Originally, this red brick quasi-Georgian town house defined its *étage noble* by a trio of marble lunettes (later replaced), as in McKim, Mead & White's Lathrop House, 120 East Bellevue Street, Chicago (1891–93). Flagg already had revived Georgian and federal architecture for hospitals

68. Ernest Flagg. Ernest Flagg House and Office (demolished), 109 and 111 East 40th Street, New York City, completed in 1908 (EFP, AL, CU).

and country houses. Now he sought to reintroduce a type of row house that had been prevalent in New York City during the 1820s and 1830s: the plain four-story house of red brick with limestone trim. But Flagg was not alone, for this revival was enjoying a current vogue. Montgomery Schuyler, in an article of 1906 entitled "The New New York House," awkwardly identified the new type as "a reversion to the high [Dutch] stoop pre-brownstone front with the high stoop left out."[20]

In the design of the private urban house, Flagg's interest focused on the role of the automobile. Here was "A New Type of City House," proclaimed the editors of *Architectural Record* in 1907 when the Flagg House with its basement garage was published.[21] It was new because the automobile was new, and because the house and carriage house had never before been integrated successfully.

Before 1903, Flagg lived with his wife and daughter in a duplex apartment at the Knickerbocker apartment house, 245 Fifth Avenue. They spent the weekends and summer months on Staten Island. From 1903 to 1907, they lived on Staten Island year-round. The move to 40th Street in 1907 was initially a step closer to the Charles Scribners, who were then living only a few blocks away at 12 East 38th Street, but who were soon to reside "uptown" at 66th Street. Flagg undoubtedly wished to remain close to the professional sector and the architectural milieu. Thomas Hastings, for example, had both his office and residence only a few blocks away on 41st Street to be near the New York Public Library.[22] Another factor, the purchase of Flagg's first automobile in 1907, a Packard, made a house with its own garage desirable.[23] Even though automobile clubs with garage facilities, including the Flagg-designed Automobile Club of America (1905–7), were being constructed in the old carriage-trade district in the west fifties, they were far removed from East Side residences.

The drama of the Flagg House was its entrance, deliberately scaled for vehicular arrivals and departures. Just inside the gate, screened with a wrought-iron grill, large French doors opened onto a vaulted porte cochere that tunneled through the building to an elevator on which the automobile might be lowered to a basement garage. The garage, whose roof and skylight are indicated on the ground floor plan, was equipped with a fireproof door, a gasoline pump room, and a storage tank beneath a concrete floor (Fig. 69).

To the editors of *Architectural Record,* the Flagg House with its integrated garage represented a type of dwelling "which will multiply greatly in the future, for it affords a practical demonstration of the possibility of

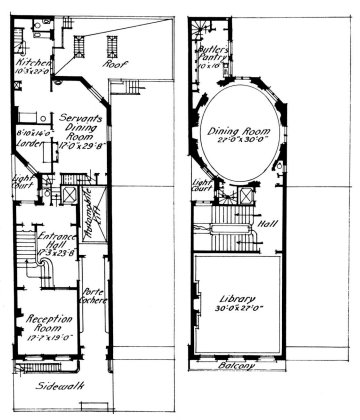

69. Ernest Flagg. Ernest Flagg House. Plans of ground floor (left) and first floor (right), 1905–7 (*Arch Rec* XXII, September 1907, p. 185).

combining with the ordinary city house a garage, the need for which is daily becoming more urgently felt.''[24] Nonetheless, Flagg's elevator scheme proved too expensive to become a standard solution to the garage problem, as the editors of *Architectural Record* had enthusiastically predicted. Yet, the concept of the integrated garage that Flagg introduced into town houses continued to intrigue other architects who came to prefer the garage on the street level. This solution was one which Flagg ultimately employed in his Morris House (1913–14). The garage also might be located a grade below, though approached directly from the street via a ramp and thereby eliminating the elevator.

The plan of the Flagg House was still organized along the lines of the American basement type. As in Flagg's town houses generally, ample space was allocated to a grand staircase with an ornamental wrought-iron railing and an entrance hall of light-colored Caen stone. Since the staircase served a ceremonial function, it was augmented by a passenger elevator, a feature shared by most Flagg town houses.[25] Of all the spaces on the *étage noble,* the octagonal dining room with an elliptical ceiling was the most impressive. Unlike the earlier town houses, the interior of the dining room was not finished in light enameled wood but in natural cherry, with black marble used for both the mantel and a series of Ionic pilasters.[26] The room was furnished with reproductions of Louis XIII and Louis XIV furniture which, along with other furniture, hardware, and lighting fixtures, were purchased in France.[27]

No sooner had 109 East 40th Street been completed than construction had begun in the summer of 1907 for a second smaller house next door at No. 111. The brickwork of both was English bond with a diaper pattern and recessed joints. To mitigate the absence of a vertical demarcation between the two houses, and to unify an awkward disparity between the heights of the two structures, Flagg replaced the marble lunettes above the windows of the *étage noble* at No. 109 with pediments similar to those on the Scribner town house. The newer town house was a good investment, as Flagg rented it from the time of its completion in 1908 until 1919 when he moved his office from the Mills Building at 35 Wall Street to the lower floors of No. 111.[28] In an effort to escape the social obligation of callers, Flagg had a passage constructed from the main floor of No. 109 to his office next door.[29]

In no other Flagg town house were utilitarian and functional aspects of design more advanced. Not only were the needs of the automobile considered, but equal care was given to heating, ventilation, and other requirements for comfort and hygiene, including a "rain bath" or shower, all of which the editors of *Architectural Record* did not fail to appreciate.[30] Flagg incorporated many of these features (except a garage) in the Robert I. Jenks House, 54 East 64th Street (1906–7; with Walter Chambers).[31]

Shortly after the completion of his own town house, Flagg received a letter from his sister, Louisa, announcing that her husband, Charles Scribner, had purchased a house at 9 East 66th Street and that she wished to have it altered.[32] Although Flagg worked on sketch plans for No. 9, nothing came of the intended alteration.[33] A year later, Flagg recorded in his diary that the Scribners had dined at 109 East 40th Street and had "looked over [Flagg's] house with an eye to their own."[34] By mid-December 1909, Flagg was able to show the Scribners a drawing of an elevation for a new house at No. 9.[35] The executed design was remarkably similar to 109 East 40th Street especially in plan. The Scribner House at 9 East 66th Street (1909–12; now Polish Delegation to the United Nations) was organized around the porte cochere entrance with a basement garage (Fig. 70). Rooms were disposed roughly according to the Flagg House plan. These included an oval dining room, which Flagg is believed to have modeled after the oval dining room of the former Scribner residence at 12 East 38th Street and which may also have served as a precedent for the dining room at 109 East 40th Street.[36] Yet, unlike the Flagg House, its exterior reflected a fusion of American and French classicism. The Scribner House elevation relied more on well-articulated fenestration, with a paneled arrangement of limestone, emphasizing the slender proportions and planar elevation of its five stories, while maintaining the same cornice line of its

70. Ernest Flagg. Charles Scribner House, 9 East 66th Street, New York City, 1909–12 (Wendy Barrows).

71.   Count László Széchényi Villa (now the Russian Embassy), 104 Andrássy
Avenue, Budapest, 1909–11. Alterations by Ernest Flagg.

more sculpturally ornate neighbor, the Shepard House at 5 East 66th Street
(1900; now Lotos Club) by Richard Howland Hunt.[37]

Following the elaborate efforts at the Flagg and Scribner houses to
provide the modern town house with its own attached garage, Flagg was
confronted with a similar problem in the alteration of a late-nineteenth-century
villa in Budapest, commissioned by Mrs. Cornelius Vanderbilt II (the former
Alice Gwynne). This town house at 104 Andrássy Avenue (now the Russian
Embassy) was purchased by Mrs. Vanderbilt as a wedding present for her
daughter, Gladys, who married Count László Széchényi in 1908 (Fig. 71).[38]
But it was not until March 1909 that Mrs. Vanderbilt sought Flagg's assistance in preparing plans for remodeling the Budapest residence.[39] These involved a number of interior designs, including the dining room, which were
similar to those of the Scribner and Flagg houses. The renovations, supervised
by an architect in the Flagg office, met Flagg's approval when he visited the
Széchényi villa during a European tour in the spring of 1910.[40]

The major thrust of the alterations focused on the design of a porte
cochere that pierced the middle of the entire structure and was enclosed by an
ornamental iron gate. In effect, the Széchényis' chauffeur drove the automobile

153

through the house, deposited his passengers at the entrance inside, continued to the other side and on to the garage located in one corner of the villa. More elaborate than those of the Scribner or Flagg town houses, the porte cochere of the Széchényi villa was vaulted in concrete and finished in marble and stucco, with eight Doric columns as interior supports.

In 1913 Flagg was given another town house commission, this for Lewis Gouverneur Morris, the descendant of a prominent New York family of political and financial leaders. Flagg prepared two house plans for a narrow lot (25 × 82 feet) at the southeast corner of Park Avenue and 85th Street. The rejected scheme was a traditional Adamesque-federal elevation dominated by an entrance with fanlight above.[41] The executed design, however, marked a departure from the traditional twentieth-century revival of federal architecture,

72. Ernest Flagg. Lewis Gouverneur Morris House (now The New World Foundation), 100 East 85th Street, New York City, 1913–14 (The New World Foundation).

while still employing its traditional materials: red brick and white limestone. The Morris House at 100 East 85th Street (1913 – 14; now The New World Foundation) might appear to be two gabled houses separated by a small open courtyard, were it not for a staircase passage in the middle connecting what are actually two wings (Fig. 72).[42] To increase its exposure to light, Flagg oriented the Morris House to its 85th Street facade. A garage on the ground level of the 85th Street block served as a pretext to exploit a split-level plan formed by the garage a half-story below the entrance level of the Park Avenue block. Inside, a broad staircase (of reinforced concrete) which joined the two blocks created a directional force through the six main levels of the house, was demarcated on the exterior with a syncopated trio of narrow lights, one set for each flight of stairs (Fig. 73). The tension within this staircase block was further complicated

73.   Ernest Flagg. Lewis Gouverneur Morris House (Wendy Barrows).

by two vertical towers appended to the facade, like the tower volumes of Flagg's St. Luke's Hospital: one, an elevator tower extending the full height of the structure and surmounted by a lantern; the other, a spiral staircase for servant use.

The Morris House with its parapet gables represents a regional interpretation of federal architecture which Flagg, no doubt, considered an appropriate character for a family long associated with the early history of New York. But other aspects of the design find no precedent in American architecture. The deliberate spatial complexity and manipulation of form, although evident in Flagg's earlier work, including the Farmington Avenue Church, represent a design approach that nineteenth-century British architects had explored. The Morris House courtyard unites the expressed volumes and is similar to William Butterfield's plan of All Saints, Margaret Street Church, London (1849–59).[43] But the design of this urban house, with its asymmetrical yet balanced disposition of parts, its tall gables interrupting the horizontal emphasis of the city block, the reflection of the interior organization on the exterior by means of bay windows and tall narrow lights, and the use of red brick with stone trim, were all residual Queen Anne elements brought into an axial alignment and clarity that was reminiscent of Richard Norman Shaw's two city houses at 180 and 185 Queen's Gate, London (1885; 1890), and his own house at 6 Ellerdale Road, Hampstead, London (1875–76).[44] Flagg may have been opposed to the "archaeology" of Queen Anne eclecticism, but not to the ingenious manipulation of form found in the best work of such architects as Butterfield, Shaw, and Lutyens. Flagg's town houses were original, functionally inventive, and responsive to their urban sites.

Flagg's country houses demonstrate an even greater freedom of style and effort to acknowledge regionalism and topographical siting than do his town houses. Unlike the R. Fulton Cutting House which employed "modern French Renaissance" forms, its contemporary, the Edwin Ginn House, located in the wooded hills near the Rangely section of Winchester, Massachusetts (1896–97; demolished), illustrated a revival of federal domestic architecture (Fig. 74). A large stable was added in 1900.[45] Like the Clark House, the Ginn House was organized according to a federal plan with a large central hall flanked by rooms on either side (Fig. 75). In an effort to express the regional associations of New England federal architecture, Flagg chose a design that treated classical elements, including the use of red brick and white marble quoins, sills, and lintels, in a picturesque way. A covered veranda and porch hemicycle were executed in the manner of McKim, Mead & White's Colonial

74.   Ernest Flagg. Edwin Ginn House (demolished), 55 Bacon Street, Winchester,
Massachusetts, 1896–97 (*Works,* fig. 61).

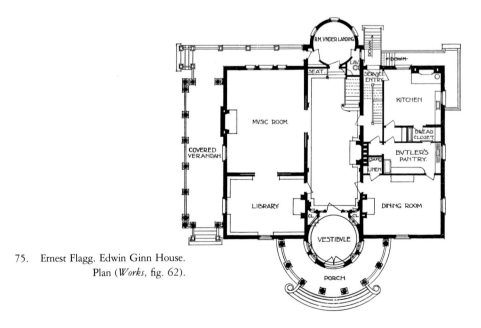

75.   Ernest Flagg. Edwin Ginn House.
      Plan (*Works,* fig. 62).

Revival country houses, especially the F. W. Vanderbilt House, Hyde Park, New York (1895–99). But while the interiors were largely Colonial Revival, they too conveyed French features. The music room addition of 1912, for example, was paneled in mahogany with oak parquet floors; it had French windows and doors.[46]

As the Ginn House achieved a new monumentality in the Boston suburb, the Frederick G. Bourne House, "Indian Neck Hall," in Oakdale, Long Island (1897–1900, 1907–8; now La Salle Military Academy), helped to establish domestic monumentality on Long Island's South Shore (Fig. 76). During a wave of Long Island and Westchester County development in the 1890s, Beaux-Arts architects designed lavishly formal country houses for the new breed of American millionaire whom Harry Desmond and Herbert Croly disparagingly characterized in their *Stately Homes in America* of 1903.[47] In the years just after Bourne became president of the Singer Manufacturing Company in 1890, he purchased land between Oakdale and Sayville which banked the estuary of the Great South Bay. By 1900 the Bourne estate was reported to comprise nearly 1,000 acres.[48] Drawn to the region by his love for outdoor sports, Bourne had been a leader in the South Side Sportsmen's Club along with W. K. Vanderbilt, W. Bayard Cutting, and Captain Nicoll Ludlow, all of whom lived on estates of comparable size.[49] There were Vanderbilt's Idle Hour in Oakdale, by Richard Howland Hunt of 1899, with later additions (the original building, begun in 1876 by Richard Morris Hunt, burned), and Cutting's Westbrook at Great River of 1886.[50] Bourne had previously lived in a fourteen-room apartment at The Dakota on Central Park West, for which he

76.   Ernest Flagg. Frederick G. Bourne House, "Indian Neck Hall" (now La Salle Military Academy), Oakdale, Long Island, 1897–1900 (ATSP, AL, CU).

is purported to have supervised the interiors when he received his start in business supervising Alfred Corning Clark's various building enterprises.[51] But with the completion of his year-round estate, "Indian Neck Hall," in 1900, Bourne gave up his Dakota apartment, substituting a pied-à-terre at the Buckingham Hotel (Fifth Avenue at 50th Street).[52]

Recalling Benjamin Latrobe's designs for the porticos of the White House — a model favored by architects of the Colonial Revival style — Flagg employed a pedimented portico for the main northeast elevation and a curved colonnaded portico for the garden or southwest elevation. Like many of its Newport counterparts of the previous decade, it faced the sea. From the Great South Bay, the southwest elevation appeared as a greatly attenuated version of the Ginn House. On the northeast side a number of elements were exaggerated: a porte cochere and steep side wings with a Palladian window on each end wall.[53] These show a calculated manipulation of form while anticipating the stiff formality of Charles Platt's country houses.

The Bourne estate was essentially a collection of buildings and artificially landscaped features, each with its own discrete function. In addition to the house itself, there were a boathouse, a stable, an artificial lake, and a bridge, not to mention a three-mile canal system originally filled with 1,200 trout.[54] All were components of large country estates circa 1900. In addition to these dependencies the house itself was planned around Bourne's recreational interests to include a greenhouse, a library, a billiard room, and a Turkish bath. The music room was dominated by a vast organ. Architecturally signifying the leisurely pace of "Indian Neck Hall" were both the large-scale porticos and a veranda that meandered around the garden facade (so that both sun and shade might be accessible at any one time), as in antebellum southern plantation houses. (Renovations of 1907 and 1908 included a greatly expanded court on the northwest wing for servants' quarters and the removal of the wooden veranda to allow for a large music room addition.) The Great South Bay facade appeared all the more monumental from its elevated position on a broad terrace, mediating between the house and both the lawn and the marshland beyond. There were no formal gardens to interrupt this vista, nor did anything disturb the appearance of the natural landscape that Bourne loved.

But as Flagg envisioned a vast uninterrupted sweep of lawn against which to foil the house, he lavished on the plan a spatial complexity in contrast to the simplicity of the landscape around it (Fig. 77). Its seemingly symmetrical exterior belied an asymmetrical interior organization. Unlike the symmetrical plans of the Ginn and Clark houses, Flagg adroitly manipulated a split axis

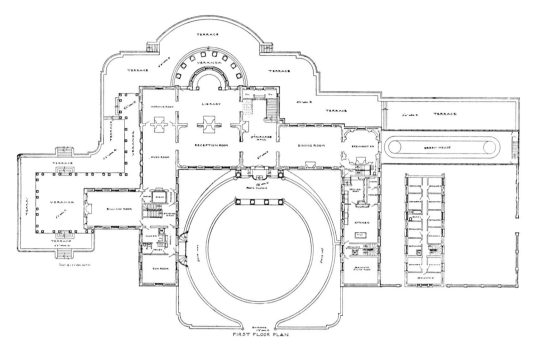

77. Ernest Flagg. Frederick G. Bourne House, "Indian Neck Hall."
Plan, 1897 (*Works,* fig. 67).

for the Bourne House plan. Here the axis created by the front (northeast) entrance with its pedimented portico ended in a staircase, and was therefore not aligned with the Great South Bay veranda. This shift of axis was more scenographically indicated on the Great South Bay elevation, where the veranda on one side was balanced on the other by a series of set-backs (like stage flats). Each volume was clearly articulated on the exterior. This spatial complexity and split axis, new in Flagg's work, were academic devices borrowed from eighteenth-century French *hôtel* planning and also common to Edwin Lutyens's domestic architecture.[55]

In contrast to the red brick and white marble exteriors of "Indian Neck Hall" and the Clark House, their interiors, like those of many Flagg town houses, used a light palette and ornamental scheme associated with the period of Louis XV, which was enjoying a vogue in France during the late nineteenth century. The airy elegance of the Bourne House interiors was a sure antidote to the ponderous gravity of earlier Victorian furniture and interiors, as well as a counterpart to the neo-Georgian and Voyseyian interiors which were popular at the turn of the century in England and consequently in America.[56] Thus the style of the Bourne House was a hybrid: neo-Georgian and Federal Revival forms for the exterior, "modern French Renaissance" for the interiors.

160

Not long after "Indian Neck Hall" was completed, Bourne made arrangements to have a summer residence constructed in the remote Thousand Islands in upstate New York which, like the Long Island shore, had then become fashionable. These islands in a luminous waterway, the so-called "Venice of America," had become the retreat of industrialists, including George M. Pullman who built "Castle Rest" near Alexandria Bay, and a hotel entrepreneur, George C. Boldt, whose "Boldt Castle" on Hart (also Heart) Island was begun in 1900, with portions remaining incomplete.[57] In season, such large summer hotels in Alexandria Bay as the Thousand Island House and The Crossman flourished.

In the summer of 1903 Bourne purchased Dark Island, Chippewa Bay, New York, near the Canadian border, and commissioned Flagg to draw up plans for a "castellated residence and other buildings" which he later called "The Towers."[58] Dark Island may have been chosen for its isolated location in the center of the five-mile-wide opening to Chippewa Bay and the heart of a former haven for wildfowl. The site afforded a unique set of conditions for Bourne to build a hunting lodge. Accessible only by water, the island location gave him the opportunity to exercise his powers of navigation, for in 1903

78. Ernest Flagg. Frederick G. Bourne House, "The Towers," Dark Island, Chippewa Bay, New York. View from the south, 1903–5 (ATSP, AL, CU).

Bourne was elected Commodore of the New York Yacht Club.[59] Sailing down the Saint Lawrence River on his yacht *Artemis,* Commodore Bourne, who was often accompanied by the Flaggs, followed the construction of his island residence for the next two years.

Viewed from the water, "The Towers" drew a sharp profile against the sky (Fig. 78). It was both prominently and dramatically sited on the ten-acre island, which Bourne had instructed to be left "extremely rugged and natural except the formal garden."[60] The sheer technology of preparing the island for construction should not be underestimated, for the erection of a seawall, docking facilities, and construction of a tunnel through the rock to create subterranean passages took approximately a year to complete. The structure was named for its two towers: a large tower facing due south; a smaller tower, round with a conical roof, facing north. The house occupied the leeward (southeast) side of the island and was approached along a series of axes and cross axes from the landing dock via an elevator tower and a bridged passage (similar to Richardson's linkage between the Allegheny Courthouse and Prison in Pittsburgh, and the porte cocheres of late-nineteenth-century resort architecture, including McKim, Mead & White's Casino at Narragansett Pier, Rhode Island). A boathouse was situated next to the landing dock but its role was strictly for show, since the real functions of shelter and repair were relegated to a much larger boathouse which was located, along with a powerhouse and ice house, on the opposite (northwest) side of Dark Island. This collection of structures, following local building techniques and employing local materials, was constructed of granite and sandstone quarried on nearby Oak Island and was roofed with terra-cotta tile.

The plan of "The Towers" is a study in controlling the picturesque. Even the addition of a squash court above the "piazza" in 1928 and a loggia added to the original breakfast room somewhat earlier did not alter Flagg's *parti.*[61] Each of the twenty-eight rooms, contained within the five stories of the original structure, is consecrated to a specific function, ordered to the whole by a rigid axial alignment and following the tenets of Beaux-Arts theory. This is best illustrated on the first floor plan (Fig. 79), where the round tower room, facing south, is assigned a predetermined function as the "Den," rather than a purely picturesque role; for it was here that the Singer Manufacturing Company president kept his vacation office, equipped with a large safe. Within the composition, this "lookout" tower room reinforced a sense of containment as the pivotal joint of two wings that interlocked at right angles. Like Flagg's institutions, the parts are discernible as legible volumes.

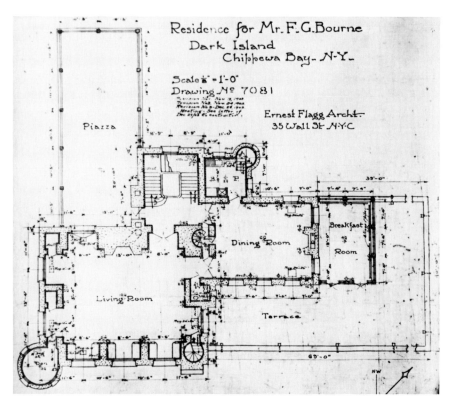

79.   Ernest Flagg. Frederick G. Bourne House, "The Towers." Plans of
first floor (top) and mezzanine (bottom), 1903–5 (ATSP, AL, CU).

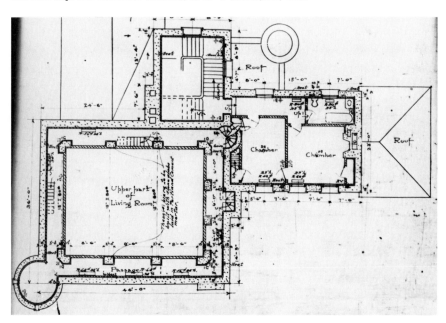

The remoteness and arcadianism of Dark Island encouraged a primi-tive romanticism and an equally primitive habitat. It also encouraged a certain theatricality, because "The Towers" was modeled not after an actual architec-tural example but after a fictional example: the Old Royal Lodge in Sir Walter Scott's historical novel *Woodstock* (1832).[62] Scott's novel, set in England in the year 1652, revolved around the religious and political factionalism after the Civil War between the forces of Cromwell and those loyal to King Charles II. It was Scott's description of the royal hunting lodge at Woodstock, an assem-blage of buildings accruing from Norman and succeeding architectural pe-riods, that inspired Flagg. Scott wrote about a subterranean "labyrinth," "secret passages," "chambers of concealment and retreat," as well as "trap-doors, and hatchways, panels, and portcullises."[63] Indeed, Flagg was so taken with Scott's architectural description of the royal hunting lodge that he adapted its two most salient aspects: a stone structure with towers inspired by Norman architecture, and a maze of secret passages. The entrance vestibule was a cavernous vaulted space. These vaults, executed by crews of Italian masons, indicated Flagg's preference for reviving medieval techniques of stone con-struction following the methods outlined by Viollet-le-Duc in his *Histoire d'une maison,* rather than for Guastavino vaulting methods routinely used in turn-of-the-century American buildings.[64] Yet the spatial complexities of the vestibule frustrated that single-purpose approach. Within a relatively con-stricted area, a number of perspective views complicated the visitor's spatial perception. The most intricate of these was produced by facing mirrors: a mirrored overmantel within the hemicycle of the arch above, and a second mirror on the opposite wall; the two reflected an infinity of reciprocal views (Fig. 80). The device has the power and mastery of form common to Lutyens's work, though less evident in the Briton's contemporaneous restoration of Lindisfarne Castle.[65] Certainly Flagg's and Bourne's mutual love of games and fable inspired this house. Moreover, the very Frenchness of this English archi-tecture — Norman corresponding to French Romanesque — accounted for Flagg's adroit handling of it and, at the same time, prevented the architecture from appearing anomalous to the rest of his work.

On the main (first) floor above the vestibule, a living room occupies center stage (see Fig. 79). It is here that the hunting lodge in Scott's novel is most literally realized. The plan indicates a large hall with a series of compart-ments or booths, each of which contains gaming tables along the southeast and southwest walls commanding a view of Chippewa Bay, not unlike the vista of Woodstock forest from the oriel windows of the royal hunting lodge, as Scott described it.[66]

80.   Ernest Flagg. Frederick G. Bourne House, "The Towers." Vestibule.

Because the height of the living room was 17 feet, Flagg planned a mezzanine floor above these compartments to contain a circumferential hidden passage (see Fig. 79). In *Woodstock* a hinged door leading to one such secret passage was concealed by a portrait of Charles I.[67] Intrigued by that idea, Flagg provided for an oval portrait of Charles I to be hung on the wainscoting of the southeast wall above the center compartment. Departing from the Scott novel, however, "The Towers" portrait was used to conceal an oval lookout which might be unhinged by anyone inside the passage to afford a vantage of the entire room. There were other such passages running both horizontally and vertically, via two spiral stone staircases. Passages in nearly every room of the house were entered from doors disguised either as wainscoting, a part of a chimney piece, or a bedroom closet wall. These doors were activated by a variety of curious devices including push buttons concealed behind lighting fixtures, thermostats, or even closet hooks. Subterranean passages led from the kitchen to the powerhouse and boathouse. Heralded as a "Castle of Mysteries" by the *New York Times,* upon its completion in the fall of 1905, "The Towers" was surrounded by a veil of secrecy which Bourne, Flagg, and the building

165

81. Ernest Flagg. Ernest Flagg House, "Stone Court" (now St. Charles Seminary), Dongan Hills, Staten Island, 1898–99 (Flagg Family Papers).

82. Ernest Flagg. Ernest Flagg House, "Stone Court." Plan (*Works,* fig. 73).

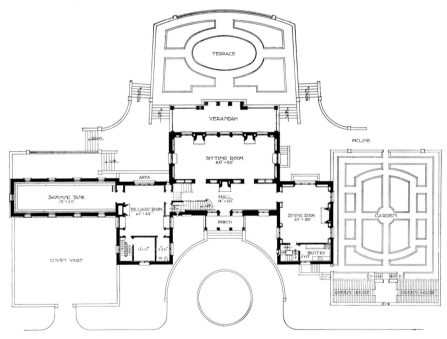

166

superintendent, Arthur Sutcliffe, all encouraged.[68] During the summer of 1905 as the house was nearing completion, Sutcliffe privately reflected on the reaction of the Italian workmen to their first experience within "the mysterious passage." "They were quite frightened," wrote Sutcliffe, "and said they would never come into the house again."[69]

While Flagg was neither a hunter nor a sportsman, the Bourne lodge nevertheless reflected a very personal statement. Within the Flagg family circle, his wife, Margaret (Margie), read novels aloud each evening promptly at 7:45. They were not the works of Dreiser, Zola, or Joyce, but those of Scott (Waverley novels), Robert Louis Stevenson, and James Fenimore Cooper.[70] Here then was architecture as theater, one which both staged and completed the narrated adventure story. Flagg apparently envied his client. As "The Towers" neared completion, Sutcliffe recorded: "Mr. Flagg repeats over and over that he regrets he did not build a similar place for himself."[71] But Flagg had already built a large stone and timber residence of an altogether different character on an island close to Manhattan.

The theme of regionalism in Flagg's work is nowhere more evident than in his own Staten Island country house, "Stone Court" (now St. Charles Seminary at 209 Flagg Place) of 1898–99 (Fig. 81). In 1897 Flagg began to purchase land on Staten Island through his association with George Cromwell, a friend of Walter Chambers, who became the first borough president of Richmond in 1898.[72] Flagg undoubtedly chose the island location because of its accessibility to Manhattan. He may also have wanted to strengthen his family ties, since the Vanderbilt presence on Staten Island was long established and Flagg's land in Dongan Hills was no more than a stone's throw from the Moravian Cemetery where the Vanderbilt ancestors were interred in a titanic mausoleum designed by Richard Morris Hunt in 1886.[73] Built along a ridge on the northeast side of Staten Island near its highest point at Todt Hill, "Stone Court" was still further elevated upon a terrace, commanding a view of Lower New York Bay, over a mile away (Fig. 82). In July 1899, Flagg (who was forty-two) and his bride, Margaret Elizabeth Bonnell (a native of Staten Island who was only seventeen), moved into the recently completed house, "Stone Court." It resembled such regional examples of Dutch colonial architecture as the fieldstone Billiou-Stillwell-Perine House (begun in 1662 with additions to 1830), the Vanderbilt farmhouse in Stapleton (demolished), and the Lake-Tysen House, Tysen's Lane (c. 1740; now Richmondtown).[74] It was also similar to the domestic architecture of the Dutch colonies in the Caribbean, monumentalized to twentieth-century standards.[75] Thus, an adjustment of the design, not only to New World Dutch colonial but also to the native architecture of Staten Island, was explicit. The gambrel roof, with its flared eave which terminated in a veranda, virtually consumed the facade. The roof (originally slate) was boldly pierced by two chimneys (reminiscent of American federal houses), a sunporch, and an observation gallery. The house was constructed of locally quarried stone, the exterior walls whitewashed like any number of indigenous colonial models.

Flagg's "Stone Court" had all the traditional components of the late-nineteenth-century leisure estate, though lacking the overall scale of his clients' houses and the theatrical elements of "The Towers." In addition to the main house, a gate and gatehouse, a greenhouse, a water tower, and stables were all constructed before 1902, mostly of local stone which maintained the

83.   Ernest Flagg. Ernest Flagg House, "Stone Court." Aerial view after 1908 (EFP, AL, CU).

84.   Ernest Flagg. Palm House, "Stone Court" (Flagg Family Papers).

vernacular quality common to other Staten Island masonry buildings.[76] Like the Bourne and Ginn houses, Flagg's residence was devoted to a number of recreational pursuits. For example, a billiard room, a bowling alley, a swimming tank, and a Turkish bath were housed in the northeast wing. Flagg's estate was far from static, since both house and grounds were continually undergoing a variety of "improvements." By the fall of 1909, these included a more elaborate terracing with a fountain, the rebuilding of roads, and a greatly enlarged main house with such additional outbuildings as a Lutyens-like palm house, greenhouses, a pump house, an ice house, a hen house, a windmill, a garage, and a stone house (Figs. 83, 84). At this time a second story was added to the porch and porticos of the end wings, further pronouncing the house's horizontality and Palladian composition. A music room wing, a breakfast room, and a palm room were axially disposed within an enlarged plan.[77] The paneled music room was the most elaborate element of the design, similar to those "modern French Renaissance" music rooms of the Ginn and Bourne estates. After 1909, the Flagg estate became a kind of building farm, more than it had ever been, as Flagg and local workmen experimented on new construction techniques for small stone houses (see Chapter IX).

169

The interiors at "Stone Court" were furnished exclusively by Flagg, who was a shrewd collector. Continually perusing a favorite auction house for good values, Flagg purchased furniture and tapestries. His clients, often ready to dispose of a spare chandelier or piece of furniture, were more direct sources. The organ that dominated Flagg's music room, for example, had belonged originally to Frederick Bourne. But Flagg's curious sense of collecting extended beyond his house to the stables. Just after the Spanish-American War, when the horses used by Roosevelt's celebrated Rough Riders were brought back to America, so the story goes, Flagg purchased three of them at auction.[78]

"Stone Court" was Flagg's fortress of culture. It was a symbol of the heritage which he had acquired through birthright, but that material wealth had made possible. Flagg's genteel love of literature, music, the fine arts, genealogy, and estate management were inherited from British culture with its links to the Renaissance. By World War I, Flagg had bought up much of the adjacent Todt Hill property and had begun to design and build a colony of houses which he called the Flegg Ridge Estate.[79] Flagg used the name "Flegg" because it reflected his own Anglo-French heritage, for he had traced his genealogy back to English yeomanry and still farther back to twelfth-century ancestors among the landed gentry of Norfolk County whose names were Flegg and de Fleg. Flagg's Norman ancestry confirmed for him, both culturally and artistically, the appropriateness of his architectural training in France and set the stage for the Anglo-French small houses he designed around "Stone Court."

Flagg's town and country houses exemplified his aspirations for the American home. No matter what historical style Flagg employed, each work was stamped by the recurring characteristics of his personal style: planar wall surfaces, spatial components clearly articulated on the exterior, rooms axially aligned and designated for specific functions, creative manipulations of forms, as well as elements of American and French classicism with English influences. Whether individual rooms or entire houses, each had comfort and elegance, and each was calculated to convey an image of upper-class professional and leisured life. Flagg lived as his clients lived. In short, his domestic architecture was marked by his personal sense of style and pattern of living, and his concern for regionalism and variety, all of which characterized his *parti* for the American house.

CHAPTER SIX

Rationalism and Aestheticism in Commercial and Utilitarian Building

IF FLAGG'S institutional and monumental works illustrated his command of academic classicism, his commercial and utilitarian buildings demonstrated his mastery over the principles and aesthetics of structural rationalism as they were understood in France during the early Third Republic. There were two interpretations. The first defined *rationalism* as a reasoned approach to architecture as decorated structure. The second regarded it as an available style, like *Néo-Grec,* which was suitable for certain building types, particularly the office building, which was essentially a product of the nineteenth century and as a result could not reflect historical precedent. Students at the Ecole des Beaux-Arts received no direct training in the design of commercial buildings, which by a long-standing tradition in France were relegated to a low status in the hierarchy of building types because they lacked the qualities associated with religious and civil architecture: monumentality, nobility, meaning, and destiny. In short, architects trained at the Ecole were encouraged to feel that commercial architecture was somehow beneath them. By the second half of the nineteenth century, however, commerce in France required a specialized building typology.[1] But not until the lectures and writings of Viollet-le-Duc did commercial architecture become the object of serious theoretical study; not until those of Julien Guadet that it was codified according to function; and not until the work of a generation of architects in the 1870s and 1880s that commercial architecture was given special consideration.

This freedom from architectural precedent was also accompanied by a freedom from traditional masonry materials. During the early Third Republic, architects trained at the Ecole were no longer principally confined to working in stone or brick, no longer taught that mass and shade were *the* desired effects. Architects reveled in the use of new materials and explored the appropriate means for their expression. Pierre Chabat in his influential publication of 1881, *La Brique et la terre cuite,* surveyed a wide range of public and private buildings in France that employed brick and terra cotta "in their technical or decorative applications."[2] For those who sought a rational expression of exposed metal, Viollet-le-Duc was influential. When using iron, he maintained, architects should find "forms suitable to its properties and manufacture; we ought not to disguise it."[3] So strong was the legacy of Viollet-le-Duc in some circles during the early Third Republic that when exposed metal was specified, often for ancillary rather than primary structural support, it posed a design as well as an engineering problem.

Flagg's commercial architecture synthesized problems of aesthetics and construction. In his widely published paper, "American Architecture as Opposed to Architecture in America," Flagg suggested that architects seek a national style of decoration to complement their "American ways of building."[4] As a group, Flagg's commercial and utilitarian buildings not only expressed the merger of technology and aesthetics, science and materialism, but also they were his most inventive. Like their French counterparts, Flagg's buildings experimented with new structural systems and new materials using combinations of masonry, terra cotta, metal, and glass. Furthermore, they showed his respect for building process and legible parts — the very qualities inherent in the French models. Consequently, both Flagg's attitude to architectural design as decorated structure, and his use of rationalism as an available style, readily distinguished him from his American contemporaries who were not of "the French school" or who, for the most part, failed to consider the specific requirements of character and function when they applied conservative classicism to commercial architecture. Much of an explanation of this lies in the pragmatic nature of Flagg's early career, in his training in France, and in his personality. Because Flagg received no formal architectural training in America, he was open to uniting a variety of architectural styles and approaches in a way that many of his American contemporaries were not. Even though his career at the Ecole proper was relatively short, his study in the Atelier Blondel and his travels in France, Italy, and England encouraged his already well-developed independent nature. Because he worked "a little outside the usual channels of the profession," Flagg must have felt freer to experiment with building techniques, materials, and ways of decorating that were new to

85.   Ernest Flagg and
Walter B. Chambers.
Firehouse Engine Co. 33,
44 Great Jones Street,
New York City, 1898–99
(Wendy Barrows).

America but for the most part reflected French methods, principles, and aesthetics.

The construction of Flagg's commercial buildings parallels the chronology of his institutions and monumental works. Numbering roughly a dozen or more significant works, these buildings date from 1893 to the Depression. In assessing their development, there are two salient points. First, the composition of Flagg's commercial and utilitarian buildings was largely the same; corners were closed and emphasized, allowing the middle to be opened up. Second, even though Flagg was influenced by Sullivan and the Chicago school

173

when he employed structural steel in his commerical buildings around 1900, he continued to use the familiar compositional format of French commercial buildings of the 1880s. Along with the vocabulary of French classicism, these elements together became hallmarks of Flagg's style.

Apart from considerations of composition and structure, these commercial buildings reflect their urban contexts. Their designs are tempered by the nature of their narrow city lots, their party walls, the streets they front, and the economic principles that condition their heights and densities. (The latter two factors are more critical determinants of the monumental skyscraper, especially Flagg's Singer Tower of 1906–8.) In considering all these factors and the diverse building types represented—firehouses, lofts, stores, office buildings, and banks—Flagg's foremost problem was to treat commercial and utilitarian building both rationally and artistically.

Masonry Firehouses

Among the early utilitarian buildings that epitomize Flagg's compositional format are two New York City firehouses designed in collaboration with Walter Chambers: Firehouse Engine Co. 67, 170th Street of 1897–98, and Firehouse Engine Co. 33, 44 Great Jones Street of 1898–99 (Fig. 85).[5] These commissions coincide with the growth of city services when the New York fire force changed from volunteer to professional manpower. A reorganization plan distributed the companies geographically throughout the boroughs of New York City.[6] Of these two similar firehouses, Engine Co. 33 was the more significant.[7] This fire station was planned as a double or two-company house with headquarters for the chief of the Fire Department, then newly appointed Edward F. Croker, a nephew of Tammany boss Richard Croker.[8]

The firehouse illustrates Flagg's adaptation of French models. Indeed, this building type had had a short but rich building tradition in France where the celebrated *pompiers* (firehouses) and *casernes* (barracks) of Achille Hermant (Jacques's father; 1823–1903), Julien Hénard (1812–87), and J. A. Bouvard were undoubtedly known to Flagg in the 1880s, as was Jacques Hermant's Caserne des Célestins (see Fig. 12) in the 1890s.[9] But at the same time, American urban conditions (the need for a fireproof structure and the constricted dimensions of the city lot) influenced the four-story firehouse design. Structurally, these firehouses of the 1890s were transitional. They employed masonry bearing walls, cast-iron columns, and steel floor beams. In spite of the utilitarian nature of Firehouse Engine Co. 33, the facade was treated artistically. A classically detailed base of limestone with two arched openings to accommodate horse-drawn fire engines defined the street level and visually supported the upper floors. Above it, a round arch of beveled limestone punctured the red brick wall surface with a monumental aperture. This manipulation of mass and void, this contrast of textures, materials, and colors—ordinary brick detailed in white limestone and crisp metal ornament—produced a dramatic effect. These elements further articulated the facade with a play of light and shade. Because the arch monumentalized the building, it brought the firehouse into civic recognition, working urbanistically as the Midwest banks of Louis Sullivan did a decade later.[10] While the firehouse's large-scale window conveyed its civic function, the cartouche symbolized the academic side of this Beaux-Arts building with a utilitarian function.

Scribner Buildings

The supreme elegance with which Flagg could approach commercial architecture in New York is perhaps no better illustrated than in two buildings for the publisher Charles Scribner's Sons: the first Scribner Building (now United Synagogue of America) at 153–157 Fifth Avenue of 1893–94, and the second Scribner Building at 597 Fifth Avenue of 1912–13 (Figs. 86, 87).[11] In spite of the two decades that separate these buildings and the differences in their respective structural systems, both Scribner buildings employ the compositional format associated with Flagg's style. They are also attempts to reflect the reasoned nature of their materials and structures.

In 1893, when Charles Scribner's Sons decided to relocate its bookstore and headquarters from 743–745 Broadway to the then fashionable Madison Square Garden district, a mixed residential and commercial area, it chose a site at 153–157 Fifth Avenue between 21st and 22nd streets.[12] This was Flagg's first commercial structure. The commission for this prestigious office building, which claimed to be "the first in America built from ground to top distinctly for the uses of a publishing-house," was due to Flagg's loyal family patrons, Charles and Arthur Scribner.[13]

The Scribner Building at 153–157 Fifth Avenue combined two distinct functions: a bookstore and an office building. Its facade brilliantly explicated the dual nature of the program. Moreover, each function operated both architecturally and urbanistically. This six-story structure was organized into a grid format to express the like office spaces of the publishing house. Two entrances gave access to the building: the uptown entrance allowed Charles Scribner to reach his private study on the fifth floor; the main entrance on the downtown side led to elevators serving all departments. In effect, this masonry

175

86.   Ernest Flagg. Scribner Building (now United Synagogue of America),
153–157 Fifth Avenue, New York City, 1893–94 (Charles Scribner's Sons).

office building enframed an elegant metal and glass storefront whose display
windows perfectly conveyed their merchandising function, and whose scholarly
ornament complemented the library-like bookstore within. The image was
deliberate. *Scribner's Magazine* likened the salesroom interior to "a particularly well-cared-for library in some great private house, or in some of the
quieter public institutions."[14] *The Independent* compared it to "a retreat of
quiet, refined and learned leisure."[15] Punctuating the store's entrance was an

176

87.   Ernest Flagg. Scribner Building, 597 Fifth Avenue, New York City,
1912–13 (Charles Scribner's Sons).

exotic metal and glass projecting marquee (now removed), not unlike that of the Knickerbocker apartment building with which Flagg was associated a decade earlier. While paired cast-iron columns visually supported the Scribner marquee, foliated wrought-iron brackets spanned the storefront. The imagery of the iron ornament, so like the wire-drawn typography of the printed page, made a symbolic reference to the publishing house. Urbanistically, the marquee announced Scribner's on Fifth Avenue by giving the store visual prominence; on a practical level, it provided temporary shelter for patrons. Thus, while the office building with its mansard roof maintained the uniform cornice line and urban scale of its Fifth Avenue neighbors, the storefront broke from such established norms, its marquee thrusting into the pedestrian space to link store with street.

Fresh from Paris and buoyant from the recent acceptance of his *Néo-Grec* design for the Corcoran Gallery and his more conservative "modern French Renaissance" scheme for St. Luke's Hospital, Flagg conceived of his first Scribner Building as equally derivative of French models. It embraced the aesthetics and techniques of French commercial architecture during the early Third Republic. In his *maison commerciale* at 3 rue d'Uzès of 1880 (see Fig. 13), Edmond Guillaume demonstrated a facility for working in masonry and metal in an effort to rationalize the classical tradition. In effect, Flagg brought back with him French commercial architecture, which already had assimilated the theory and design of Viollet-le-Duc. But when Flagg returned to America in 1891, commercial architecture had not yet been fully affected by the impact of the French rationalist. The American publication in 1875 of the first volume of Viollet-le-Duc's *Entretiens,* translated by Henry Van Brunt, had only a minimal effect in spreading rationalist theory in America. Viollet-le-Duc's influence, principally among Richard Morris Hunt's students, was largely confined to domestic, rather than commercial or utilitarian, architecture. Moreover, the American architects he influenced relied upon traditional as opposed to new materials. Ware & Van Brunt's Memorial Hall at Harvard University (1874–78), with its timber trusses and ornamental iron finials, summarized this early influence in America of Viollet-le-Duc's Gothic rationalism, even though it was also Ruskinian. No one more broadly interpreted Viollet-le-Duc's theory within a variety of architectural contexts than did Hunt's student, Frank Furness (1839–1912). His commercial buildings of the 1880s emulated the curiosities of Viollet-le-Duc's decorated masonry, metal structural supports, and foliated iron ornament.[16] However, in spite of his reverence for the master, Furness never explored in his commercial architecture those daring metal structural supports and glass spans that Viollet-le-Duc's publications had suggested and which had influenced French practice. This aspect of Viollet-le-Duc's influence in his native France was not incorporated into American commercial building until Flagg combined masonry, metal, and glass to produce wide spans.[17] The impact on commercial building rapidly followed the first American publication in 1881 of the second volume of the *Entretiens,* translated by Benjamin Bucknall.

In terms of composition, structure, and the reasoned use of materials, the Scribner Building of 1893–94 was thoroughly French. There, the French formula for a commercial structure — a load-bearing masonry cage with emphasized corner piers that enframed ornamental iron girders for spanning purposes — appeared in America. This French use was ultimately derived from Viollet-le-Duc's project for a Town Hall (see Fig. 9), illustrated in the second volume of the *Entretiens,* which was published in 1872.[18] Similarly, Flagg spanned the wide storefront with foliated metal brackets, even though they were strictly confined to the exterior and were nonstructural.

Like Guillaume's *maison commerciale,* for example, the Scribner Building used interlocking small- and large-scale elements of masonry and metal to articulate a composition divided into bays as well as a planar facade to reinforce the urban character of the street. The prestigious nature of the Scribner Building, however, called for a more hierarchical expression of character than a commercial building ordinarily would have warranted. Flagg, therefore, chose to define the facade with a series of horizontal elevations. A combination of *Néo-Grec* ornament, similar to that of the Corcoran, and a proliferation of classical details on the facade complemented the crisp lithic quality of its Indiana limestone. Independent from the masonry facade, classically detailed iron columns and foliated cast- and wrought-iron ornament on the storefront assumed exotic roles appropriate to the store's literary function as a symbol of high art and culture.

When Charles Scribner's Sons, in a similar move two decades later, relocated its bookstore and offices to 597 Fifth Avenue, Flagg was called upon, once again, to design the new building (see Fig. 87).[19] This move, like the earlier one from Broadway to Fifth Avenue, was prompted by a wave of fashionable settlement uptown. The relocation of Charles Scribner's Sons was part of a larger "leapfrog" development up the Fifth Avenue spine.[20] The new site, near the corner of 48th Street, was undoubtedly chosen for its proximity to the New York Public Library, completed in 1911, and to Grand Central Terminal, then under construction. Later, in the years just prior to 1930 when

179

Scribner's considered a possible move still farther north, the firm decided against relocating when it anticipated that Rockefeller Center would be a stable cultural and commercial anchor for the area.[21]

In designing the new ten-story skyscraper in 1912, Flagg's problem was fundamentally different from 153–157 Fifth Avenue, which had not employed skeletal construction.[22] Flagg's concern was to monumentalize the office building, distinguish its architectural character, and, above all, express the frame. The Scribners' concern was to model the new store after the image of the old. By adapting the masonry, metal, and glass components of the old store to a more monumental structure, the new Scribner Building would retain its former Fifth Avenue identity. There were, however, several critical differences. While the new building also employed limestone for the facade, this was clearly treated as a thin veneer, in contrast to the earlier building in which

88.   Ernest Flagg. Scribner Building, storefront, 597 Fifth Avenue (Princeton University Library).

89.   Ernest Flagg. Scribner Building, bookstore, 597 Fifth Avenue
(Princeton University Library).

masonry bearing walls were defined by a deep reveal. Furthermore, the interrelationship between masonry and metal was dissimilar. The masonry of the new
building no longer served as a supporting cage. Instead, the metal and glass
storefront extended to the party walls, thus identifying the steel frame as the
primary, not an ancillary, support. In both cases the rational premise of Flagg's
design was uncompromised. Like 153–157 Fifth Avenue, the new Scribner
Building is a classically proportioned and articulated ensemble "with a scale
and elegance of detailing," as Henry-Russell Hitchcock observed, "that be-
longs to the new century."[23]

The metal and glass storefront was at once the building's most salient
and most controversial feature (Fig. 88). During a series of planning discussions with clients Charles and Arthur Scribner in the spring of 1912, Flagg had
proposed a design with more than one entrance for the bookstore.[24] But as
Arthur regularly vetoed the idea, "still holding to the one entrance," presumably on the grounds that the store would lose valuable display space, Flagg
reflected, "my best and most original feature is lost."[25] Nonetheless, the
storefront design is still one of striking originality and unmistakably Flagg's.
Taking his cue from the organization of 153–157 Fifth Avenue, Flagg

181

divided the shopfront "grill," as he called it, into the familiar bay system of emphasized corners with the center opened up.[26] But now the storefront became a field of metal and glass. Orchestrated by a geometry of perfectly proportioned parts, Flagg's metal grid dominated the facade's first two stories and mezzanine. A central arch focused the composition. It was as if Flagg had taken the metal and glass marquee at 153 – 157 Fifth Avenue, tilted it upright, and pressed it into the grill. Factory windows, over which Flagg expressed some anxiety because of his clients' objections when they "threatened to kick on the windows but did not," were louvered to allow for natural ventilation.[27] Although suggesting prefabrication and standardization, these factory windows, on the contrary, illustrated the essence of custom design. What accounted for the opulence and exoticism of the metal and glass front of the new Scribner store, as with the old, may have been Viollet-le-Duc's direct influence. In his project for a Town Hall (see Fig. 9), Viollet-le-Duc expressed his intentions for ornamenting the metal trusses of the interior. "Supposing the iron-work to be painted and gilt," he asserted, "we can readily imagine that the effect would be extremely rich."[28] It is possible that Flagg took the theoretician's suggestion literally when he privately expressed the hope that the Scribners "will let me use a little gold on the front of their building."[29] The resulting black metal grill, with its wrought-iron foliated and scroll ornament and cast-iron columns trimmed in gold, was executed by Whale Creek Iron Works.[30] It remains today a serenely eloquent statement and, along with the earlier Scribner's, a reminder of numerous metal and glass marquees and metal storefronts in New York which no longer survive.

The interior of the bookstore, like the exterior of the building, realized a complex interplay of spatial elements in which the image of 153 – 157 Fifth Avenue was retained (Fig. 89). Like the old Scribner bookstore, the interior of the new store was similar to the browsing space of a small library. The eighteenth-century treatment of the interior reinforced its intended character. The bookstore was axially planned with columns on either side of a central aisle and a grand staircase to the rear which led up to a balcony level. Flagg gave the monumental space with its 30-foot-high vaulted ceiling a human scale by the scenographic interrelationship of its parts. A series of bays linked the storefront to a mirrored end wall which, while casting light back from the Fifth Avenue display window, reflected the whole interior in perspective.[31]

Flagg considered the Scribner Building at 597 Fifth Avenue a great personal triumph. "I think the building is the best thing I ever did," he said, "and I am glad I lived long enough to have this opportunity."[32] Coming at a low point in his career, with few new prospects and significant reductions in the office force following the completion of the U.S. Naval Academy in 1908, the Scribner Building gave Flagg renewed "hopes of that as a boost to my reputation."[33] He was right. The Scribner Building of 1912–13 did boost his reputation, not with the immediate and tangible reward of new business, but in designing an architectural *tour de force* on Fifth Avenue.

Toward a Rational Ideal: Singer Loft Building and Automobile Club of America

The change from load-bearing masonry and iron construction to the steel frame around 1900, as illustrated by the two Scribner buildings, confirmed a dramatic reversal in Flagg's attitude toward skyscraper technology. The six-story Scribner Building of 1893–94 was tangible proof of his trust at that time in the safety of masonry bearing walls from the standpoints of structural stability and fireproofing. In his influential "white paper" of 1896, "The Dangers of High Buildings," Flagg advocated the "urgent need of a law providing that the outer walls of fireproof buildings . . . be real walls, capable of supporting themselves."[34] His opposition to skeletal construction before the late 1890s reflected a broader and peculiarly New York suspicion about exposed or encased metal buildings. The long tradition of employing cast-iron fronts for commercial buildings, firmly established in New York from the 1860s, had been thrown into question by the devastating fires of Chicago (1871), Boston (1872), and Worth Street, New York (1879). Cautious observers like Flagg believed that during such fires, buildings employing thick masonry walls not only had survived, but also had deterred the spread of fire. Skeletal construction, so Flagg and others argued in the mid-1890s, was not a viable alternative. Such steel framework, Flagg maintained in his "Dangers" article, could not withstand the test of fire or corrosion. In a large conflagration, the thin slabs of masonry or fireproofing material would "peel off almost immediately, the steel framework would become warped, and the whole construction would fall over."[35] Further, he argued, because "the steel framework is imbedded in masonry, where it cannot be examined," it was always endangered by the possible hazard of rust and corrosion from water damage.[36] Most of the ideas in Flagg's article, which popularized the opposition to skeletal construction, were actually put forth earlier by the architect George B. Post, at a meeting of the Architectural League of New York in August 1894 and later that year, with Thomas Hastings and others, at the annual convention of the American Institute of Architects held in New York.[37]

90. Louis Sullivan. Bayard
(Condict) Building, 65 Bleecker Street,
New York City, 1897–98
(Richard Nickel).

Conservative opposition notwithstanding, the decade of the 1890s
marked the acceptance of the skeletal frame for commercial building. While
cast-iron architecture prevailed into the decade, New York instituted a building code in 1899 requiring cast-iron fronts to be backed with masonry, which
effectively eliminated their subsequent use.[38] In 1894–95 Bruce Price's
twenty-story American Surety Building at Broadway and Pine Street, New
York, "introduced the first complete steel frame."[39] During the 1890s Flagg's
commercial buildings, employing masonry bearing walls, cast-iron columns,
and steel beams, were structurally transitional. By the end of the decade New
York architects, as Montgomery Schuyler observed in his article of 1899, "The
'Sky-scraper' up to Date," had at last accepted the inevitable: the modern
skyscraper with its steel frame and elevator. But what Schuyler deplored about
these New York commercial buildings was their "conventional" treatment of

184

the facade into a tripartite division which denied the reality of the frame. He further lamented that "the solution of a building problem so new as that presented by the steel-framed tall building should have apparently so largely ceased to be experimental."[40] His only hope for New York commercial building was the promise of Louis Sullivan's newly completed Bayard (Condict) Building, New York, of 1897–98 (Fig. 90). There, Schuyler maintained, Louis Sullivan had "adhered so strictly to the unpromising facts of the steel cage," for the Bayard Building was "the nearest approach yet made, in New York, at least, to solving the problem of the sky-scraper."[41] The premise on which Sullivan and Schuyler argued was clearly one of finding an appropriate decoration to identify the steel frame. Indeed, the Bayard Building became an emblem in Manhattan of the formidable Chicago tradition which Schuyler appreciated.[42] Architects of "the French school" like Flagg, however, sought an alternative approach to Sullivan's articulation of the tall building.

At roughly the same time that Montgomery Schuyler publicly deplored the conventionality of skyscaper design, Ernest Flagg was calling for an American style of architecture which he applied to commercial building. In his "American Architecture as Opposed to Architecture in America," Flagg observed that while there had been "American ways of building, as for instance, our high buildings with the skeleton construction, and the cast-iron fronts of thirty or forty years ago," there had not yet been "decorative features" of comparable "nationality." Either they had been "used in accordance with passing fashions, supposedly modeled on European usage," he argued, or they were "extraordinary attempts by individuals at originality." "None of these attempts," Flagg maintained, "has met with popular favor." Only when decoration could approximate construction in "nationality," Flagg inferred, could American architecture begin to evolve into "the *parti* for America."[43] The result would be modern; it would be "architecture" and not "archaeology."

Nowhere in Flagg's commercial architecture is his promised *parti* — "the logical solution to the problem from his [the architect's] dual standpoint as constructor and artist" — so well illustrated as in the Singer Loft Building at 561 Broadway, New York, of 1902–4 and his Automobile Club of America, New York, of 1905–7 (Figs. 91, 92). As prototypes for his *"parti* for America," the Singer Loft Building and Automobile Club of America, with their hybrid of American skeletal construction and French-derived composition and decoration, represent two rational experiments in ornamented construction.

185

91. Ernest Flagg. Singer Loft Building, 561 Broadway, New York City, 1902–4 (© John Ebstel).

92. Ernest Flagg.
Automobile Club of
America (demolished),
247–259 West 54th
Street, New York City,
1905–7 (*Brickbuilder*
XVI, May 1907,
pl. 65).

In February 1902, Flagg was commissioned by the Singer Manufacturing Company, through its president, Frederick G. Bourne, to design a twelve-story office and loft building for an L-shaped lot at the corner of Broadway and Prince Street, New York.[44] The Singer Loft Building, when it first appeared on Broadway, was a startling event, even though it has often since been dismissed mistakenly as just another cast-iron building, undistinguished from its neighbors in the district south of Houston Street now popularly known as SoHo. Close observation, however, reveals that both image and structure emanate from an entirely different concept. The Singer Loft is clearly unrelated to the earlier development in standardization where prefabricated

187

modular units of cast iron were joined together and painted, and so disguised as the homogenous and repetitive elevation of a stone palazzo. In this respect alone, it had much in common with Richard Morris Hunt's customized design for two storefronts on Broadway, namely, Tweedy & Co., 476 Broadway (1871–72; demolished), and Hammerslough Brothers, 478–482 Broadway (1873–74; now Roosevelt Building). Although both were constructed of cast iron, they did not imitate Italianate palazzos but frankly explored the decorative possibilities of iron, employing *Néo-Grec* and Moorish motifs. "Each," Montgomery Schuyler observed, "had the fundamental merit of being unmistakably designed for its material."[45] Nonetheless, largely due to fire precautions, the use of a load-bearing system of exposed metal in New York was effectively banned in 1899, only a few years prior to Flagg's design for the Singer Loft.

In a radical departure from the normative use of exposed metal for bearing walls in previous commercial building, Flagg's solution accommodated a steel frame to the compositional format of French commercial architecture. Here, proportioned parts were conditioned by French classicism: a two-storied base defined by an ornamental wrought-iron arch, a shaft of nine stories terminated by a second arch of exotic ironwork to monumentalize the entire facade, and an attic story completed by a row of urns to effect an ordered but picturesque profile. Corners were emphasized to allow the center to be opened up. This design was further complicated by its two facades: the principal Broadway facade with a frontage extending 50 feet served a public function, while a second facade of 35 feet on Prince Street, directed to shipping and receiving, quoted the Broadway elevation on a diminutive scale. Moreover, the nature of the L-shaped site, with its party walls abutting the corner building and the extensive excavating and shoring-up procedure involved, which lasted approximately a year, made this design extremely impractical.[46]

In plan, a precociously wide span between pairs of steel columns on the facade permits floor-to-ceiling glass (Fig. 93). Though an unrelated development, this use prefigures the window wall of Willis Polk's Hallidie Building of 1915 and ultimately the curtain wall of the 1920s.[47] However, Flagg's placement of steel columns serves as a cage to enframe balconies and window wall, rather than as a support for cantilevering.

This experimental design for the Singer Loft Building operates principally as structural expression. The use of a rational system of ornament makes explicit the positioning of each steel column within its masonry and terra-cotta enclosure. An axonometric drawing indicates the structural column at the core,

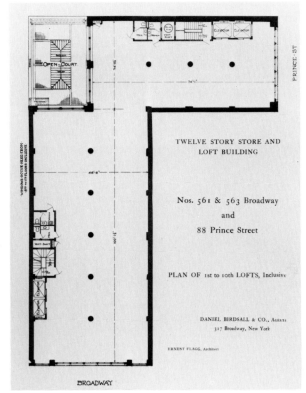

TWELVE STORY STORE AND
LOFT BUILDING

Nos. 561 & 563 Broadway
and
88 Prince Street

PLAN OF 1st to 10th LOFTS, Inclusive

DANIEL BIRDSALL & CO., Agents
317 Broadway, New York

ERNEST FLAGG, Architect

OPEN COURT

WINDOWS FROM OUTER WALLS FROM 8TH to 11TH FLOORS INCLUSIVE

PRINCE ST

BROADWAY

93. Ernest Flagg. Singer
Loft Building. Plan
(*The Singer Building*
[promotional brochure];
ATSP, AL, CU).

wrapped in a fireproofing material and faced with unglazed terra-cotta panels, with a thin trellis of steel straps and angles to encase them (Fig. 94).[48] Polychromed materials — orange terra cotta and metal painted green — stamp the building with the period colors of the Singer logo for corporate identification.

Clearly there were no American precedents for Flagg's French-inspired approach to structural expression. Sullivan's Bayard (Condict) Building (see Fig. 90) on Bleecker Street had only recently been completed just a few blocks away from the Singer Loft. Flagg must have been impressed by its forceful use of skeletal construction and Sullivan's approach to rationalism. But Flagg's objective in 1902 was to express his familiar compositional format — emphasized corners and a monumental arched opening in the center — while employing a steel frame and fireproofing it. To Flagg, finding an American style of decoration was a difficult task. Instead of adopting Sullivan's all-terra-cotta facade, Flagg chose a different program of ornament which articulated

189

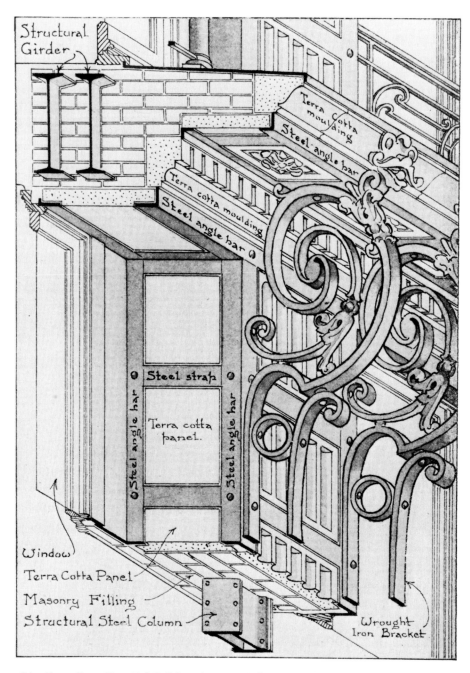

Structural Girder

Terra Cotta moulding

Steel angle bar

Terra cotta moulding

Steel angle bar

Steel angle bar

Steel strap

Steel angle bar

Terra cotta panel.

Window

Terra Cotta Panel

Masonry Filling

Structural Steel Column

Wrought Iron Bracket

94.   Ernest Flagg. Singer Loft Building. Axonometric drawing (*Arch Rec* XV, March 1904, p. 278).

the structure through discrete parts of terra cotta, metal, and glass. In effect, this style of decoration was more French than American.

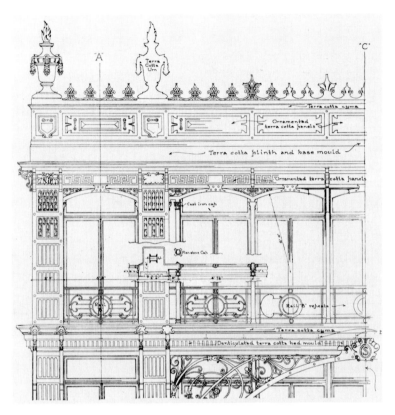

95.   Ernest Flagg. Singer Loft Building. Line drawing of attic
(*Arch Rec* XV, March 1904, p. 282).

Precedents for Flagg's experimental approach, his brand of structural
rationalism, and use of materials are found in the writings of Viollet-le-Duc.
Yet even though Flagg must have admired Viollet-le-Duc's use of a modern
structural system and new materials in his project for a Town House and tiled
shopfront, illustrated in the second volume of the *Entretiens* (see Fig. 10),
Flagg's design did not proceed directly from any visionary work, but rather
from a realized project.[49] His decorative approach is specifically schooled by
Jean-Camille Formigé's twin cultural buildings, the *Palais des arts libéraux*
and *Palais des beaux-arts,* at the 1889 Paris exposition. A comparison between
one bay of the *Palais des arts libéraux* and the attic story of the Singer Loft
illustrates how closely Flagg followed the Parisian model (Fig. 95; see Fig. 15).
However, Flagg adapted Formigé's design so that the terra cotta, metal, and
glass of the Singer Loft would read as an ornamental appliqué to the enclosed
skeletal frame.

Formigé's system called for structural columns of exposed metal with

191

polychromed terra-cotta tile infill. The separation of tiles by means of horizontally placed straps of metal recalls a sixteenth-century classical motif originating with the theory and design of Philibert de l'Orme. In an effort to establish a reasoned French order, de l'Orme argued in his *Architecture* of 1567 for the substitution of limestone for marble. He also specified that columns use decorative banding to disguise the joints between their superimposed drums.[50] Typical of this interpretive treatment of columns by sixteenth- and seventeenth-century French architects is one of the Louvre portals from which Guadet extracted a detail (Fig. 96).[51] Here, column flutes are filled with a decorative floral motif and punctuated by horizontal banding. In a surprising transformation, the modern use of a steel trellis and fluted tiles in Formigé's design and Flagg's comparable scheme for the Singer Loft represent an anagrammatic adaptation of the fluted column and horizontal bands of the sixteenth-century motif, and a further attempt to rationalize French classicism. At the same time, the piers of Formigé's and Flagg's designs are now engaged symbolically by the horizontal placement of steel straps. In their substitution of metal and terra cotta for masonry — that is, modern materials and modern

96. Porte Jean Goujon, Louvre, Paris. Detail of column (Guadet, *Eléments et théorie de l'architecture,* vol. 1, fig. 137).

methods of construction—Formigé and Flagg were, in effect, following the reasoned practice to which de l'Orme and others were committed in the sixteenth century and Viollet-le-Duc and his followers in the nineteenth century.

Flagg obviously chose the Formigé source for the similarity of its building typology. The program at 561 Broadway—a series of open lofts for operational showroom and office functions—closely approximated the shed-like space of a model exposition structure, though forcibly accommodated to the vertical exigencies of the skyscraper format. In effect, the Singer Loft housed a permanent exhibition of Singer machines. So suggested a promotional brochure of the period which urged "public exposition" of the Singer machines in operation "for here is undoubtedly the most extensive and complete installation to be found."[52]

Flagg may even have designed the Singer Loft Building as an intentional, combative, and rational response to the Chicago fair of 1893 and its successors in Buffalo (1901) and Saint Louis (1904). Ironically, the World's Columbian Exposition, which was immediately hailed as the triumph of a burgeoning Beaux-Arts classicism by American critics, was bitterly repudiated by French analysts and by Flagg.[53] Due to such criticism, it is not surprising that Flagg was excluded from participation in either of the two subsequent fairs which attempted to rival Chicago's lead in character, opulence, and scale, as well as in program and organization.[54] Thus, given Flagg's disdain for American exposition architecture, given his professional barring from the A.I.A. (the sponsoring organization of the Buffalo and Saint Louis fairs), given his involvement in the Architectural League of America, given his unqualified respect for French criticism, and, finally, given the similarity in building typology between commercial and exposition architecture, had Flagg designed a building for one of the recent American fairs, he would have used an aesthetic similar to the Singer Loft Building.

Flagg, like Formigé and Saulnier before him, was overcome by the advantages of construction which Viollet-le-Duc described for buildings such as his project for a Town House and tiled shopfront (see Fig. 10). "They would," he promised, "be quite finished in builders' yards, the factories and workshops before being put up, and consequently they would be erected very quickly, without mishaps, obstruction, or great annoyance to the neighbourhood."[55] The Singer Loft design with its synthesis of legible parts and its impression of a prefabricated method of assemblage, like the Formigé exposition models, in fact belied the actual nature of the construction. Far from

Viollet-le-Duc's prediction, the Singer Loft was literally plagued with construction obstacles. Due in part to its irregular L-shaped plan, in part to the intricacies and scale of the design, and in part to the complexities of orchestrating the various trades with a work force totaling two hundred, the Singer Loft was slow to be constructed, fraught with mishap, and of great annoyance to the neighborhood. During the two years of construction, Arthur Sutcliffe, who superintended the work and was himself the victim of an on-the-job leg injury, recorded no less than ten serious accidents and several comic ones. Certainly the most "colorful" of these incidents was, according to Sutcliffe, "the upsetting of a pot of bright green paint by one of our painters working on a scaffold at the 12th story of the Broadway front. The wind scattered the paint like rain and many in the crowded street below were sprinkled with it. First, they crowded in the store and made a lively demonstration there but were sent up to me. I sent them on to see the painter foreman on whom they vented their wrath. His efforts to remove the paint from 14 people were unsuccessful and some law suits result[ed] from the ruined suits."[56]

Critical response to the Singer Loft was mixed. A number of progressive critics praised it: Harry Desmond of *Architectural Record* labeled it "A Rational Skyscraper," and Montgomery Schuyler called it "the logical skyscraper."[57] The admiration of both critics centered on the Singer Loft's frank recognition of its frame as an enlightened effort in solving skyscraper design. Desmond singled out Flagg, as he did Hastings, from among the "importers of French modes" for his "real appreciation of the French mental process of dealing with things architectural, its lucidity and directness."[58] Characterizing the Singer Loft as "structural expression," Desmond further praised Flagg for seeking a new solution to the skyscraper "directly on logical instead of traditional lines, relying rather upon the 'principles' inculcated at the Ecole than upon any established set of patterns."[59]

Critics of the Singer Loft clearly recognized parallels with the work of Louis Sullivan, especially his Bayard (Condict) Building. Desmond regarded both as attempts to define rationally the nature of the metal frame by allowing the structure to be structure, the decoration, decoration. Yet even though Desmond saw the promise of a new rationalism — Sullivan entering from a "highly personal" approach, Flagg reflecting the process of French design — he still recognized weaknesses inherent in their respective work. Desmond criticized Sullivan for failing to "adhere to his own principle that form should follow function," when he allowed "the functionless arch" in some of his designs.[60] Desmond was less specific in his criticism of Flagg's skyscraper of

1902–4. Other journal editors were not.

Commentary about the Singer Loft Building focused on the functional use of metal for construction and decoration. In 1904 the editors of the Boston *Architectural Review* applauded Flagg's efforts to "develop a consistent style from the exigencies of fireproof construction." But they also viewed the building's "excessive" use of wrought iron with "no structural import" as an inadequate solution to the skyscraper.[61] In 1909 the editors of *Architectural Review* challenged Montgomery Schuyler for his support of the Singer Loft as "the logical sky-scraper." Although they praised Flagg's building, which "frankly recognized the use of a steel framework," they questioned the "rationalism" of a design calling for fireproofing material secured with metal straps. The editors misunderstood the Singer Loft design, the structure of which, they thought, was "employed in much the way half-timber was first used in France, filling the spaces between the supporting framework with another structural material, generally brick."[62] In effect they confused the Singer Loft design with the structural use of exposed metal which Viollet-le-Duc described and Saulnier, Formigé, and others employed in France where architects were not restricted by law.[63] The editors were convinced that when the metal was subjected to weather, it would rust, and when subjected to fire, it would warp, thus exposing and thereby endangering the structural steel. Yet as the axonometric drawing of the Singer Loft demonstrated, Flagg intended the structural steel columns, encased in a brick fireproofing material, or "masonry filling," to be independent of the exposed terra-cotta panels and decorative wrought-iron trellises (see Fig. 94). But in spite of these measures, the hazard from fire or weather in theory could affect the structure as well as the decorative enclosure; for although the steel columns seemed to be adequately fireproofed, it was questionable how much the steel girders were protected. Moreover, the Singer Loft's exposed iron also required continual maintenance, particularly painting. Even Flagg's building superintendent, Arthur Sutcliffe, had his doubts about the Singer Loft withstanding a conflagration as intense as the Baltimore fire of 1904.[64]

If critics were alert to the Singer Loft's structure, they were sparing about the building's real strength: its exotic ornament. Only Desmond appreciated it for embracing the rationalist canon of decorated structure. He praised its ornamentation for being "confined entirely to such expression as rightfully can be imparted to terra cotta and iron."[65] "To fulfil its proper function," Flagg wrote some two decades later, "ornament should soften, add interest, beauty, refinement, and grace to the thing ornamented."[66] Combining new materials of metal, terra cotta, and glass for the Singer Loft, Flagg frankly identified and fully exploited their decorative properties. Exotic wrought-iron ornament defined the compositional elements of the design while it enlivened the surfaces with cast shadows.[67] Terra cotta was not treated as a substitute for stone, but was candidly and discretely stated largely as tile. Luxfer prism glass on the ground floor of both the Broadway and Prince Street facades introduced an early use of the material, then considered to be functional as well as decorative.

The meaning of the Singer Loft is, therefore, the fusion of a native structural system with an imported ornament which Flagg hoped would become nationalized. Together these would form the prototypical *"parti* for America." Even though Flagg ultimately failed in his proselytizing mission, the Singer Loft nonetheless demonstrated an attempt to adapt the decorative possibilities of French structural rationalism to American skeletal construction.

With a commission the following year to design a new clubhouse-garage for the Automobile Club of America at 247–259 West 54th Street (demolished; see Fig. 92), Flagg mastered the planning requirements of a building more complex than the Singer Loft.[68] In an effort to formulate a rational *parti,* Flagg also expressed the structural and functional demands of this new building type. Indeed, the automobile garage complex was a uniquely twentieth-century structure confined in the first decade to a few major cities, including New York, London, and Paris. In New York, for example, a whole section of the city was reserved for the marketing, garaging, and servicing of automobiles. The area near Broadway, roughly between 54th and 59th streets, served as the focus of what was contemporaneously described as the automobile district and which had formerly served the carriage trade.[69] Within this limited area, structures with combined showrooms and garages were erected for automobile dealers to accommodate the full-service needs of their customers. As the district spread east and west of Broadway, buildings of this new type, including the Automobile Club of America, now existed side by side with the brownstone houses of this formerly mixed residential-commercial neighborhood.

When the Automobile Club of America, founded in 1899, decided to move its headquarters from Fifth Avenue at 58th Street to the new automobile district, it commissioned Ernest Flagg to design a combined clubhouse and garage for three hundred vehicles to serve both the social and practical needs of its members.[70] Flagg may have received the commission through a socially prominent leader of the organization, Courtlandt Field Bishop, whose town

97. Ernest Flagg. Automobile Club of America. Garage interior
(*Scientific American* XCVI, April 27, 1907, p. 349).

house at 15 East 67th Street Flagg had recently completed.[71] An automobile
enthusiast himself, Flagg was a member of the club.[72]

With his design for the Automobile Club of America, Flagg once
again explored the problem of articulating the frame both artistically and
rationally. It was one further attempt to adapt French decoration to American
skeletal construction and thereby both perfect and evolve Beaux-Arts design in
America. Resolving many of the inconsistencies present in the earlier loft
building, Flagg clarified the Automobile Club's structural system with a steel
frame sheathed in concrete for practicable fireproofing and concrete floors to
support heavy loads. Not only did the need for adequate fireproofing dictate
the improved skeletal frame, but it also required a cautious plan. Unlike most
other garages of the period where gasoline was stored within the building
proper, Flagg's design restricted its storage to an underground tank independent of the garage structure.[73] This and other precautionary measures which
characterized Flagg's entire plan prefigured fire protection regulations governing such garages.[74]

This seven-story structure with combined clubhouse and garage facilities signified the merger of two modern technologies: the skyscraper and the
automobile. Its skeletal frame provided the ideal matrix for the storage of
vehicles (Fig. 97). While the Automobile Club was not the first building to
join together these technologies, it was one of the first large structures of
reinforced concrete erected in New York.[75] But it was a *tour de force* for

programmatic, not for structural, reasons; not only did it successfully integrate a utilitarian garage with an elegant clubhouse, but its facade also explicitly stated the dual nature of the interior organization.

Following Beaux-Arts principles, Flagg ingeniously planned the discrete programmatic requirements of separate pedestrian-club and vehicular-garage functions using a hierarchy of design elements, scale, scenography, materials, and polychromed decoration to suggest their respective character. Club members entering on foot would pass through the weighty pedimented entrance consecrated by the organization's cartouche, proceed to the vestibule, and ascend the staircase to the second floor containing the members' assembly hall (Fig. 98) and grill, which occupied the height of two stories. Its scale, ceremonial sequencing of spatial experience, and opulent, French Renaissance-inspired decoration were elements of Beaux-Arts design appropriate to the character of a socially exclusive club. Members entering by car would roll through one of three vehicular entrances. Sole access from the garage to the

98. Ernest Flagg. Automobile Club of America. Assembly hall
(*AABN* XCI, May 4, 1907).

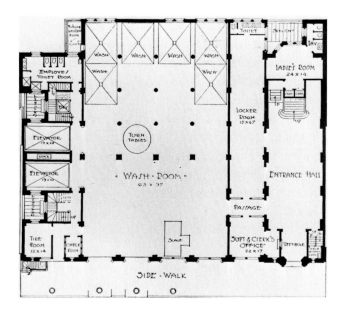

99. Ernest Flagg.
Automobile Club of America.
Ground floor plan
(*Brickbuilder* XVI, May
1907, pl. 67).

clubhouse was gained by a connecting passage to the vestibule (Fig. 99). Once inside, the scenario of the automobile was predictably different. A turntable and elevators ensured ease of circulation to one of the storage areas on floors three to six, or to the service department on the top floor. In contrast to the members' rooms, the character of the garage — with its tiled floors, revealed structure, and array of Fairbanks scales and dynamometers — was clinical (see Fig. 97).

Within the compositional format long associated with his work, Flagg keyed to the facade the programmatic distinctions between the clubhouse and garage. A band of lunette windows and a pedimented entrance of white granite were conditioned by the bold ornament of French classicism which suggested the ceremonial use of the clubhouse and its corresponding character. The economized grid of the remaining structure and the presence of standardized factory windows acknowledged the utilitarian character of the garage. Flagg's repetition of the Formigé-inspired ornament that had characterized the Singer Loft Building, further signified the artistic and rational potential of the ornament. Terra-cotta panels held in place by metal angles — this time avoiding the possibility of endangering the steel frame through the use of a concrete enclosure — once again rationally articulated the skeletal structure.[76] Polychromed materials appropriately expressed those properties associated with each character of this binary program. The Automobile Club employed white granite for the ground floor, and white enameled brick with green-and-white terra-cotta ornament above it to convey both the purity of the garage and the opulence of the clubhouse.[77] Like the Singer Loft Building, the Automobile Club of America illustrated Flagg's effort to introduce a rational architecture by uniting the best of America (the skeletal frame) with the best of France (logical decoration).

In another loft building of this period, the Scribner Manufacturing and Printing Press at 311–319 West 43rd Street, New York (1905–7), Flagg continued to use the same compositional format as a way of treating the utilitarian structure in architectural terms. Identifying the rational aspects of the Scribner loft design, Russell Sturgis praised Flagg for "enclosing his lantern-like wall of windows between two more massive vertical members, upright towers, as it were."[78]

The facade of the Automobile Club garage does not explicitly reflect the influence of contemporaneous European or American garages, even though their structural and mechanical systems were similar. On the one hand, Flagg could not eliminate the Beaux-Arts role of ornament as Auguste Perret had achieved in his severely abstract Garage-Ponthieu, 51 rue de Ponthieu, Paris (1905; demolished) or Albert Kahn in his Packard Garage at Broadway and 61st Street, New York (1906–7; demolished).[79] On the other hand, Flagg did not disguise the reinforced concrete frame of the Automobile Club in a casement of indifferent masonry too elaborate to convey its functional character, as Snelling & Potter had done for its garage on West 93rd Street, New York, of 1906.[80]

Flagg's successful integration of the automobile and the skyscraper was just one extension of his long-standing interest in the future of the automobile. In formulating the Automobile Club *parti,* Flagg sought to unite the roles of the constructor and the artist. He also considered the problems of civil engineering and bridge design.[81] In a competition of 1899 for a Memorial Bridge across the Potomac, Flagg served as consulting architect to the engineer, W. R. Hutton, for designs that were artistic and illustrated the ideals of structural rationalism. The Hutton-Flagg team submitted two designs which were characteristically Beaux-Arts.[82] The first was the more inventive of the two, for it was a double-decker arrangement employing both a vehicular roadway and pedestrian walkway above, and a street-car railway below. Like the Automobile Club, modern materials and methods of construction were joined together to create a sumptuous effect for the Memorial Bridge. A richly embellished dome of bronze, steel, stone, and concrete crowned the draw span.

Flagg's design approached the spirit of the metal pavilions of the 1878 and 1889 Paris expositions, but his project met with understandably little success among American critics.[83] Even though Montgomery Schuyler published the first design in his article of 1901, "Monumental Engineering," he actually preferred the second design which was favored also by the selection committee.[84] With the substitution of simple stone piers for the exotic masonry and metal dome of the first design and without the multilevel organization, the second design was dull if more economical by comparison. Schuyler nonetheless praised it for its "straightforwardness and expressiveness which belong to monumental as well as to utilitarian engineering."[85]

In the years following the completion of the Automobile Club of America, Flagg's interests also embraced the problems of road construction. These years coincided with the enormous proliferation of automobile traffic in large cities. The superiority of European methods of road construction and maintenance appeared obvious to Flagg in the summer of 1908 when he made his first return visit to England and France since his student days nearly two decades before. Touring in the Packard with his family and the chauffeur, Alfred Beaver, Flagg observed English and French methods of road paving and maintenance during his three months of travel.[86] In a series of articles written on his return, Flagg urged that a British and French type of stone pavement (called Durax in England), with its promise of high performance and durability, be substituted for asphalt in areas of heavy traffic. New York City streets would be a case study.[87] Although Flagg sparked the interest of the City Club and New York officials, his plan called for such extensive changes in the existing methods of road construction and maintenance that officials could not support it.[88]

Prestige Office Buildings and Speculative Lofts

Flagg's concern to express architectural character in the prestige office building remained constant. In his Produce Exchange Bank Building at 10 Broadway, New York, of 1904–5 (demolished; Fig. 100) and Gwynne Building, Cincinnati, of 1913–14 (Fig. 101), Flagg further explored the office building *parti*: the steel skeleton was expressed, the facade was opened up, and surfaces were defined by rich textures and lyrical embellishments of masonry, metal, and glass. Once again, his frank expression of the skeletal frame did not act as the *raison d'être,* but rather as the vehicle for an elegant and well-articulated enclosure. To express architectural character, Flagg chose deluxe masonry facing materials like those on the two Scribner buildings.

201

100. Ernest Flagg. Produce Exchange Bank Building (demolished), 10 Broadway, New York City, 1904–5 (*Architecture* XII, October 1905, pl. LXXXIV).

Flagg's Produce Exchange Bank Building occupied an irregular lot on the northeast corner of Broadway and Beaver Street at Bowling Green.[89] In spite of its commercial ties with the New York Produce Exchange (1881–85; demolished) directly opposite, Flagg's building eschewed George B. Post's earlier use of dark red brick and terra cotta. Two decades after its completion, Post's Produce Exchange looked old-fashioned when compared to a new public structure being constructed on the southern tip of Bowling Green: Cass

202

101. Ernest Flagg. Gwynne Building, Sixth and Main streets, Cincinnati, 1913–14 (Procter and Gamble Company).

Gilbert's U.S. Custom House (1900–1907).[90] To most observers, the light granite exterior and robust decorations of the Custom House, as opposed to the ponderous quality of the Late-Victorian Produce Exchange, must have seemed the symbol of a new era of aestheticism in commercial architecture. Like the Custom House, Flagg's Produce Exchange Bank Building demonstrated a spirit of materialism and *architecture luxe*.

The Produce Exchange Bank Building defined the nature of an office building, the first floor of which was occupied by a bank. Flagg's Beaux-Arts approach called for materials to be assigned specific roles in the composition: weighty granite for the base, light-colored brick with metal and glass infill forming vertical shafts, and a picturesque stone cornice with urns supported by richly ornamented cast-iron brackets to terminate the structure. The articulation of the attic was similar to the Singer Loft Building, although its proportions were awkward. Otherwise, the design, with its canonical tripartite division of stacked elevations, followed the classical formula for a skyscraper. There, a comparatively extravagant display of materials on the facade at street level was typical of Flagg's conservative classicism at the United States Naval Academy or the work of his contemporaries in England, including Mewès, Shaw, and Belcher. To economize the office building above, brick was substituted for stone (as it was at the Naval Academy). This demarcation of architectural character recognized the programmatic divisions between the bank and the rest of the building closed off from it, with provisions for separate entrances on Broadway and Beaver Street.[91] Earlier, Flagg had arrived at a similar articulation of the two functions, bank and office building, in his First National Bank Building, Hartford (1897–99). With masonry bearing walls, instead of skeletal construction, the First National Bank Building employed a heavily rusticated stone base for the banking floor and economical brick for the upper floors, ornamented with stone and wrought iron. A mansard roof capped the seven stories of this office building, which inaugurated the "Beaux-Arts style" in Hartford.[92]

The undulating walls, corner location, tripartite division of the facade, and rusticated base of the Produce Exchange Bank Building recalled the design of D. H. Burnham & Co.'s Fuller ("Flatiron") Building of 1901–3, farther north on Broadway. But there the similarities ceased. Whereas the metal and glass bays of the Produce Exchange Bank broke out from the masonry wall plane, the window bays of the "Flatiron" Building gave the illusion of a solid masonry wall, thereby disguising its metal frame. By contrast, Flagg's elevation, with tiers of wall alternating with metal and glass bays, and further defined by piers and spandrels, emulated Sullivan's allusion to the support and infill system of the skeletal frame.[93] However, Flagg inverted the pier-spandrel motif with alternate bays projecting rather than receding from the wall plane. By using one such tier of metal and glass bays to turn the corner of Broadway and Beaver Street, Flagg not only candidly identified the steel frame of the Produce Exchange Bank Building, but also brilliantly expressed its prominent site and bank entrance. In contrast to Sullivan's tall buildings, including the

Bayard, which called for terra cotta as the decorative and functional enclosure, Flagg's Beaux-Arts design suggested that he considered the wholesale substitution of terra cotta for masonry inappropriate to convey the architectural character of the prestige office building.

Flagg's final interpretation of the prestige office building was another family commission, the Gwynne Building, Sixth and Main streets, Cincinnati, of 1913–14. Just before Christmas Day in 1912, when Flagg's office was in a state of depression for lack of work, the architect received a letter from "Cousin Alice" (Mrs. Cornelius Vanderbilt II) stating that she wished him "to make plans for an office building for Cincinnati."[94] In his diary, Flagg noted the urgency of this commission which "comes in the nick of time and so worth more to me now than a much larger order would have formerly."[95] Flagg's office manager at the time, Arthur Sutcliffe, was even more candid: "It was like a hungry man getting a bit of bread."[96]

The Gwynne Building, named in honor of Alice Gwynne Vanderbilt's Cincinnati ancestors, is informed by a prevailing regionalism: its tower and broad dimensions follow a well-established midwestern urban type.[97] During a visit to Cincinnati in January 1913, Flagg entered in his diary a rough sketch of the new building indicating an elevation of only three bays.[98] When Alice Vanderbilt was able to purchase additional land to increase the size of the lot and frontage on Main Street, the building was expanded to four-by-thirteen bays (58 × 162 feet).[99] A tower on the northwest corner of the building was integrated into the design of the Main Street elevation.

Thus unlike the New York skyscraper, which had to conform in plan to the narrow and comparatively shallow lots of the Manhattan grid, the Cincinnati building could take advantage of the generous dimensions of midwestern blocks. Towers had been associated with American industrial and commercial buildings and had been integral to the development of Manhattan skyscraper design, beginning with Richard Morris Hunt's Tribune Building of 1873–75. The tower had long established itself as a signifying element of the Chicago school's commercial architecture. For example, the towers of McKim, Mead & White's New York Insurance Company Building, Omaha (1887–90), and Adler & Sullivan's Auditorium, Chicago (1887–89), were expressed as pergola-like temples integrated into their designs.[100] Although the Gwynne Building's tower was largely symbolic, it contained a water tank as in the dome of St. Luke's Hospital. As elegant as the Scribner Building of 1912–13, the Gwynne Building, with its all-limestone veneer, metal trim, and polychromed mosaic decorations, reflected a Beaux-Arts attitude toward permanence and

102. Ernest Flagg. Gwynne
Building. Detail of facade.

sumptuousness characteristic of the prestige office building. Once again the skeletal frame was secondary to the role of ornamental detailing which maintained a surface planarity. Stone carvings, reminiscent of the *Néo-Grec* details of the Corcoran Gallery and the Scribner buildings, were dispersed across the elevations as bas-reliefs. Bronze grills spanned 9 feet across each window while metal brackets anchored the copper and stone cornice. Enameled mosaic panels "in Venetian gold and colors" provided rich embellishment to the buff-colored surfaces (Fig. 102).[101] These ornamental details recall Early Christian and Renaissance mosaic decoration and Viollet-le-Duc's approach to decorative relief in his chapter on masonry in the second volume of the *Entretiens* (Plate XX).

Flagg's commercial architecture was not limited to the patronage of the Singer Company or the Scribner and Vanderbilt families, even though, as his diary recorded, he was most concerned about these commissions.[102] Flagg himself acted as both principal designer and developer for two loft buildings.

206

When the firm he organized in 1909, the Model Fireproof Tenement Company, found the subsequent demand for low-income housing greatly diminished, it diversified its interests to include commercial building. In 1911 Flagg designed a storage and loft building at 645–651 Eleventh Avenue, New York, although it was not until 1913 that construction began. Again in 1927–28, Flagg designed and helped to finance the construction of a second loft, adjacent to the first, at 653–659 Eleventh Avenue (Fig. 103).

In these two loft buildings, Flagg continued to apply the policies that had operated so successfully for tenement houses: economy, quality construction, and fireproofing. For them, Flagg specified flat-slab concrete construc-

103. Ernest Flagg. Loft buildings, 645–651 and 653–659 Eleventh Avenue, New York City, 1911–14 and 1927–28 (ATSP, AL, CU).

tion. The earliest of the two was technologically precocious since it purportedly employed "for the first time in New York the cantilever flat slab type of construction."[103] While this method was proven a success in the Midwest by the pioneering Turner Construction Company, it remained largely untried in the East when contracts were signed in 1913 with the Phoenix Concrete Steel Company, and a reluctant New York Buildings Department eventually approved plans.[104] For this storage-loft facility, the advantages of flat-slab construction appeared self-evident. It offered ease of construction, fireproofing, and the capacity to bear heavy loads.[105] Unlike the deluxe office building where ornament defined character, the speculative loft building called for ornament to assume a comparatively minimal role. Indeed, the intrinsic purity of the mushroom-columned interior suggested that such utilitarian buildings conveyed a fully functionalist aesthetic. Thus Flagg's commercial and utilitarian buildings were especially revealing for the Beaux-Arts manner in which their character was determined by use.

Together, Flagg's commercial and utilitarian buildings illustrate his efforts to apply rationalist ideals to modern American building practice, thereby evolving a *"parti* for America." In 1909 Flagg stated: "If we will approach our problem in precisely the same spirit that the mediaeval architects approached theirs, allowing ourselves to be led by the dictates of common sense, we shall have taken the first step in what may be a truly national style of architecture. Let us then give to each material forms which are logically appropriate to it and build structures which express what they are and which show how they are made."[106] This then was Flagg's personal struggle to introduce to America a rational architecture whose design would be based on Beaux-Arts principles, whose decoration would arise out of the exigencies of construction, and whose *parti* would reconcile science and art. Although Flagg's architecture fell short of his goal, it was still remarkably inventive. It celebrated new technology and new materials. Unlike many firms, including both McKim, Mead & White and Carrère & Hastings, which employed the ingenious, but comparatively simple, technology of Guastavino vaulting and also preferred stone construction whenever possible, Flagg freely specified reinforced concrete for vaults (for example, at the United States Naval Academy Chapel) as well as for the flat-slab frame (for speculative loft buildings), and frankly expressed skeletal construction. But as advanced as his structural systems were, they remained, in most cases, secondary to the use of such legibly and sumptuously combined materials as masonry, terra cotta, metal, and glass.

CHAPTER SEVEN

The Singer Tower
and Skyscraper Reform

WITH THE Singer Tower at 149 Broadway, Ernest Flagg originated the first of the skyscrapers of needle-like proportions that later characterized the spectacular New York skyline of the 1920s and 1930s (Fig. 104). The Singer Tower was celebrated also for the number of records it held. When completed in 1908, the Singer Tower was the tallest building ever constructed; in 1967–68, as it was disappearing from the Manhattan skyline, it received the questionable distinction of being called the tallest building ever demolished.[1] It took only twenty months to build this "eighth wonder of the world," as the Singer Manufacturing Company advertised it, and nearly a year to demolish the structure.[2] Ironically, its brief life of sixty years hardly fulfilled the promise of Flagg's alleged prediction that his work was "as solid and lasting as the Pyramids."[3] A symbol of corporate identity, the Singer Tower's future was doubtful in 1962 when the Singer Company as owner-manager vacated its headquarters for a then more prestigious Rockefeller Center location. Within a few years the new owner, United States Steel Corporation, planned the demise of the Beaux-Arts landmark and replaced it with a fifty-story slab by Skidmore, Owings & Merrill, now One Liberty Plaza.[4] The very forces which created the Singer Tower — imagery, corporate identity, land values, technology, and style — were also factors that caused its demolition sixty years later. But the lasting significance of the Singer Tower was its influence on the New York Zoning Resolution of 1916 which contained Flagg's influential ideas on height and area restrictions for the American skyscraper.

The great Singer Tower, built between 1906 and 1908, was the culminating feature of an extensive building complex, designed entirely by Flagg and executed in two phases nearly a decade apart. The first phase began

104. Ernest Flagg. Singer Tower (demolished), 149 Broadway, New York City, 1908 (The Singer Company).

in 1896 when Flagg was authorized to prepare plans for a ten-story office structure at the northwest corner of Broadway and Liberty Street, known as the Singer Building.[5] To develop this valuable site further, Singer president, Frederick G. Bourne, acquired adjacent land and commissioned the architect to design the fourteen-story Bourne Building at 85–89 Liberty Street, constructed between 1898 and 1899 (Fig. 105). In a second building phase beginning in 1906, another fourteen-story structure, the Bourne Building Addition at 91–93 Liberty Street, was linked to the complex at 85–89 Liberty Street; and the original Singer Building was dramatically reconstructed

105. Ernest Flagg. Singer and Bourne buildings (demolished), 149 Broadway and 85–89 Liberty Street, New York City. Photograph taken before 1906 (New-York Historical Society).

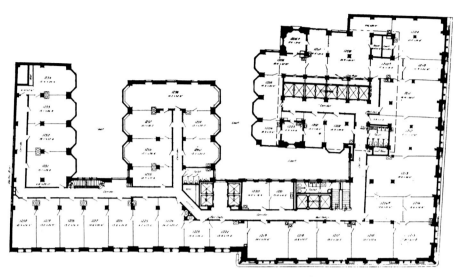

106. Ernest Flagg. Singer Tower and Bourne buildings, 149 Broadway, 85–89 and 91–93 Liberty Street. Plan, 1908 (*Architects' and Builders' Magazine* IX, July 1908, p. 430).

to the height of the new buildings and enlarged along Broadway to incorporate a forty-seven-story Singer Tower (Fig. 106).[6]

The original Singer Building, commissioned in 1896 and built in 1897–98, essentially conditioned the design of all subsequent Singer and Bourne buildings. This ten-story mansarded office building, although strongly textured with the strident polychromy of red brick and limestone trim, had little to do with the style of such earlier commercial buildings as Richard Morris Hunt's Tribune Building of 1873–75.[7] By the mid-1890s the French mansard with its convex roof surmounting an ornamented block was strongly evident in New York domestic architecture, including the American châteaux on Riverside Drive and Flagg's own town houses, for example, the O. G. Jennings House (see Fig. 65). It was also similar to the original conception of the Naval Academy buildings. Labeled "modern French," the Singer Building reflected the contemporaneous revival of interest in eighteenth-century domestic architecture, especially the French *hôtel particulier,* now adapted to the prestige office building.[8] Several Flagg-designed office buildings followed the Singer model.[9] As owner-manager, the Singer Manufacturing Company occupied the top four floors while the basement and ground floor were headquarters for a bank.[10] Sumptuous, showy, and richly appointed, the Singer Building was the kind of office building that corporate clients demanded. Above all else,

212

it was good business in an age of big business.

Consistent with the method of construction for most of his commercial and utilitarian buildings during the 1890s, Flagg employed masonry bearing walls with interior iron columns and steel floor beams for the Singer Building.[11] Premised on Flagg's conviction that the "outer walls of fireproof buildings shall be real walls, capable of supporting themselves," the Singer Building illustrated the arguments in his manifesto of 1896, "The Dangers of High Buildings."[12] Fixed at a height of ten stories, the Singer Building served as a model for voluntary height restriction that the city of Paris had enforced by statute. Flagg contended, "How can a building whose height is out of all proportion to the width of the street, which is punched full of holes, and which has greed written all over it, be a work of art?"[13] Moreover, based on the need for masonry construction and its corresponding demand for more massive foundation walls, a ten-story building, so Flagg insisted, was more economically viable than one of fifteen or twenty stories. With the assurance of enough light and air for this low-rise solution, all areas of the building were habitable, not just the upper stories.[14] While Flagg's views received a favorable first reaction, progressive critics soon recognized the obsolescence of bearing-wall construction coupled with the need for tall buildings. Among them, Montgomery Schuyler had already rejected the premise of Flagg's argument by 1899. Yet he could not help but praise the aesthetics of Flagg's Singer solution; for even though "it is questionable whether it was worth doing [it] has been unquestionably well done."[15] By 1898, however, as the Bourne Building was being constructed, Flagg still limited the height of the office building (to fourteen stories), but converted to skeletal steel construction.[16] Thereafter, Flagg continued to argue the dangers of high buildings, not from the standpoint of fire and safety, but from a lack of height and density restriction.

The building campaign on the Broadway and Liberty Street site, initiated during the presidency of Frederick G. Bourne (1889–1905), roughly coincided with the last phase of Singer's expansion on the international market. Due to a new European nationalism which encouraged high protective tariffs, Singer constructed factories in Russia and Germany which necessitated new regional sales and management offices. Flagg was responsible for the designs of two such offices.[17] Following the completion of the Podolsk Factory in Russia in 1901, the Singer Company commissioned Flagg to design a new showroom and offices on Nevskii Prospekt in Saint Petersburg (1902–4; now *Dom Knigi* or "House of Books"). But by December 1902, Singer executives had contracted with a local architect, P. Iu. Siuzor, to complete the building, evidently

107.　Ernest Flagg. Singer Tower under construction, August 17, 1907 (author's collection).

along the lines of the Flagg model (published in *Architectural Record*), but with some substantial alterations.[18] Flagg's design may have influenced Siuzor's use of steel frame construction and floors of reinforced concrete. Although a small dome in the Flagg model celebrated a prominent corner site, the dome of Siuzor's building was a more flamboyant display of metal and glass.[19] Another foreign Singer building, located in Berlin (East), of 1904–6 was fully executed according to Flagg's design, but did not survive the Second World War.[20]

The record height of the 612-foot Singer Tower was scarcely arbitrary. In May 1902, Flagg was "asked to make plans for the Broadway addition to the Singer Building" (1896–98).[21] As early as February 1903 he intended the future Singer Tower, "over 35 stories high," to be "the tallest in the world."[22] But Flagg's executed design for the forty-seven-story Singer Tower still demonstrated his reform solution to high density within the commercial district and his continued opposition to the unrestricted skyscraper. As an architectural statement, the Singer Tower was more important for its imagery and organization than for its technology; more important for planning reform than for significant design.

The aggregate of Singer and Bourne buildings posed a major problem of integration and uniformity, both functionally and stylistically. In order to link all buildings within the complex, the original Singer Building of 1896–98 was increased from ten stories to fourteen. At the same time, its mansard roof and brick walls were partially peeled away to accommodate structural reinforcement for the Singer Tower addition, thus changing the load-bearing masonry exterior of the original building to complete skeletal construction (Fig. 107). Now the forty-seven-story tower was encased by a fourteen-story block which for structural reasons would diminish wind pressure and promote stability. Internally, vertical integration was assured by an elevator bank serving both base and tower. Four cars were designated for the tower, one car ascending to the top story, stopping at the observation deck on the fortieth floor. Externally, the Singer Tower retained the "modern French" design of the original building to promote a continuity of style among these diverse parts. Now a mansarded dome quoted the roof of its fourteen-story base.

The tower, 65 feet square and set back approximately 30 feet from its base, was a unique solution to the New York skyscraper. The tower portion did not "grow" from its base as Richard Morris Hunt's Tribune Building had done. Nor was it an isolated tower which "appears frankly from [its] base," as Francisco Mujica had called the tower addition to the Metropolitan Life

Insurance Company Building, completed in 1909.[23] Rather, like McKim, Mead & White's Madison Square Garden (1889–91), an impressive tower surmounted its base. In addition to their adaptation to American buildings, Beaux-Arts towers were common vehicles for conveying landmark status and monumentality in Europe. The clock tower of D. H. Toudoire's Gare de Lyon, Paris, of 1899, formed a quasi mansard. In adopting the mansard solution for the Singer Tower, Flagg did more than just evoke his Beaux-Arts training. He sought specific associations of architectural character. The Singer Company's Kilbowie Factory, built in 1882 at Clydebank, Scotland (near Glasgow), was the manufacturing base of its European operations. This red brick mill building, so like its American counterparts, was surmounted by a 200-foot-high clock tower with a mansarded dome (Fig. 108).[24] Thus in one blow, Flagg's Singer Tower could recall the image of the European manufacturing center at the American home office.

As with much of his work, especially commercial architecture, Flagg employed the compositional format of emphasized corners and a central arched opening on each of the tower's four faces to monumentalize it. Yet, unlike the

108.   Singer Manufacturing Company Kilbowie Factory, Clydebank, Scotland, 1882 (The Singer Company).

Singer Loft Building in which its composition rationally expressed its structural steel columns, the Singer Tower's similar composition did not strictly articulate the skeletal frame beneath its masonry envelope. With the tower raised to new heights, the need to combat increased wind pressure caused Flagg and his structural engineer to apply steel cross-bracing to the corners. Although cross-bracing was part of the standard repertory of structural reinforcement by 1900, Flagg's system was especially elaborate. The Singer Tower, so *Scientific American* reported, "may be considered as made up of four corner towers, each 12 feet square in plan, and a central tower inclosing the elevator well."[25] This trussed structure was remarkably similar to the Eiffel Tower of the 1889 Paris exposition.[26] But while it was predictable for Flagg to adapt French engineering to the skeletal grid of an American skyscraper, it was another matter to design a perfectly logical enclosure for it. Schuyler noted the way in which Flagg conveyed a "sense of the skeleton behind the padding by artful devices such as the variation in material and color, and the lightening and opening of the fenestration . . . to denote that the central part is not a wall, but a mere screen quite incapable of supporting itself."[27] In effect, Flagg spaced the cross-bracing so that it would not interrupt the placement of corner windows, and thereby accommodated structure to composition (see Fig. 107). In contrast to the masonry corners, the center was opened up by an uninterrupted vertical shaft of metal and glass. This compositional format was common to French architecture of the early Third Republic and a consistent element of Flagg's style. Earlier, Flagg had employed a vertical linkage of windows to rationalize wall surfaces: in the Clark House, in Bancroft Hall (by the addition of metal spandrels), and in the Produce Exchange Bank Building (see Figs. 66, 49, 100). He continued to compose in this way for the Scribner Building of 1912–13 (see Fig. 87). Flagg, of course, was aware of the critical success of Carrère & Hastings' Blair Building, New York (1902–3; demolished), which had employed a similar motif: a thin veneer of masonry combined with shafts of metal and glass in the center to express its skeletal construction.[28] Of the two other towers to hold the height record before the First World War, Napoleon Le Brun & Sons' Metropolitan Life Insurance Company Tower of 1905–9 and Cass Gilbert's Woolworth Building of 1911–13, the Woolworth Building employed the more logical enclosure. Gilbert organized the facade into a series of bays with a terra-cotta envelope which directly expressed the building's uniformly spaced and distributed frame, a combination of portal and knee bracing. Schuyler maintained that the Woolworth's Gothic enclosure "most unmistakably denotes its skeleton."[29]

217

109.   Ernest Flagg. Singer Tower. Lobby, 1908 (Semsch, ed., *A History
of the Singer Building Construction,* p. 104).

Along with these changes to the Singer Building's scale and structure,
the old main entrance on Liberty Street was replaced by a new Broadway
entrance. Accompanying the new orientation was a two-story lobby which led
from the revolving doors of the entrance to the rear staircase (Fig. 109). A series
of vaults, each with its own glazed saucer dome, like the staircase of Mahan
Hall (see Fig. 55), formed a perspective view. Sixteen piers, which supported

218

the domed ceiling, were covered in a revetment of Pavonazzo and silver-gray Montarenti Sienna marble and detailed with bronze medallions bearing the Singer logo. The opulence of this circulatory space complemented the "modern French" details of the exterior. Moreover, the light color scheme and wall surfaces in the spirit of eighteenth-century French design recalled the splendors of French exposition architecture, especially the relatively restrained buildings of Charles Mewès (1860–1914) at the 1900 Paris fair. The celestial radiance of the Singer lobby, touted as "the most beautiful and impressive ever erected in a great commercial building in the City of New York," set a new standard for such interiors.[30] Skyscraper towers were symbols of prestige in the commercial district and the public spaces of these buildings reinforced that intended character. A few years later, the Gothic design of the Woolworth lobby promoted the image of the secular cathedral.[31]

The achievement of the "record" Singer Tower, as Schuyler called it in 1909, was a matter of organizational expertise in both the management of the Flagg office and the synchronization of the various building trades during construction.[32] Like most large architectural offices of the period, the Flagg office force, reduced to a staff of forty-seven early in 1908, followed the D. H. Burnham organization, with separate departments for drafting, engineering, and specifications. But unlike other offices, Flagg's made the daring addition of a department of construction in 1907 because there was no general contractor for the Singer Tower. Each department, in spite of its seeming autonomy, was inextricably interdependent. The progress of one department depended on the progress of another; and the success of this interaction accounted for the speed with which the Singer Tower advanced in design and construction.[33] To an unparalleled degree, problems of engineering and construction were centralized in the Flagg office. Flagg's chief engineer, Otto Francis Semsch, headed the engineering department, which obviated the need for a structural consultant under contract. This procedure departed from the norm. The Woolworth Building's architect, Cass Gilbert, for example, signed a contract for its foundations and steel frame with Gunvald Aus, a structural engineer with whom Gilbert had been previously associated.[34] Moreover, with no general contractor, the head of the department of construction in the Flagg office, Frank P. Whiting, supervised construction of the Singer Tower and the synchronization of the building trades.[35] Because of the unparalleled height of the Singer office building, problems of safety and efficiency for the construction workers were essential concerns. Building crews were coordinated in their work pace, and were dispersed geographically throughout the structure, often at perilous

219

heights.[36] With swelling pride in their managerial achievement, the Flagg office and Singer executives announced through their spokesman, Semsch, that "not a single important piece of material was dropped during the erection and there was not a single fatal accident."[37] The increasing emphasis on the bureaucratization of the office force and these construction practices paralleled Bourne's enlightened, if paternalistic, management and marketing practices.[38]

Flagg and the Singer Manufacturing Company envisioned the Singer Tower as an isolated pinnacle whether seen as part of the New York skyline or at the closer vantage point of Broadway at Liberty Street. But once construction was under way, their vision of an isolated tower was soon marred. The consequences of unrestricted zoning, which Flagg and others had already vigorously opposed, were becoming dramatically apparent. In a construction photograph of October 5, 1907, the Singer Tower was seen with a neighboring structure, the forty-three-story City Investing Company Building, wrapped around it (Fig. 110). Hailed as "The Largest Single Office Building in the World," the City Investing Company Building had an area capacity far in excess of the Singer Tower.[39] Thus, even before its completion, the Singer Tower — an example of a reform solution to the New York skyscraper, voluntarily restricted in its density — was impaired by the commercial greed of its neighbor. Flagg learned a sobering lesson that propelled him toward a five-year crusade for zoning reform in New York City.

The skyscraper reform movement in the first decades of the twentieth century focused on a method of restricting height and area without destroying urban land values. The Singer Tower had been particularly instructive. It was located in what the *New York Times* in 1907 described as "the heart of the new Manhattan . . . two blocks in area on the west side of Broadway, between Cortlandt Street and Trinity Church [Wall Street]." There, the intensity of building activity was a new phenomenon. "Never before in the history of the world," the report continued, "has so much steel, brick, stone, mortar, and terra cotta been piled up in such a small space."[40] In 1903, the year after the Singer Company completed its acquisition of the entire parcel, these two blocks, and those running east of Broadway toward Nassau Street and along Wall Street, received the highest valuation within the commercial district.[41] Land values in this area had been determined by a number of principles: historical proximity to the old business center, concentration of utility, and accessibility to transportation.

In 1908 Flagg set down his provisions for skyscraper reform and began to lobby for them. In his capacity as chairman of two committees on the

110. Ernest Flagg. Singer Tower under construction, October 5, 1907 (author's collection).

building code, the first for the Society of Beaux-Arts Architects and the second for the New York Chapter of the American Institute of Architects, Flagg became the dominant spokesman among New York architects. Sponsored by these organizations that year, Flagg addressed the Committee on the Limitation of Height and Area of the Building Code Revision Commission of New York City. There he fixed his position on skyscraper reform. Based in part on

221

his earlier manifesto, "The Dangers of High Buildings," Flagg outlined the provisions for restrictive legislation which he advocated in an article in *American Architect*. His plan would restrict building to 75 percent of the area of a plot, which was "not to exceed once and a half the width of the street on which it faces, with a maximum of one hundred feet."[42] The remaining 25 percent would be unrestricted in height. The resulting tower solution, based on the Singer model, would thus strike a delicate balance between the demand for return on capital investment where land values were high, and the need for legislated safeguards. An additional provision of the Flagg plan allowed for "the purchase and sale between adjoining owners of the right to build high within the limit stated" — essentially the current notion of a transfer of air rights.[43] This would deter owners from erecting what Montgomery Schuyler called a "spite skyscraper."[44] Finally, if a tower were to be unrestricted in height, Flagg saw the need to require that all its sides be "treated architecturally," and that the structure be fireproof, with no wood used in its construction.[45] Flagg's proposal was articulate, popular, and widely published in architectural journals and the daily press.[46]

In all likelihood the Flagg plan would have been adopted had it not been for an opposing scheme put forth in 1908 by D. Knickerbacker Boyd, president of the Philadelphia Chapter of the American Institute of Architects. Although the principles of restrictive zoning paralleled those in Flagg's proposal, Boyd's called for a building height no more than one and a quarter times the width of the street. To allow light and air to reach the street and limit building density, the Boyd plan proposed two alternatives, each involving a formula: one called for a "stepped facade," or set-back treatment; the other, for an "absolutely continuous front," the building line at ground level adjusted proportionally to the building height. The second scheme, which Boyd favored, would have the advantage of widening the sidewalk and thus permitting maximum light and air to penetrate the street.[47]

Of those critics who followed the debate, Schuyler was most perceptive in illuminating the advantages and defects of both the Flagg and Boyd proposals. In his article of 1908, "To Curb the Skyscraper," Schuyler summarized the implications of both while championing the Flagg scheme. Schuyler cited Flagg's objectives to " 'citify,' to regularize, in a word, to Parisianize the city." By contrast, Boyd's scheme would, according to Schuyler, promote "diversity and variegation." Schuyler preferred the control offered by Flagg's design. Given "the actual race of architectural practitioners and the reasonable probabilities of our street architecture," Schuyler noted cynically, he saw more promise in "a regular cornice line and a street front in a single plane . . . than a sawtoothed skyline and a higgledy piggledy of alignment." Schuyler's preference for Flagg's Beaux-Arts solution showed his bias for "aesthetic results," as he himself admitted.[48]

The debate over zoning ensued for five years. Then in 1913 Flagg and Boyd each submitted statements to and appeared before the Heights of Buildings Commission of New York City whose conclusions and recommendations shaped the Zoning Resolution of 1916. In its report, the Commission recommended a hybrid of the Flagg and Boyd schemes. It adopted the set-back provision, the major element of the Boyd plan, while allowing an unlimited development on 25 percent of the site, the Flagg contribution.[49]

During its deliberations, the Commission chose to relegate the question of aesthetics to a peripheral role. Commission member and municipal reformer Lawrence Veiller motioned that " 'aesthetic consideration' be struck entirely out of the program, on the ground that even the mention of the term would cause the public and law-making bodies to feel that the Commission was wasting time, as the courts of New York do not recognize aesthetic considerations." Opposition by fellow Commission members, however, modified the program so that "aesthetic considerations" in the context of their "relation to rentability and the value of land," would be permissible.[50] Nonetheless, the Commission's decision clearly disadvantaged the most salient aspect of Flagg's proposal: the uniform cornice line. If adopted, the uniform cornice line would have promised a majestic image for New York: avenues regularized in height by orderly blocks, like Parisian boulevards, and the skyline punctuated with New World towers.

The defeat of Flagg's Beaux-Arts scheme in 1913 reflected a broader effort to overcome the formalities of City Beautiful planning which had dominated public thinking during the first decade of the century when the New York City Improvement Commission, a municipal planning organization founded by Seth Low, issued a series of proposals calling for the reorganization of Manhattan. In 1904 Flagg had proposed his own scheme for Manhattan calling for a ten-mile parkway similar to the Champs-Elysées in Paris, the Unter den Linden in Berlin, and the Ringstrasse in Vienna. Extending from Christopher Street to the Harlem River and bisecting the island, Flagg's parkway plan also entailed a partial demolition of Central Park. Flagg's efforts to mitigate the constraints of the grid-iron plan and to integrate and rationalize green spaces in relation to buildings received enthusiastic support, but his proposal to destroy portions of Central Park was justifiably controversial.

However misguided it may seem today, Flagg's plan to replace the naturalistic mid-nineteenth century urban park with a formal garden followed such celebrated precedents as the Mall in the Senate Park Commission plan for Washington, D.C., of 1901.[51]

No firm in the history of corporate building capitalized more on the fame of its tower than did the Singer Manufacturing Company. No American skyscraper had previously commanded such popular attention. Every phase of its construction "from foundation to flag pole" was assiduously reported by an enthusiastic press and encouraged by the zealous Singer public relations staff — perhaps because it knew from the beginning that the Singer height record would be ephemeral (Fig. 111). Long before construction was completed, the daily press announced that the Metropolitan Life Insurance Company Tower would top the Singer Tower's 612 feet.[52] Singer had only eighteen months in which to promote its image. Fast on the heels of the Metropolitan Life skyscraper, completed in 1909, came the Woolworth Building. The power of the Singer's landmark status and corporate identity was overwhelmingly persuasive to American businessmen, among them Frank Woolworth. His deci-

111. The Singer Tower in comparison with other tall structures in the world in 1908 (Semsch, ed., *A History of the Singer Building Construction,* p. 5).

224

112. Victoria Falls and Niagara Falls compared with the height of the Singer Tower, 1907 (*Scientific American* XCVI, June 29, 1907, p. 525).

sion to build the Woolworth Building as a rival tower to "advertise the Woolworth five-and-ten-cent stores all over the world" was a direct response to the Singer image.[53]

Even before the anticipated Singer Tower was completed, progress reports were accompanied by a flood of height comparisons. "With the exception of the Eiffel Tower," reported the *New York Times* on February 22, 1906, "the Singer Building will be the loftiest structure in the world; [it] will be higher than all existing skyscrapers by from 200 to 300 feet, and will be about 40 feet higher than Washington Monument."[54] The Singer Tower soon became the measure of all things. At first its 612 feet formed a unit of comparison. It was summoned to measure, for example, the relative heights of Victoria Falls and Niagara Falls with the skyline of New York. "Only the Singer Building's Tower Rises Above the Crest," boasted *Scientific American* in 1907 (Fig. 112).[55] Even the most eccentric comparisons were made. *Scien-*

113. Singer Tower. Crown, 1908 (Semsch, ed., *A History of the Singer Building Construction*, p. 41).

tific American also measured in graphic terms such abstractions as steam-power capacity or meat consumption in the United States against the height of the Singer Tower.[56]

The tower solution dominated the skyscraper before the First World War as architects and their clients sought identifiable images for skyscrapers on the Manhattan skyline. There, art and business — aesthetics and capitalism — and architects and corporate leaders formed an unprecedented alliance. The Singer, Metropolitan, Banker's Trust, and Woolworth towers each identified with a different stylistic theme: Beaux-Arts, Italian Renaissance, or Gothic.[57]

Napoleon Le Brun & Sons chose an Italian Renaissance campanile for its Metropolitan Tower, as did Trowbridge & Livingston for its Banker's Trust Building (1909–12), while Cass Gilbert and his client, Frank Woolworth, preferred the expressive power of Gothic for the Woolworth Building. The ornamented attic was the distinguishing feature of such New York skyscrapers, as Barr Ferree predicted as early as 1904.[58]

The crown of the Singer Tower (Fig. 113), with its unorthodox mansarded dome and concentration of French Second Empire ornament, recalling Visconti's and Lefuel's pavilions of the new Louvre (see Fig. 6), made it a signifying element in the urban landscape. Although domes had traditionally appeared in France to define major corners, the Singer Tower did not actually celebrate its own corner at street level. Instead, its dome contributed a striking silhouette to the Manhattan skyline (Fig. 114) and provided Broadway with a prominent punctuation mark. Thus Flagg transformed a French solution for a corner site into an aerial landmark through his conviction that all facets of such towers be "treated architecturally." To emphasize the summit of the tower, the dome displayed a confection of sculptural embellishments, hip rolls, *oeils de boeuf,* dormer windows and specially reinforced "curved" windows, as well as Maine roofing slate; it was crowned with a lantern of richly ornamented copper. Singer's individualized tower and crest asserted the com-

114.   The Singer Tower and the Manhattan skyline, 1911 (Library of Congress).

227

115. Singer Tower by night, 1908 (Byron collection, Museum of the
City of New York).

pany's corporate identity with a lavish show of big business consumption.
Flagg's exuberant use of French decoration was an appropriate expression of
this.

228

Flagg conceived of the Tower in two contrasting images: the Singer by day and the Singer by night. A stately image by day, the Singer's red brick and limestone polychromy emphasized its solidity and permanence. But by night, it could be dematerialized into a luminous column of light visible for forty miles (Fig. 115). It was an electric image, one produced by thirty projector searchlights throwing their beacons upon the shaft of the tower and 1,600 incandescent lamps outlining the sculptural relief of the mansarded dome with garlands of light.[59] This same use of electric lights had transformed the Paris exposition of 1889 and succeeding American fairs including the Chicago fair of 1893 and the Pan-American Exposition, Buffalo, of 1901. Whether by day or by night, a 30-foot-long white pennant with the name "SINGER" in red letters flew from the flagpole as a banner of corporate public relations. The device was enormously popular (see Fig. 104).

The Singer Tower not only illustrated the principles of Flagg's skyscraper reform, but it also encouraged the possibility of an entire city of towers, which Flagg hoped would determine the character of New York as a future metropolis. The potentially extendable tower, by virtue of its available technology, could satisfy the need for high density on commercially prime land, while at the same time imposing restrictions to allow requisite amounts of light and air. The altruistic tower, as Flagg saw it, was a thing of the present as well as the future. No sooner had the 612-foot skyscraper firmly established its dominance over the profile of Manhattan, than the press reported that Flagg was preparing plans for a 1,000-foot tower which would, according to the *New York Times*, "put the Singer tower down in a valley" and compel the Eiffel Tower "to give up its place as the world's loftiest structure."[60] This rival skyscraper was planned on the site of George B. Post's Mills Building, on Broad and Wall streets at Exchange Place, where Flagg's office was then located. Little is known of this project, which was never executed. Again in 1911, Flagg was at work on another design for a 1,100-foot tower, planned for Broadway and Morris Street, which also was not realized.[61]

During the New York building boom that lasted from 1900 to the Depression, architects like Flagg saw Manhattan as the model city of the future and focused their imagination on what it might look like. As Flagg advanced his views on height and area restrictions, he also envisioned a metropolis of the future permeated with towers resulting from such zoning regulations. In one visionary drawing of about 1908 Flagg depicted the future skyline of New York. Its appearance in Semsch's *A History of the Singer Building Construction* was accompanied by the statement: "Mr. Flagg would have New York a veritable city of towers."[62] This future profile of New York also embodied Flagg's vision of a "City of the Twentieth Century" which he described in his article of 1908, published in *American Architect*. When seen from a distance on the skyline, the city's towers, "carried to their logical conclusion" and standing on well-proportioned bases, would appear "picturesque"; whereas on the street level, they would have "the appearance of order and sobriety which comes of a uniform height and continuous cornice line."[63] Finally, Flagg's

116.   Harry M. Pettit.
"King's Dream of New York,"
1908 *(King's Views
of New York)*.

230

drawing envisioned a future multilevel circulation system integrating transportation and architecture. Overhead bridges would link buildings at breathless heights and dirigibles could be moored to lofty flagpoles. The regulated but still visionary conception of the future city which Flagg had so clearly articulated in his speeches and writings was actually far closer to Louis Sullivan's then little-known project of 1891 for a set-back skyscraper city than it was to D. H. Burnham's Plan of Chicago (1907–9).[64]

Flagg's drawing was only one of several utopian schemes for the metropolis of the future. But if Flagg's study for a "city of towers" of 1908 only briefly outlined his plan, it flowed from a common theoretical underpinning. Harry M. Pettit's drawing, "King's Dream of New York," published by Moses King the same year, was an even more fantastic view of future New York microscopically rendered, along a Broadway-like thoroughfare (Fig. 116).[65] Although this imaginary "Cosmopolis of the Future" was a city of towers — attenuated versions of the Singer Tower and Adler & Sullivan's Schiller Building were among them — there was no effort to regulate their scale and density. It might be day above, but within the canyon of Broadway it was already night.

The sustaining power of Flagg's vision of the city in 1908 is reflected in a project of 1927, a still-future city of towers. Responding to Manhattan's uncurbed growth in the 1920s, Flagg called for the planning of highways, buildings, and sidewalks to reduce congestion in American cities. Looking to the future, Flagg argued, "if cities three times the[ir] former height are to be built successfully, street capacity must be proportionately increased."[66] Based on the New York City model which he knew best, Flagg's "City of the Future" of 1927 integrated three components of the modern skyscraper city: the steel frame, the elevator, and the automobile (Fig. 117). Calling for a radical alteration in city streets to relieve traffic congestion, Flagg's proposal specified three classes of traffic, each to "move independently at its proper speed and without interruption."[67] Slow-moving vehicles would run on the surface, with adjoining sidewalks giving direct access to shops. Express through traffic would pass on a narrower elevated roadbed, reached by ramps. Pedestrians would use an elevated superstructure with bridges carried over cross streets and connected to shops above ground level. This multilevel approach to circulation was undoubtedly influenced by similar studies of Harvey Wiley Corbett, Frederick A. Delano, and others that appeared together with Flagg's in Thomas Adams's *Regional Plan of New York* of 1931.[68] Flagg's "City of the Future" called for new zoning regulations which would have had dramatic consequences for new

231

117. Ernest Flagg. "The City of the Future," 1927 (*Scientific American* CXXXVII, October 1927, fig. 1).

construction. Because his plan necessitated a street wider than its Manhattan model, the building line of the first two stories had to be stepped back 25 feet. Flagg specified that "one third of the rest of the plot [be restricted] to four stories and the remainder unrestricted as to height."[69] Because his plan required new height and area restrictions, it would only be adopted in new districts within cities. In advocating the tower solution a decade after its defeat in 1916, Flagg justified its use on economic and aesthetic grounds, for the set-back solution, he argued, resulted in "loss [of area] and ugliness."[70] With their picturesque crests, the skyscrapers in Flagg's "City of the Future" nostalgically recalled the Singer Tower, and the elevated bridges beside them were reminiscent of nineteenth-century cast-iron structures.[71]

In contrast to Flagg's regularized Beaux-Arts image and city of towers, the Boyd plan as implemented in the early and mid-1920s produced an irregular streetscape of set-back skyscrapers which such architects and visionaries as Harvey Wiley Corbett and Hugh Ferriss regarded as a positive gain.[72] Ultimately, however, Flagg's tower solution to the skyscraper and the imagery that accompanied it were more sustaining than the set-back solution, for the great skyscrapers of the late 1920s — the Chrysler, Chanin, and Empire State buildings — returned to the earlier aesthetic and proportions of individualized towers and crests. A similar return to the identifiable crest in the 1980s (after years of the post-Second World War undifferentiated slab) is evident in New York's recent skyscrapers, notably Johnson & Burgee's American Telephone and Telegraph Building. But the permissive zoning regulations of 1961 have compromised the positive contributions of the tower solution by permitting increased density and encouraging plazas which establish incoherent relationships with streets and neighboring buildings. A recent recognition of this problem has resulted in a revision of the New York code introducing daylight zoning and acknowledging the positive benefits of such restrictions which the Singer Tower voluntarily adopted in 1908. Although the Singer Tower no longer survives, its example sets a civic-minded precedent for the tower solution in Manhattan.

The Singer Tower made the Singer Manufacturing Company famous, and it also made Flagg famous. Never before had the Singer image been so vigorously promoted, nor corporate boosterism reached such "heights." Flagg's efforts, too, were rewarded as he gained respect within New York architectural circles and professional organizations, which embraced his ideas on skyscraper reform. While his architectural career had already peaked by 1908, Flagg had not previously represented his profession in a capacity of leadership. It was a role he welcomed. This affiliation and the example of his Singer Tower established his reputation within the skyscraper reform movement.

CHAPTER EIGHT

Urban Housing Reform: "An Incentive to Build"

A T THE SAME time that Flagg launched his architectural career with large commissions, including the Corcoran Gallery and St. Luke's Hospital, he pioneered efforts in model tenement housing. An ardent spokesman for the housing reform movement, he promoted his ideas on scientific planning over a span of forty years with a series of model tenements, workingmen's hotels, and apartment complexes. I. N. Phelps Stokes, a fellow tenement-house architect, later honored Flagg as "the father of the modern model tenement in this country."[1]

Flagg's contributions were far-reaching. He devised a light-court plan which applied the principles of apartment house design to tenements and broke with the existing pattern of tenement housing. Flagg's model plan with its increased space, light, and air, as well as its fireproofing, encouraged higher minimum standards for tenements, eventually mandated by the Tenement House Law of 1901. Moreover, the popularity of Flagg's work encouraged other architects to specialize in tenement house design. Widely adopted by Flagg's contemporaries, his light-court plan endured from the 1890s to the Depression, both in New York and in other large cities. The Flagg model plan marked an essential phase in the evolution of low-rise housing from the single lot before 1894 to the entire New York city block of the 1920s.

Flagg's involvement in housing reform was unique among fellow architects because he originated a model plan and formed a building company to execute his designs. In 1894 the editors of *Record and Guide* noted that until Flagg's efforts at reform, there prevailed a "long and total indifference of our architects toward the tenement house problem in this city."[2] Flagg was guided by two compelling, if often conflicting, motives: his social conscience and his desire for profit. Although a few architects, including Edward Tuckerman Potter, George B. Post, and Calvert Vaux, were deeply committed reformers, their writings and their work had relatively little impact.[3] Flagg was among the first Beaux-Arts-trained architects to specialize in tenement housing. Although Richard Morris Hunt is credited with five Manhattan tenements in the late 1880s, his were not progressive designs but standard office work.[4] Most of the large firms avoided tenement planning; McKim, Mead & White got no closer to the problem than its multiple dwellings for middle-income families, the King Model Houses, on West 138th and 139th streets, Harlem (1891–92).[5] I. N. Phelps Stokes (1867–1944), who studied for the entrance exams to the Ecole des Beaux-Arts in several preparatory ateliers from 1894 to 1897, was one of the few architects who succeeded Flagg in demonstrating a strong commitment to tenement house design. Earlier, as a special student in the program in architecture at Columbia University during the academic year 1893–94, Stokes had decided to specialize in the economic planning and construction of housing for the working classes. Stokes's early decision to seek a career of "useful service" was consistent with the interest in philanthropic reform of his socially prominent family.[6]

If Flagg's concerns were unusual, so was his background. Flagg's early experiences in business, land and building speculation, as well as living among low-income groups on the Lower West Side had enabled him to observe the New York tenement house problem firsthand. "I had seen it at close range," he remarked in later years, "and regarded it as an evil of the first magnitude."[7] No one was more keenly aware that tenements were traditionally designed by one class and built for another. In advocating more economical plans than those put forth by the investment philanthropists around him, Flagg contended, "it is almost impossible for one, not a tenement dweller himself, to see the matter from the tenant's standpoint."[8] So Flagg was in a unique situation, at once insider and outsider.

The Model Tenement House and Flagg's Light-Court Plan of 1894

From the 1860s, the urban housing reform movement in America followed two paths. The first was the path of enlightened capitalism and private funding. The second was the path of restrictive legislation and public funding. Flagg's background in building speculation prepared him to join forces with the private investor-reformer to design model tenement houses, financed and constructed through building companies. The solution to the housing crisis, Flagg later maintained, lay in the construction and management

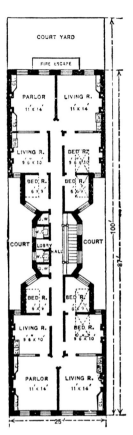

118. James E. Ware. First-prize plan in tenement house competition of 1879 (De Forest and Veiller, eds., *The Tenement House Problem*, vol. 1, p. 101).

of tenement houses based on "sound economic principles" where the investor-reformer was given "an incentive to build" through "a profit upon rents," but within "reach of the great mass of people."[9] Flagg believed in laissez-faire economics, even though he also supported legislation favoring certain types of planning restrictions and amenities. Flagg was an arch-paternalist in an age of paternalism.

When Flagg joined the urban housing reform movement in the 1890s, there was little enforced legislation governing tenement house construction. Building speculators responded to market demands. The most significant regulatory reform had been the Tenement House Law of 1879, sponsored by the Association for Improving Conditions of the Poor (AICP), which encouraged the construction of model tenements as it limited building density.[10] Model tenements differed from speculative tenements because they were financed by private investor-reformers with voluntary limits on profit and higher

236

standards of sanitation.[11] The Tenement House Law of 1879, which super-
seded a more permissive law of 1867, restricted building to a maximum of 65
percent coverage of the lot and favored tenement construction on the prizewin-
ning plan of James E. Ware (Fig. 118).[12] Ware's design came to be known as
the "dumb-bell" plan because it conformed to the standard city lot (25 × 100
feet) with narrow air shafts (4 feet 8 inches wide) between buildings. But the
"dumb-bell" epithet soon became as descriptive of its effectiveness as of its
plan form. Even though interior bedrooms might have some access to light and
air, the narrow unfireproofed shaft, which acted like a flue, proved to be a fire
hazard, a convenient receptacle for garbage, and a conduit for cooking odors.
Moreover, with little enforcement of the 1879 code, the dumb-bell "model"
tenement routinely occupied 75 to 90 percent of its lot.[13] Thus, rather than a
restrictive solution, Ware's popular plan, serviced by ineffective air shafts,
encouraged development into clusters of high-density blocks. In short, Ware's
plan tended to retard, rather than advance, tenement house reform.[14]

Flagg recognized that the chief defect of existing tenement house
design lay in its adherence to the historical pattern of land usage, calling the
division of blocks into standardized lots, fixed by the Commissioners' Plan for
Manhattan of 1811, "the greatest evil which ever befell New York City."[15]
The lot plagued the city: the narrowness of it, the depth of it, and the rigidity of
it. Convinced that he had arrived at a progressive planning solution, Flagg took
his case to the public. In an article of 1894, "The New York Tenement House
Evil and Its Cure," published in *Scribner's Magazine,* he denounced existing
plans, especially the dumb-bell, because they were based on the standard lot
which satisfied the requirements of single family dwellings, but not those of
multiple dwellings. By contrast, Flagg's plan combined four standard city lots
into a square plot (100 × 100 feet) with a 28-foot-square central light-court
containing corner stairs set in at an angle (Fig. 119). The plan recalled Henry J.
Hardenbergh's plan for The Dakota Apartments on Central Park West between 72nd and 73rd streets of 1880–84 (Fig. 120). Statistically, Flagg
demonstrated that his square plan was more economical than the prevailing
rectangular one, since it employed less wall enclosure, the corner stairs further
eliminating the space usually occupied by corridors and partitions.[16] It also
provided greater room space, more light, ventilation, and fire protection. With
three apartments per floor for each lot, instead of the dumb-bell's four, Flagg's
light-court plan permitted larger rooms (25 percent more space). In spite of a
building's lower density, Flagg maintained that such economical planning and
construction would result in lower rents (15 percent less) and lower vacancy

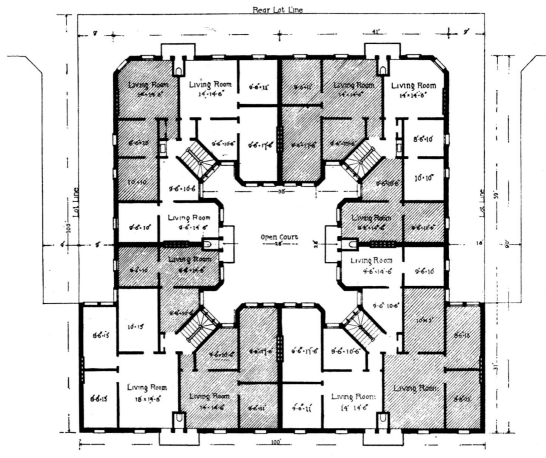

119.   Ernest Flagg. Plan for a tenement house with a frontage of 100 feet
(*Scribner's Magazine* XVI, July–December 1894, p. 112).

rates than in the dumb-bell. Moreover, the light-court plan effectively allowed
more light and air to reach interior rooms and even direct sunlight to penetrate
the upper floors. Unlike the dumb-bell tenements, in which apartment units
were divided by air shafts whose walls were perforated with windows, Flagg's
plan separated each cluster of three apartments with an interior fire wall.[17]
Apart from its functional advantages over the dumb-bell, the new plan on a
100-foot-square plot, or its variations on 75- or 50-foot frontages, was informed by Flagg's Beaux-Arts training. It was biaxially symmetrical, employed modular design, and, like all his plans, according to Flagg, was conceived as a "mathematical proposition."[18]

    Yet as popular as it was among model tenement house reformers and

238

tenants, Flagg's light-court plan was ignored by speculative builders, who continued to use the higher-density dumb-bell plan.[19] Flagg argued that his solution could be successful if landlords would recognize the economy and desirable features of the light-court plan and if restrictive legislation would mandate that all tenements, not just model dwellings, adopt the provisions of his plan.[20] Stokes called Flagg's 1894 plan, and his subsequent buildings which employed it, "the starting point in the designing of modern low-rent model tenements in New York."[21] But only after the passage of the Tenement House Law of 1901 did the Flagg light-court plan become the low-cost urban housing model in Manhattan.

120.   Henry J. Hardenbergh. The Dakota, New York. Plan, 1880–84 (*Plumber and Sanitary Engineer* II, 1885, p. 271).

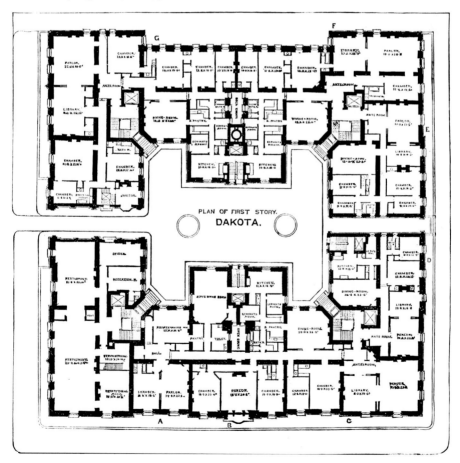

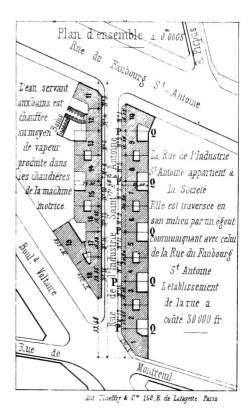

121. Emile Leménil. Plan of worker housing for the Société des immeubles industriels, rue des immeubles industriels, 1878 (Muller et Cacheux, *Les habitations ouvrières en tous pays*, pl. 27).

When Flagg devised his aggregate plan with its central courtyard, he set a new standard for economical and healthful tenement housing in America by applying French planning principles. The courtyard plan had long been an established feature of two classes of European multiple dwellings: tenements and apartments. Now it was pressed into service for even higher-density living, conforming to Manhattan's rigid block and lot pattern. By the late 1860s in America, the difference between a tenement house and an apartment house was evident in the plan and focused on the idea of a "common right" to halls, stairways, and toilets.[22] The provisions of the 1901 Tenement House Law maintained such distinctions.[23]

In arriving at his *parti,* Flagg claimed that he simply adopted the type of plan employed for French apartment and tenement houses, dividing a plot into four sections with two L-shaped apartment groups in front facing the street, and two in the rear receiving light from a central court (*cour, grande cour,* or *courette*) or a rear court.[24] In this way, the French planner consolidated the open space into one square court large enough to provide light for all rooms

240

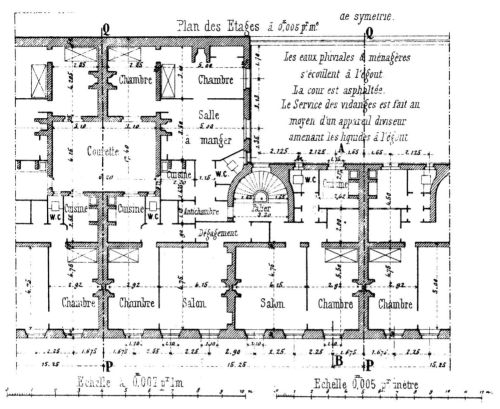

122.   Emile Leménil. Worker housing for the Société des immeubles industriels,
rue des immeubles industriels. Plan of apartment units, 1878 (Muller et
Cacheux, *Les habitations ouvrières en tous pays,* pl. 27).

facing it. Through this method of lighting the building, "the owner depends
entirely upon his own property for light," rather than "upon his neighbor's
land," which, Flagg assumed, was seldom dependable.[25]

Such principles of French planning informed housing practices during
the early Third Republic, where the light-court plan continued to be employed
not only for apartment houses, but also for worker and subsidized middle-
income housing. During his student years in Paris, Flagg lived in an apartment
building with a light-court.[26] Whether he had special knowledge of French
tenement or worker housing which employed light-courts is unknown. Yet, he
could have visited several widely published examples of worker housing that
employed light-court plans, including Emile Leménil's housing for the Société
des immeubles industriels located on both sides of the rue de l'Industrie
Saint-Antoine, now rue des Immeubles industriels (Fig. 121). Leménil's plan

grouped clusters of tenement units around light-courts containing corner stairs (Fig. 122). Such light-court housing projects figured prominently in the exposition of 1878 and in that of 1889, which Flagg attended.[27]

Similarly, the light-court plan distinguished J. B. André Godin's factory housing, *the familistère,* at Guise, France, which was based on the theories of Charles Fourier and his workers' community, or *phalanstère.* The five-story units of Godin's workers' housing estate, built in stages from 1859 to 1883, had both glazed light-courts and corner staircases. Although Flagg might have been influenced by the social possibilities of Godin's courtyard plan, he was unmistakably motivated by the "sound economic principles" of capitalism, as opposed to the communitarian values of Fourierism.[28]

By the mid-1890s the New York apartment house, unlike the tenement house, had already employed the light-court plan for several decades, Flagg having had direct experience with it while assisting in the design of the Fifth Avenue Plaza Apartments. The French origins of the New York courtyard apartment, with its light-court and covered driveway, or porte cochere, have been well established.[29] Richard Morris Hunt is long acknowledged to have incorporated the French courtyard into the first apartment house in America, the Stuyvesant Apartments at 138–146 East 18th Street (1869–70; demolished).[30] To distinguish the one-story living units of this "walk-up" from the ordinary tenement house, the Stuyvesant became known as the "French Flats." It contained four stories of apartments with studios in its mansard. Even earlier, Hunt had designed the Studio Building at 51–55 West 10th Street (1857; demolished) with combined studio and living units grouped around a central glazed court.[31] During the last quarter of the century, middle- and upper-middle-income New Yorkers favored such French flats, many employing the courtyard plan with both elevators and corner stairs. Henry J. Hardenbergh designed two such apartment buildings, the Vancorlear on Seventh Avenue (1879; demolished) and The Dakota (see Fig. 120).[32] Even Flagg's former associates in the firm of Hubert, Pirsson & Hoddick published a light-court housing project which they called "French Flats." These duplex apartments, with their staircases and elevators at the corners, were financed through cooperative ownership, similar to the firm's earlier Central Park Apartments.[33]

Initially, model housing reformers during the nineteenth century favored the light-court plan for its salubrious effects. Like the pavilion plan that dominated nineteenth-century hospital design, the light-court plan for tenements responded to the prevailing belief in the miasmic theory of disease, calling for maximum ventilation to expel disease-causing vitiated air and replenish it with a fresh supply. For this reason British planners in the 1830s and 1840s advocated courtyards. Among those executed plans, Henry Roberts's Model Houses in Streatham Street, Bloomsbury (1849), employed an open quadrangle (30 × 70 feet), surrounded on three sides by apartments. Access to them was obtained by a single staircase leading to galleries on each floor. By eliminating interior corridors, the Streatham's apartment units were effectively disconnected "to prevent the communication of contagious diseases."[34] During the 1860s and 1870s planners in Britain, including George Peabody (an American financier and philanthropist) and Sir Sidney Waterlow (a politician and reformer), continued to use open staircase towers and balconies to maximize fresh air, but often at the expense of exposure to light.[35] The use of open staircase towers and balcony plans, especially Waterlow's Langbourne Buildings, Mark Street, Finsbury (1863; demolished), was transported to New York by a Brooklyn merchant, Alfred T. White. White put both British planning and management principles into practice in America with two tenements constructed in Brooklyn: Home Buildings (1876–77) and Riverside Buildings (1890). Not constrained by the Manhattan gridiron plan, White's Riverside Buildings employed a perimeter scheme containing blocks of apartment units, two rooms deep, surrounding a park-like open space.[36]

Ironically, by the 1890s, long after the germ theory of disease had ceased to justify the hygienic priority given to natural ventilation, the courtyard plan increased in popularity. Epidemics of cholera, tuberculosis, and other diseases, especially in New York in the 1890s, cautioned reformers against the ever-present threat of contagion.[37] For Flagg, Potter, and other tenement house reformers in the 1890s, maximum ventilation still continued to be a prerequisite for salubrious multiple dwellings.[38] As with the pavilion plan for hospitals, Flagg considered the light-court plan, in conjunction with new methods of hygiene, a fail-safe approach to disease prevention. Moreover, European planners reached conclusions similar to those of their American counterparts. For example, during the same month in which Flagg published his *Scribner's* plan, a similar light-court plan for a dense block of tenements in Naples appeared in the French architectural journal, *La Construction Moderne*.[39] About the same time, consolidated light-court plans also appeared in such cities as Gothenburg (Sweden) and Berlin.[40] Like Flagg, these Continental tenement house designers relied upon French precedents in scientific planning.

In sum, the light-court plan had long been a fixture of the apartment house, as well as subsidized middle-income and worker housing in France.

Variations of light-court plans had also been used by British housing reformers during the nineteenth century in their efforts to militate against the spread of disease among the tenement population. In adopting the courtyard plan — heretofore associated with middle-income housing in America — to model tenement houses, Flagg applied the principles of French planning and improved the standard of economical and healthful low-income dwellings.

The Alfred Corning Clark Buildings and Other Light-Court Tenement Houses

The superiority of Flagg's model plan of 1894 was self-evident to housing reformers; the *Scribner's* article had, in Flagg's words, "attracted a great deal of attention."[41] But it was not until 1896 that Flagg's plan had hopes of being realized. That year a group of reformers responded to the Report of the Tenement House Committee of 1894, under the chairmanship of Richard Watson Gilder. The report dramatically demonstrated that "New York possessed the worst tenement system in the world."[42] In March 1896 these reformers founded the Improved Housing Council. Following a period of social unrest which culminated in the McKinley-Bryan election in November that year, the council's Committee on Model Apartment Houses sponsored a model tenement house competition. The council, in turn, organized the City and Suburban Homes Company, a building company based on the British models of George Peabody and others.[43] According to reformer Lawrence Veiller, it was founded "for the purpose of building model tenement houses in New York as a business investment."[44] In the days before high inflation, the company's prospectus was inviting. Its objectives were "to offer . . . a safe 5 per cent investment and at the same time supply to wage earners improved, wholesome homes at current rates." With three-fourths of the capital stock made public, shares were fixed at $10, low enough, company directors insisted, "to make the shares popular and within the reach of wage-earners." While encouraging tenant investment, these directors altruistically (but erroneously) maintained that "the enterprise was conceived wholly in the interest of such toilers."[45]

The City and Suburban Homes Company members came, for the most part, from the council and other reform organizations including the AICP and the Improved Dwelling Association. The company's first president, Elgin R. L. Gould (1860–1915), was an academic rather than a philanthropist. He received his doctorate in political science from Johns Hopkins University and was a lecturer at that institution (1892–97) and a professor of statistics at the University of Chicago (1895–96).[46] Gould was the author of a statistically comprehensive report on housing in Europe and America for the United States Department of Labor, *The Housing of the Working People,* published in 1895.[47] In it, Gould demonstrated that model houses were a financial success.[48] Other officers and directors of the City and Suburban Homes Company included Samuel D. Babcock, R. Fulton Cutting, W. Bayard Cutting, Adrian Iselin, Jr., Darius Ogden Mills, Cornelius Vanderbilt II, and Alfred T. White.[49] Several of them were already, or soon would be, Flagg's patrons.

By November 1896, the City and Suburban Homes Company had acquired its first site on West 68th and 69th streets when Mrs. Alfred Corning Clark, an heir to the Singer Manufacturing Company fortune, turned over land from the Clark Estate in exchange for shares in the building company. Subsequently, twenty-eight architectural firms submitted tenement house plans to a jury consisting of Gould and other housing reformers.[50] Unlike previous competitions, the program required that these plans cover a whole city block (200 × 400 feet). The jury recommended to the City and Suburban Homes Company two plans which employed light-courts: one by Flagg, another by the dumb-bell tenement architect, James E. Ware. Flagg's entry, which had side courts facing the street instead of the yard, was based on an improved 100-foot courtyard plan of 1895 which he had published in an anthology on urban reform, *The Poor in Great Cities* (Fig. 123).[51] Ware's plan also contained a central light-court and sides open to the street, features which were borrowed from Flagg's improved plan of 1895 but also encouraged by the competition's program (Fig. 124).[52] In comparing the two plans, Stokes called Ware's "a refinement of the Flagg plan."[53] Although the committee appreciated the economy and scientific planning of the Flagg design, they favored Ware's arrangement of suites and his use of a passage from the main entrance facing the street through to the central court, elements which identified it as a "French plan."[54] (Flagg claimed that these features sacrificed space and were, therefore, too costly for ordinary tenement dwellers to afford.) Even so, Flagg was appointed architect, evidently not because his plan was preferred to Ware's, for in accepting it, the committee required him to modify it. Rather, he received the commission because, as Flagg tells us, "it was through me that the land had been acquired," his ties to Mrs. Clark, the Singer Company, and the Clark Estate having been previously well established.[55]

The competition caused Flagg and Ware to draw swords. Years later Flagg recalled: "Mr. Ware was told that I had accused him of copying my plans." Flagg self-righteously insisted that the charge was "amply justified." According to Flagg's understanding of the events that followed, Ware retali-

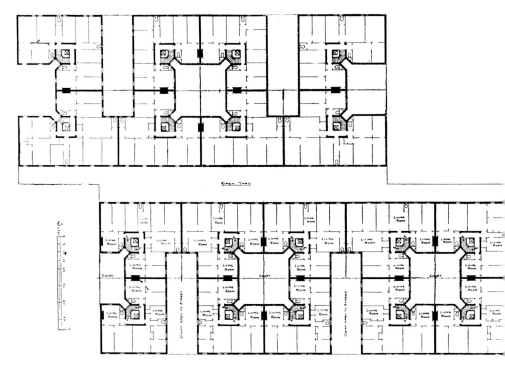

123. Ernest Flagg. First-prize plan as adopted for the Alfred Corning Clark
Buildings or City and Suburban Homes Company Model Tenements, 217–233 West
68th Street and 214–220 West 69th Street, New York City, 1896 (*Architecture and
Building* XXVI, January 2, 1897, p. 8).

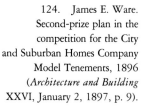

124. James E. Ware.
Second-prize plan in the
competition for the City
and Suburban Homes Company
Model Tenements, 1896
(*Architecture and Building*
XXVI, January 2, 1897, p. 9).

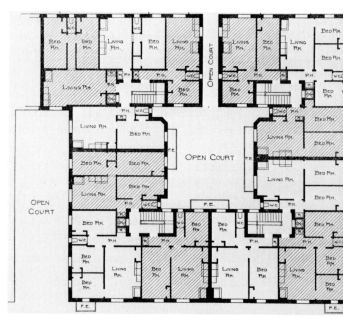

ated by soliciting the signatures of leading architects, including McKim, Mead, and White, to a petition stating that Flagg had "no monopoly of any plan." Without an opportunity to defend himself, Flagg later recalled, "I appeared to be condemned by practically the entire architectural profession of the city."[56] This affair, sandwiched between both the earlier St. Luke's Hospital and Corcoran competitions and the subsequent events surrounding the New York Public Library commission, further damaged Flagg's already weakened professional standing.

Completed in 1898, the Alfred Corning Clark Buildings occupied nineteen city lots on West 68th and 69th streets, between Amsterdam and

125. Ernest Flagg. Alfred Corning Clark Buildings or City and Suburban Homes Company Model Tenements (demolished), 214–220 West 69th Street, New York City, 1896–98 (Zeisloft, *The New Metropolis,* p. 287).

West End avenues (Fig. 125). (They were demolished in the late 1950s to make way for the Lincoln Towers urban renewal project.)[57] The company later applauded Mrs. Clark, the donor-investor, for anticipating the economic, as well as the social, advantages of such an investment.[58] But Flagg was most likely responsible for that investment. Well experienced in land and building speculation, he undoubtedly alerted Mrs. Clark to the strategic location of the Clark Estate lots and persuaded her to invest.

From the 1870s the West Side had experienced dramatic growth. The completion of the Ninth Avenue elevated railroad in 1871 encouraged real estate development in the vicinity of its Columbus Avenue route. Middle- and upper-middle-class residents moved into the area above West 70th Street. Brick and brownstone row houses as well as apartment buildings, some part of the Clark Estate, accommodated these dwellers.[59] The tenement population, however, was becoming increasingly congested in the area below West 68th Street. The Clark Estate site was situated only a few hundred feet from two of the most crowded tenement blocks in New York City.[60] The Clark tenement houses were thus wedged between these two residential zones, with the denser tenement zone expanding at a faster rate northward. The City and Suburban Homes Company saw these model tenements as a panacea. They would relieve congestion and deter neighborhood decline. The company predicted that conditions in the adjacent middle-class neighborhood, in terms of both its property values and its hygiene, would militate against "degenerating influences."[61] In effect, these model tenements formed an advantageous buffer zone; for what was good for them was good for the property values of the Clark Estate's vast holdings in the west seventies and eighties.

Like all of Flagg's designs, the Clark tenements illustrated his objectives: to fuse French scientific planning with Beaux-Arts aesthetics, while adapting both to American building problems. In an age which praised efficiency and scientific management, Flagg was widely recognized for his successful application of science to planning problems.[62] Lawrence Veiller applauded Flagg's "study of scientific tenement house plans," and the Clark tenements as an example of it.[63] Stokes regarded the new type of light-court plan as "much the best and most scientific."[64] Even the New York press recognized the intentions of the City and Suburban Homes Company to make all the houses of the Clark Estate "as perfect as science to date can make them."[65] It proclaimed that buildings on 100-foot-square sites, which employed the light-court plan as opposed to the dumb-bell plan, clearly distinguished "scientific from unscientific plannings."[66]

If the Alfred Corning Clark Buildings were regarded as scientific, it was because they met the reformers' objectives to eliminate tenement house evils by providing (1) large apartments through economic planning, (2) hygiene and sanitation, (3) amenities, (4) family privacy and home comfort, and (5) skillful management. The Clark buildings comprised a colony of six-story buildings, configured to 100-foot-square plots with 30-foot central light-courts and corner staircases. The complex included a total of 373 apartment units with four stores and an office. Although of nonfireproof construction — a point on which Flagg vehemently disagreed with the company — the model tenements had firewalls and fireproofed staircases.[67]

Observers noted that these model tenement houses promoted, rather than retarded, good health. The courtyard plan on a 100-foot-square plot was regarded during the period as the form which produces "almost perfect hygienic results." Long dark corridors were eliminated and stairways were well lighted. Good drainage and ventilation further promoted sanitation. Because these model tenements were the last word in terms of amenities, they illustrated a new concept of the autonomous tenement unit. Previously, the independent unit with its own washing, bathing, and toilet facilities had been integral only to middle-income housing in America. "Every apartment whether it have two, three, or four rooms is complete in itself, with its private water closet, laundry, tubs," announced the *New York Times*. Comfort, so Flagg, Gould, and the other reformers believed, was also a tenement dweller's right. The *New York Times* further noted that "special attention is given to all the little 'human nature' features, such as closets, pantries."[68] By challenging the traditional notion of common rights for tenement housing, Flagg and the City and Suburban Homes Company advanced the cause of individual rights so fundamental to the Progressive Era in America.

Like other aspects of the Clark tenements, their planning and management adhered to capitalist notions of "sound economic principles." Stokes praised Flagg for bringing his "business experience" and "common sense" to such problems of economic planning.[69] Flagg's ability to economize space and construction permitted rents to be kept realistically, not artificially, low. They averaged about one dollar per room per week, comparable to ordinary tenement houses in the same neighborhood.[70] Under Gould's direction, the City and Suburban Homes Company promoted a rigorous system of tenement house management based on the British model of "friendly rent collection" developed by Octavia Hill.[71] The company was proud of its low vacancy rate.[72] Due to their high standard of planning, construction, and amenities provided, the Clark model tenements attracted a stable tenantry of, what Veiller called, "the better class of working people."[73] Not only were families welcome, but also widows and working women, the latter housed in a building at 220 West 69th Street specially reserved for them.[74] If the tenants were satisfied with such humane aspects of tenement life, the investors were gratified by their return. Dividends on the capital stock for the first five years averaged about 4 percent, the same percentage as the company's mortgage, although one point below what its officers had promised.[75]

Flagg brought to the tenement house not only his knowledge of scientific planning, but artistic expression as well. Like their Parisian counterparts, the six-story Clark tenements maintained a uniform cornice line for Manhattan streets. Their planar brick surfaces conveyed a domestic character as in the model tenements of the Peabody Trust, London. Yet the tenement buildings of the Clark Estate were discrete blocks.[76] In designing the obligatory metal fire escapes, Flagg emphasized their compositional and artistic possibilities, not just their functional role. An ornamental wrought-iron balcony stretching across each facade defined the attic story while providing an emergency fire exit. As in his other buildings of this period, Flagg's application of French classicism also dominated the decorative aspects of the *parti*. The model tenement houses were constructed of light-reflecting brick, like St. Luke's Hospital, and trimmed with Indiana limestone. Each of the round-arched entrances was crowned with a Beaux-Arts cartouche. Furthermore, the symmetrical elevation of each block corresponded to its symmetrical plan and to the regular shape of its rooms. Flagg considered these features essential as much for their "beauty of form" as for their scientific planning.[77]

In spite of the overall success of its first model tenement, the City and Suburban Homes Company did not award further tenement commissions to Flagg. The company disagreed with a number of the principles Flagg endorsed, including fireproof construction and the use of shops for the entire ground floor.[78] Instead, the company chose Ware as its principal architect, adopting his 1896 competition plan (popularizing the Flagg light-court model) for many of its subsequent tenement houses, including the earliest buildings of the First Avenue Estate on First Avenue between 64th and 65th streets, built in 1899–1900.[79]

Thus unable to put his ideas fully into practice, Flagg persuaded one of the City and Suburban Homes Company investment philanthropists, Darius Ogden Mills, to organize a new building company. Flagg's objective was to demonstrate to building speculators, as well as to investment reformers, that

126.   Ernest Flagg. New York Fireproof Tenement Association Model
Tenements (partially demolished), 567–569 Tenth Avenue, New York City,
1899–1901 (New York Public Library).

tenement buildings which employed both fireproof construction and his model
plans could yield a more favorable return on an investment, thereby eliminating philanthropic practices and housing subsidies.[80] In 1899 Flagg formed the
New York Fireproof Tenement Association (later the Model Fireproof Tenement Company), which purchased land and built the first fireproof model
tenements in New York.[81] Called the New York Fireproof Tenements (after
the organization), this group of eleven buildings (now partially demolished)
was constructed on Tenth Avenue between 41st and 42nd streets in a crime-
ridden area known as DeWitt-Clinton, popularly named Hell's Kitchen (Fig.
126).[82] Although similar in plan, scale, amenities, and rentals to the West
68th and 69th streets Clark tenements, the Tenth Avenue tenements, housing
470 families, followed the French pattern of mixed use with shops to provide
higher rentals and alleviate vacancies on the ground floor. Here Flagg demonstrated the advantages of fireproof construction: low maintenance and insurance rates, economy of space, and endurance of materials.[83] The founder and
strongest believer in the company, Flagg soon subscribed to one-quarter of the
stock and later bought out the other shareholders. The financial success of the

251

venture was also due to shrewd management. The Tenth Avenue tenements employed the Octavia Hill system of management which Gould had instituted earlier at the Clark tenements. Because of it, losses were kept below 1 percent.[84] Flagg maintained that the company was operated as "a purely business venture," rather than as a philanthropic investment for its dividends were not limited.[85]

As architect, planner, and developer, Flagg used the company as an investment tool to build five additional model fireproof tenements dispersed throughout Manhattan. The largest and most technologically advanced of these was a 132-unit complex located at 506–516 West 47th Street near Tenth Avenue (1911; demolished) which employed a light-court plan for a series of 50-foot-wide lots, fireproof construction of steel and reinforced concrete, as well as the placement of shops on the ground floor.[86] Flagg maintained that the higher cost of fireproof construction was more than offset by its economic benefits: the elimination of costly fire escapes and an increase in the number of stories in a tenement house. The West 47th Street tenements also used especially thin (1½ inches) but solid wall partitions, employing a wire lath and plaster technique that Flagg patented, thereby gaining a greater economy of floor space.[87] Yet Flagg distinguished these salmon-colored brick buildings through the use of white marble for window sills and entrance columns.

Although an economic investigation into the practices of such building companies lies beyond the parameters of this study, a preliminary examination of the Model Fireproof Tenement Company's records indicates short-term economic success. From 1909 to the Depression the company consistently showed impressive earnings and dividends (up to 12 percent).[88] In his history of the company, Arthur Sutcliffe confirmed the early success of Flagg's venture. As the company's secretary and treasurer, Sutcliffe observed that by 1920 the company's investment objective — to give a higher return on fireproof tenements than on nonfireproof tenements — had been met.[89]

In an effort to promote his theory and design of tenement housing outside Manhattan, Flagg sought the assistance of a loyal client, the Boston publisher Edwin Ginn. Following a trend toward philanthropic investment in Boston's West End neighborhood, Ginn purchased a site on the Charlesbank in 1901.[90] It was not until 1909 that Ginn commissioned Flagg to design a five-story fireproof model tenement house, Charlesbank Homes, at the southeast corner of Charles and Poplar streets (Fig. 127).[91] In 1911, just before the completion of the building, Ginn formed a management corporation, Charlesbank Homes, Inc. Unlike its New York counterparts, Charlesbank Homes was

127.   Ernest Flagg. Charlesbank Homes (demolished), Charles and Poplar
streets, Boston, 1909–11 (Charlesbank Homes).

founded as a purely philanthropic venture since its charter prohibited dividends to members of the corporation.[92] Charlesbank Homes also employed
fireproof construction of steel and reinforced concrete, as well as Flagg's
patented partitions. Due to a generous plot of land (145 × 110 feet) and
patron support, Flagg could employ the more costly French plan he admired,
now incorporating a passage from the street to the light-court. Moreover, this
five-story walk-up had access to Charlesbank, a park-playground designed by
Frederick Law Olmsted (1887–92), and commanded a view of the Charles
River. Charlesbank Homes operated successfully for nearly a half-century. But
in 1960, during a sweep of urban renewal in Boston's West End, the Boston
Redevelopment Authority took over the building by eminent domain, dis-
placed its tenants, and demolished Charlesbank Homes.[93]

The New York Tenement House Law of 1901 and the Survival of the Light-Court Plan

The building of model tenements through philanthropic investment
was a positive contribution toward, but not a solution to, meeting housing
needs. By 1900 philanthropic reform had provided only a fraction of the

82,652 tenement houses in the five boroughs, 42,700 in Manhattan alone.[94] Any broad-based reform would need to come from the public rather than the private sector, from enforceable legislation rather than isolated instances of philanthropic housing, however exemplary they might be.

The survival of Flagg's light-court plan from 1894 to the Depression was not due to its adoption by model tenement companies, but rather to a wave of enforced legislation that reshaped New York building practices from the beginning of the twentieth century. With the sponsorship of the Charity Organization Society (COS), the urban reformer Lawrence Veiller founded a Tenement House Committee in 1899 for the purpose of securing tenement house legislation and enforcing it, as well as for promoting the construction of model tenement houses on a large scale and improving existing housing conditions. The committee, consisting of housing specialists and other reformers, included Robert W. de Forest, president of the COS, and Richard Watson Gilder, Jacob Riis, E.R.L. Gould, I.N. Phelps Stokes, and Ernest Flagg. The following year they proposed a housing code, organized a landmark tenement house exhibition, and held a model tenement competition. Politically, Veiller had no intention of blocking the private effort to construct model tenements. Yet he was convinced that only legislated means could assure any significant increase in their numbers. Fundamentally, he believed in the obligation of government to impose fair housing practices on all.[95]

Veiller pressed for tight legal restrictions on housing. By contrast, Flagg favored only minimal regulatory standards which he believed to be economically feasible for all builders to employ and which would result in affordable tenements.[96] Veiller and Flagg were diametrically opposed on this issue, Flagg considering the construction and management of tenement houses a business, Veiller rejecting the capitalist approach.[97] Because of their differences and what the members regarded as his "heretical views," Flagg later recalled, he was "speedily dropped" from participation in the Tenement House Committee.[98] He was not invited to the fifteen-member New York State Tenement House Commission of 1900, although he did testify at a commission hearing on the "General Evils of the Tenement House System."[99] Through the efforts of the COS Tenement House Committee and the state commission which followed, the legislature implemented their recommendations with the passage of the Tenement House Law of 1901 and the formation of the New York City Tenement House Department to enforce it.[100]

While the broad provisions of the Tenement House Law of 1901 upgraded existing buildings (so-called old-law tenements), their most radical reforms were in new construction (new-law tenements). The 1901 law was largely informed by a study of the plans submitted in the Tenement House Committee's competition of 1900 (based in turn on both Flagg's and Ware's light-court plans of 1896) and also of new plans by Flagg and Stokes, prepared at the request of the Tenement House Committee.[101] Adhering closely to the Flagg model, the law's most significant provisions limited the area to be occupied by a tenement house to 70 percent of the lot (with inner courts 24 X 24 feet for buildings on 100-foot-square plots), mandated fireproof construction for tenements in excess of 60 feet (six stories), and established minimum room sizes.[102] The 1901 law did not prohibit building on the standard 25 X 100-foot lot, but the larger courts now specified by the code made the city lot economically impractical for multiple dwellings employing the dumb-bell or any other plan. Under the new law, which applied to apartment houses as well as tenements, several building patterns emerged.[103] In effect, until the passage of the Multiple Dwelling Law in 1929, the 1901 law favored the survival of Flagg's light-court plan for three categories of multiple dwellings: model tenements, apartment houses, and speculative tenements.

In the first two decades of the twentieth century, model tenement house architects continued to prefer the light-court plan, improving on and often adapting it to special needs. Ware used it repeatedly for the City and Suburban Homes Company-sponsored tenements of the First Avenue Estate. Today blocks of such Flagg- and Ware-inspired light-court tenement houses, constructed by that company from 1900 to 1915, stand near the East River from the mid-sixties to the upper seventies.[104] I. N. Phelps Stokes (with his partner, John Mead Howells) used the light-court plan for the Tuskegee tenement at 213–215 West 62nd Street (1901), as did the architect Grosvenor Atterbury for the Phipps House at 325–335 East 31st Street (1906–7).[105] Henry Atterbury Smith also sought the curative effects of light-courts and corner staircases when he employed them for his East River Homes, or Shively Sanitary Tenement (now Cherokee Apartments), on East 77th and 78th streets (1909–11).[106]

Because the new law applied to all multiple dwellings, the light-court plan with its compact perimeter massing continued to suit middle-class apartment houses. Taking up the legacy of Hunt, Hardenbergh, and others, New York architects found the tall courtyard apartment ideal for development along Manhattan's residential thoroughfares, especially on Broadway and Central Park West. An early example is Clinton & Russell's high-rise apartment house, The Apthorp, 2101–2119 Broadway (1908). In a later development on the East Side, after the New York Central Railroad depressed its tracks, Park Avenue became a grand residential boulevard lined with such courtyard apartment buildings as Warren & Wetmore's 270 Park Avenue (1918; demolished) and McKim, Mead & White's 277 Park Avenue (1925; demolished).[107]

The third category of multiple dwelling, speculative tenements, employed the light-court model, especially after the Zoning Resolution of 1916 made it more advantageous for developers to do so.[108] They chose one version of Flagg's light-court plan, using a 50-foot-wide module which the new law favored. In 1911 Flagg had used that plan successfully for his West 47th Street tenements in which he skillfully obtained twenty-eight rooms per floor, the greatest number of rooms achieved under the provisions of the 1901 law and equal in number to the dumb-bell plan.[109]

After the First World War a new housing pattern emerged. Architects now focused on the economical and social value of organizing the entire Manhattan block according to residential needs. Some, like Stokes, still admired the light-court plan. In surveying its forty-year history in 1936, Stokes concluded that in spite of improvements to Flagg's model plan, "no better type of walk-up tenement for the independent 100′ × 100′ city lot has ever been devised."[110] But as early as 1901 Stokes had prepared, as part of the Report of the Tenement House Commission, a perimeter block plan for "park tenements" modeled after nineteenth-century British philanthropic housing and A. T. White's Brooklyn tenements. There the long sides of an entire New York City block were lined with tenement buildings leaving the interior reserved for gardens and playgrounds.[111] Although Stokes never executed his plan, other architects after the First World War adapted it to philanthropic and middle-class housing. The most innovative proponent of the plan, Andrew J. Thomas, used it for the Dunbar Apartments at 149th and 150th streets, between Seventh and Eighth avenues (1926–28), financed by John D. Rockefeller for black families on a cooperative plan.[112] As the originator of the middle-class "garden apartment," Thomas made it a fixture of New York City boroughs as exemplified by the Homewood Garden Apartments, Brooklyn (1919), sponsored by the City and Suburban Homes Company.[113]

The light-court plan was a critical step in the evolution of housing standards from the 25 × 100-foot lot of the late nineteenth century to the perimeter block plan of the 1920s. While Flagg developed the principle of the aggregate lot, limiting it to a discrete tenement building module, Stokes and others expanded the notion by developing an entire block as a residential unit. Yet Flagg considered the development of a whole city block economically unfeasible because of the capital it required for land acquisition and building construction. After the First World War there were two avenues open to

128.   Ernest Flagg. Mills House No. 1 (now The Atrium), 160 Bleecker Street, New York City, 1896–97 (New-York Historical Society).

257

developers: private investment in residential quarters away from the center of Manhattan (as, for example, the Dunbar Apartments), or municipal acquisition of land for urban renewal. Flagg's laissez-faire attitude toward government intervention kept him from endorsing the second approach.

Mills Houses

Both Flagg's model plan and the concept of investment philanthropy extended to lodging houses for single men — so-called workingmen's hotels. In 1896, Darius Ogden Mills, the New York banker, philanthropist, and politician, commissioned Flagg to design two workingmen's hotels: Mills House No. 1 at 160 Bleecker Street (now remodeled as ''The Atrium,'' a condominium) of 1896–97 (Fig. 128), and Mills House No. 2 on the Lower East Side at Rivington and Chrystie streets (1896–98; demolished).[114] Philanthropic incentive was no different for workingmen's hotels than for model tenements. Following the principle of the Rowton Houses, London, the Mills hotel enterprise was, according to D.O. Mills, ''in no sense a charitable concern,'' and that it was to be managed ''in a strictly business way.''[115]

Mills House No. 1 was the earlier, larger, more complex, and celebrated of Flagg's two hotels. It joined together two ten-story blocks with a tower.[116] This workingmen's hotel shared with Flagg's model tenement houses a similar structure, use of materials, and plan. Of brick construction with concrete floors, Mills House No. 1 was considered fireproof. Each block contained its own 50-foot-square light-court (Fig. 129). Banking the perimeter of its two courtyards were 1,500 bedroom cubicles, each measuring a

129. Ernest Flagg. Mills House No. 1. Plan of upper floors (*Works*, fig. 40).

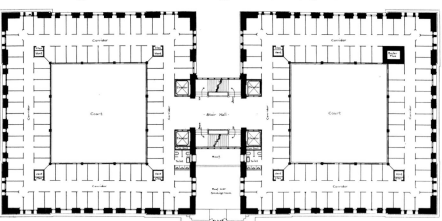

130.   Ernest Flagg. Mills House No. 1. Court smoking and lounging room
(Zeisloft, *The New Metropolis,* p. 245).

131.   Ernest Flagg. Mills House No. 1. Plan of mezzanine (*Review of
Reviews* XV, January 1897, p. 60).

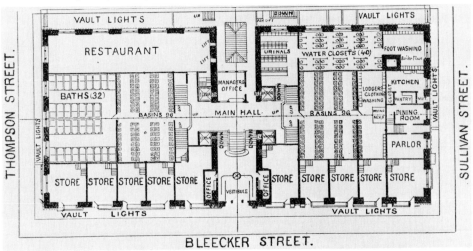

cramped 5 × 7 feet. Flagg regarded the bedroom cubicle as the module. Like the autonomous apartment unit of the tenement house, each bedroom had access to light and air through a window, either on the street or on the court. Flagg composed the windows of the facade into groups of six to alleviate "a jail-like appearance."[117] Metal played an ornamental as well as a structural and a functional role, with wrought-iron brackets defining the cornice. Metal-and-glass-covered light-courts, embellished with palms and other plants, provided gentlemanly sitting rooms (Fig. 130). These served the same social function as the glazed courts of Godin's workers' housing in France. The Mills hotel demonstrated Flagg's notion of scientific planning. With stores on the ground and mezzanine levels, residential and commercial functions were mixed. Areas were specified according to function: a basement restaurant served four hundred men; reading and smoking rooms occupied the first floor, while a second restaurant, baths, a complete self-service laundry, and washrooms were ingeniously planned on the mezzanine (Fig. 131). Elevators serviced all floors.[118]

Such business and community leaders as D. O. Mills used the model lodging house to promote social control. Similar to other New York institutions in the nineteenth century, especially the Young Men's Christian Association (YMCA), the founding of the Mills houses was underscored by a desire to regulate conduct and to achieve moral betterment and upward mobility for single workingmen. Like the YMCAs, the Mills houses responded to the swelling migration of unattached young workingmen from rural areas to New York City during the last decade of the century, increasing the supply of cheap lodging through the construction of new buildings.[119] Aside from the absence of recreational facilities, the program and amenities of Mills House No. 1, with its glazed light-court and bedroom cubicles, served as a model for YMCA design.[120]

In keeping with the management principles of model tenement houses, lodgers would include only "the class that are seeking work and have not found steady employment, or . . . those whose wages require that they live cheaply and economically."[121] The daily press reported that "tramps and objectionable persons will be rigidly excluded."[122] When the Mills houses opened, their clients were clerks, salesmen, and professional men.[123] These hotels offered an unparalleled opportunity for the male "bachelor" in New York City. In 1897 a lodger could receive a room at No. 1 for twenty-five cents a night and a meal for fifteen or twenty cents with, as the ads promised, "no exasperating extras."[124] In return, a guest was subjected to community standards — the Mills house rules. Indeed, during working hours from nine to five, lodgers were barred from their own rooms.[125] Some compared the service at the Mills houses to the service at first-class hotels. But first-class hotels they were not.

Reaction to the two Mills hotels was mixed. On the one hand, they provided the city with a total of nearly 2,000 rooms, or 12 percent of the cheap single lodging supply, thereby helping to stabilize a drifting urban population.[126] They also attempted to alleviate the problems associated with single males in tenement houses who, as one writer charged, were "threatening the health of the families and frightfully corrupting the morals of the girls."[127] On the other hand, such superior lodgings might only encourage desertion of married men to these surrogate homes. Some reformers deplored the fact that similar inexpensive accommodations were not equally available to women or married couples. In looking beyond the individual merits or defects of the hotels, one observer blamed the industrial system which favored the employment of unmarried men who were often willing to work for less pay. Because the system "puts a premium on celibacy," he argued, "such an hotel is necessary."[128] In sum, the Mills hotels responded effectively to the short-term housing needs of a small but significant number of men. However much a reformer such as Jacob Riis criticized the first Mills house, or its system of enlightened capitalism, he still recognized the value of "a business concern that simply strives to give the poor lodger his money's worth."[129]

Flagg Court

Paternalism and philanthropic investment, two motivating factors in the construction and management of tenement houses and workingmen's hotels, also shaped Flagg's interest in middle-class apartment houses during the Depression. When the New York Central Railroad acquired rights to about half of the Tenth Avenue tenements and the entire group of tenements at 506–516 West 47th Street, their forced sale in 1931 and subsequent demolition obliged the Model Fireproof Tenement Company and Flagg (who owned the 47th Street tenement outright) to reinvest their capital to avoid a taxable gain.[130] That year, without federal assistance, they courageously purchased a plot of land in the Bay Ridge section of Brooklyn and Flagg set out to design garden apartments.[131] Completed in 1937, Flagg Court at 7200 Ridge Boulevard occupied the entire block between 72nd and 73rd streets, although only six of the intended eight apartment houses were ever constructed (Fig. 132).[132] Housing 425 families, Flagg Court was an exceptional enterprise by any

132. Ernest Flagg. Flagg Court, 7200 Ridge Boulevard, Bay Ridge,
Brooklyn, 1932–37.

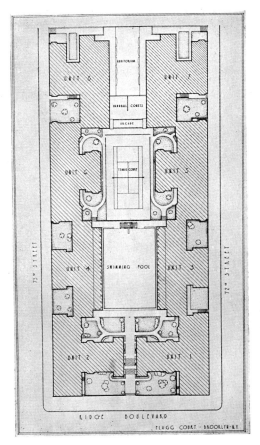

133. Ernest Flagg.
Flagg Court. Plan (*Addition
to Flagg Court,* p. 12).

standards, but particularly by those of the Depression years. The name "Flagg Court," like Rockefeller Center (a commercial counterpart of the period), connoted the paternalistic objectives of its owner. In contrast to the work of speculative builders, who required a complete and immediate return on their capital, Flagg Court was conceived as a long-term investment and praised for its fireproof construction, quality equipment, and amenities.[133] Flagg held the property until his death in 1947. A year later his estate sold it for $2.1 million.[134]

In its massing, use of materials, and plan, Flagg Court followed the recent precedents of Andrew Thomas and of Flagg's own Celtic Park Apartments, Long Island City, built in 1932 for the City and Suburban Homes Company.[135] The towers of Flagg Court with their roof-top pergolas followed the example of the Knickerbocker Village on the Lower East Side (designed,

263

built, and financed by the Fred. F. French Company in 1933–34), which, in turn, derived from Sir Edwin Lutyens's Grosvenor House, Park Lane, London, of 1930.[136] In effect, Flagg developed the garden apartment into a middle-class counterpart of a grand hotel.

Flagg Court grouped together nine-story apartment buildings to form a perimeter block plan around an open courtyard. Each building was indented on both the street and courtyard sides to allow small garden courts and a greater exposure to light and air (Fig. 133). In an effort to mitigate the institutional effects of such cliff-like buildings, Flagg applied (often inappropriately) picturesque details associated with small houses. Limestone string courses, a scalloped molding supported by metal brackets, and a brick parapet with ornamental perforations linked together the indented masses. Clinker bricks produced richly textured wall surfaces. Like Andrew Thomas's garden apartment, The Towers at Jackson Heights (1924), Flagg's courtyard was depressed below grade.[137] It demonstrated Flagg's further debt to Lutyens. The courtyard employed three elements of Lutyens's imagery, especially in his buildings for the capital at New Delhi, completed in 1931: the arcaded veranda, pool garden, and *chattri* (a Hindu pergola or sun shelter).[138] But Flagg transformed Lutyens's formal elements into recreational ones. The focus

134. Ernest Flagg. Flagg Court. Swimming pool (Flagg Family Papers).

of the Brooklyn courtyard was a swimming pool with *chattris* strategically positioned (Fig. 134). A tennis court and auditorium were axially disposed behind the pool. Access to recreational rooms on the basement level was through the arcaded veranda.

With its "healthful surroundings," Flagg Court offered opportunities for the urban middle class to enjoy the illusion of suburban life.[139] For example, tiled surfaces and sun shelters on the roof of Flagg Court allowed tenants to enjoy a "breeze from off the ocean."[140] But its suburban amenities were also a means for social control. Flagg Court's paternalism was as self-evident in the facilities and services it offered — a restaurant, a dance academy, clubrooms for boys and girls, even a day-care center to supervise children for "shopping mothers," as opposed to working ones — as in the management's policies, particularly the discriminatory selection of tenants.[141]

In applying the principles of scientific planning to apartment houses, which Flagg had developed through four decades of model tenement house design and construction, he demonstrated that they could be built and managed on a competitive basis. With its concrete-frame and hollow-tile construction, the ceiling heights of Flagg Court were reduced to 8 feet, thereby obtaining nine stories from building heights usually required for seven.[142] Flagg's notion of science also extended to his own patented inventions. These apartment houses were ingeniously equipped with reversible fans inserted in the wall and rolling window shades mounted on the outside in the French manner (see Fig. 143).[143]

In assessing the housing reform movement from 1894 to the Depression, one sees Flagg's role as fraught with contradiction. Although Flagg served only briefly as a member of the COS Tenement House Committee, he used his influence successfully to promote the tenement house legislation of 1901, which favored the adoption of his plan. Later he charged that the new law overregulated tenements, a view eventually shared by Stokes.[144] Because they were too costly to construct and rent, such tenement houses, according to Flagg, were economically "beyond the means of the ordinary tenement dweller."[145] Flagg said that he wanted to provide low-cost affordable housing for the blue-collar tenant, and yet, like the City and Suburban Homes Company, he always strove for what Veiller described as "the best class of working people."[146] If there was discrimination in tenant selection, there were conflicts in his motives. Flagg wanted to cure "the tenement house evil," but he also wanted to make a profit; science would provide a way out of the dilemma through economy of design and construction. Flagg's notions of science em-

265

braced three aspects of his work: first, a light-court plan based on French design; second, the new American technology of structural steel and reinforced concrete construction, even though they were more expensive to employ and were often not yet accepted in the building trades; and, third, his own patented "custom-designed" devices, such as wall partitions. While his light-court plan was easily transmitted and highly influential, making Flagg a paternal figure in the tenement house reform movement, other aspects of his design which promised economy were not so easily transmitted, especially to speculative builders. Flagg benefited financially from his system. It was through his full or partial ownership of several tenements, two loft buildings, and Flagg Court, rather than through his architectural practice, that he attained economic status as a man of wealth and property.

Given the strengths and weaknesses of the New York housing reform movement during the Progressive Era, Flagg's light-court plan and the tenement houses and workingmen's hotels which employed it were nevertheless extremely effective contributions. Flagg's aggregate plan had been naturally adapted to Manhattan's street grid. In applying the planning concepts of upper-class housing to low-income realities, the Flagg model raised the standard of the cheap housing stock. In the absence of restrictive legislation and public support for such multiple dwellings, perhaps the only failure of the Flagg model was to provide insufficient housing with the private capital it required. After the First World War, with adequate enforceable legislation and increased investment capital, tenements and garden apartments, such as Flagg Court, employed the perimeter block plan as a preferred solution to high-density residential needs.

CHAPTER NINE

Small Houses of Modular Design

IN THE DESIGN and construction of small stone houses, Flagg formed a tenuous alliance between theory and practice. His interest in small houses began about 1908 with the first of a series of building experiments on his Staten Island estate at Dongan Hills. Later, with the help of other architects, builders, magazine editors, and writers who supported his ideas, Flagg's designs were employed for single houses in the New York region, for government-sponsored housing in Pennsylvania during the First World War, and for whole colonies of houses as far away as Los Angeles. In the face of postwar housing shortages and rising building costs, Flagg attempted to make new housing affordable to the middle class. The decade of the twenties marked a resurgence of stone houses in suburban areas and on country estates by housing specialists including Mellor, Meigs & Howe, and Aymar Embury. But Flagg's objectives, like those of Grosvenor Atterbury, Clarence Stein, and Henry Wright, were more comprehensive; his impact extended beyond individual houses to entire communities.

Flagg's small stone houses looked deceptively simple, for their vernacular appearance actually belied a high level of formalism which conditioned their design. Four elements comprised Flagg's aspirations for the small house: the use of a module, or fixed unit of measure, to facilitate design; a system of proportional relationships that he claimed to derive from Greek architecture; economical methods of construction (using Flagg's patented inventions); and the possibility of self-building. In applying such formalism to the comparatively simple, even banal, requirements of small-house design and construction, Flagg forged an uneasy merger of theory and practice. In the end, it was their regional and vernacular characteristics that gave these houses their cohesive sense of place.

Flagg's interest in small houses followed the gradual decline of his large architectural practice with the completion of the United States Naval Academy and the Singer Tower in 1908. It also coincided with a building recession, the so-called panic of 1907. Throughout the following four decades until his death in 1947, Flagg enjoyed greater leisure time to devote to projects outside his office practice. He kept a daily diary (1908–14), patented over thirty inventions (most relating to construction techniques), pursued civic and professional activities, managed his estate, and lived comfortably from property investment income.[1] He was surrounded by a devoted family and was, in turn, a devoted, if autocratic, husband and father. The Flaggs traveled to Europe in the summers of 1908, 1910, and 1924. Flagg also published three books which together summarized his current interests in small-house design and construction, Flagg family genealogy, and the principles of Greek architecture: *Small Houses: Their Economic Design and Construction* (1922), *Genealogical Notes on the Founding of New England: My Ancestors Part in that Undertaking* (1926), and *The Parthenon Naos* (1928). But the role of Flagg's family and estate were central. Toward the end of his life, as he openly professed his atheist position on religion, he wrote, "I can say without fear of any . . . consequences that . . . heaven is a happy home, with freedom from bodily ills and financial embarrassment, and that hell is the opposite of that condition."[2]

The notion of a module in architectural design preoccupied Flagg as an object of serious study from about the time of the First World War, although he had discovered the advantages of using a module much earlier and, like most other things, had done so in a pragmatic way. Even though many architects employed modular design, Flagg claimed that he had first learned to rely on the module as a shortcut method of design when he was at the Ecole des Beaux-Arts: "I first drew in all the axial lines of the plan. They formed squares so nearly equal that I decided to make them equal . . . that perhaps in this way harmony of proportion might be obtained with certainty."[3] Throughout his long architectural career, Flagg consistently applied a modular method of design to virtually all building types. A module of 2 feet 2¾ inches was used for St. Luke's Hospital. At the Corcoran Gallery of Art, the module was 3 feet 6 inches; its "lines were indicated on the structure, by the points of the cheneau." At the United States Naval Academy, a larger module of 8 feet 4 inches "governs both the plans of the buildings themselves and their arrangement on the grounds."[4]

In his articles, books, and ongoing research for two unpublished manuscripts, "The Recovery of Art" and "Stone Houses of Modular Design,"

Flagg sought to understand Greek principles of design and the writings of Vitruvius, the Roman architect and theorist.[5] Although Flagg accepted Vitruvius's theory of harmonic proportions based on the human form and on a study of Greek architecture, he took a too literal interpretation of Vitruvius's "doctrine [which] relates to the lower diameter of the column as the module and to his various formulas for the design of the orders."[6] Flagg failed to understand Vitruvius's appreciation for the flexibility of the module in Greek architecture. Taking his cue from Julien Guadet, Flagg attacked Vitruvius's theory, as he understood it, for its deleterious effect on classicism: "Instead of a simple way of obtaining harmony and preserving rhythm in architecture by measure, as in music and in poetry, we have been taught *architecture chiffrée* [a mathematical approach to architecture], as Guadet says."[7] Using the data of European architects and archaeologists, Flagg attempted to replace Vitruvius's theory of the module with one using standard measurements and correspondingly simple proportional relationships.[8]

Flagg's theory of the module was keyed to a particular measurement, such as the width of a bay, which might govern the proportions of a single temple. In the Parthenon, Flagg showed how the width of the bay, as well as the length and width of the top step of the stylobate, were dimensions based on the number 13. Flagg identified this number as the module and, therefore, "the key of the Parthenon peristyle."[9] Ironically, Flagg's notion of the module relied as much on specific numbers as did his interpretation of Vitruvius's theory; and his charge that Vitruvius's notion of the module was too rigid could be applied to his own theory. Moreover, although Flagg claimed to have identified simple proportional relationships in Greek design (1 to 2, 2 to 3, 3 to 4), he also found proportional relationships that were not so simple. In his own mind, Flagg's understanding of Greek principles of design justified (after the fact) variations in the sizes of modules in his building types. In formulating his modular theory based on actual measurements, Flagg thought that he was proceeding in a manner that was rational, scientific, and French. Yet Flagg's idiosyncratic understanding of the Greek use of the module was at odds both with his own time and with contemporary theory. Thus, in the 1920s when Flagg misinterpreted and rejected Vitruvius's notion of the module, he was militating against a broadly accepted theory. In 1924 Flagg traveled to Paris and presented his findings before a meeting of the Institut de France. His reception bristled with hostility.[10]

In short, to find evidence of the module, Flagg looked to Greek architecture because it illustrated the most elementary principles of design. But

Flagg failed to explain why his use of the module was particularly Greek. It could have come equally from J.N.L. Durand or from a long tradition of classicism. Moreover, Flagg superimposed the module on a system of proportional relationships, derived from Greek architecture; but his explanation of the way in which the module was related to them was confused, his allusions often too intellectualized or implausible. In spite of its shortcomings, Flagg's use of the module became increasingly significant in his own work through its application to the design and construction of small houses. Flagg's notion of the module sheds further light on his personality, for he worked in isolation. Flagg was immensely creative. But he was also frequently naive, often arrogant, and usually stubborn. These characteristics encouraged his original ideas, but worked to limit his influence.

Yet Flagg was not the only one seeking to understand either Greek principles of design or modular theory; for this had been a preoccupation not only of French architects, but also of American artists and architects of his generation. Among them, Jay Hambidge (1867–1924) maintained that Greek art and architecture were consciously based on mathematical principles of proportion which he called "dynamic symmetry." In a series of publications he, like Flagg, applied Greek principles to modern design.[11] Claude Bragdon (1866–1946) also published studies on proportional systems, including *The Beautiful Necessity* (1910). Flagg, Hambidge, and Bragdon pursued a course which each predicted to be comprehensive and revolutionary but was, actually, of limited significance. A number of architects also shared Flagg's efforts to apply modular principles of design to economical methods of construction. E. T. Potter, for example, designed a housing system based on a module. Frank Lloyd Wright's Usonian houses most nearly paralleled Flagg's small houses; the Usonian houses of the thirties and forties employed modules, eliminated attics and large cellars, and employed innovative low-cost methods of construction including the possibility of self-building.[12]

First on Flagg's Staten Island estate, later for paying clients, for government-sponsored housing toward the end of the First World War, and even for other architects and developers who adopted his methods of modular design and construction, hundreds, perhaps thousands, of these small stone houses were built.[13] In their design and construction, Flagg applied a module of 3 feet 9 inches. When compared with the modules of Flagg's designs for institutions, the small-house module was relatively large. Flagg justified it on the basis of a convenience to standardized building materials; for example, the 3-foot 9-inch module would adapt itself to "standard lengths of lumber . . . graded at two-foot intervals."[14] The dimension of this module would allow a margin for any inconsistencies in the length of precut lumber.

In preparing working drawings, Flagg used yellow-lined graph paper which he had specially prepared. The 3-foot 9-inch module was divided into five parts, each 9-inch part corresponding to a line on the graph paper. Flagg's French training influenced him to rationalize the design process, using graph paper *(papier quadrillé)*. He was especially aware of Durand whose *Précis des leçons* Flagg credited with "setting forth the advantages of this method of planning," namely economy and utility—the same reasons that compelled Flagg to use it.[15] Guadet also recommended the use of *papier quadrillé*.[16] Flagg may also have known that earlier Thomas Jefferson was similarly influenced by his French experience to employ graph paper.[17]

From 1897 when he purchased his first parcel of land on Staten Island, until his death a half-century later, Flagg was continuously engaged in an aggressive campaign of land acquisition. By the Second World War his holdings on Staten Island were so vast that in 1946 he could offer 17 of his 300 acres of land in the Todt Hill section as a site for the new United Nations.[18] Such land acquisitions were extensions of Flagg's interest in estate management and attempts to consolidate his position on Staten Island.

After 1908, when his large office practice began to decline, Flagg lived in his Manhattan town house and retreated to Staten Island on weekends and during the summer to pursue leisure activities, which for him consisted of building. Flagg thought of his estate as an experimental building farm, the house and grounds continually undergoing what he called "improvements." These included a first wave of extensive alterations to "Stone Court" (from 1907 to 1909) and the earliest of Flagg's small stone houses.

The remodeling of the Gate House into a two-story house, completed in the spring of 1908, and the construction of another house on the estate launched Flagg's enduring interest in small stone houses.[19] The second of these, a two-and-a-half story stone house adjacent to the greenhouses, was the gardener's cottage. This L-shaped house with its stone wall formed an enclosed courtyard. There Flagg claimed to be using a "new approach," which anticipated a type of house he called in 1910 the "cloister house," designed "about a hollow square."[20] That year Flagg also began to design a small colony of cloister houses for Edwin Ginn near his house in the Rangely section of Winchester, Massachusetts (see Fig. 74). This project for thirteen cloister houses was still under discussion in the last years before Ginn's death in 1914.[21]

271

During the First World War, as increasing leisure was forced upon Flagg, he continued to design and supervise the construction of other small stone houses employing the same materials as "Stone Court" and picturesquely sited in relationship to it. From 1906, Flagg was assisted by his chauffeur and estate superintendent, Alfred Beaver, a former seaman and a native of Staten Island. With Beaver and a crew of workmen, Flagg realized his theories and his patented inventions with actual construction. Even though he continued to employ locally quarried soapstone, Flagg adapted it to concrete construction techniques.

During the winter of 1916–17 Flagg began to build what Sutcliffe called "the new type of houses . . . on the delightful sites he has for cottages on his large estate."[22] These were "Bowcot" (1916–18) at the corner of Flagg Place and West Entry Road (Fig. 135); Tower House on Flagg Place (1920–22; demolished); and "House-on-the-Wall" or "Wallcot" (1918–22) on Flagg Place (Fig. 136).[23] With their structural, aesthetic, and financial success

135.   Ernest Flagg. "Bowcot," Flagg Place, Staten Island, 1916–18 (Flagg Family Papers).

272

(Flagg rented them), he continued to develop his property into a colony of small stone houses, an Anglo-French village he called the Flegg Ridge Estate. Photographs and drawings of completed houses, as well as designs for future ones, appeared in his deluxe handbook of 1922, *Small Houses: Their Economic Design and Construction.* Flagg conceived of his book as a building prospectus for the Flegg Ridge Estate. Three other houses, including the South Gate House at 180 Coventry Road (formerly Todt Hill Road; 1921), first occupied by Alfred Beaver; Hickling Hollow, 309 Flagg Place (1922); and the McCall House at 1929 Richmond Road (1924), occupied by Flagg's secretary, Agnes Tehan, were clustered around the periphery of "Stone Court" on Flagg's estate (Fig. 137).[24] There are several more Flagg-designed houses on Staten Island, built for paying clients. The Paul Revere Smith House at 143 Four Corners Road (1923–24) was built for a sailor at a cost of $15,000.[25] Behind it is situated the so-called Honeymoon Cottage, built for the artist Florence Frank at 143½ Four Corners Road (1926).[26] The John W. Morris House at 208

136.   Ernest Flagg. "House-on-the-Wall," or "Wallcot," Flagg Place, Staten Island, 1918–22 (Flagg Family Papers).

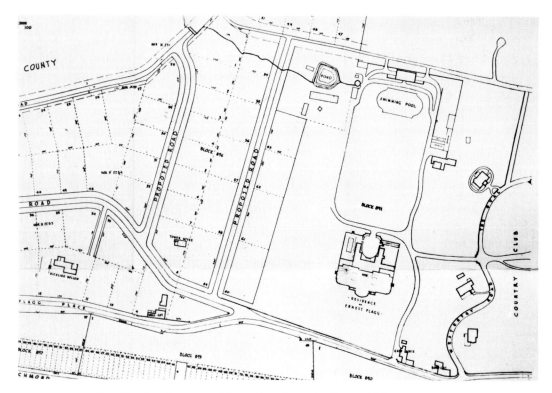

137. Plan from Prospectus of Ernest Flagg Properties, Dongan Hills,
Staten Island, c. 1940 (author's collection).

Neal Dow Avenue (1924–25) was built in the Westerleigh section of Staten
Island.[27]

These local examples demonstrated Flagg's prime objectives of finding
economical means for improving the design and construction of small houses.
Alternating chapters on the theoretical and the practical in Flagg's book, *Small
Houses,* illustrated his original methods. Remaining true to his Beaux-Arts
training, Flagg charged these modest homes with the high ideals of classicism
and rationalism. Renewing his allegiance to the legacies of Charles Blanc,
Viollet-le-Duc, Julien Guadet, and even John Ruskin, Flagg demonstrated
how to obtain "truth" and "beauty" economically through "architectural"
means, rather than "applied ornament," and "archaeological methods."[28] He
regarded his stone houses as examples of "artistic construction."[29] They illustrated the ideals of decorated structure and the rational premise of his sustained
commitment to architecture as opposed to archaeology. Flagg's small stone

274

houses also confirmed his belief in the fundamental principles of Beaux-Arts classicism including varied symmetry, order, and balance.[30]

Flagg's use of the module also relied on the same simple harmonic proportions, such as 2 to 3 or 3 to 4, that he had observed both in Greek temples and in the modest houses of American colonial builders.[31] "These people," Flagg insisted, "were obtaining unconsciously the same kind of proportions as used by the Greeks."[32] Flagg chose similar elementary harmonics for his own small houses. In a typical working drawing on graph paper of the South Gate House, the modules help to establish those simple proportional relationships (Fig. 138).

The practical elements of Flagg's architecture buttress theory in a very personal way. Due to the rising cost of wood, its decreasing supply after the First World War, and its potential as a fire hazard, Flagg advocated "stone for

138. Ernest Flagg. South Gate House, Coventry Road, Staten Island. Working drawing (original on yellow-lined graph paper), 1921 (Flagg, *Small Houses: Their Economic Design and Construction,* p. 2; No. 1).

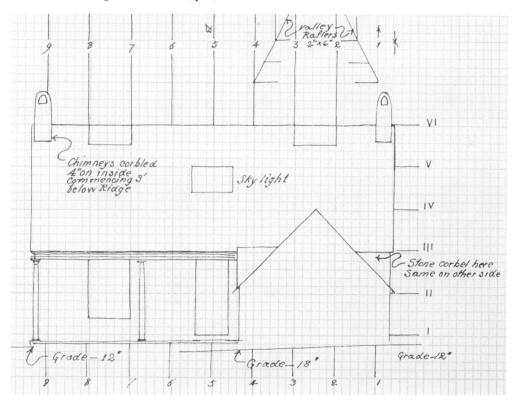

139. Flagg method of
board-forming (Flagg, *Small
Houses: Their Economic
Design and Construction,*
p. 19, No. 9).

ordinary houses."[33] Although Flagg may have regarded these small houses as
"ordinary," his building methods and his designs were not. Construction in
stone, "king of building materials," Flagg proclaimed, needed an economical
method of building walls.[34] Flagg devised one. Using a locally quarried
serpentine soapstone backed with concrete, Flagg employed a technique of
formwork to construct walls. Although its origins were classical, the use of
forms or temporary boards for casting concrete, revived in the nineteenth
century, had become a traditional American method of construction.[35] Yet
Flagg made no mention of its modern use in his publications and chose instead
to acknowledge a technique of formwork which he understood the Romans
had used. For practical problems, like theoretical ones, Flagg consulted French
interpreters of Roman methods, in particular Auguste Choisy, the French
engineer and writer who influenced Le Corbusier at about the same time. In his
L'Art de bâtir chez les Romains of 1873, Choisy explained how the Romans
had used forms for building walls, but only for simple stone ones, and not for
concrete walls faced with stone.[36] However, Flagg believed that the Romans

276

had also used formwork for stone-and-concrete walls—views confirmed by recent scholarship.[37] He thus adapted a Roman system of concrete wall construction employing reusable wood shuttering and patented his design.[38] A foundation wall was first aligned to modular lines marked on the ground. Standardized wooden forms, consisting of uprights and cross-pieces, were secured to foundation sleepers (without the use of nails) to form a trough. Stones were placed inside the trough with their flat sides flush with the outer face of the wall to form a mosaic pattern. Concrete was subsequently poured around the dry stones to form the backing (Fig. 139). The wood shuttering (like the Roman model) was later removed and reassembled at a higher point in the wall. The finished wall, which Flagg called "mosaic rubble," was about 12 inches thick.[39] The technique of setting stone in concrete resulted in a cross between a poured concrete wall and a masonry wall; a similar concept was later used by Wright at Taliesen West, near Phoenix, Arizona (1938–59), and by Eero Saarinen at Morse and Stiles colleges, Yale University in New Haven (1960–62).

The small stone houses that Flagg designed were unique because of their methods of design and construction, as well as their use of Flagg's patented inventions and distinctive construction details. Since the economy of stone construction dictated low rather than high walls, Flagg designed tall spreading roofs that were steeply pitched. To allow light to reach the upper spaces of these atticless houses in a manner he believed the Greeks to have used in lighting the interiors of their temples, Flagg invented a so-called ridge-dormer window, situated along the ridge of the roof (Fig. 140).[40] As a means of natural ventilation, the ridge-dormer was designed to be opened each spring, closed each fall.[41] Interiors were dramatically altered both by the ridge-dormer (Fig. 141) and by Flagg's other inventions, including fireproof wall partitions, which he first patented in 1908. Each partition, only about 1¾ inches thick, consisted of plaster applied to both sides of a jute, burlap, or wire screen, stapled to the floor and ceiling, without wooden studs (Fig. 142).[42] Among the fifty or more details and methods of construction that Flagg published in his manuals, *Small Houses* and "Standard Details of Construction" (1928), were patented designs for rolled roof coverings, hinges and locks, and outside window shades (Fig. 143), in addition to those for concrete wall construction, ridge-dormers, and fireproof partitions.[43] At the fringe of the efficiency movement, Flagg's crusade was a private affair.

At the same time that Flagg worked on inventions for small houses, he also obtained patents for a sleeping car containing roomettes with "duplex" berths. Earlier, such architects as H. H. Richardson and Bruce Price had applied their skills to railroad car design.[44] But among the architects of his own generation, Flagg was unusual in the breadth of his design interests. The Pullman Company in Chicago and the Canadian National Railways in Montreal maintained lengthy negotiations with Flagg from 1924 to 1938. They even went so far as to make models of Flagg's design with its duplex berths and patented treadle-operated urinal. The Canadian National Railways also issued a promotional brochure illustrating "The Flagg Car" (Fig. 144). In the end, however, neither company adopted his patented sleeping car.[45] By the Depression the railroad sleeping car was on the decline and such companies were forced to retrench.[46]

Flagg's patented details of construction made his small stone houses distinctive for their time. But other characteristics, including their concern for human comfort and energy efficiency, make them distinctive today. These small stone houses have thick masonry walls, some with porches and overhanging roofs on the south and west sides (which block the summer sun), in

140. Ernest Flagg. "Bowcot," ridge-dormer (Flagg, *Small Houses: Their Economic Design and Construction*, p. 9, No. 4).

141.   Ernest Flagg. "Bowcot," interior with ridge-dormer (Flagg, *Small Houses: Their Economic Design and Construction*, p. 9, No. 5).

addition to shutters, outside window shades, and ridge-dormers. As Wright had advocated earlier, Flagg omitted large cellars because they were damp and attics because they were hot in summer and cold in winter and wasted space.[47]

  Flagg's aspirations for these small houses involved two spheres of activity: the private realm within his Dongan Hills estate, and the public arena

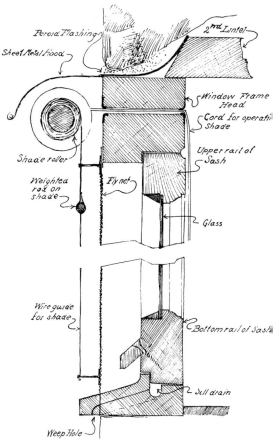

142.   Ernest Flagg. Fireproof partition (Flagg,
*Small Houses: Their Economic Design and
Construction,* p. 30, No. 19).

143.   Ernest Flagg. Outside window shade (Flagg,
*Small Houses: Their Economic Design and
Construction,* p. 38, No. 12, fig. 2).

of his office practice. Within the first sphere, these small houses represented
Flagg's consummate effort to develop an ancestral estate while perpetuating
the colonial, topographical, and vernacular building tradition of Staten Island.
In theory, they relied on the same simple harmonic proportions that Flagg
recognized in the houses of American colonial builders. In practice, the designs,
details, and scale of these houses looked back both to eighteenth-century
classicism (including Anglo-American, Dutch, and Huguenot) and to more
distant examples of Anglo-French or Norman and Romanesque architecture.
With their masonry walls of locally quarried stone, steeply pitched roofs,
turrets, and tall chimneys with curved ventilation caps, all picturesquely
designed, Flagg's small houses emulated both the Norman architecture of the
Cotswold Hills in England and the Romanesque architecture in the regions of

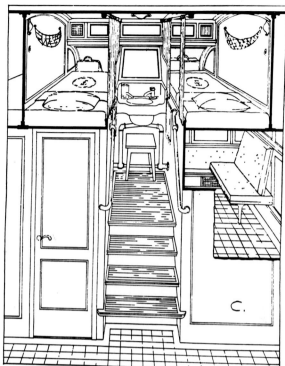

144. Ernest Flagg. Sleeping
Car with "duplex" berths.
Section drawings (*The Flagg Car,*
p. 4; ATSP, AL, CU).

C.

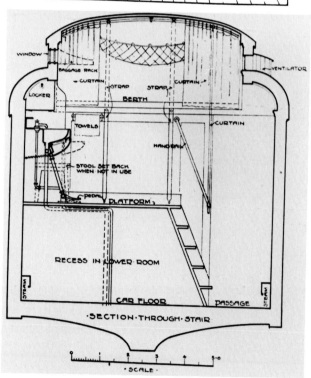

WINDOW
BAGGAGE RACK
CURTAIN
STRAP   STRAP
CURTAIN
VENTILATOR
LOCKER
BERTH
TOWELS
CURTAIN
HANDRAIL
STOOL SET BACK
WHEN NOT IN USE
PEDAL
PLATFORM
STEAM
RECESS IN LOWER ROOM
STEAM
CAR FLOOR   PASSAGE
·SECTION·THROUGH·STAIR·

·SCALE·

145.   Ernest Flagg. Memorial Church of the Huguenots (now Huguenot Reform Church), Amboy Road and Huguenot Avenue, 1923–24 (Flagg Family Papers).

Normandy and Brittany in France. Using French *Guides Joanne* and other guidebooks, Flagg studied Norman and Romanesque architecture firsthand during his student years from 1888 to 1890. On a return visit to France and England in 1908, Flagg purposely renewed his interest in the domestic architecture of the Ile-de-France, Normandy, and Brittany. His diary recorded visits to towns in Normandy (Evreux, Caen, Bayeux, and Mayenne) and Brittany (Pontivy) where he often photographed examples of domestic architecture as models for later house designs.[48] For example, the Governor's House at Coucy-le-Château in France served as the model for Hickling Hollow, Design No. 4 in *Small Houses,* while a house at Bayeux informed Design No. 42, which is similar to the Paul Revere Smith House.[49] As in vernacular examples of Norman and Romanesque architecture, Flagg's houses employed local materials; they were strategically sited, and they responded to topographical adjustments, changes in level, and existing landscape features such as stone walls. Flagg integrated the "House-on-the-Wall" with an existing retaining wall. Similarly, Flagg designed "Bowcot," as its name suggests, to conform to the bend in Flagg Place. René de Blonay, a Swiss architect working in the Flagg office during the twenties, later remarked that Flagg "was proud of the way these houses followed the road; he thought it very continental."[50] The names "Bowcot" and "Wallcot" derive from the vernacular stone cottages of the Cotswolds. Ingeniously sited, the design of "Bowcot" "empathized" with the topography and public character of the street. It was oriented to the garden, especially to terraces and courtyards. The house has no street entrance at all; access to it is from the garden or terrace. Like the domestic work of Mellor, Meigs & Howe in America or Edwin Lutyens in England, Flagg's houses conveyed an architecture of mood. The Anglo-French character of the Gate House, gardener's cottage, other outbuildings and small houses on Flagg's land, and the dozens of drawings for projects in *Small Houses,* confirm Flagg's intention to establish a Norman village on Staten Island as if it were his own ancestral village, the Flegg Ridge Estate. In effect, Flagg saw himself as a modern Huguenot, building with new construction techniques and thereby creating the illusion of an evolving architectural tradition native to Staten Island.

146.   Ernest Flagg. Memorial Church of the Huguenots (now Huguenot Reform Church), interior (Flagg Family Papers).

283

Flagg's objectives were further confirmed in his design for a Reformed Dutch church to commemorate the first settlement of French Huguenots and Walloons on Staten Island. As in his small houses, the Memorial Church of the Huguenots (now Huguenot Reform Church), Amboy Road and Huguenot Avenue of 1923–24, demonstrated Flagg's application of modular theory to concrete and mosaic rubble wall construction (Figs. 145, 146).[51] With its northern spire, ridge-dormers, curved ventilator caps, and skylight construction, this vaulted masonry and concrete structure illustrated Flagg's own brand of medievalism. Moreover, the church's stone vault, dramatically punctuated with oculi, was also reminiscent of the Roman cryptoporticus. Stone for the church was quarried on the site of an iron mine within Flagg's Todt Hill estate. Like the Paul Revere Smith House of the same period, the rich autumnal color of the stone was due to its high iron content and Flagg's method of cleaving it. When he synthesized a theory of classicism with vernacular forms from the Middle Ages, as in this church, Flagg recalled the abstract designs of his contemporary, Edwin Lutyens; and when he applied concrete construction to both ancient and medieval forms, he proceeded in the rational spirit of Viollet-le-Duc.

The second arena of Flagg's involvement in small houses concerned his office practice. Flagg intended his book, *Small Houses,* and his numerous articles to reach a wide audience. He publicized his methods of design and construction, but attempted to keep control over them. Those wishing to use his "processes and devices" were instructed to apply directly to Flagg for a license since many were covered by U.S. patents.[52]

Flagg's small houses demonstrated to other architects and builders some clear advantages of his unique methods of design and construction, but their full promise — sociological, economical, and functional — was not always realized. Flagg may have intended them to be affordable to all middle-income families, but most of his plans suggest a stratified household arrangement more characteristic of families of greater means. Of the fifty designs in *Small Houses,* forty-one contained accommodations for two or more servants.[53] Only six were servantless. In the Beaux-Arts manner, Flagg's plans specified six functional divisions: public part (living room and dining room), private quarters (bedrooms), service areas (kitchen and dependencies), communication, storage, and outdoor areas.[54] These divisions are clearly evident in the plans of "Bowcot" indicating rooms for two servants (Fig. 147).[55] On the one hand, Flagg thought that his most important contribution to American life was to reduce the cost of building, to make individual home ownership affordable

284

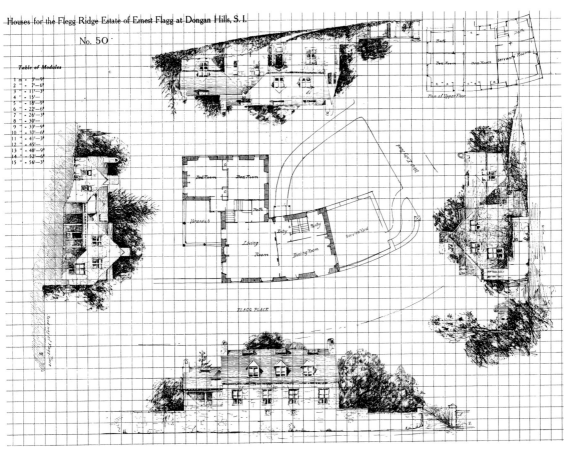

147.   Ernest Flagg. "Bowcot." Plans, 1916 (Flagg, *Small Houses: Their Economic Design and Construction*, p. 145, No. 50).

(in many instances he proved this to be so), and thereby bring stability to family life.[56] On the other hand, his designs for "small" houses requiring servants were still conditioned by class consciousness.

Although Flagg intended his methods to become widely adopted, his highly customized approach to design often impeded, rather than facilitated, his objectives. The Flagg method of stone and concrete construction using formwork eliminated expensive cut stone and thus the need for skilled masons. This gave the system a clear edge. But in other areas of design, execution, and maintenance, the Flagg method had its drawbacks. Even though Flagg insisted that his modular system of planning and his details of construction had the advantage of standardization and interchangeable parts, it made a more convincing theory than practice. Flagg's method depended on special graph paper and licenses to use his patented devices, obtainable only from his office. Moreover, many standard builders' dimensions were altered to fit the module. A standard 3-foot 3-inch door, for example, when widened to meet the 3-foot 9-inch module, created problems in hinging.[57] Flagg's methods of construction, according to a housing specialist of the period, were "wastefully expensive in materials."[58] Also, the soapstone was porous. To combat the inevitable problem of damp walls, owners resorted to the practice, in some cases annually, of painting the exteriors or repairing interior walls. The ridge-dormers leaked and the wall partitions did not adequately buffer sound.[59] Once again in Flagg's work, these small stone houses demonstrated a conflict between rationalism and functionalism, theory and practice.

Other architects and builders were nonetheless attracted to the aesthetics of these stone houses, as well as to their promise of economy and standardization. Flagg's methods, spread through the press in both popular journals and architectural publications, received national attention in the 1920s and 1930s. For example, *McCall's Magazine* ran a series in 1923, 1924, and 1925 which inspired Flagg to build the "McCall Demonstration House" or McCall House (1924) on Richmond Road.[60] Although there were many popularizers of Flagg's modular method of design and stone house construction, Harold Cary and Frazier Forman Peters were the most important.[61] Cary was Flagg's first and most ardent booster. In a series of articles and a best-selling book, *Build a Home — Save a Third* (1924), Cary exceeded Flagg's modest assertion that his methods of concrete and stone construction were "more economical in the long run" than either wood frame construction or conventional methods of masonry construction.[62]

In two articles for *Scientific American* and *Collier's*, Cary exaggerated Flagg's accomplishments and boldly claimed that Flagg had "put up more than 500 attractive houses at a savings of one-third their ordinary building cost."[63] In an effort to prove the economic value of Flagg's methods, *Collier's* financed the construction of two small houses which Cary, a writer with no prior experience in building, supervised. In 1924 the first Collier's House, located in Croton, New York, was constructed in seven months. It cost $10,767, a savings of one-third over conventional stone houses, but about the same cost as either stucco or frame construction.[64] A second Collier's House, smaller and more compact in plan, was built for $8,914, demonstrating the economic value of Flagg's method and the possibilities of self-building.[65] But other magazines such as *House Beautiful* published articles which sought to discredit Cary's exaggerated claims and even its own previous reports on Flagg's methods.[66]

Another popularizer of Flagg's methods, a builder named Frazier Forman Peters, constructed several houses in Westport, Connecticut, with Warren Matthews as architect.[67] Peters's first book, *Houses of Stone,* of 1933 enjoyed a wide circulation.[68] In it he accepted Flagg's methods of concrete and stone construction, but modifed the formwork. In subsequent books Peters continued to publicize the advantages of this method of construction over traditional masonry, but he shed any illusions as to the economic benefits of stone over frame houses.[69] By the late 1940s Peters had built nearly two hundred stone houses based on Flagg's methods of design but eliminating most of his idiosyncratic details and building techniques.[70] Other builders followed Peters.[71] Publicized by Flagg's *Small Houses,* as well as by Cary's articles and influential book and by Peters's books, Flagg's methods spread nationwide. Flagg had contractual agreements or direct associations with the construction of small houses based on his methods and designs as far away as Saint Louis, Los Angeles, and Milwaukee.[72] In his later years Flagg recollected with mixed emotion how "so called Flagg houses sprang up in many parts of the country which had little resemblance to the genuine article."[73]

In addition to the impact of Flagg's methods on middle-class housing, his system influenced several generations of self-sufficient homesteaders, among them Helen and Scott Nearing. Although the Nearings did not know Flagg personally, they shared his belief that "people of limited means and experience could build permanent, beautiful dwellings out of native stone."[74] Following their retreat to Vermont in the 1930s, the Nearings built their own stone houses at Forest Farm (1934–35) which they described and illustrated in their book of 1954, *Living the Good Life.*[75] Using Flagg's *Small Houses* as a guide, they "accepted the principles and applied them to *family* building — not professional — with skilled help of carpenters, electricians, etc."[76] Thus, even by those laymen who were most committed to implementing Flagg's ideas, skilled specialists were still required. Moreover, in some cases, the Nearings simplified and further economized the Flagg method by replacing Flagg-specified scaffolding and studs with furring strips to support the forms and eliminating his highly personal details.[77] A younger generation of self-builders in the 1960s and 1970s revived Flagg's methods for small houses because they considered them "alternative" building systems.[78] However, the most recent trend for self-builders is toward standardized techniques, rather than customized ones.[79]

Flagg's system was not generally accepted by established architects; but the Chicago-school architect, William Gray Purcell, was an exception. Impressed by what he called the "integrated system" outlined in Flagg's *Small Houses,* Purcell sent for sheets of Flagg's graph paper in 1927.[80] In a series of small stone houses built in the Northwest — the Bradford, Bastian, and Bell houses (Portland, Oregon) and the Todd House (Salmon Creek, Washington), all of 1927; and the Arnold House (Vancouver, Washington) of 1928 — Purcell adapted Flagg's methods of design and construction.[81] Most of the Purcell houses followed the simple massing of the Flagg model. Some, like the Todd House, even incorporated Flagg's patented details such as ridge-dormers. Most, however, used conventional rather than modular working drawings, since Purcell found that he "could not make firm contracts on Flagg drawings."[82] In acknowledging the merits of Flagg's book, *Small Houses,* Purcell later recalled that it "greatly influenced my approach to the American assembly."[83]

Flagg was given the opportunity to apply his methods to the wartime housing needs of an industrial village in 1918 with an order to design 650 houses for the Sun Shipbuilding plant at Chester, Pennsylvania.[84] This project, one of seventy-nine sites across the country, was sponsored by the U.S. Shipping Board's Emergency Fleet Corporation as part of a large program to ease the housing shortage by providing government housing for shipworkers.[85] In effect, such projects marked the government's first efforts to build public housing for wartime industrial workers.[86] Although Flagg, a staunch Republican, was opposed to the practice of government-financed housing, he made a patriotic (and self-interested) exception and solicited the work. In May 1918, Frederick L. Ackerman, Supervisor of Design for the U.S. Shipping Board, visited Flagg's Dongan Hills stone houses. Sufficiently convinced that the design and methods of construction of these houses, complete with their patented wall partitions and other Flagg-invented details, could be adapted to wartime housing, Ackerman retained Flagg as architect.[87]

In the Chester project called Sun Village, Flagg was commissioned to design fifteen types of multiple dwellings including two- and four-family houses, apartments, and houses with ground floor stores. Even though the street grid had largely been determined, Flagg was able to adjust the placement of units "in small groups about partly enclosed squares and on courts recessed from the streets," sharing the objectives of such garden city architects and planners as Grosvenor Atterbury, Clarence Stein, and Henry Wright (Fig. 148).[88] Some of Flagg's designs for multifamily houses (without servants) at

Sun Village were similar to those for single-family dwellings (with servants) in *Small Houses* (Fig. 149).[89] They shared a similar scale, massing, and many customized details such as ridge-dormers. At the same time, some of the Chester houses substituted red brick for more expensive stone, while others used frame construction, sometimes with stucco walls and generally with flared eaves reminiscent of the colonial architecture of the Dutch and Pennsylvania German settlements.[90]

Recalling the tensions of Flagg's early architectural career, this housing project became the object of an architect-client dispute. In spite of its initial acceptance of the Flagg-invented details of construction, the U.S. Shipping Board specified only standard details after June 1918, but Flagg was determined to continue using his own.[91] When his first houses were completed that year, they were officially condemned and the Board terminated its contract with Flagg.[92] Following the November armistice, the Sun Village housing project, then over 75 percent constructed, was completed by the government.[93] It was ready for occupancy in February 1919 and was subsequently transferred to the private sector.[94]

In sum, Flagg's preoccupation with modular design and a Greek theory of proportions during the last twenty-five years of his life fulfilled a

148.   Ernest Flagg. Sun Village, Chester, Pennsylvania. Perspective, 1918 (*Architecture* XXXVIII, October 1918, pl. CLXXII).

289

149.   Ernest Flagg. Design No. 20, House A (Flagg, *Small Houses: Their Economic Design and Construction,* p. 61, No. 20).

dream of his years at the Ecole des Beaux-Arts. His studies of the Parthenon and other Greek temples culminated his architectural career in much the same way as Prix de Rome winners Paul Blondel and Louis Duc culminated their student careers with studies of the restorations of the Temple of the Concord, Hadrian's Villa, and the Colosseum. But unlike his French mentors, Flagg transformed such classical studies through their practical application to small house design and construction in a manner that was literal — too literal. Flagg's modular theory never became the universal system he intended it to be, and its practical application was ultimately flawed by the idiosyncracies of his methods. There was nothing uniquely Greek about his use of a module.

290

Moreover, the module was not suited to stone construction, but to the technique of formwork. Instead, Flagg's theory of the module based on classical proportions was principally a vehicle for his own personal expression. John Summerson once observed of Le Corbusier and his "Modulor": "there are types of extremely fertile, inventive mind which need the tough inexorable discipline of such systems to correct and at the same time stimulate invention. And the fate of these systems seems, on the whole, to confirm this; they rarely survive their authors and users. . . . That, however, in no way diminishes their importance."[95] The same could be said of Flagg and his module.

Flagg's application of concrete technology to masonry construction, resulting in more economical small stone houses and the possibilities of self-building, was innovative. His concept of good design eliminated sham construction; structure and materials were self-evident, with ornament intrinsic, rather than applied, to them. Flagg's sensitivity to region and topography was exemplary; his use of passive solar elements, far-sighted. Although his patented inventions were unique, they had defects, both economical and functional. His patented processes and devices cautioned conventional builders, but self-builders were challenged by their assurance of custom design.

Flagg's system thus provided the client with a choice between professional building and self-building. His objective to provide affordable housing to middle-income families was a democratic ideal.[96] Flagg's principles of design and construction for small houses remained constant; only the size and the amenities changed. Yet all builders did not achieve Flagg's promised economies. Ironically, published figures on cost overruns for his small stone houses eventually made the middle class realize that such houses were too expensive.

Flagg's Staten Island houses endure as his most personal architectural statement. As in "Stone Court," Flagg's "Bowcot" and "House-on-the-Wall" seem obsessively concerned with self-reflection. Flagg was as much an outsider to Staten Island society as he was a loner within his profession. His spreading estate, therefore, established his presence among the Vanderbilts, Bayards, and de Forests. As components of the Flegg Ridge Estate, these houses combined associations of ancestry with those of experience and education. By imposing a grand theory on ordinary house design and construction, Flagg broadly applied his Beaux-Arts education. These small houses synthesized American colonial and Anglo-French medieval architecture. Yet through his notion of applied science — his methods and patented inventions — Flagg thought that he was guiding the evolution of the Renaissance into a modern age. In theory and practice, Flagg approached each design problem as a scientific experiment to be worked out empirically. His methods combined a certain naiveté with intellectual capacity. Although highly customized and idiosyncratic, these small stone houses illustrated Flagg's ideals of artistic construction and the promise of American architecture as opposed to archaeology.

Ernest Flagg regarded his personal life and his career as an architect, inventor, and author with the profound optimism that characterized the Progressive Era. An indication of his personal aspirations is contained in his unpublished autobiography, "One Hundred and One Observations and a Century of Life," which was written during the last decade of his life. Although Flagg did not live long enough to fulfill the prediction of the book's title, he did reach a formidable ninety years of age. While still pursuing his study of Greek temples, working on plans for additional housing units to complete Flagg Court in Brooklyn, and actively seeking to interest United Nations officials in his Dongan Hills property, Flagg suffered a fatal heart attack at his Manhattan house on the afternoon of April 10, 1947. According to his close associate, "he had spent the morning at his desk in the office and died as he wished — suddenly and yet active."[97]

Flagg looked back to the prevailing belief during the late nineteenth century that inventions were, according to Leo Marx, "evidence of man's power to impose his will upon the world."[98] In Progressivist thought inventions demonstrated that the world had a specific rational purpose and that the inventor was in control. Flagg's most active years of inventing from 1916 to 1934, which roughly coincided with a period of "full mechanization" in America, confirmed his notion of progress with its roots in the nineteenth century.[99] René de Blonay, an architect who knew Flagg well, ascribed to him that quality which every genius possesses, namely that he is "ignorant of the world around him."[100] Flagg lacked interest in his fellow American architects and their work. Instead, he was drawn to the work of Thomas Edison and Henry Ford. Like them, Flagg represented the American myth of the self-made man who through intelligence, ingenuity, and determined individualism could establish his own path. But unlike these inventors Flagg had little following. He was isolated from his fellow architects because he ignored social conventions and architectural politics.

Flagg's faith in progress strongly conditioned his attitude toward both his own work and the role of the architect in society. In his view, the Bourne residence, "The Towers," of 1903–5 was superior to "Stone Court" of

1898–99; Pomfret School of 1906–11 was better than the U.S. Naval Academy a decade earlier; the Scribner Building of 1912–13 was "the best thing I ever did"; and his study of Greek theory during his late career was the crowning achievement of his life. Flagg's efforts to advance the cause of French classicism challenged a generation of American architects to turn away from imitation and archaeological revivalism by applying the reasoned and scientific principles of Beaux-Arts theory and practice. These accomplishments, together with his pragmatic methods for providing economic solutions to housing problems, made him one of the most innovative Beaux-Arts architects in America.

THE FLAGG FAMILY TREE*

Dr. Henry Collins Flagg (1742–1801)
m.1784, Rachel (Allston) Moore (1757–1839)
[m.1775, Captain William Allston, first husband
Mary Allston, Washington Allston, William Moore Allston]

Henry Collins Flagg (1790–1863)
m.1811, Martha Whiting (1792–1875)

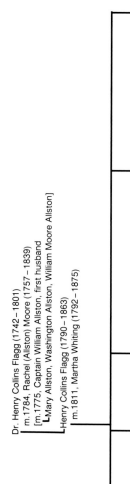

Henry Collins Flagg (1811–1862)
m.1836, Olivia Moss Sherman

Mary Allston Flagg (b. 1814)
m.1836, George Sherman

George Whiting Flagg (1816–1898)
m.1849, Louisa Henriques

William Joseph Flagg (1818–1898)
m.1851, Elizabeth Longworth

Jared Bradley Flagg (1820–1899)
m.(1)1841, Sarah R. Montague, d. 1844
└ Montague Flagg (1842–1915)
m.(2)1846, Louisa Hart (1828–1867)
m.(3)1869, Josephine Bond (no issue)
Charles Noel Flagg (1848–1916)
m.1874, Ellen Annie Earle (1852–1920)
└ Montague (1883–1924)
└ Charles Noel Flagg II (1881–1949)
Jared Bradley Flagg (1853–1926)
Ernest Flagg (1857–1947)
m.1899, Margaret Elizabeth Bonnell
(1882–1978)
└ Betsy Flagg (b.1900)
  m. John Melcher
  └ Pamela Melcher
  └ Ursula Ward Melcher
Washington Allston Flagg (1860–1903)
m.1886, Anna Davis Robins
Louisa Flagg (1862–1948)
m.1882, Charles Scribner (1854–1930)
└ Charles Scribner (1891–1953)
  m. Vera Bloodgood
└ Charles Scribner, Jr.
└ Julia Scribner
Louise Scribner (1882–1963)
  m. George D. Schieffelin
  └ George McKay Schieffelin
Rosalie Allston Flagg (1866–1950)
m. 1890, William D. Jaffray

Rachel Moore Flagg (1822–1884)
m.1840, Abraham Evan Gwynne
└ Alice Moore Gwynne
  m.1867, Cornelius Vanderbilt II
  └ William Henry Vanderbilt II
  └ Alice Gwynne Vanderbilt
  └ Cornelius Vanderbilt III
  └ Gertrude Vanderbilt
  └ Alfred Gwynne Vanderbilt I
  └ Reginald Claypole Vanderbilt
  └ Gladys Moore Vanderbilt
    m.1908, Count László Széchényi

Edward Octavius Flagg (1824–1911)
m.(1)Eliza W. McNeill
m.(2) Mary Lettia Ferris

* This schematic family tree is drawn from two studies: Ernest Flagg,
*Genealogical Notes on the Founding of New England: My Ancestors Part
in that Undertaking*; Helen D. Perkins, "Descendants of Jared Bradley
Flagg, 1820–1899," unpublished manuscript, June 1972. I wish to thank
Miss Perkins for making her study available to me. Alan Burnham's
"Ernest Flagg Tree" was also very helpful (American Architectural Archive).

Works

Ernest Flagg's major architectural works are listed in chronological order. Although many sources were used in compiling this chronology, a few were most valuable. A partial list of buildings designed in Flagg's office (with some inaccurate dates) is among the Arthur T. Sutcliffe Papers. The diaries of Flagg and Sutcliffe also aided the preparation of the chronology. Building permits and docket books in the New York City Buildings Department and the Bureau of Buildings, Borough of Richmond, also were consulted. All buildings are extant unless otherwise noted.

Samuel J. Tilden Tomb   1892
     New Lebanon, New York

Corcoran Gallery of Art   1892–97
     Seventeenth Street between New York Avenue and E Street,
     Washington, D.C.

St. Luke's Hospital   1892–97
     Morningside Drive between 113th and 114th streets, New York City

William Cullen Bryant Monument   1893
     Central Park, New York City

Scribner Building (now United Synagogue of America)   1893–94
     153–157 Fifth Avenue, New York City

Tamalpais Apartment Building (with Walter B. Chambers)   1894
     4300 S. Calumet, Chicago, Illinois

St. Margaret Memorial Hospital   1894–98
     265 46th Street, Pittsburgh, Pennsylvania

R. Fulton Cutting House   1895–97
     Madison Avenue and 67th Street, New York City
     Demolished

St. Nicholas Skating Rink (with Walter B. Chambers; now American   1895–98
     Broadcasting Companies, Broadcast Operations and Engineering)
     57 West 66th Street, New York City

Mills House No. 1 (now The Atrium)   1896–97
    160 Bleecker Street, New York City

Edwin Ginn House and Stable   1896–97;
    55 Bacon Street, Winchester, Massachusetts   stable, 1900
    House demolished

Mills House No. 2 (with Walter B. Chambers)   1896–98
    Rivington and Chrystie streets, New York City
    Demolished

Alfred Corning Clark Buildings or City and Suburban Homes Company   1896–98
    Model Tenements
    217–233 West 68th Street and 214–220 West 69th Street,
    New York City
    Demolished

Singer Building   1896–98
    149 Broadway and Liberty Street, New York City
    Demolished

United States Naval Academy   1896–1908
    Annapolis, Maryland

Firehouse Engine Co. 67 (with Walter B. Chambers)   1897–98
    170th Street, New York City

D. O. Mills Tenements   1897–98
    183–185 Sullivan Street, New York City

YMCA Building (now Village Offices)   1897–98
    Cooperstown, New York

Farmington Avenue Church (George M. Bartlett, associate architect;   1897–99
    now Immanuel Congregational Church)
    10 Woodland Street and Farmington Avenue, Hartford, Connecticut

First National Bank Building (George M. Bartlett, associate architect;   1897–99
    now Northeast Savings)
    50 State Street, Hartford, Connecticut

Frederick G. Bourne House, "Indian Neck Hall"   1897–1900;
    (now La Salle Military Academy), and Stable   alterations, 1907–8
    Oakdale, Long Island

Bourne Building   1898–99
    85–89 Liberty Street, New York City
    Demolished

Firehouse Engine Co. 33 (with Walter B. Chambers)   1898–99
    44 Great Jones Street, New York City

O. G. Jennings House (with Walter B. Chambers;
    now Lycée Français de New York)
    7 East 72nd Street, New York City
	1898–99

Ernest Flagg House, "Stone Court," and Gatehouse
    (now St. Charles Seminary)
    209 Flagg Place, Staten Island
	1898–99;
	additions, 1907–9

Alfred Corning Clark House and Stable
    Riverside Drive and 89th Street, New York City
    Demolished
	1898–1900

Soldiers' and Sailors' Monument New Britain, Connecticut	1899
Lawrence Library (with Walter B. Chambers) Pepperell, Massachusetts	1899–1901

New York Fireproof Model Tenements
    500–512 West 42nd Street, 505–515 West 41st Street,
    567–569 Tenth Avenue, New York City
    Partially demolished
	1899–1901

Rectory St. Mark's Church, Second Avenue and 11th Street, New York City	1900
Riverside Pumping Station Location unknown	1900
Sheldon Library St. Paul's School, Concord, New Hampshire	1900–1901

Connecticut Mutual Life Insurance Building (George M. Bartlett,
    associate architect)
    Hartford, Connecticut
    Demolished
	1900–1902

Bishop Tenements 58–62 Hester Street, New York City	1901–2
Frederick G. Bourne Tomb Greenwood Cemetery, Brooklyn, New York	1902
Monroe Street Tenements Monroe Street, New York City	1902

William C. Sheldon House
    38 East 40th Street, New York City
    Demolished
	1902–3

Singer Loft Building 561 Broadway and 88 Prince Street, New York City	1902–4

Singer Tower   preliminary design, 1902;
    149 Broadway, New York City   constructed, 1906–8
    Demolished

Officers' Houses   1903
    Naval Hospital, Brooklyn Navy Yard, Brooklyn, New York

Courtlandt F. Bishop House (now Regency Whist Club)   1903–4
    15 East 67th Street, New York City

Arthur Scribner House   1903–4
    39 East 67th Street, New York City

Frederick G. Bourne Residence, "The Towers"   1903–5
    Dark Island, Chippewa Bay, New York

Naval Hospital (now The Bureau of Medicine and Surgery)   1903–6
    23rd and E streets, Washington, D.C.

Plant Pavilion   1903–6
    St. Luke's Hospital, New York City

Masters Sisters' Residence   1904–5
    McMahan Island, Five Islands, Maine

Produce Exchange Bank Building   1904–5
    10 Broadway, New York City
    Demolished

Singer Building   1904–6
    22 Kronenstrasse, Berlin (East)
    Demolished

Naval Hospital   1904–7
    Annapolis, Maryland

Automobile Club of America   1905–7
    247–259 West 54th Street, New York City
    Demolished

Ernest Flagg House   1905–7
    109 East 40th Street, New York City
    Demolished

Bourne Building Addition   design, 1905;
    91–93 Liberty Street, New York City   constructed, 1906–9
    Demolished

Scribner Manufacturing and Printing Press   1905–9
    311–319 West 43rd Street, New York City

O. G. Jennings House   1906
    Fairfield, Connecticut

Robert I. Jenks House (with Walter B. Chambers)   1906–7
   54 East 64th Street, New York City

De Forest Fireproof Tenements   1906–7
   203–205 East 27th Street, New York City

Bishop Building   1906–7
   125th Street and Eighth Avenue, New York City

Pomfret School   1906–11
   Pomfret, Connecticut

Ernest Flagg Office   1907–8
   111 East 40th Street, New York City
   Demolished

Robert L. Burton Houses No. 7 and No. 8   1908
   Woodmere, Long Island   (date houses were published)

Jared Bradley Flagg and Louisa Hart Tombs   1908
   Evergreen Cemetery, New Haven, Connecticut

Stollwerk Factory   1908
   Stamford, Connecticut

Travers Pavilion   1908–16
   St. Luke's Hospital, New York City

Charlesbank Homes   1909–11
   Charles and Poplar streets, Boston, Massachusetts
   Demolished

Count László Széchényi Villa (now Russian Embassy)   1909–11
   104 Andrássy Avenue, Budapest, Hungary

Charles Scribner House (now Polish Delegation to the U.N.)   1909–12
   9 East 66th Street, New York City

Princeton University Press Building (now Scribner Building)   1910–11
   William and Charlton streets, Princeton, New Jersey

Model Fireproof Tenement Company Tenements   1911
   506–516 West 47th Street, New York City
   Demolished

Loft Building (Model Fireproof Tenement Company)   design, 1911;
   645–651 Eleventh Avenue, New York City   constructed, 1913–14

Scribner Building   1912–13
   597 Fifth Avenue, New York City

Gwynne Building   1913 – 14
    Sixth and Main streets, Cincinnati, Ohio

Moran Garage   1913 – 14
    62nd Street and Eighth Avenue, New York City

Lewis Gouverneur Morris House (now New World Foundation)   1913 – 14
    1015 Park Avenue (100 East 85th Street), New York City

Universal Films   1914 – 15
    Fort Lee, New Jersey

Paragon Films   1915
    Leonia Heights, New Jersey

Scribner Loft for Bonwit Teller   1916 – 17
    10 – 12 East 38th Street, New York City

"Bowcot"   1916 – 18
    Flagg Place and West Entry Road, Staten Island

Sun Village, Emergency Fleet Corporation Housing Project   1918 – 19
    Chester, Pennsylvania

"House-on-the-Wall" or "Wallcot"   1918 – 22
    285 Flagg Place, Staten Island

Tower House   1920 – 22
    Flagg Place, Staten Island
    Demolished

The Temple Baptist Church   1920 – 24
    Charleston, West Virginia

South Gate House   1921
    180 Coventry Road (originally Todt Hill Road), Staten Island

North Baptist Church   1921 – 24
    King Street, Port Chester, New York

Hickling Hollow   1922
    309 Flagg Place, Staten Island

Memorial Church of the Huguenots (now Huguenot Reformed Church)   1923 – 24
    5475 Amboy Road and Huguenot Avenue, Staten Island

Paul Revere Smith House   1923 – 24
    143 Four Corners Road, Staten Island

McCall House   1924
    1929 Richmond Road, Staten Island

John W. Morris House	1924–25
208 Neal Dow Avenue, Staten Island	
St. Mary of the Angels, Scribner Chapel	1925
Morristown, New Jersey	
Demolished	
St. Luke's Hospital Convalescent Hospital	1925–27
Greenwich, Connecticut	
Scrymser Pavilion	1925–28
St. Luke's Hospital, New York City	
Honeymoon Cottage	1926
143½ Four Corners Road, Staten Island	
Loft Building (Model Fireproof Tenement Company)	1927–28
653–659 Eleventh Avenue, New York City	
Stanley Stanger House	1928
Queen Mary Road, Montreal, Canada	
Celtic Park Apartments	1931–32
Long Island City, New York	
Flagg Court	1932–37
7200 Ridge Boulevard, Brooklyn, New York	

Patents
Filed by Ernest Flagg

U.S. Patent No.

907,024 Fireproof Partition Construction, December 15, 1908

946,211 Reinforced Partition Walls, January 11, 1910

1,174,703 Sleeping Cars, March 7, 1916

1,176,532 Support for Cement Material, March 21, 1916

1,224,625 Compartment Sleeping Cars, May 1, 1917

1,238,658 Methods for Building Sleeping Car Partitions, August 28, 1917

1,276,632 Roof Coverings, August 20, 1918

1,465,899 Roof Structures, August 21, 1923

1,479,705 Hinge Constructions, January 1, 1924

1,484,484 Constructing Concrete Walls, February 19, 1924

1,485,262 Partition Constructions, February 26, 1924

1,489,074 Building Forms for Concrete, etc., April 1, 1924

1,489,995 Sleeping Car Constructions, April 8, 1924

1,507,475 Nose Washers, September 2, 1924

1,511,956 Lock Mechanism, October 14, 1924

1,517,205 Door Hinges, November 25, 1924

1,553,228 Door Frame Construction, September 8, 1925

1,608,381 Skylight Construction, November 23, 1926

1,622,944 Fireplace Construction, March 29, 1927

1,622,997 Building Constructions, March 29, 1927

1,634,181 Improvement in Hinge, June 28, 1927

1,675,262 Improvement in Hinges, June 26, 1928

1,675,263 Urinal, June 26, 1928

1,722,204 Improvement in Hinges, July 23, 1929

1,736,709 Gauges for Applying Hinges, November 29, 1929

1,788,287 Lock and Latch Mechanism, January 6, 1931

1,850,747 Compartment Vehicles, March 22, 1932

1,907,403 Hinges, May 2, 1933

1,933,476 Partition Wall Construction, October 31, 1933

1,973,617 Compartment Vehicles, September 11, 1934

Canadian Patent No.

237,714 Outside Window Shades, February 12, 1924

237,715 Hinge Construction, February 12, 1924

238,651 Partition Construction, March 18, 1924

238,652 Constructing Concrete Walls, March 18, 1924

238,653 Roof Structures, March 18, 1924

238,819 Building Forms for Concrete, etc., March 25, 1924

238,978 Methods & Apparatus for Heating, April 1, 1924

240,351 Fireplace Construction, May 27, 1924

243,935 Lock Mechanism, October 28, 1924

254,512 Sleeping Car Construction, October 13, 1925

272,074 Improvement in Hinges, July 5, 1927

French Patent No.

498,034 Improved Roof Coverings, April 8, 1919

579,130 Sleeping Car Constructions, March 22, 1924

589,612 Improvements in Hinge, etc., November 25, 1924

627,028 Improvement in Hinge, January 3, 1927

Belgian Patent No.

316,591 Sleeping Car Constructions, March 25, 1924

British Patent No.

226,410 Improvements in Sleeping Car Constructions, December 24, 1924

238,424 Improvements in Bracket and Hinge, November 18, 1924

265,560 Improvement in Hinges, October 13, 1927

German Patent No.

415,232 Sleeping Car Construction, March 21, 1924

Abbreviations

AABN	*American Architect and Building News; American Architect*
Arch Rec	*Architectural Record*
Arch Rev	*Architectural Review* (Boston)
ATSP, AL, CU	Arthur T. Sutcliffe Papers, Avery Library, Columbia University
Delaire	E. Delaire, *Les Architectes élèves de l'Ecole des Beaux-Arts 1793–1907* (Paris: Librairie de la Construction Moderne, 1907)
DAB	*Dictionary of American Biography* (New York: Charles Scribner's Sons)
EFP, AL, CU	Ernest Flagg Papers, Avery Library, Columbia University
JAIA	*Journal of the American Institute of Architects*
JRIBA	*Journal of the Royal Institute of British Architects*
JSAH	*Journal of the Society of Architectural Historians*
"Observations"	Ernest Flagg, "One Hundred and One Observations and a Century of Life," unpublished manuscript (Flagg Family Papers and EFP, AL, CU)
"Works"	H. W. Desmond, "The Works of Ernest Flagg," *Architectural Record* XI (April 1902) pp. 1–104

Selected Writings by Ernest Flagg

1893   "Description of St. Luke's Hospital as it Will be When Completed," *History of St. Luke's Hospital with "A Description of the New Buildings"* (New York: Wynkoop & Hallenbeck, 1893), pp. 18–35.

1894   "Society of Beaux Art[s] Architects," October 2, 1894, unpublished manuscript (EFP, AL, CU).

"The Ecole des Beaux-Arts," *Arch Rec* III, First Paper (January–March 1894), pp. 302–13; Second Paper (April–June 1894), pp. 419–28; IV, Third Paper (July–September), pp. 38–43.

"The New York Tenement-House Evil and Its Cure," *Scribner's Magazine* XVI (July 1894), pp. 108–17.

"Influence of the French School on Architecture in the United States," *Arch Rec* IV (October–December 1894), pp. 210–28.

1895   "The New York Tenement-House Evil and Its Cure," in *The Poor in Great Cities* (New York: Charles Scribner's Sons, 1895), pp. 370–92.

1896   "The Dangers of High Buildings," *The Cosmopolitan* XXI (May 1896), pp. 70–79.

1898   "The Bonding of Brickwork," *Brickbuilder* VII (December 1898), pp. 259–61.

Letter to the Editor, *The Sun* (New York), December 18, 1898, II, p. 3.

1899   Published letter in answer to the question circulated on January 13, 1899, by Albert Kelsey, "An Unaffected School of Modern Architecture in America — Will it come?" *Catalogue of the T Square Club Exhibition and Architectural Annual for the year 1898* [Philadelphia, 1899], pp. 20–22; reprinted as "A Letter by Ernest Flagg" in *Architectural Annual 1900,* pp. 31–32.

"The New Naval Academy," *Proceedings of the United States Naval Institute* XXV (December 1899), pp. 865–73; reprinted in *Architects' and Builders' Magazine* I (April 1900), pp. 227–34.

1900   "American Architecture as Opposed to Architecture in America," *Inland Architect and News Record* XXXV (June 1900), p. 36; *AABN* LXVIII (June 23, 1900), p. 93; *Southern Architect and Contractor* XI (July 20, 1900); *Arch Rec* X (October 1900), pp. 178–90; *Architectural Annual 1900,* pp. 31–32.

1903   "The Planning of Hospitals," *Brickbuilder* XII (May 1903), pp. 90–95; (June 1903), pp. 113–19.

         "The Planning of Apartment Houses and Tenements," *Arch Rev* X (August 1903), pp. 85–90.

1904   "The Plan of New York, and How to Improve it," *Scribner's Magazine* XXXVI (August 1904), pp. 253–56.

1906   "The Best Method of Tenement Construction," *Charities and the Commons* XVII (October 1906), pp. 77–80.

1908   "The Future American Style," *The Western Architect* XI (April 1908), p. 36.

         "The Limitation of Height and Area of Buildings in New York," *AABN* XCIII (April 15, 1908), pp. 125–27.

         "Fireproof Buildings," *AABN* XCIII (April 29, 1908), pp. 141–42.

         "New Buildings for the United States Naval Academy, Annapolis, Md.," *AABN* XCIV, Part I (July 1, 1908), pp. 1–7, pls. 1–18; Part II (July 8, 1908), pp. 9–13, pls. 19–32.

         "Stone Pavements in Two Cities," Letter to the Editor, *The Sun* (New York), November 1, 1908, p. 8.

1909   "American Architecture of the Future," *New York American Souvenir Edition,* September 18, 1909, p. 4.

         "Road Building and Maintenance," *The Century Magazine* LXXIX (November 1909), pp. 139–49.

         Prospectus of the Model Fireproof Tenement Co. [1909] (ATSP, AL, CU).

1910   *Roads and Pavements* (New York: The De Vinne Press, 1910).

1911   "Public Buildings," *New York Architect* V (June 1911), pp. 105–10.

1918   "Housing of the Workingmen," *Architecture* XXXVIII (October 1918), pp. 269–70.

1920   "The Module System in Architectural Design," *Architecture* XLII (July 1920), pp. 206–9.

1921   "Architectural Design by the Use of a Module," *Architecture* XLIV (October 1921), pp. 315–18.

         "Economy with Beauty in the Country House," *Country Life* XL (October 1921), pp. 44–46.

1922   *Small Houses: Their Economic Design and Construction* (New York: Charles Scribner's Sons, 1922).

"The Justification of the Architect is Architecture," *AABN* CXXI (March 29, 1922), pp. 245–48.

"Stone Walls and Their Construction," *Country Life* XLII (May 1922), pp. 73–80.

1924   "The New McCall House, Step by Step," *McCall's Magazine* (October 1924), scrapbook (EFP, AL, CU).

"New Light on Greek Art; Vitruvius and His Module," *JRIBA* XXXII (December 6, 1924), pp. 57–65.

1925   "New Light on Greek Art," *JAIA* XIII (January 1925), pp. 1–4.

1926   "Building Regulation, Sanity and Congestion," from an address at the Meeting of the Sub-Committee on Housing, Zoning and Distribution of Population, New York, November 11, 1926 (Frances Loeb Library, Graduate School of Design, Harvard University).

Genealogical Notes on the Founding of New England: My Ancestors Part in that Undertaking (Hartford: Case, Lockwood & Brainard Co., 1926).

1927   "The City of the Future," *Scientific American* CXXXVII, Part 1 (September 1927), pp. 238–41; Part II (October 1927), pp. 334–37; *Safety* XIII (September–October 1927), pp. 114–23.

1928   "Standard Details of Construction" in *New Garden Homes* (Philadelphia: Ladies Home Journal [1928]).

"The Flagg Car," prospectus [c. 1928] (ATSP, AL, CU).

The Parthenon Naos (New York: Charles Scribner's Sons, 1928).

1930   "The Basis of Greek Design," *Architecture* LXII (September 1930), pp. 127–32; (October 1930), pp. 207–10.

"Adaptability of Greek Methods to Modern Use," *Architecture* LXII (December 1930), pp. 335–38.

1931   "Adaptability of Certain Ancient Methods to Modern Use," *Architecture* LXIII (February 1931), pp. 99–102; (April 1931), pp. 224–26.

"Modern Adaptation of Ancient Methods for Plan Making," *Architecture* LXIII (June 1931), pp. 347–50.

"Commensurability and Walls," *Architecture* LXIV (August 1931), pp. 101–4.

1936   "A Plan for Unaided Low-Rent Housing," *Real Estate Record* (December 19, 1936), pp. 35–38.

      Again the New York Tenement House Evil and Its Cure (ATSP, AL, CU).

[c. 1937] *Addition to Flagg Court* [c. 1937] (author's collection).

1945   "A Fish Story: An Autobiographical Sketch of the Education of an Architect," *JAIA* III (May 1945), pp. 182–88.

1946   "The German Conquest of Taste," *JAIA* V (January 1946), pp. 42–44.

Unpublished Manuscripts:

      "One Hundred and One Observations and a Century of Life," (Flagg Family Papers and EFP, AL, CU).

      "The Recovery of Art" (EFP, AL, CU).

      "Stone Houses of Modular Design" (EFP, AL, CU).

Notes

ARCHIVES

Due to the extensive use of primary source material, chapter notes contain full bibliographical references. The greatest concentration of Flagg documents, the Ernest Flagg Papers (EFP, AL, CU) and the Arthur T. Sutcliffe Papers (ATSP, AL, CU), are at Avery Library, Columbia University. The Ernest Flagg Papers contain the major portion of the Flagg Family Papers, owned by the architect's widow, Mrs. Ernest Flagg, until 1978. The Ernest Flagg Papers include Flagg's diaries, letters, a scrapbook, published articles, unpublished manuscripts, a list of patents, photographs, and other documents. Institutions or companies that commissioned buildings by Ernest Flagg maintain historical files of varying depths. Where material has been drawn from them, credit has been given in the notes. The American Architectural Archive, Greenwich, Connecticut, also contains much useful information. The Singer Manufacturing Company Papers are located at the State Historical Society of Wisconsin in Madison. Documents pertaining to two important government-sponsored commissions, the United States Naval Academy at Annapolis and the Emergency Fleet Corporation housing project, Sun Village, in Chester, Pennsylvania, are contained in the National Archives, Washington, D.C. The Charles Scribner's Sons Archives are located at Princeton University, Princeton, New Jersey. Most of Flagg's architectural drawings no longer survive, owing to a fire in the Flagg office and the dispersal of the office papers following the architect's death in 1947. Among the very few extant drawings by Flagg's hand are those of the Corcoran Gallery of Art contained in the Gallery's collection (see Figs. 22 and 25).

INTRODUCTION

1. Ernest Flagg, *Small Houses: Their Economic Design and Construction* (New York: Charles Scribner's Sons, 1922), Preface.

2. "Current Periodicals," *Arch Rev* III (1895), p. 39.

3. H. Van Buren Magonigle, "A Half Century of Architecture," *Pencil Points* XV (January 1934), p. 12.

4. *Exposition Universelle 1900, Jury International, Rapports,* Groupe II, Oeuvres d'art, classe 10, architecture (Paris: Imprimerie Nationale, 1904), p. 117. "Art Awards at Paris," *New York Times,* August 28, 1900, p. 2.

5. Letter, Charles F. McKim to Richard Morris Hunt, August 30, 1894, Box 1, p. 320 b (McKim Collection, Library of Congress).

CHAPTER ONE

1. Invitation, Committee on Awards (Leopold Arnaud, Philip L. Goodwin, Gerald A. Holmes), New York Chapter of the A.I.A., to Ernest Flagg, February 14, 1945 (EFP, AL, CU). "Awards," *Architectural Forum* LXXXII (April 1945), p. 80.

2. Both organizations were located at 115 East 40th Street. Arthur Cort Holden, interview with author, December 10, 1982.

3. Arthur T. Sutcliffe Diary, March 21, 1945 (ATSP, AL, CU).

4. Arthur Cort Holden, interview with author, December 10, 1982.

5. "Honors to Architects," *JAIA* III (April 1945), p. 153.

6. Arthur Cort Holden, interview with author, December 10, 1982.

7. Letter, Hugh Ferriss to Ernest Flagg, March 20, 1945 (Box 41, President's Correspondence, Architectural League of New York, Records, Archives of American Art). Arthur T. Sutcliffe Diary, March 29, 1945 (ATSP, AL, CU). Ernest Flagg, "A Fish Story: An Autobiographical Sketch of the Education of an Architect," *JAIA* III (May 1945), pp. 182–88. Flagg was made an Honorary Member of the Architectural League of New York in the fall of 1946. Letter, Wallace K. Harrison to Ernest Flagg, October 23, 1946 (EFP, AL, CU).

8. Jared Bradley Flagg's father, Henry Collins Flagg (1790–1863) of Charleston, South Carolina, and New Haven, was the half brother of Washington Allston. Jared B. Flagg, *The Life and Letters of Washington Allston* (New York: Charles Scribner's Sons, 1892), pp. 6–7. For a genealogical history, see Ernest Flagg, *Genealogical Notes on the Founding of New England: My Ancestors Part in that Undertaking* (Hartford: Case, Lockwood, & Brainard Co., 1926), pp. 135–38 (hereinafter cited as *Genealogical Notes*), and Flagg Family Tree. See also "Jared Bradley Flagg," *National Cyclopaedia of American Biography,* VII (New York: James T. White & Company, 1897), p. 549; J.M.H. [Jean McKinnon Holt], "Jared Bradley Flagg," *DAB,* VI (1931), p. 449; "Jared Bradley Flagg," obituary, *New York Times,* September 26, 1899, p. 7.

9. Jared Bradley Flagg, unpublished autobiography, p. 5. This typed manuscript is in the possession of the Rev. Dr. Thomas J. Bigham. Although undated, the manuscript was probably written in the late 1880s. A copy of it is in the Stowe-Day Foundation library, Hartford. See also Helen D. Perkins, *An Illustrated Catalogue of known portraits by Jared B. Flagg, 1820–1899,* Stowe-Day Foundation, 1972. I am grateful to Miss Perkins for her assistance with the Flagg family history.

10. Jared Bradley Flagg autobiography, p. 5.

11. Flagg, *Genealogical Notes,* pp. 135–36. *National Academy of Design Exhibition Record, 1826–1860,* vol. 1 (New York: New-York Historical Society, 1943), p. 164. Polk later

became a bishop and Confederate general. Joseph H. Parks, *General Leonidas Polk C.S.A.* (Louisiana: Louisiana State University Press, 1962). Although Jared Bradley claimed to have exhibited a portrait of his father at the National Academy of Design when he was only sixteen, the annual exhibition catalogue for 1836 contains no record of it.

12. Jared Bradley Flagg autobiography, p. 12.

13. Ibid., pp. 13–106.

14. Jared Bradley Flagg autobiography, p. 97. H. W. French suggests that Jared Bradley and his brother, George Whiting, "both enjoyed the advantages of association with their uncle Washington Allston" (*Art and Artists in Connecticut* [Boston: Lee and Shepard, 1879], p. 106).

15. Jared Bradley Flagg autobiography, p. 39.

16. Ibid., pp. 47–109. Flagg, *Genealogical Notes,* p. 135.

17. Jared Bradley Flagg autobiography, pp. 110–12, 147–48.

18. Jared Bradley Flagg became an Honorary Member, Professional, in 1847 and a National Academician in 1849. Eliot Clark, *History of the National Academy of Design 1825– 1953* (New York: Columbia University Press, 1954), p. 255.

19. Ernest Flagg, "New Britain," unpublished manuscript, p. 41 (EFP, AL, CU).

20. Jared Bradley Flagg autobiography, p. 148.

21. Record of the Annual Meeting of the Trustees of Trinity College, Hartford, July 15, 1857, *Records Washington College,* p. 138 (Archives, Trinity College). Letter, Paul R. Palmer (Columbiana Collection, Columbia University, New York) to author, July 27, 1979.

22. Jared Bradley Flagg autobiography, pp. 163–64.

23. Ibid., p. 165.

24. Jared Bradley's letter confirms that "the sole cause of my resignation is the loss of my wife's health, which, in the opinion of most competent medical advisors, cannot be restored by any means short of a change of residence & of climate" (Vestry Minutes, October 20, 1863). In accepting his resignation the Vestry expressed their "deep sorrow" and "regret that he is compelled to sever a relation which has been so agreeable to them" (Vestry Minutes, October 22, 1863 [Grace Church, Brooklyn]). Both H. W. French and Ernest Flagg give this version of Jared Bradley Flagg's resignation. See French, *Art and Artists in Connecticut,* p. 107; and Flagg, "A Fish Story," p. 182.

25. Flagg, *Genealogical Notes,* p. 135.

26. See *National Academy of Design Exhibition Record 1826–1860,* vol. 1, pp. 164–66, and *The National Academy of Design Record 1861–1900,* vol. 2, Maria Naylor, ed. (New York: Kennedy Galleries, 1973), pp. 305–6.

27. *International Exhibition 1876, Official Catalogue,* Part II (Philadelphia: John R. Nagle

and Company, 1876), p. 29. Although Jared Bradley executed several portraits of the Commodore, this painting was owned by William Henry Vanderbilt.

28. "Hester Prynne" was a popular subject in the 1880s and 1890s. Jared Bradley's brother, George Whiting, painted one in 1883 and his son, Charles Noel, in 1886. See *The National Academy of Design Record 1861–1900,* vol. 2, Naylor, ed., pp. 304–6.

29. French's *Art and Artists in Connecticut* contains brief biographies of the five Flagg artists, pp. 81–82, 91–94, 106–8, 155–56, 159. See also J.M.H. [Jean McKinnon Holt], "George Whiting Flagg," *DAB,* VI (1931), pp. 448–49; "Montague Flagg," obituary, *New York Times,* December 25, 1915, p. 7; "Charles Noel Flagg," obituary, *New York Times,* November 11, 1916, p. 9. The artist James Montgomery Flagg was not closely related to Ernest Flagg.

30. Flagg, *Genealogical Notes,* p. 195.

31. See Flagg Family Tree.

32. Ernest Flagg, "Farm at Whitneyville," unpublished manuscript, p. 33 (EFP, AL, CU).

33. Flagg, "A Fish Story," p. 182. For a brief biography of Ernest Flagg, see Alan Burnham, "Ernest Flagg," *DAB,* Supplement Four 1946–1950 (1974), pp. 280–82.

34. Flagg, "A Fish Story," p. 182.

35. Ibid., pp. 182–86.

36. See entry in Flagg's diary, "Memorandum of Events in the Life of Ernest Flagg," January 1876 (EFP, AL, CU).

37. Flagg, "A Fish Story," pp. 183–84. In November 1881, for example, Ernest Flagg lived at the Cosmopolitan Hotel at the corner of West Broadway and Chambers Street on the Lower West Side. "Memorandum of Events in the Life of Ernest Flagg," November 1881 (EFP, AL, CU). "Business Embarrassments," *New York Times,* March 9, 1881, p. 8.

38. Flagg, "A Fish Story," pp. 185–86. H. Stuart Hughes, *Consciousness and Society: The Reorientation of European Social Thought 1890–1930* (New York: Alfred A. Knopf, 1958), pp. 318–23.

39. Several studies discuss the introduction of the apartment house in New York City: "Apartment Houses I," *AABN* XXIX (September 27, 1890), pp. 194–95; "Apartment Houses II," *AABN* XXX (November 15, 1890), pp. 97–101; "Apartment Houses III," *AABN* XXXI (January 10, 1891), pp. 20–23; "Apartment Houses IV," *AABN* XXXI (January 17, 1891), pp. 37–39. George Hill, "Apartment House," in Russell Sturgis, ed., *A Dictionary of Architecture and Building,* vol. 1 (New York: Macmillan Company, 1901), pp. 82–89. Andrew Alpern, *Apartments for the Affluent* (New York: McGraw-Hill Book Company, 1975). Robert A. M. Stern, "With Rhetoric: The New York Apartment House," *VIA* IV (1980), pp. 78–92.

40. "A New Apartment House," *Record and Guide* XXXI (February 17, 1883), p. 63.

41. Estimates for The Dakota's cost of construction alone ranged from $1 million to $1.5 million. See "The Dakota," *New York Architecture* (HABS No. NY-5467), prepared by Diana S. Waite (National Park Survey, July 1969), p. 57. See also "Vast Apartment Houses," *Record and Guide* XXIX (June 3, 1882), p. 550.

42. For a biographical sketch of Philip G. Hubert, consult G. Matlack Price, "A Pioneer in Apartment House Architecture: Memoir on Philip G. Hubert's Work," *Arch Rec* XXXVI (July 1914), pp. 74–76.

43. "Progress in Building," *New York Times,* September 24, 1882, p. 3.

44. In June 1880 the Hubert Home Club (as owner) and Hubert, Pirsson & Co. (as architects) announced their prospective cooperative apartment house. The following year Jared B. Flagg was mentioned as the owner of the land for the West 57th Street site. "Buildings Projected," *Record and Guide* XXV (June 26, 1880), p. 608. See also land transactions in *Record and Guide* XXV (April 3, 1880), p. 316; XXVII (January 29, 1881), p. 98; XXVII (February 26, 1881), p. 180; Flagg, "A Fish Story," pp. 185–86. In a publication by Hubert, Pirsson & Co., the Rembrandt heads a list of nine apartment houses financed under the "Home Club" system or "co-operative plan." The other eight follow: the Hubert, the Hubert annex, the Hawthorne on 59th Street, the Central Park or Navarro buildings on Seventh Avenue between 58th and 59th streets, the Mount Morris on 130th Street, the building at 30th Street and Madison Avenue (121 Madison Avenue), the building at 28th Street and Madison Avenue (80 Madison Avenue), and the Chelsea building on 23rd Street. See Hubert, Pirsson & Co., *Where and How to Build* (New York [1892]), p. 74.

45. Jared Bradley was associated with at least four cooperative apartments for which Hubert, Pirsson & Co. were architects: the Rembrandt, 57th Street; 80 Madison Avenue (northwest corner of 28th Street: 1881–82); 121 Madison Avenue (northeast corner of 30th Street; 1882–83); the Knickerbocker, 245 Fifth Avenue (southeast corner of 28th Street; 1882–83). In "A Fish Story" (p. 186), Flagg maintained that his uncle, William J. Flagg, also speculated with Hubert, Pirsson & Co. on an apartment house at the northeast corner of Madison Avenue and 28th Street. At the death of James A. Pirsson in 1885, the firm became Hubert, Pirsson & Hoddick.

46. For a description and illustrations of the Central Park apartments, see Hubert, Pirsson & Co., *Where and How to Build,* pp. 78–80.

47. "The Central Park Apartments," *Building* II (December 1883), p. 33.

48. Ibid.

49. Press reports indicated that units in the first four houses of the Central Park apartments sold immediately. "The Prospect for Apartment Houses," *Record and Guide* XXXII (October 27, 1883), p. 830.

50. For a distinction between the apartment house and tenement house, circa 1900, see Hill, "Apartment House," and "Tenement House," in Sturgis, ed., *A Dictionary of Architecture and Building,* vol. 1, pp. 82–89; vol. 3 (1902), pp. 777–81.

51. Following his trip to Paris in 1879 to study French apartment house design, Richard Norman Shaw introduced the duplex system in England. Shaw's Albert Hall Mansions, London (1879–81), employed a duplex plan. "Apartment Houses III," pp. 21–22. Andrew Saint, *Richard Norman Shaw* (New Haven and London: Yale University Press, 1976), pp. 197–200. Stern, "With Rhetoric: The New York Apartment House," pp. 80–81.

52. First and second floor plans were published in "The Central Park Apartments," p. 33. On the extensive use of this arrangement, see Hubert, Pirsson & Co., *Where and How to Build,* p. 74.

53. "Buildings Projected," p. 608.

54. Flagg, "A Fish Story," p. 186. "Two Notable First Class Apartment Mansions," *Record and Guide* XXX (November 4–11, 1882), p. 61.

55. "Apartment Houses IV," p. 39.

56. "Cooperative" entailed the formation of a joint stock company in which occupants bought their units in addition to a monthly maintenance fee fixed at 15 percent of the purchase price. Further details of the two apartment houses are given in "Two Notable First Class Apartment Mansions," p. 61.

57. Flagg, "A Fish Story," p. 186. "Two Notable First Class Apartment Mansions," p. 61. "Vast Apartment Houses," p. 550. Jared Bradley Flagg purchased the land. For a report of this transaction, see *Record and Guide* XXIX (March 4, 1882), p. 194.

58. Interiors that were renovated in 1940 no longer reflect the duplex plan. Alpern illustrated 121 Madison Avenue, see *Apartments for the Affluent,* pp. 14–15.

59. "A New Apartment House," p. 63.

60. The firm was reluctant to credit Flagg with the improved two-story duplex, even though they did not dispute his authorship. Hubert, Pirsson & Co., Letter to the Editor, *Record and Guide* XXX (November 11–18, 1882), p. 73.

61. Contrary to published reports, Ernest Flagg was not the Knickerbocker's architect.

62. "Two Notable First Class Apartment Mansions," p. 61. Transactions of land and buildings to Jared B. Flagg and subsequently to the Knickerbocker Apartment Co. were reported in *Record and Guide* XXIX (April 22, 1882), p. 394; (April 29, 1882), p. 423; (May 6, 1882), p. 456; XXX (July 8, 1882), p. 666; XXXI (April 7, 1883), p. 225.

63. "Two Notable First Class Apartment Mansions," p. 61.

64. This land transaction, a sale of the Anderson estate, was reported in *Record and Guide* XXX (December 23–30, 1882), p. 139.

65. *Prospectus of the Fifth Avenue Plaza Apartments,* New York, 1883 (New York Public Library); D. H. King, Jr., is also named as builder. See also Sarah Bradford Landau, *Edward T. and William A. Potter: American High Victorian Architects* (New York and

London: Garland Publishing, 1979), p. 477, n. 72. I am very grateful to Professor Landau who informed me of the existence of this prospectus and generously provided me with a text of it.

66. Published plans by the architect Carl Pfeiffer for a subsequent project on the same site, the Plaza Apartment House, indicate a light-court and dimensions which approximate the specifications of the Fifth Avenue Plaza prospectus. "The 'Plaza' Apartment House, New York, N.Y.," *AABN* XVI (July 5, 1884), p. 6, pl. 445. The Pfeiffer plan was also similar to Henry J. Hardenbergh's light-court plan for the Vancorlear Apartment House, Seventh Avenue (1879). See "Apartment Houses IV," pp. 37–39.

67. "The Prospect for Apartment Houses," p. 830.

68. "The Duplex Apartment House," *Arch Rec* XXIX (April 1911), p. 327.

69. "Tired of Living in Flats," *New York Times,* September 20, 1885, p. 5.

70. Mrs. Ernest Flagg, interview with author, New York, October 30, 1974.

71. Flagg, "A Fish Story," p. 187. Flagg also applied his skills as a planner to a design for a National Library (Library of Congress) about the time Congress finally approved Smithmeyer & Pelz's design in 1886 (see Chapter III).

72. Flagg, "A Fish Story," p. 187. See also Montgomery Schuyler, "The Vanderbilt Houses," in William H. Jordy and Ralph Coe, eds., *American Architecture and Other Writings* (Cambridge, Mass.: Harvard University Press, 1961), vol. 2, pp. 488–501.

73. Flagg, "A Fish Story," p. 187.

74. Ibid. Newspapers document alterations to the Cornelius Vanderbilt II residence with George B. Post, architect, and David H. King, Jr., builder. See "Mr. Vanderbilt's New Home," *New York Times,* November 26, 1893, p. 21; "Cornelius Vanderbilt's House," *New York Times,* March 5, 1892, p. 8; and "Mr. C. Vanderbilt's Palace," *New York Times,* January 28, 1893, p. 10.

75. Flagg, "A Fish Story," p. 187.

76. Richard Howland Hunt, Richard Morris Hunt's son, began his studies at the Ecole in 1885. Delaire, p. 297.

CHAPTER TWO

1. H. Stuart Hughes provides a comprehensive synthesis of the period. See especially Chapter 2, "The Decade of the 1890's: The Revolt against Positivism," in his *Consciousness and Society: The Reorientation of European Social Thought 1890–1930* (New York: Alfred A. Knopf, 1958), pp. 33–66.

2. See Neil Levine, "Architectural Reasoning in the Age of Positivism: The *Néo-Grec* Idea

of Henri Labrouste's Bibliothèque Sainte-Geneviève" (Ph.D. diss., Yale University, 1975); and "The Romantic Idea of Architectural Legibility: Henri Labrouste and the *Néo-Grec*," in Arthur Drexler, ed., *The Architecture of the Ecole des Beaux-Arts* (New York: Museum of Modern Art, 1977), pp. 324–416.

3. For illustrations of these buildings, see Drexler, ed., *Architecture of the Ecole des Beaux-Arts,* pp. 80, 424–29.

4. Richard Chafee and Richard Moore have both analyzed the reform movement of 1863 and the reactionary reforms that followed. See Chafee, "The Teaching of Architecture at the Ecole des Beaux-Arts," in Drexler, ed., *Architecture of the Ecole des Beaux-Arts,* pp. 97–106; Richard A. Moore, "Academic *Dessin* Theory in France after the Reorganization of 1863," *JSAH* XXXVI (October 1977), pp. 145–74.

5. See David Van Zanten, "Architectural Composition at the Ecole des Beaux-Arts from Charles Percier to Charles Garnier," in Drexler, ed., *Architecture of the Ecole des Beaux-Arts,* p. 272; and Robin Middleton, "19th Century French Classicism," *Architectural Design* XVII, p. 10.

6. David Van Zanten describes "the monumental path of movement" in Garnier's Opera. See his "Architectural Composition" in Drexler, ed., *Architecture of the Ecole des Beaux-Arts,* p. 272.

7. David Van Zanten has analyzed the "fundamental social relationship" of theater participants, which Garnier describes in his book, *Le Théâtre,* of 1871. Ibid., p. 278.

8. Moore, "Academic *Dessin* theory," p. 160.

9. [Eugène-Emmanuel] Viollet-le-Duc, *Entretiens sur l'architecture,* vol. 1 (Paris: A Morel et Cie, 1863); vol. 2 (Paris: Vve A. Morel & Cie, 1872).

10. I am grateful to Neil Levine for sharing with me his knowledge of the *Néo-Grec* movement.

11. Compare an example of Viollet-le-Duc's domestic architecture, the Maison Courmont, 26 rue de Liège, Paris (1846–48), with projects for domestic architecture in the second volume of the *Entretiens.* The Maison Courmont is illustrated in "Eugène-Emmanuel Viollet-le-Duc, 1814–1879," *Architectural Design Profile* (1980), pp. 72, 74.

12. Anatole de Baudot's Saint-Jean de Montmartre is illustrated in Marc Emery, *Un siècle d'architecture moderne en France 1850–1950* (Horizons de France, 1971), pp. 23–24.

13. See P. Planat, "Le Lycée Lakanal," *La Construction Moderne* I (February 20, 1886), pp. 217–19; "Le Lycée Racine," *La Construction Moderne* III (March 24, 1888), pp. 283–84, and (March 31, 1888), pp. 293, 295.

14. Viollet-le-Duc, *Entretiens,* vol. 2, p. 289.

15. Eugène-Emmanuel Viollet-le-Duc, *Discourses on Architecture,* vol. 1, Henry Van Brunt, trans. (Boston: James R. Osgood and Company, 1875), p. 245.

16. Van Zanten, "Architectural Composition," in Drexler, ed., *Architecture of the Ecole des Beaux-Arts,* p. 254.

17. E. Rivoalen, "La Nouvelle Sorbonne," *La Construction Moderne* IV (August 3, 1889), pp. 505–8; (August 10, 1889), pp. 519–21; (August 31, 1889), pp. 559–60; V (March 29, 1890), pp. 292–94, pl. 7; (April 5, 1890), pp. 304–6, pl. 58; (April 26, 1890), pp. 337–40, pl. 59.

18. For illustrations of Guadet's Hôtel des Postes, see Louis Hautecoeur, *Histoire de l'architecture classique en France* (Paris: A. et J. Picard et Cie, 1957), vol. 7, p. 377, fig. 329; and E. D., "Le Nouvel Hôtel des Postes à Paris," *Encyclopédie d'architecture* III.2 (1886–87), pls. 1123, 1124, 1130. For illustrations of Pascal's Faculté de Médecine et de Pharmacie, Bordeaux, see *L'Architecture* VIII (December 21, 1895), pls. I–VI.

19. Foreign, rather than French, observers labeled Ginain's Bibliothèque de la Faculté de Médecine as "neo-grec." See, for example, Schuyler "A 'Modern Classic,'" in William H. Jordy and Ralph Coe, eds., *American Architecture and Other Writings* (Cambridge, Mass.: Harvard University Press, 1961), vol. 2, p. 592, n. 151.

20. Hautecoeur reproduces several views and a plan of Notre Dame d'Auteuil in *L'architecture classique,* vol. 7, pp. 365–66, figs. 313–15. For a photograph and a plan of the Lycée Buffon, see Drexler, ed., *Architecture of the Ecole des Beaux-Arts,* [p. 458].

21. "Reconstruction de la Gare Saint-Lazare," *La Construction Moderne* III (January 21, 1888), pp. 174–75; pls. 28, 29. J. Lisch, "La Nouvelle Gare Saint-Lazare, à Paris," *Encyclopédie d'architecture* IV.1 (1888–89), pp. 20–22, pls. 5,7.

22. "La Gare du Havre," *La Construction Moderne* III (March 17, 1888), p. 271, pl. 38. This railroad station recalled Lisch's earlier Gare du Champ-de-Mars at the 1878 Paris exposition, illustrated in *Encyclopédie d'architecture* II.7 (1878), pls. 510, 524, 533, 541, 542, 549.

23. Viollet-le-Duc, *Entretiens,* vol. 2, p. 327, n. 1. Saulnier's Chocolate Mill was extensively published in *Encyclopédie d'architecture* before 1878. For a series of illustrations and an explanatory text by Saulnier, see "Usine Menier, à Noisiel (Seine-et-Marne)," *Encyclopédie d'architecture* II.6 (1877), pp. 91–93 (see p. 91 for a list of plates published after 1874); II.7 (1878); See also Cervin Robinson, "Usine Menier," *Architectural Forum* CXXXVI (May 1972), pp. 20–23.

24. In contrast to the dual nature of Nénot's design, those of his fellow entrants in the competition of 1883, Albert Ballu and Louis-Ernest L'heureux, liberally employed exposed metal structural supports and conveyed a consistently higher level of rationalism throughout. A. de Baudot, "Reconstruction et agrandissement de la Sorbonne," *Encyclopédie d'architecture* III.2 (1883), pp. 28–32, pls. 872, 874.

25. See "Caserne des Célestins," *L'Architecture* XV (July 5, 1902), pp. 223–34, pl. 37.

26. "Maison commerciale rue d'Uzès, No 3, à Paris," *Revue Générale de l'Architecture et des Travaux Publics* XXXVII (1880), pp. 247–50. The first two floors have been altered.

27. Hautecoeur, *L'architecture classique,* vol. 7, p. 413.

28. Ernest Flagg, "Influence of the French School on Architecture in the United States, *Arch Rec* IV (October–December 1894), p. 218.

29. Paul Gout, "Coup d'oeil rationaliste sur l'Exposition Universelle," *Encyclopédie d'architecture* IV.2 (1889–90), pp. 91–94.

30. H. Chaîne, "L'Exposition Universelle de 1889," *Encyclopédie d'architecture* IV.1 (1888–89), pp. 91–92. Frantz Jourdain noted the rational expression of monumental decoration in "La Decoration & le rationalisme architecturaux à l'Exposition Universelle," *Revue des Arts Decoratifs* X (1889–90), pp. 33–38.

31. For an illustration of Bouvard's *Palais des Industries Diverses,* see *La Construction Moderne,* IV (July 13, 1889), pl. 89. See also René de Cuers, "J. A. Bouvard," *Arch Rec* X (February 1901), pp. 290–312.

32. Flagg arrived in Paris between April 1888 and June 2, 1888, the latter established by his letter of reference from the U.S. Legation. See Flagg dossier, Archives de l'Ecole Nationale Supérieure des Beaux-Arts, section architecture, série antérieure au 31 décembre 1895, AJ-52-365, p. 182 (Archives Nationales). I am grateful to Richard Chafee who made notes of Flagg's dossier available for my dissertation before I was able to consult it in Paris.

33. See document entitled "No. 1080 d'Inscription, Mr. Flagg," Paris, June 13, 1888 (EFP, AL, CU). For information on the Ecole calendar, see Alexis Lemaistre, *L'Ecole des Beaux-Arts dessinée et racontée par un élève* (Paris: Librairie Firmin-Didot et Cie, 1889), p. 127. The dates for these examination periods were subject to change. At the very end of the century they were held in October–November and again in April–May. See Henry Guédy, *L'Enseignement à l'Ecole nationale et spéciale des beaux-arts, section d'architecture* (Paris: Librairie de la Construction Moderne [1899]), p. 5.

34. Richard Chafee, "Richardson's Record at the Ecole des Beaux-Arts," *JSAH* XXXVI (October 1977), p. 175.

35. Flagg, "A Fish Story," pp. 187–88.

36. Ibid., p. 188. Flagg, therefore, took the exams on three occasions, rather than the two he discusses.

37. Flagg dossier, Feuille de Renseignements, AJ-52-365, p. 185 (Archives Nationales).

38. Flagg's student number 4147 denotes class rank when admitted. Registres matricules des élèves de la section d'architecture, 1800–1925, AJ-52-240 (Archives Nationales). Flagg is inaccurate when he maintains in "A Fish Story" (p. 188) that he "entered No. 5 on the list!"

39. The rue de Seine address appears on Flagg's *carte d'élève,* while the rue Séguier address appears on the Ecole register, as well as on his diary of 1890 (EP, AL, CU).

40. Arthur T. Sutcliffe Diary, October 14, 1904 (ATSP, AL, CU).

41. Even among the best students, the length of study required for the *diplôme* varied enormously. Georges Chédanne received his diploma in six years (1881–87); Tony Garnier in nine years (1890–99); Paul Bigot in eleven years (1889–1900). See Delaire pp. 181, 213, 270.

42. After June 27, 1887, the diploma gained value when all living Grand Prix de' Rome winners in architecture were given diplomas. See Chafee, "Teaching of Architecture," in Drexler, ed., *Architecture of the Ecole des Beaux-Arts,* p. 105.

43. See Registres matricules des élèves de la section d'architecture, 1800–1925, AJ-52-240 (Archives Nationales). Herbert Dudley Hale placed twenty-eighth among the thirty-six entrants in the second class in 1889. Joseph H. Freedlander entered the Atelier Daumet in the first class in 1890. John Vredenburgh Van Pelt entered the second class in 1890 as a student of Douillard-Thierry and Deglane. Both Freedlander and Van Pelt completed the program at a rapid pace, within five years. See also Delaire, pp. 265, 288, 419.

44. Eugène Müntz, "Historique" in Guédy, *L'Enseignment à l'Ecole nationale,* p. xx.

45. Flagg dossier, AJ-52-365, pp. 181–85 (Archives Nationales). *Carte d'élève* (EFP, AL, CU).

46. Müntz, "Historique," in Guédy, *L'Enseignement à l'Ecole nationale,* p. xx.

47. Flagg dossier, AJ-52-365, p. 184 (Archives Nationales). Flagg's student drawings do not survive.

48. Certificates (EFP, AL, CU).

49. "Memorandum of Events in the Life of Ernest Flagg," August 1890 (EFP, AL, CU).

50. See Brockway entry (4062), Registres matricules des élèves de la section d'architecture, 1800–1925, AJ-52-240 (Archives Nationales). Ernest Flagg Diary, September 9, 1890 (EFP, AL, CU). Delaire, pp. 40, 197.

51. See Chambers entry (4160), Registres matricules des élèves de la section d'architecture, 1800–1925, AJ-52-240 (Archives Nationales). Delaire, p. 41.

52. Delaire, pp. 208, 261.

53. Ernest Flagg Diary, November 21, 1890 (EFP, AL, CU).

54. Flagg owned a copy of Paul-Marie Letarouilly's *Edifices de Rome Moderne.* Ernest Flagg Diary, November 6, 1890 (EFP, AL, CU).

55. A list of books, which Flagg presumably owned before his departure from France, appears in his diary of 1890 (EFP, AL, CU). Flagg's impressive library of over 200 volumes is no longer intact.

56. For a list of foreign students at the Ecole until 1907, see Delaire, pp. 478–80. A chronological, although incomplete, list of American students appears in James Philip Noffsinger, *The Influence of the Ecole des Beaux-Arts on the Architects of the United States*

(Washington, D.C.: Catholic University of America Press, 1955), pp. 106–10.

57. Ernest Flagg, "The Ecole des Beaux-Arts," *Arch Rec* III (January–March 1894), First Paper, pp. 302–13; (April–June 1894), Second Paper, pp. 419–28; IV (July–September 1894), Third Paper, pp. 38–43.

58. Later the most authoritative reference for the Ecole's entrance requirements and curriculum was Henry d'Herville's *La Section d'Architecture à l'Ecole Nationale et Speciale des Beaux-Arts* (Paris: Librairie de la Construction Moderne, 1896). This was succeeded by Henry Guédy's publication of 1899. Both represent more serious accounts than Lemaistre's informal survey.

59. Cf. Eugène Müntz, *Guide de l'école nationale des beaux-arts* (Paris: Maison Quantin [1889]).

60. The most significant of these subsequent accounts was published in a special issue of *Architectural Record;* see Beaux-Arts Number (January 1901). Articles by Eugène Müntz, Walter Cook, John Mead Howells, and Thomas Hastings expand and revise Flagg's earlier contribution. Several accounts of the Ecole des Beaux-Arts precede Flagg's. See F.L.V. Hoppin, "An Architectural Knockabout–VI," *AABN* XXVI (August 24, 1889), pp. 89–90 (one of seven parts); and Albert Kahn, "Our Travelling Scholar," *AABN* XXXIII (July 18, 1891), pp. 39–41. For a historical perspective and a discussion of the *réglements,* see Chafee, "Teaching of Architecture," in Drexler, ed., *Architecture of the Ecole des Beaux-Arts,* pp. 61–108.

61. Flagg, "The Ecole des Beaux-Arts," Second Paper, p. 419.

62. Ibid., p. 422.

63. Ibid., pp. 421–22.

64. For a list of ateliers, see Chafee, "Teaching of Architecture," in Drexler, ed., *Architecture of the Ecole des Beaux-Arts,* pp. 500–501.

65. See Paul R. Baker, *Richard Morris Hunt* (Cambridge, Mass.: MIT Press, 1980), pp. 25, 29–31.

66. "Francis Ward Chandler Dead," *AABN* CXXX (September 20, 1926), p. 16; *JAIA* (October 1926), p. 504. After 1869 Chandler became associated with the architectural program at M.I.T., newly established by William Robert Ware in whose office (Ware & Van Brunt) Chandler had worked from 1864, prior to his Paris study. See also "Ecole Nationale des Beaux Arts Prix de Reconnaissance des Architectes Americains, List of American Students of Architecture in the Paris Ateliers" [1846–1885], (Frances Loeb Library, Graduate School of Design, Harvard University). Robert Swain Peabody, who graduated from Harvard in 1866, had already entered the Ecole des Beaux-Arts in the fall of 1867 when his friend McKim arrived in Paris. It was probably due to Peabody's influence that McKim also joined the Atelier Daumet. See Charles Moore, *The Life and Times of Charles Follen McKim* (Boston: Houghton Mifflin Company, 1929), pp. 21–23. See also Delaire, pp. 334, 367.

67. While Daumet continued in his role as *patron,* two French students, Charles Girault and Pierre-Joseph Esquié, assumed direction of the atelier in 1885 and 1888 respectively. See Chafee, "Teaching of Architecture," in Drexler, ed., *Architecture of the Ecole des Beaux-Arts,* p. 501.

68. Delaire, pp. 297, 428, 417, 334. For McGuire's account of his student life in the Atelier Daumet, see Mildred E. Lombard, "The Beaux-Arts Institute of Design," *Légion d'Honneur Magazine* IX (July 1938), pp. 81–83.

69. The spirit of Chantilly and other French châteaux closely paralleled the work of his father, Richard Morris Hunt, in a number of residences designed before 1885, notably the William Kissam Vanderbilt House, New York (1879–81). See Hautecoeur, *L'architecture classique,* vol. 7, pp. 427–29.

70. Moore, *The Life and Times of Charles Follen McKim,* pp. 33–34. Draftsmen who had worked in McKim's office prior to their training at the Ecole des Beaux-Arts chose a number of different ateliers. Edward Tilton and William Boring were both students of J. L. Pascal.

71. Louis H. Sullivan, *The Autobiography of an Idea* (New York: Press of the American Institute of Architects, 1926), p. 233.

72. Delaire, pp. 408, 392, 428, 331, 219.

73. Although Constant Moyaux succeeded André as *patron* of his official atelier, most students chose to join the independent Atelier Laloux. See Delaire, p. 124. Richard Chafee discusses official ateliers in his "Teaching of Architecture," Drexler, ed., *Architecture of the Ecole des Beaux-Arts,* pp. 90–91, 501.

74. Delaire, pp. 289–90, 344.

75. Delaire, pp. 295, 198, 206, 234. Most draftsmen in Richardson's office never trained in Paris. Of those besides Howard who attended the Ecole des Beaux-Arts subsequent to their work in Richardson's studio, only one student, Welles Bosworth, entered and joined the Atelier Redon in 1897. See Delaire, p. 189. For a discussion of Richardson's studio, see James F. O'Gorman, "The Making of a 'Richardson Building,' 1874–1886," *H. H. Richardson and His Office* (Cambridge, Mass.: Harvard College Library, 1974), pp. 4–13.

76. For a published, but incomplete, tabulation of the numbers of American students in each of the Ecole ateliers, see Noffsinger, *Influence of the Ecole des Beaux-Arts,* pp. 89–91.

77. In 1889 the three official ateliers were those directed by Jules André, Léon Ginain, and Julien Guadet. For a discussion of their founding, see Moore, "Academic *Dessin* Theory," p. 151.

78. Flagg, "The Ecole des Beaux-Arts," Second Paper, p. 422.

79. Ibid., pp. 422–23.

80. Ibid., p. 423.

81. Ibid.

82. Following Paul Blondel's death in 1897, L. Scellier de Gisors succeeded him as *patron*. With its line of successor *patrons*, the atelier continued until 1968. See Chafee, "Teaching of Architecture," in Drexler, ed., *Architecture of the Ecole des Beaux-Arts*, p. 501.

83. See Delaire, pp. 163, 168, 354, 391. Stephen Codman, George B. de Gersdorff, Cary Selden Rodman, Pennington Satterthwaite, C. W. Wheelwright, and C. C. Zantzinger were also American students of Paul Blondel. See Delaire, pp. 217, 274, 390, 399, 429, 430.

84. Delaire, pp. 183–84. CH.L. [Charles Lucas], "Nécrologie M. Paul Blondel," *La Construction Moderne* XII (May 1, 1897), pp. 371–72. Historians have consistently confused Paul Blondel with his contemporary, Henri Blondel (1832–97), even though they were not related. Henri Blondel, who did not train at the Ecole, was the architect of a number of significant works combining masonry, metal, and glass. Among his commercial buildings to receive an enthusiastic and extensive press are the Belle Jardinière department store (1878), the Bourse de Commerce (1888–89), which replaced the former Halle aux Blès, and an urbanistic complement to Garnier's Opera: a corner pavilion on the avenue de l'Opéra and the rue du Quatre Septembre for the Société de Dépôts et de Comptes Courants. See [Charles Lucas], "Nécrologie M. Henri Blondel," *La Construction Moderne* XII (September 18, 1897), p. 612; P. Vauthier, "Maison de la Belle Jardinière," *Revue Générale de l'Architecture et des Travaux Publics* XXX (1873), pp. 11–17, pls. 8–11; E. Rivoalen, "La Bourse de Commerce à Paris," *La Construction Moderne* V (December 21, 1889), pp. 121–24, pls. 23, 25; and "Société de Dépôts et de Comptes Courants," *Revue Générale de l'Architecture et des Travaux Publics* XXX (1873), pp. 199–200, pls. 47–49.

85. In addition to receiving the Prix Deschaumes (1868), the Prix Rougevin (1869), the Prix Blouet (1872), and the Prix Achille Leclère (1873), Blondel won a Deuxième Grand Prix in the competition of 1875 for a Palais de Justice.

86. From 1881 until Blondel's death in 1897 at the age of fifty, scores of students passed through his atelier. Tony Garnier (1869–1948) was the most celebrated. He joined the Atelier Blondel and entered the first class in 1890, the year of Flagg's departure. After Blondel's death, Garnier maintained his allegiance to the Atelier Blondel under the direction of Scellier de Gisors. In 1899 Tony Garnier, like his two *patrons*, culminated his Ecole career by winning the Grand Prix de Rome. See Delaire, p. 270.

87. Blondel also served as Architecte du Palais du Louvre et des Tuileries and Architecte de la Cour de Cassation. See Delaire, pp. 183–84. See also [Charles Lucas], "Nécrologie M. Paul Blondel," *La Construction Moderne* XII (May 1, 1897), pp. 371–72.

88. Flagg, "The Ecole des Beaux-Arts," Second Paper, p. 423.

89. *Grands Prix de Rome, d'Architecture de 1850 à 1900* (Paris: Armand Guerinet [1900]), vol. 1, pp. 5–6; vol. 2, pls. 266–74.

90. *Gazette des Architectes et du Bâtiment,* XV (Paris: Librairie des Imprimeries Réunies, 1886), p. 188.

91. For illustrations of Blondel's design and an astute criticism supporting his entry, see E.R. [Rivoalen], "Le Concours de l'Opéra-Comique," *La Construction Moderne* VIII (August 12, 1893), pp. 530–33, pls. 93, 94.

92. Among Paul Blondel's works in Mulhouse are a bank, a clinic, a public library, and several *hôtels.* See Delaire, pp. 183–84, and [Charles Lucas], "Nécrologie M. Paul Blondel," p. 371.

93. This notion of *parti* was loosely akin to Freud's theory of creativity, Henri Bergson's use of intuition as "personality," and Max Weber's use of intuition as *verstehen,* or understanding. See Hughes, *Consciousness and Society,* pp. 117, 310–11.

94. Flagg, "The Ecole des Beaux-Arts," Third Paper, p. 39.

95. Moore, "Academic *Dessin* theory," pp. 156–57.

96. Flagg, "The Ecole des Beaux-Arts," Third Paper, p. 39.

97. Ibid.

98. Ibid.

99. See David Van Zanten's analysis of composition and *parti:* "Architectural Composition," in Drexler, ed., *Architecture of the Ecole des Beaux-Arts,* pp. 112–15.

100. Quatremère de Quincy, *Architecture* (Paris: Agasse, 1825), vol. 3, pp. 80–81.

101. Georges Gromort, *Essai sur la théorie de l'architecture* (Paris: Vincent, Fréal & Cie, 1946), p. 144.

102. Flagg, "The Ecole des Beaux-Arts," Third Paper, p. 39.

103. Ibid., p. 40.

104. Charles Blanc, *Grammaire des arts du dessin* (Paris: Renouard, 1880; orig. pub. 1867), p. 67.

105. Ibid.

106. Ibid., p. 72.

107. Ibid., p. 70.

108. Ibid., pp. 70–71. Blanc's notion of character derived principally from eighteenth-century classical theory, especially the synthesis that Jacques-François Blondel formulated in his *Cour d'Architecture,* but also by examples, both visionary and actual, of the *architecture parlante* of such Revolutionary Classicists as Etienne-Louis Boullée and Claude-Nicolas Ledoux. For a discussion of character in Blondel's *Cour d'Architecture,* see Robin Middleton, "Jacques François Blondel and the *Cours d'Architecture,*" *JSAH* XVIII (December 1959), pp. 140–48. In the *Grammaire,* (p. 95), Blanc cited Le-

doux's Prison at Aix-en-Provence as an illustration of the predominance of solids over voids to effect a sober and imposing character.

109. Blanc, *Grammaire des arts du dessin,* pp. 71, 76.

110. Ibid., p. 76.

111. Ibid.

112. J[ulien] Guadet, *Eléments et théorie de l'architecture,* 4 vols. (Paris: Librairie de la Construction Moderne, 1929; orig. pub. 1901–4). In 1894 Guadet assumed the post of professor of theory. His lectures were later published as this four-volume work.

113. Ibid., vol. 1, pp. 8, 117–36.

114. See Guadet's address, "Leçon d'ouverture du cours de théorie de l'architecture à l'école des beaux-arts," ibid., vol. 1, p. 88.

115. Ibid., p. 108.

116. Ibid., p. 9.

117. Ibid., pp. 100–101.

118. Ibid., pp. 238, 365.

119. Ibid., p. 132.

120. Ibid.

121. Ibid., p. 133.

122. Colin Rowe, review of Talbot Hamlin, ed., *Forms and Functions of Twentieth Century Architecture,* in *Art Bulletin* XXXV (July 1953), p. 170.

123. Guadet, *Eléments et théorie de l'architecture,* vol. 1, pp. 134–35.

124. Viollet-le-Duc, *Discourses,* vol. 1, pp. 93–94.

125. See Morton G. White, *Social Thought in America: The Revolt Against Formalism* (New York: Viking Press, 1949), p. 12; and Henry F. May, *The End of American Innocence* (Chicago: Quadrangle Books, 1964), pp. 30–31.

126. Charles Garnier, *A travers les arts* (Paris: Librairie de L. Hachette et Cie, 1869), p. 69, as quoted and translated in Van Zanten, "Architectural Composition," in Drexler, ed., *Architecture of the Ecole des Beaux-Arts,* p. 279.

127. Charles Garnier, *Le Nouvel Opéra de Paris* (Paris: Ducher, 1878–80), vol. 1, p. 122, as quoted and translated in Van Zanten, ibid., p. 286.

128. Viollet-le-Duc, *Discourses,* vol. 1, p. 175.

129. Flagg, "Influence of the French School," p. 222.

130. Blanc, *Grammaire des arts du dessin,* p. 305, translated and quoted by Flagg in

"Influence of the French School," p. 222.

131. Flagg, "The Ecole des Beaux-Arts," Third Paper, p. 41.

132. Flagg, "Influence of the French School," p. 223.

133. Ibid., p. 226

CHAPTER THREE

1. For a discussion of American culture in the decade of the 1890s, see John Higham, *Writing American History* (Bloomington, Ind.: Indiana University Press, 1970), pp. 88–89.

2. See Henry F. May's analysis of idealism and progress as the dominant articles of American faith during the years just before the First World War in *The End of American Innocence* (Chicago: Quadrangle Books, 1964), pp. 9–29.

3. Flagg made his last entry in a diary of this period from Paris on December 28, 1890. He had returned from Italy the previous week.

4. James Philip Noffsinger records the names of 364 American students of architecture at the Ecole during these years. See *The Influence of the Ecole des Beaux-Arts on the Architects of the United States* (Washington, D.C.: Catholic University of America Press, 1955), pp. 106–9. Richard Chafee has expanded the list.

5. "Ecole Nationale des Beaux Arts Prix de Reconnaissance des Architectes Americains, List of American Students of Architecture in the Paris Ateliers" [1846–1885], (Frances Loeb Library, Graduate School of Design, Harvard University). Noffsinger, *Influence of the Ecole des Beaux-Arts,* p. 106.

6. See Delaire for a list of American Ecole alumni, pp. 479–80.

7. An account of one American, Joseph McGuire, describes the social meetings of Ecole *élèves* in a number of Parisian cafés, notably the Café d'Orsay. See Mildred E. Lombard, "The Beaux-Arts Institute of Design," *Légion d'Honneur Magazine* IX (July 1938), pp. 81–86. The society officially commemorated Thanksgiving Day in 1890 when a group of American Ecole students and alumni held a dinner at the Café d'Orsay at which they pledged to meet a year later in New York; but it was not until 1893 that a permanent organization was to grow out of the resulting annual dinners. A copy of the Café d'Orsay Thanksgiving Dinner menu was signed by all those allegedly present. I am grateful to Richard Chafee for drawing to my attention an account of the annual meeting of November 21, 1911, at which Flagg exhibited a copy of the original menu signed by the following Ecole students: John P. Benson, Evans Preston, J. W. Lavalle, A. L. Brockway, Joseph H. McGuire, John W. Bemis, Edward L. Tilton, Ernest Flagg, Whitney Warren, J. Donaldson, George Cary, Edgar A. Josselyn, Thornton Floyd Turner, Austin W. Lord, Louis de Sibourg, T. R. Plummer, S.B.P. Trowbridge, and

William A. Boring. "Annual Meeting of the Society of Beaux-Arts Architects," *AABN* C (December 6, 1911), p. 4.

At the annual dinner of the society in 1911, Flagg, who had just been elected president, delivered a brief talk on that historic Café d'Orsay meeting. Unfortunately, the recollection of those events is riddled with inaccuracies. While Flagg is purported to have taken credit for "the suggestion to perpetuate the annual dinner in a Society," and is allegedly recorded as present at the 1890 Thanksgiving meeting in Paris, he was actually in Italy at the time. There is no doubt, however, about Flagg's contributions to the society's permanent organization as a trustee, treasurer, and officer of the first Committee on Education when the Society was legally founded. The Paris meeting, on one hand, might largely be interpreted as a commemorative beginning since the founding organization in New York of 1894 was the product of six trustee-officers who, with the exception of William Boring, were not actually present at that Thanksgiving gathering. Arthur T. Sutcliffe, Flagg's office manager, recorded the anniversary event. "The annual dinner of the Beaux-Arts Society was held at the Brevort Hotel tonight together with the election of officers. Mr. Flagg who was the one who first suggested it was elected president tonight. He made a little historical sketch going back to a dinner at the Café d'Orsay in Paris 21 years ago when it was first suggested that they meet a year hence in N.Y.C. and then Mr. Flagg made the suggestion to perpetuate the annual dinner in a Society" (Arthur T. Sutcliffe Diary, November 21, 1911 [ATSP, AL, CU]). Ernest Flagg recorded his own presence in Rome from November 6 to November 28, 1890, when he arrived in Naples. Ernest Flagg Diary (EFP, AL, CU).

8. "For a Club of Architects," *New York Tribune*, April 4, 1893. William A. Boring presided and G. T. Snelling (Columbia College School of Mines), Thomas Hastings, and Emmanuel-Louis Masqueray gave addresses. The article also reports the presence of the following architects: James Brite, A. B. Dillon, A. W. Lord, Edward P. Casey, Joseph H. McGuire, John Carrère, John W. Lavalle, John W. Bemis, George Cary, S.B.P. Trowbridge, Holland Anthony, E. D. Lindsey, W. B. Chambers, Edward Tilton, John P. Benson, and Albert L. Brockway. See newspaper clipping (EFP, AL, CU).

9. In addition to these officers, Richard Howland Hunt served as first corresponding secretary and John M. Carrère as chairman of the Committee on Education. These architects, as well as the four officers, served as trustees for the first year. *Society of Beaux-Arts Architects, Incorporated January, 1894* [1916], pp. 4, 52–55.

10. The society's corporate name was not legally changed until 1912 during Flagg's term of office as president. "Amendment to Articles of Incorporation," February 22, 1912, *Society of Beaux-Arts Architects, Incorporated January, 1894* [1916], pp. 5–6. Flagg was elected president for two terms, 1911–12; 1912–13.

11. The trustees regarded the social functions of the new society to be ancillary to its educational role. The society's objectives were "to cultivate and perpetuate the associations and principles of the Ecole des Beaux-Arts of Paris and to found an Academy of Architecture for the purpose of architectural exhibitions and training, and to establish and maintain a library of architecture, also a club house for social usages" (*Society of*

Beaux-Arts Architects, Incorporated January, 1894 [1916], p. 3). They were similar to those in Flagg's 1893 report. See "To Found an Academy of Architecture," *New York Times,* January 23, 1893, p. 4, and a notice in *AABN* XLIII (February 3, 1894), p. 49.

12. Though not an alumnus of the Ecole des Beaux-Arts, Ware had been one of the students in Hunt's studio and had established his own office atelier in Boston when he formed a partnership with Henry Van Brunt in 1863. To develop the M.I.T. curriculum, Ware traveled to Europe to observe European schools, particularly the Ecole des Beaux-Arts. See William A. Coles, ed., *Architecture and Society* (Cambridge, Mass.: Harvard University Press, 1969), p. 16. See also Leopold Arnaud, "Columbia Dean Recalls this Century Brought 'Beaux Arts' Schools to United States," Letter to the Editor, *Progressive Architecture* XXX (January 1950), p. 9.

13. Catherine Clinton Howland Hunt, *The Richard Morris Hunt Papers,* Alan Burnham, ed., p. 161 (American Architectural Archive). See also Steven M. Bedford, "History 1: the founding of the School," and David G. De Long, "William R. Ware and the pursuit of suitability," in Richard Oliver, ed., *The Making of an Architect 1881–1981* (New York: Rizzoli, 1981), pp. 8–16.

14. F. H. Bosworth, Jr., and Roy Childs Jones, *A Study of Architectural Schools* (New York: Charles Scribner's Sons, 1932), p. 3.

15. *AABN* XLIII (February 3, 1894), p. 49.

16. "Society of Beaux Art[s] Architects," October 2, 1894, unpublished manuscript (EFP, AL, CU).

17. Ibid.

18. For Hunt's studio, see Paul R. Baker, *Richard Morris Hunt* (Cambridge, Mass.: MIT Press, 1980), pp. 100–107; Henry Van Brunt, "Richard Morris Hunt," in Coles, ed., *Architecture and Society,* pp. 332–33; James F. O'Gorman, *The Architecture of Frank Furness* (Philadelphia: Museum of Art, 1973), pp. 23–30. Two of Hunt's students, William Robert Ware and Henry Van Brunt, carried the studio tradition to Boston where in 1863 they established an atelier in conjunction with their office practice. See T.F.H. [Talbot Faulkner Hamlin], "William Robert Ware," *DAB,* XIX (New York: Charles Scribner's Sons, 1936), pp. 452–53. See also James F. O'Gorman, *H. H. Richardson and His Office* (Cambridge, Mass.: Harvard College Library, 1974), pp. 4–13.

19. Like those before it, this atelier partnership largely reflected Richard Morris Hunt's influence. From 1891, both Masqueray and Chambers had been employed in Hunt's office as draftsmen for Biltmore, the George Washington Vanderbilt House near Asheville, North Carolina. For a survey of Masqueray's career at the Ecole, see Delaire, p. 342. Hunt's paternalism toward Chambers was longstanding. Chambers's father and Hunt were friends and fellow members of the Century Club. Hunt played an advisory role in the family decision that Chambers pursue architectural studies, first in Munich, then Paris. See Francis S. Swales, "Draftsmanship and Architecture as Exemplified by

the Work of Walter B. Chambers," *Pencil Points* IX (September 1928), pp. 543–56.

20. *The Brochure Series* III (1897), p. 111.

21. Both Carrère & Hastings and Flagg directed ateliers associated with their offices where students received instruction in return for drafting assistance. Flagg's office atelier, however, was short-lived. See *The Brochure Series* I (1895), pp. 9, 11. Flagg's address to the Society of Beaux-Arts Architects on October 2, 1894, indicates that he had already dissolved his office atelier. "Many of the members of the society have had pupils in their offices, but this arrangement has serious drawbacks," Flagg observed. "If the office is busy, very great inconvenience and disorganization results. In my own case I have had to abolish the practice" ("Society of Beaux Art[s] Architects," October 2, 1894, unpublished manuscript [EFP, AL, CU]).

22. "A Too-Vaulting Ambition," *AABN* LXXXVIII (December 30, 1905), p. 210.

23. "A School of Architecture, Columbia University," ibid., p. 212.

24. "History," *Ball of the Fine Arts* [Beaux-Arts Ball program], March 11, 1920, the Society of Beaux-Arts Architects and the Beaux-Arts Institute of Design (National Institute for Architectural Education).

25. Ibid.

26. The Society of Beaux-Arts Architects was eventually recognized by the Ecole des Beaux-Arts in Paris when the society founded the Paris Prize in 1904. Awarded by competition, the American recipient was automatically received into the first class at the Ecole without taking the usual entrance exams. See "History," *Ball of the Fine Arts*. See also Noffsinger, *Influence of the Ecole des Beaux-Arts,* pp. 54–64. In 1954 the National Institute for Architectural Education became the successor organization to the Beaux-Arts Institute of Design.

27. Otto J. Teegen, "The B.A.I.D. — Its Past and Future," *JAIA* XX (October 1953), p. 184.

28. Flagg, "Influence of the French School on Architecture in the United States," *Arch Rec* IV (October–December 1894), p. 226.

29. Ibid.

30. R. S. [Russell Sturgis], "Style," in Sturgis, ed., *A Dictionary of Architecture and Building,* vol. 3 (New York: Macmillan Company, 1902), p. 671.

31. Ibid.

32. Flagg, "Influence of the French School," p. 211.

33. Ernest Flagg, "American Architecture as Opposed to Architecture in America," *Arch Rec* X (October 1900), p. 178.

34. Thomas Hastings, "The Relations of Life to Style in Architecture," *Harper's New Monthly Magazine* LXXXVIII (May 1894), p. 959.

35. Ibid.

36. Ibid., p. 960.

37. Ernest Flagg, "The Truth About American Architecture," unpublished manuscript, pp. 7–8 (EFP, AL, CU).

38. Ibid., p. 7.

39. Flagg, ibid., pp. 7–8. Thomas Hastings, "Architecture and Modern Life," *Harper's New Monthly Magazine* XCIV (May 1897), p. 404.

40. Hastings, "Relations of Life to Style," p. 960.

41. Ibid., p. 957.

42. Flagg, "American Architecture as Opposed to Architecture in America," p. 180.

43. Ibid.

44. Ibid.

45. Flagg, "Influence of the French School," p. 218.

46. M. S. [Montgomery Schuyler], "Schools of Architecture and the Paris School," *Scribner's Magazine* XXIV (December 1898), p. 765.

47. Ibid., pp. 765–66.

48. Ibid., p. 766.

49. David Van Zanten illustrates and discusses Emile Bénard's Premier Grand Prix design of 1867, *Un Palais pour l'exposition des Beaux-Arts* (A Palace for an Exhibition of Fine Arts). See his "Architectural Composition at the Ecole des Beaux-Arts from Charles Percier to Charles Garnier," in Drexler, ed., *Architecture of the Ecole des Beaux-Arts,* where Atwood's Fine Arts Building and the other structures of the World's Columbian Exposition of 1893 also are discussed and illustrated, pp. 240–41, 252–54, 470–74.

50. Ernest Flagg, Letter to the Editor, *The Sun,* December 18, 1898, II, p. 3.

51. Ibid.

52. Van Brunt, "The Historic Styles and Modern Architecture," in Coles, ed., *Architecture and Society,* pp. 303–4.

53. Fiske Kimball, *American Architecture* (Indianapolis and New York: Bobbs-Merrill Company, 1928), pp. 147–68. I am grateful to William Jordy for revealing the significance of this essay and for sharing his observations with me.

54. Ibid., p. 166.

55. Ibid., p. 149.

56. Ibid., chapter, "The Triumph of Classical Form," pp. 171–87.

57. Jean Paul Carlhian discusses some of the departures from French classicism that American architects made. "Beaux Arts or 'Bozarts'?," *Arch Rec* CLIX (January 1976), pp. 131–34.

58. Kimball, *American Architecture*, p. 163.

59. Among those who attacked the archaeological basis of McKim, Mead & White's architecture, Herbert Langford Warren made a forceful argument. See "The Use and Abuse of Precedent," *Arch Rev* II (April 3, 1893), p. 23.

60. "A Letter by Ernest Flagg," *Architectural Annual,* Albert Kelsey, ed., 1900, p. 31.

61. Ibid., pp. 31–32.

62. The Architectural League of America has been the subject of a study by David Van Zanten who kindly supplied me with the text of his lecture, "Beaux-Arts Architecture and the American Renaissance," delivered at the National Collection of the Fine Arts, March 26, 1977. At least two members of the Society of Beaux-Arts Architects attended the League's first convention in Cleveland in 1899: John E. Howe and Alexander Buell Trowbridge. Howe was a member of the society's Committee on Education in 1895 and its corresponding secretary in 1896 and 1897–98. A. B. Trowbridge, a professor at Cornell University, served as the society's secretary from 1909 to 1912. *The Society of Beaux-Arts Architects, Incorporated January, 1894* [1916], pp. 53–55. For the roster of clubs, see *Architectural Annual,* Kelsey, ed., 1900, p. 279.

63. The Architectural League of America is purported to have pursued architectural education "without in any way infringing upon the prerogatives of the American Institute of Architects," but implications of their partisanship made them suspect. "Convention Architectural League of America," *Inland Architect and News Record* XXXV (June 1900), p. 35.

64. See Flagg's letter in answer to the question circulated on January 13, 1899, by Albert Kelsey to a number of prominent architects, "An Unaffected School of Modern Architecture in America — Will it come?" *Catalogue of the T Square Club Exhibition and Architectural Annual for the year 1898* [Philadelphia, 1899], pp. 20–22; reprinted as "A Letter by Ernest Flagg" in *Architectural Annual,* Kelsey, ed., 1900, pp. 31–32.

65. Taking his cue from Flagg, Kelsey counseled the delegates: "The advancement of American architecture, as opposed to architecture in America, should be our common purpose." Albert Kelsey, "The Advancement of American Architecture," *AABN* LXV (July 8, 1899), p. 13.

66. Louis H. Sullivan, "The Modern Phase of Architecture," *Inland Architect and News Record* XXXIII (June 1899), p. 40.

67. "Second Annual Convention of the Architectural League of America," *Inland Architect and News Record* XXXV (June 1900), p. 43. Flagg did not attend either convention.

68. Flagg's paper, "American Architecture as Opposed to Architecture in America," was

first published in the *Inland Architect and News Record* XXXV (June 1900), p. 36. Other leading architectural journals subsequently published the article. See *AABN* LXVIII (June 23, 1900), p. 93; *Southern Architect and Contractor* XI (July 20, 1900); and *Arch Rec* X (October 1900), pp. 178–90. Future citation of Flagg's paper refers to its publication in *Architectural Record*. Louis Sullivan delivered an address at the Chicago convention. The text, "The Young Man in Architecture," appeared in the *Inland Architect and News Record* XXXV (June 1900), pp. 38–40.

69. William Gray Purcell, "Biographical Notes," November 7, 1949, p. 26 (New-York Historical Society). See also David Gebhard, "Purcell and Elmslie," in Adolf K. Placzek, ed., *Macmillan Encyclopedia of Architects* (New York: Free Press, 1982), vol. 3, pp. 500–503.

70. William Gray Purcell, "Biographical Notes," November 7, 1949, p. 27 (New-York Historical Society).

71. Letter, William Gray Purcell to Wayne Andrews, February 18, 1950 (New-York Historical Society).

72. Flagg, "American Architecture as Opposed to Architecture in America," p. 178.

73. David Gray, *Thomas Hastings* (Boston: Houghton Mifflin and Company, 1933), p. 34.

74. For illustrations of these buildings, see "The Work of Messrs. Carrère & Hastings," *Arch Rec* XXVII (January 1910), pp. 1–120; and Curtis Channing Blake, "The Architecture of Carrère and Hastings," (Ph.D. diss., Columbia University, 1976), pls. 66, 149, 163, 164, 177.

75. Curtis Channing Blake argues the issue of planarity in "The Architecture of Carrère and Hastings," pp. 48–49. See also H. W. Desmond, "A Beaux-Arts Skyscraper — The Blair Building, New York City," *Arch Rec* XIV (December 1903), pp. 436–43.

76. Eugène-Emmanuel Viollet-le-Duc, *Discourses on Architecture,* vol. 1, Van Brunt, trans. (Boston: James R. Osgood and Company, 1875), p. 245.

77. Hastings, "Architecture and Modern Life," p. 407.

78. For illustrations of Boring & Tilton's Ellis Island buildings, see "The New York Immigrant Station," *Arch Rec* XII (December 1902), pp. 726–33. Grand Central Terminal is illustrated in Wayne Andrews, *Architecture in New York* (New York: Atheneum, 1969), pp. 120–22.

79. See illustrations in Flagg, "American Architecture as Opposed to Architecture in America," pp. 181–90.

80. For a discussion of Colonial and Federal Revival architecture in the formation of a national style, see Mardges Bacon, "Toward a National Style of Architecture: The Beaux-Arts Interpretation of the Colonial Revival," in Alan Axelrod, ed., *The Colonial Revival in America* (New York: W. W. Norton & Co., 1985).

81. Letter, Ernest Flagg to Henry Saylor, November 23, 1945 (American Institute of Architects).

82. Each of the five architects would receive $400. The general invitation to architects stipulated that no compensation would be made for their services, unless one of their plans was selected. *Board of Managers Minutes,* April 25, 1892, pp. 609–15 (St. Luke's Hospital).

83. The Building Committee also served as jury for the competition. Its members were Samuel D. Babcock, chairman; Henry A. Oakley; George A. Crocker; Hugh N. Camp; F.W.G. Hurst; Aaron Ogden, secretary. Ex-officio members included George Macculloch Miller, president of the Board of Managers; George Norrie, treasurer of the Board of Managers; and Cornelius Vanderbilt II, chairman of the Executive Committee. *Thirty-Fourth Annual Report,* Board of Managers, St. Luke's Hospital (year ending October 18, 1892), pp. 8–9.

84. Wayne Andrews, *The Vanderbilt Legend* (New York: Harcourt, Brace and Company, 1941), p. 350. The Board of Managers sent a letter to Vanderbilt "expressive of the sympathy of the Board with him in the loss he has sustained in the death of his son" (*Board of Managers Minutes,* May 26, 1892, p. 619 [St. Luke's Hospital]).

85. *Thirty-Fourth Annual Report* (year ending October 18, 1892), p. 8. Of the five architects originally invited to compete, James Renwick and Charles W. Clinton did not submit entries. Other architectural firms which submitted plans were Charles A. Gifford; Sinclair, Doan & Horsfall; Thom, Wilson & Schaarschmidt; William Halsey Wood; Henry R. Marshall; and George Keller.

86. *Board of Managers Minutes,* September 26, 1892, p. 620 (St. Luke's Hospital). Plans by the other six competitors were exhibited at the Germania Building at the corner of William and Cedar streets, New York.

87. Matthew Daly, Letter to the Editor, *New York Times,* August 29, 1892, p. 3.

88. W. B. Chambers, "Architects' Plans for New St. Luke's," *The Mail and Express* (New York), September 7, 1892, p. 7. The article is dated August 31, 1892.

89. The arrangement specified that Flagg would assume Clinton's architectural fees. *Executive Committee, Board of Managers Minutes,* November 28, 1892 (St. Luke's Hospital).

90. H. W. Desmond, "Introduction" to "The Works of Ernest Flagg," *Arch Rec* XI (April 1902), p. [1].

91. Ibid.

92. Vanderbilt never fully recovered from an illness in 1896 and died in 1899 at the age of fifty-six. *The Board of Managers Minutes* contain a eulogy of Vanderbilt, praising his service as an associate of the hospital for twenty-four years. See entry for September 25, 1899, pp. 401–2 (St. Luke's Hospital).

93. Letter, J.Q.A. Ward to Frederick B. McGuire [Corcoran trustee], October 19, 1891, and a sequel to the letter, J.Q.A. Ward to Frederick B. McGuire, undated (#7260, Corcoran Gallery of Art Archives).

94. *Proceedings of Meeting of the Board of Trustees,* April 9, 1892, p. 1, Corcoran Gallery of

Art Archives (hereinafter cited as *Proceedings Corcoran*). Carrère had shown an interest in the new Corcoran from the time of his earliest inquiry to the trustees in the spring of 1891. Letter, Carrère & Hastings to "Trustees Corcoran," April 22, 1891 (#7440, Corcoran Gallery of Art Archives).

95. Three "Washington architects, Paul J. Pelz, Hornblower & Marshall, and W. B. Gray were invited to present suggestions for $200 compensation each" (*Proceedings Corcoran*, June 9, 1892, p. 2). Three more architects submitted drawings without compensation. *Proceedings Corcoran*, January 31, 1893, p. 4.

96. Letters, F. S. Barbarin to Ernest Flagg, May 23, 1892, May [27], 1892, June 22, 1892, October 11, 1892 (Letter Pressbooks, pp. 489–90, 497–99, 545–46, 608–9); Ernest Flagg to Edward Clark, April 6, 1892 (#7450); Ernest Flagg to Dr. Barbarin, April 20, 1892, May 16, 1892, May 17, 1892, May 20, 1892, May 24, 1892, May 27, 1892, May 28, 1892, June 15, 1892, June 23, 1892, July 6, 1892, July 7, 1892, July 12, 1892, October 13, 1892 (#7466, 7485, 7492, 7496, 7501, 7525, 7539, 7544, 7602, Corcoran Gallery of Art Archives).

97. "Report of the Special Committee on Plans for the New Gallery," April 10, 1893, *Proceedings Corcoran*, p. 17.

98. Letter of reply, Ernest Flagg to Dr. F. S. Barberin [sic], April 19, 1893 (#7811, Corcoran Gallery of Art Archives); "The New Corcoran Gallery," *Evening Star* (Washington, D.C.), April 15, 1893 (Corcoran Gallery of Art Archives).

99. "Exhibit of Competitive Plans for the New Corcoran Gallery of Art," *AABN* XLIII (January 27, 1894), pp. 44–45.

100. "Glover, Charles Carroll," *The National Cyclopaedia of American Biography*, 1945, XXXII, p. 338.

101. The Committee Minutes of April 30, 1894, record that "on motion of Mr. Glover it was ordered that Mr. Flagg see Mr. J. S. Larcombe [clerk of the works] with authority to engage his services" (*Proceedings Corcoran*, p. 61).

102. Letter, Ernest Flagg to the Building Committee, October 16, 1896 (#9299, Corcoran Gallery of Art Archives).

103. Ernest Flagg, "The Corcoran Gallery of Art," essay in unpublished manuscript, "One Hundred and One Observations and a Century of Life," hereinafter cited as "Observations" (EFP, AL, CU).

104. Norcross Brothers was awarded the contract with the lowest bid of $349,434. See Contract (between James H. Norcross and Orlando W. Norcross of Worcester, Massachusetts, and the Trustees of the Corcoran Gallery of Art), June 23, 1894 (#8326, Corcoran Gallery of Art Archives).

105. Letter, Norcross Brothers to F. S. Barbarin, October 7, 1896, in Committee Minutes, October 15, 1896, *Proceedings Corcoran*, p. 221.

106. Committee Minutes, July 16, 1896, *Proceedings Corcoran,* p. 215; and October 15, 1896, *Proceedings Corcoran,* pp. 219–21.

107. Telegram, Norcross Brothers to F. S. Barbarin, October 7, 1896, reported in Committee Minutes, October 15, 1896, *Proceedings Corcoran,* p. 221. James F. O'Gorman has identified Orlando Whitney Norcross, a principal in the Norcross Brothers firm, as H. H. Richardson's "Master Builder." See O'Gorman's article, "O. W. Norcross, Richardson's 'Master Builder': A Preliminary Report," *JSAH* XXXII (May 1973), pp. 104–13.

108. Letter, Carlisle & Johnson, to Ernest Flagg, October 16, 1896 (#9297, Corcoran Gallery of Art Archives).

109. Telegram, Ernest Flagg to Carlisle & Johnson, October 16, 1896 (#9299, Corcoran Gallery of Art Archives).

110. Letter, Ernest Flagg to Carlisle & Johnson, October 16, 1896 (#9299, Corcoran Gallery of Art Archives).

111. Letter, Carlisle & Johnson to Ernest Flagg, October 19, 1896, reported in Committee Minutes, October 19, 1896, *Proceedings Corcoran,* pp. 247–49.

112. Letter, Ernest Flagg to F. B. McGuire, August 11, 1896 (#9209, Corcoran Gallery of Art Archives). In his article on O. W. Norcross, James F. O'Gorman states that "Norcross had a reputation for the accuracy of his estimates" ("O. W. Norcross, Richardson's 'Master Builder,' " p. 113, n. 32).

113. Letter, Ernest Flagg to Barbarin, June 26, 1896. This letter is one of several in which Flagg defended his position (#9155, Corcoran Gallery of Art Archives).

114. In its claims against the Corcoran's Board of Trustees, Norcross Brothers maintained: " . . . our records show an expenditure of $460,653.64 for the work finished, adding 10% to which, for conducting the operations, makes $506,719 — a charge in no way unreasonable for the building as built. We have received in cash on account $362,689.24, leaving a balance from the above amount of $144,029.76" (Letter, Norcross Brothers to Frederick B. McGuire, June 26, 1897 [#9751, Corcoran Gallery of Art Archives]). Norcross Brothers submitted to the Corcoran trustees at least two offers of compromise. On April 8, 1899, the Corcoran settled the claim with Norcross Brothers for the comparatively small sum of $16,981.70. Norcross thus received a total of $379,670.94. See "Norcross Brothers," April 8, 1899, *New Gallery Account 1893–1897* (Corcoran Gallery of Art Archives). According to Flagg's office records, the actual cost of construction amounted to $459,525.07, a figure which approached Norcross's sum of $460,653.64. See *Ernest Flagg Account Book* (ATSP, AL, CU). Perhaps in an effort to overstate their losses to the Corcoran trustees for the sake of the claim, Norcross Brothers' own documents indicate that its losses were actually less. One document listing contracts completed during the years from 1881 to 1907 includes the Corcoran Gallery of Art with a contract price of $382,850 and a loss on the project of $44,353 (exclusive of a 10 percent fee for "conducting the operation"). Letter, Philip

Norcross Gross to author, June 22, 1976.

115. Letter, Ernest Flagg to Charles C. Glover, May 14, 1920 (Corcoran Gallery of Art Archives).

116. John Bigelow, "The Tilden Trust Library: What Shall it Be?" *Scribner's Magazine* XII (September 1892), pp. 287–300. Arthur J. Dillon, "The Proposed Tilden Trust Library," *Arch Rev* I (September 12, 1892), pp. 69–72. Both Phyllis Dain and Curtis Channing Blake chronicle the planning of the New York Public Library. See Dain, *The New York Public Library* (New York: New York Public Library, 1972), and Blake, "The Architecture of Carrère and Hastings," pp. 203–50.

117. Bigelow, "The Tilden Trust Library: What Shall it Be?" p. 293.

118. Ibid.

119. "City Hall in Bryant Park," *New York Sun,* February 26, 1893, and "The Old City Hall," *New York World,* February 27, 1893, newspaper clippings in scrapbook (EFP, AL, CU). See also John Bigelow, "The New York City Hall and the Tilden Library," *The Library Journal* XVIII (March 1893), pp.77–80.

120. See Blake, "The Architecture of Carrère and Hastings," p. 213, and Dain, *The New York Public Library,* pp. 53–56.

121. Dain, *The New York Public Library,* pp. 155–56.

122. Ibid., pp. 87–88, 160.

123. Ibid., pp. 158–59.

124. Ibid., pp. 161–62 and n. 69 in reference to Bigelow's Diary entries of May 3 and May 8, 1897.

125. On July 27, 1897, the Committee invited the following six architects to compete: McKim, Mead & White; George B. Post; Carrère & Hastings; Cyrus L. W. Eidlitz; Charles C. Haight; and Peabody & Stearns. See Harry Miller Lydenberg, *History of the New York Public Library, Astor, Lenox and Tilden Foundations* (New York: New York Public Library, 1923), p. 448. See also Dain, *The New York Public Library,* p. 167.

126. Dain, *The New York Public Library,* p. 168.

127. Blake, "The Architecture of Carrère and Hastings," pp. 218–19.

128. Letter, G. L. Rives to Calderon Carlisle, May 8 [1897] (Board of Trustees Letters, Manuscripts Division, New York Public Library).

129. "Special Meeting of the Board of Trustees" [Minutes], May 13, 1897, *Journal of the Official Proceedings of the Trustees of the Corcoran Gallery of Art,* II, pp. 434–35 (Corcoran Gallery of Art Archives).

130. John Bigelow Diary, June 4, 1897, p. 208 (Manuscripts Division, New York Public Library). Earlier, the Corcoran Trustees withdrew their threat to dismiss Flagg as

architect, as conveyed to Ernest Flagg in a letter from Carlisle & Johnson on October 19, 1896, *Proceedings Corcoran,* p. 247:

> Your letter of the 18th from Pittsburgh has been laid before the Committee and they instruct us to say that the Committee has the highest appreciation of your taste and talents as an artist and having never wished to do any injustice are now particularly anxious not to do you any unnecessary damage. In view therefore of the satisfactory agreement of the present difficulty directed with Messrs. Norcross, while the Committee have felt it right to make clear to you their view of your conduct, they deem it just under the circumstances to rescind the resolution of the 16th inst. dispensing with your services, and direct us to announce to you the fact.

131. John Bigelow Diary, June 4, 1897, p. 209 (Manuscripts Division, New York Public Library).

132. Henry Y. Satterlee, *The Building of a Cathedral* (New York: Edwin S. Gorham, 1901), p. 91. Richard T. Feller and Marshall W. Fishwick, *For Thy Great Glory* (Culpeper, Va.: Community Press, 1965), p. 98.

133. "The Style for a New Cathedral," *AABN* XLIX (August 17, 1895), p. 71.

134. See Feller and Fishwick, *For Thy Great Glory,* p. 15.

135. "Plans for the Great Cathedral," *New York Herald,* January 19, 1896, p. 2. "The New Cathedral at Washington," *Harper's Weekly* XL (January 25, 1896), p. 91.

136. Before May 6, 1895, Flagg also submitted plans for a proposed Hearst School for Girls, which he published along with cathedral plans a year later in *Architecture and Building.* While progress on the building program for the cathedral was temporarily halted for land to be purchased and building funds accumulated, approval for the Hearst School for Girls was given. But Flagg was not chosen as architect. Between May 6, 1895, and the year that followed, relations with Calderon Carlisle and Charles Glover had deteriorated beyond adequate repair. By the fall of 1898 when the building contract was signed, cathedral trustees had approved a Renaissance design by another architect, Robert W. Gibson. Letter, Ernest Flagg to Rev. Dr. George William Douglass [sic] (cathedral trustee), May 6, 1895 (Archives, Washington Cathedral). See illustration, *Architecture and Building* XXIV (May 16, 1896), no. 20. See also Feller and Fishwick, *For Thy Great Glory,* p. 9, and Satterlee, *The Building of a Cathedral,* p. 35.

137. Feller and Fishwick, *For Thy Great Glory,* pp. 15–16.

138. William Morgan, *The Almighty Wall: The Architecture of Henry Vaughan* (New York and Cambridge, Mass.: Architectural History Foundation and MIT Press, 1983), pp. 73–75; David Verey, "George Frederick Bodley: Climax of the Gothic Revival," in Jane Fawcett, ed., *Seven Victorian Architects* (London: Thames and Hudson, 1976), p. 100; Feller and Fishwick, *For Thy Great Glory,* pp. 16–19.

139. The Ware-Flagg dispute is discussed in Chapter VIII.

140. Letter, Charles F. McKim to Ernest Flagg, May 26, 1897, Box 2, p. 77 (McKim Collection, Library of Congress). I wish to thank J. A. Chewning for informing me

about this correspondence and for generously supplying me with the text of McKim's letters cited here.

141. Ibid.

142. Letter, Charles F. McKim to Walter Cook, May 26, 1897, Box 2, p. 76 (McKim Collection, Library of Congress).

143. *AABN* LVIII (October 9, 1897), p. 9. Many of the competition drawings are illustrated in John Galen Howard's article, "The Paris Training," *Arch Rev* V (January 1898), pp. 4–7, pls. I–X.

144. See membership list in Eliot Clark, *History of the National Academy of Design 1825– 1953* (New York: Columbia University Press, 1954), pp. 246–75. Flagg's older brother, Charles Noel Flagg (1848–1916), was elected an associate of the National Academy in 1909, see Clark, p. 254.

145. Letter, Charles F. McKim to Geo. B. Post, Esq. and others, Competitors, National Academy of Design, July 1, 1897, Box 2, p. 154 (McKim Collection, Library of Congress); in same source, see also Letter, Charles F. McKim to Ernest Flagg, July 1, 1897, Box 2, p. 153.

146. The results of these competitions were announced in *AABN* LVIII (November 20, 1897), p. 61.

147. See Lois Craig et al., *The Federal Presence: Architecture, Politics, and Symbols in United States Government Building* (Cambridge, Mass.: MIT Press, 1978), pp. 202–3.

148. "New Annapolis to be Keystone of Arch of the New Navy," *Washington Times,* July 24, 1904, III, p. 9.

149. Although Glenn Brown was also Architect of the Capitol, he wrote on behalf of the A.I.A. using the stationery of the Office of the Secretary. See Letter, Glenn Brown to John D. Long, March 26, 1900, *General File 5474/43,* Box 267, General Records of the Department of the Navy, Record Group 80, National Archives Building.

150. Letter, F. W. Hackett to the Secretary of the Navy [John D. Long], August 1, 1900, *General File 5474/49,* Box 267, RG 80, NA.

151. Ibid.

152. See Frank Lloyd Wright, "Competitions," *An Autobiography* (London: Longmans, Green and Company, 1933), pp. 152–53. Flagg's skepticism did not include the first competition for the State Capitol, Olympia, Washington, which he won. Columbia professor William Robert Ware served as principal juror. In his report of January 5, 1894, Ware ranked Flagg's design in first place as "the most elegant and scholarly that the competition has called forth." Ware concluded that "the whole treatment of the problem inspires confidence in its author as does the paper which accompanies the drawings; and it would seem as if the committee could hardly make a mistake if they intrusted the work to his hands" ("Report of Prof. W. R. Ware," *Inland Architect and*

News Record XXIII [June 1894], pp. 54–55). But soon after the foundations were laid, the project was abandoned due to insufficient funds. It was not until 1910 that there were renewed efforts to build a State Capitol. Invited to compete, Flagg reluctantly agreed, even though "it seems useless to do so in view of the fact that I have not won a competition in 17 years" (Ernest Flagg Diary, October 30, 1910 [EFP, AL, CU]). Flagg presented a new design for a group of buildings that persuaded state officials in Olympia to support him. They assumed that Flagg's original contract was still valid until members of the Washington State Chapter of the A.I.A. challenged it in 1911 and Flagg was effectively excluded. Henry-Russell Hitchcock and William Seale, *Temples of Democracy* (New York and London: Harcourt Brace Jovanovich, 1976), pp. 226, 257–60. In the midst of preparing the Capitol plans and skeptical of the results of the competition, Flagg recorded twenty-four "unsuccessful competitions," adding that "these have all been done during the last 17 years and have cost me more than $20,000 and lots of hard work." Flagg also listed ten "cases where I have done lots of work with no pay" (Ernest Flagg Diary, January 11, 1911 [EFP, AL, CU]).

153. The City and Suburban Homes Company's model tenement house competition of 1896 is discussed in Chapter VIII.

154. See Jared B. Flagg, *Flagg's Flats,* privately printed, 1909. Following a raid on Jared Flagg's office by postal inspectors in 1911, he was convicted of using the mails to defraud and served eighteen months in a federal prison. In 1926 Jared died during another fraud inquiry. "Jared Flagg," obituary, *New York Times,* August 27, 1926, p. 17.

155. Ernest Flagg Diary, April 12, 1911 (EFP, AL, CU).

156. Ibid., February 26, 1909.

157. Ernest Flagg Diary, January 10, 1911 (EFP, AL, CU). An examination of the New York Chapter by-laws corroborates the change in election procedures so that the "secret letter-ballot" of 1909 was discontinued by 1911. Cf. *Yearbook New York Chapter of the American Institute of Architects,* By-Laws, Article VIII, Section 7, 1909, pp. 63–64; 1911, pp. 64–65.

158. Ernest Flagg Diary, November 21, 1911 (EFP, AL, CU). In 1910 Flagg recorded that he was to be "placed on the Executive committee of the Beaux-Arts Society this year with a view to making the President next year" (Ernest Flagg Diary, November 15, 1910 [EFP, AL, CU]).

159. John P. Benson's name appears on the office letterhead in 1891. Letter, Ernest Flagg to S. H. Kauffmann, October 24, 1891 (#7260, Corcoran Gallery of Art Archives).

160. Albert L. Brockway's name was added to the office letterhead in 1892. Letter, Ernest Flagg to Dr. Barbaran [sic], May 24, 1892 (#7496, Corcoran Gallery of Art Archives).

161. Both Benson and Brockway had been present at the Café d'Orsay Thanksgiving dinner in 1890. In 1893 they joined Flagg at a meeting of American Ecole alumni for the purpose of discussing a permanent organization which led to the formation of the Society

of Beaux-Arts Architects, see "For a Club of Architects." John P. Benson was also a "witness" to the "Articles of Incorporation," *Society of Beaux-Arts Architects, Incorporated January, 1894* [1916], p. 4.

162. The publication in 1894 of the Tamalpais Apartment House, Chicago, by *Inland Architect and News Record* XXIV (November 1894), is the earliest evidence of their collaboration. Informed by an Italian, as opposed to a French classicism, the design of the Tamalpais Apartment House is characteristic of Chambers's, rather than Flagg's, architecture.

163. Extant office correspondence forms the basis of this chronology. Flagg carried office stationery with two separate letterheads: one with his name alone, the other with those of his partners added.

164. Swales, "Draftsmanship and Architecture as Exemplified by the Work of Walter B. Chambers," p. 553.

165. Ibid.

166. When Flagg pressed Arthur T. Sutcliffe to become his office manager, Flagg summed up his relationship with Chambers in 1907: "Mr. Chambers has not left and has no intention of leaving but devotes himself entirely to his own clients. Formerly he gave most of his time to my affairs on an agreement between us which ran out and was not renewed. He now has an interest in my work and I have an interest in his" (Letter, Ernest Flagg to Arthur T. Sutcliffe, January 29 [1907], [ATSP, AL, CU]). Their association was largely financial rather than artistic.

167. Walter Chambers held memberships in the Scroll and Key Society at Yale University, the Century and University clubs, New York. See "Walter B. Chambers," obituary, *New York Times,* April 21, 1945, p. 13.

168. Letter, Robert B. O'Connor to author, March 6, 1981. For McKim's support of the Tarsney Act, see Leland M. Roth, *McKim, Mead & White, Architects* (New York: Harper & Row, 1983), pp. 182, 395, n. 6.

CHAPTER FOUR

1. For discussions of materialism and the cult of progress in America, see John Higham, "The Reorientation of American Culture in the 1890's" in *Writing American History* (Bloomington: Indiana University Press, 1970), pp. 49, 73–102.

2. Years later Flagg wrote about this project in an unpublished essay entitled "The Corcoran Gallery of Art": "When I was in Paris I made a design for an art gallery for New York. I had in mind as a location for it the block between Madison and Vanderbilt Avenues and 43rd and 45th Streets which was then vacant. I knew that there was great need for such a place and thought that when I returned I might be able to interest The National Academy of Design in it. In making the drawings I had the criticism of my

patron M. Paul Blondel'' (EFP, AL, CU).

3. Eliot Clark, *History of the National Academy of Design 1825–1953* (New York: Columbia University, 1954), p. 255.

4. Ibid., pp. 142ff. Sarah Bradford Landau, *P. B. Wight: Architect, Contractor, and Critic, 1838–1925* (Chicago: Art Institute of Chicago, 1981), pp. 16–21.

5. Again, Flagg tells us his version of the story in ''The Corcoran Gallery of Art'': ''When I returned I showed what I had done to the members of the Council of the Academy who became very much interested in it but they saw no way to secure the necessary funds.

At this time the trustees of the Corcoran Gallery of Art in Washington had under contemplation the erection of a new building and Mr. J.Q.A. Ward the sculptor spoke to them about the design mentioned and was so enthusiastic in his praise of it that I was consulted by the Corcoran trustees'' (EFP, AL, CU).

In a letter to one Corcoran trustee, Ward lent his full support to Flagg's design: ''The young architect of whom I spoke had spent much time during and since his studies in the Beaux Arts, in preparing studies for a New Academy Building here in New York. He had the best professional advice in Paris, and seemed to have gone over the ground in a very careful and thorough manner'' (Letter, J.Q.A. Ward to Frederick B. McGuire [#7260, Corcoran Gallery of Art Archives]).

6. ''A Brief History of the Corcoran Gallery of Art,'' unpublished manuscript (Corcoran Gallery of Art Archives).

7. Land was purchased on April 3, 1891, ibid.

8. Flagg's presentation drawings, of which a ''perspective view'' and a section survive in the Corcoran collection, were judged on January 31, 1893, by a Special Committee of the Board of Trustees (Corcoran Gallery of Art Archives). See also a photograph (No. 1) of the main elevation on 17th Street which corresponds to the ''perspective view'' and section drawing (see Fig. 22 herein). *Report of the Special Committee on Plans for the New Gallery Presented to the Board of Trustees, April 10, 1893*, p. 19 (Corcoran Gallery of Art Archives). Letter, Ernest Flagg to Dr. F. Sinclair Barbarin, May 28, 1892, (#7501, Corcoran Gallery of Art Archives). Flagg also modeled a room arrangement after one in the Louvre. Letter, Ernest Flagg to F. S. Barbarin, July 6, 1892 (#7539, Corcoran Gallery of Art Archives).

9. *AABN* LVIII (October 9, 1897), p. 9. Clark, *History of the National Academy of Design 1825–1953,* p. 145.

10. Clark, *History of the National Academy of Design 1825–1953,* pp. 145–47; Landau, *P. B. Wight: Architect, Contractor, and Critic, 1838–1925,* pp. 20–21.

11. Compare Flagg's descriptions of the Corcoran and National Academy of Design which accompanied the competition drawings: [Ernest Flagg] ''Description of Drawings Submitted by Ernest Flagg'' (#7666, Corcoran Gallery of Art Archives); [Ernest Flagg] ''Design [for the New National Academy of Design building, 1897] Submitted by Ernest Flagg, Architect'' (Archives of the National Academy of Design). I would like to

thank Sarah Bradford Landau for locating Flagg's description of his National Academy of Design building and for sending me a copy of it.

12. For another drawing of Flagg's entry in the National Academy of Design competition, see John Galen Howard, "The Paris Training," *Arch Rev* V (January 1898), p. 7, pl. X.

13. Letter, Ernest Flagg to Dr. F. S. Barbarin, October 13, 1892 (#7602, Corcoran Gallery of Art Archives).

14. The clear sweep from the Corcoran to the Capitol was broken as the McMillan Commission plan of Washington, D.C. (1901), began to be carried out.

15. Flagg's original plan was published subsequent to its exhibition, along with other drawings in the Corcoran Gallery of Art competition, at the headquarters of the Washington Chapter of the A.I.A. "Exhibit of Competitive Plans for the New Corcoran Gallery of Art," *AABN* XLIII (January 27, 1894), pp. 44–45. The second phase of Flagg's plan was never implemented. An addition on that site was constructed, according to the design of Charles Platt (1925–27), to house the Clark Collection. "A Brief History of the Corcoran Gallery of Art" (Corcoran Gallery of Art Archives).

16. In his first letter to S. H. Kauffmann on October 24, 1891, Flagg sent a sketch plan, letter #7260. See correspondence between Ernest Flagg and Dr. F. S. Barbarin, letters #7466, 7485, 7492, 7496, 7501, 7539, 7544, 7602; 489–90, 497–99, 545–46, 608. See also *Proceedings of Meeting of the Board of Trustees,* April 9, 1892, through April 10, 1893, pp. 1–23 (Corcoran Gallery of Art Archives).

17. Letter, Ernest Flagg to Dr. F. S. Barbarin, February 14, 1893 (#7735, Corcoran Gallery of Art Archives); "The New Corcoran Gallery," *Evening Star* (Washington, D.C.), February 20, 1897, newspaper clipping (Corcoran Gallery of Art Archives).

18. A section drawing of Louis Duc's Atrium Court of the Palais de Justice is reproduced in Louis Hautecoeur, *Histoire de l'architecture classique en France* (Paris: A. et J. Picard et Cie, 1957), vol. 7, p. 129, fig. 95.

19. *Report of the Special Committee on Plans for the New Gallery Presented to the Board of Trustees, April 10, 1893,* pp. 17–21 (Corcoran Gallery of Art Archives).

20. Many American building precedents employ a similar massing and response to their sites. Ware & Van Brunt's nineteenth-century Gothic Memorial Hall at Harvard University (1865; 1874–78) contains a comparable program of three parts: auditorium (theater) linked to a main block (refectory) by a transept (Civil War memorial). Hunt recognized Ware & Van Brunt's use of French precedents, Renaissance as well as Gothic, and similar massing a few hundred feet away at the Fogg Art Museum. Richardson also employed a similar massing in his libraries. Yet to express a corner site, Richardson often used cylindrical forms gratuitously, as in his study plan of 1884 for a Young Men's Association Library, Buffalo; see James. F. O'Gorman, *H. H. Richardson and His Office* (Cambridge, Mass.: Harvard College Library, 1974), p. 170, cat. no 29c. In the vicinity of the Corcoran Gallery of Art, another building responds similarly to its site: Thornton's Octagon House (1798–1800). The uniting of cylinder and block at a

corner was a device also common to Greek Revival buildings. Strickland's Philadelphia Exchange (1832–34) and Soane's Tivoli Corner (1804–6) of the Bank of England, London, forcefully express the geometry of these two forms with a refined treatment and the drama of the corner intersection.

21. *Harper's Weekly* called the style of the building *Néo-Grec* and published a drawing of the 17th Street elevation, see "The Corcoran Gallery of Art," XXXVII (April 29, 1893), p. 392.

22. Several engravings of Chambord are contained in Jacques Androuet's Du Cerceau's *Les plus excellents bastiments de France,* 2 vols. (Paris, 1576 and 1579). Flagg owned both volumes.

23. It was not until the appearance of Charles B. Atwood's Fine Arts Building at the World's Columbian Exposition in Chicago in 1893 that a new wave of classicism, however "archaeological," began to dominate American museums.

24. The editors responded to photographs of the Corcoran that were published in *Inland Architect and News Record* XXIX (May 1897). "Current Periodicals," *Arch Rev* IV, no. 4 (1897), p. 31.

25. A similar motif appears on the corner piers of Louis Duc's Salle de Harlay facade of the Palais de Justice.

26. Flagg's partner Albert L. Brockway became a student of Ginain in 1888 when he entered the Ecole. Delaire, p. 197.

27. Neil Levine, "The Romantic Idea of Architectural Legibility: Henri Labrouste and the *Néo-Grec,*" in Arthur Drexler, ed., *Architecture of the Ecole des Beaux-Arts* (New York: Museum of Modern Art, 1977), pp. 350–57.

28. In a letter of December 14, 1894, to Edward Clark, chairman of the Building Committee, Flagg submitted his list of twelve artists: "In the frieze of the main entablature of the new building there is a band of lettering composed of the names of the greatest artists; the chief objective of these letters is to decorate the frieze, but at the same time the names should be selected with care, I have tried to make them representative of the world and have therefore taken one or two names only for each nation; it seems to me America should be represented and for that reason I have introduced the name of 'Allston,' as I think he, both by his works and character would fittingly represent this country" (Letter #8496, Corcoran Gallery of Art Archives). Among the essays in Flagg's unpublished manuscript, "Observations," is one on Washington Allston which also expresses this conviction. "Washington Allston," in "Observations" (Flagg Family Papers). Jared Bradley Flagg's biography of Washington Allston appeared only two years before.

29. Letter, Ernest Flagg to Edward Clark, December 14, 1894 (#8496, Corcoran Gallery of Art Archives). The following notations appear at the end of the letter:

Referred to Committee on Works of Art.
Reported with recommendations Jan 19, 1895
Approved by Board of Trustees Jan 28, [1895]

The Corcoran trustees made several revisions in the list of names, deciding upon eleven all told; but Allston's remained in the final list.

30. The decision was approved by the Corcoran trustees on January 14, 1896: "On motion of Mr. McGuire it was ordered that Mr. Flagg be allowed to have his name as Architect cut on the lower right hand corner of the Building" (*Proceedings of Meetings of the Board of Trustees,* Committee Minutes, January 14, 1896, p. 199 [Corcoran Gallery of Art Archives]).

31. I would like to thank Neil Levine for information about the French practice of signing buildings.

32. William H. Jordy, *American Buildings and Their Architects, Progressive and Academic Ideals at the Turn of the Twentieth Century,* vol. 3 (Garden City, N.Y.: Doubleday & Company, 1972), pp. 338–39.

33. *AABN* LVIII (October 2, 1897), p. 2.

34. "Mercator," Letter to the Editor, *AABN* LVIII (October 9, 1897), p. 20. A decade later, a special committee of the A.I.A. adopted the position that if a building were of sufficient importance and public character, it would be appropriate for the architect's name to appear on the facade. "Report of Committee on Signing Buildings and Using Institute Initials," *AABN* XCI (January 19, 1907), p. 43.

35. The Scribner Building, 597 Fifth Avenue, New York (1912–13), also is signed.

36. Boullée's Royal Library is illustrated in Emil Kaufmann, "Three Revolutionary Architects, Boullée, Ledoux, and Lequeu," *Transactions of the American Philosophical Society* XLII, (October 1952), p. 468, fig. 43.

37. Duban's Quai Malaquais (Seine) facade is illustrated in *L'Architecture* XXXIII (January 1920), p. 20, fig. 7.

38. See Ernest Flagg, "Specification of Granite Work . . . " (#8022, Corcoran Gallery of Art Archives).

39. Ibid.

40. Photographs of the Lenox Library appear in Drexler, ed., *Architecture of the Ecole des Beaux-Arts,* pp. 464, 465.

41. William Jordy discusses McKim's pictorial approach and "The Thrice Sanctioned Front" of the Boston Public Library in his *American Buildings and Their Architects,* vol. 3, pp. 333–44.

42. For illustrations of the United States Naval Observatory and Hunt's design for the Statue of Liberty, see Paul R. Baker, *Richard Morris Hunt* (Cambridge, Mass.: MIT Press, 1980), figs. 109, 83. See also Marvin Trachtenberg's discussion of Hunt's pedestal in *The Statue of Liberty* (New York: Viking Press, 1976), pp. 151–78.

43. Henry Van Brunt, *Greek Lines, and Other Architectural Essays* (Boston and New York:

Houghton, Mifflin and Company, 1893).

44. A plan and elevations for Hunt's Fogg Art Museum were first published in *Arch Rev* III (1894), pls. XIX, XX. The building was completed in 1895. Paul Baker cites criticism the Fogg Art Museum received, see his *Richard Morris Hunt,* pp. 376–79.

45. "The Ten Most Beautiful Buildings in the United States," *The Brochure Series,* VI (January 1900), pp. 2–4; A.D.F. Hamlin, "The Ten Most Beautiful Buildings," *The Brochure Series,* VI (January 1900), p. 15.

46. *Thirty-Fourth Annual Report,* Board of Managers, St. Luke's Hospital, New York (year ending October 18, 1892), p. 8. Illustrations of St. Luke's Hospital appear in *AABN* LXIII (February 25, 1899), p. 63, pl. 1209. See also *Works,* pp. 13–22, figs. 10–19.

47. *Thirty-Third Annual Report,* Board of Managers, St. Luke's Hospital, New York (year ending October 18, 1891), p. 8; "Instructions to Architects," *Board of Managers Minutes,* April 25, 1892, pp. 611–14 (St. Luke's Hospital).

48. "St. Luke's New Hospital," *Harper's Weekly* XXXVII (January 7, 1893), p. 20.

49. Katherine Hoffman, "A Model Hospital," *Munsey's Magazine* XXII (January 1900), p. 487.

50. Ibid.

51. Ernest Flagg, "Description of St. Luke's Hospital as it will be when completed," in *History of St. Luke's Hospital* (New York: Wynkoop & Hallenbeck, 1893), p. 19.

52. For a perspective drawing and a plan of James Brown Lord's entry for St. Luke's Hospital, see *AABN* XLI (August 26, 1893).

53. W. B. Chambers, "Architects' Plans for New St. Luke's," *The Mail and Express* (New York), September 7, 1892, p. 7.

54. *King's Handbook of New York City* (Boston, 1893), p. 472. Nathan Silver illustrates but incorrectly identifies the architect of [old] St. Luke's Hospital in *Lost New York* (Boston: Houghton Mifflin Company, 1967), p. 94.

55. "St. Luke's, Old and New," *New-York Daily Tribune,* January 19, 1896, p. 21. The cornerstone for John W. Ritch's St. Luke's Hospital was laid in 1854, see "St. Luke's Hospital" *New York Times,* May 8, 1854, p. 4. Here the architect is identified as Jno. W. Ritch.

56. Harold Kirker, *The Architecture of Charles Bulfinch* (Cambridge, Mass.: Harvard University Press, 1969), pp. 315–17, figs. 145, 146.

57. The dome, eroded and weakened by air pollution, was demolished in 1967 when architects for the Service and Research Building feared its collapse during new construction.

58. In his "Description of St. Luke's Hospital as it will be when completed," Flagg acknowledged his debt to the Luxembourg Palace: "The general appearance of the

pavilions will be somewhat similar to those of the Luxembourg, in Paris" (*History of St. Luke's Hospital,* p. 34). During two return trips to France, Flagg recorded visits to the Luxembourg Gallery, Ernest Flagg Diary, August 7, 1908, and June 8, 1910 (EFP, AL, CU).

59. On April 24, 1893, the Board of Managers announced the names of each building: "'The Muhlenberg Pavilion' in honor of the founder of the Institution, the Rev. William Augustus Muhlenberg D.D. . . . 'The Minturn Pavilion' in memory of the first President of the Hospital, Mr. Robert B. Minturn . . . 'The Norrie Pavilion' in memory of Mr. Adam Norrie, who, for over twenty-nine years was Treasurer of the Hospital . . . 'The Vanderbilt Pavilion' in memory of Mr. William H. Vanderbilt, whose legacy of $100,000 received by this Hospital in 1886 was in large part used for the erection in the connection with the present Hospital, of the Vanderbilt Annex" (*Board of Managers Minutes,* April 24, 1893, p. 33 [St. Luke's Hospital]).

60. Subsequently three pavilions were constructed with Flagg as architect: Plant Pavilion (northwest corner 113th St. and Morningside Drive; 1903–6), Travers Pavilion (114th St., east of Chapel; 1908–16), and Scrymser Pavilion (southeast corner of 114th St. and Morningside Drive; 1925–28). For this expansion program east of the original buildings toward Morningside Drive, Flagg generally followed his master design of 1892–93. In the 1950s and 1960s a new building program involved the demolition of the pavilions west of Muhlenberg and Chapel. Norrie, demolished in the early 1950s, was replaced by Stuyvesant which opened in 1956. Vanderbilt was demolished in 1965–66 to provide a site for the Service and Research Building which was completed in 1971. The vacant land along Amsterdam Avenue, originally intended for two pavilions in Flagg's scheme (never constructed), provided a site for the Clark Building (1951–56). Letter, Andrew McGowan, St. Luke's Hospital Center, to author, August 3, 1976.

61. Walter Chambers did not fail to chide the other entrants for their shortsightedness, even though the program did not call for a hospital on the scale of Flagg's scheme. "The architect," Chambers observed, "is at liberty to plan a building for the entire lot, erecting only such a part as will cover the desired area and making that part conform to the instructions. Only in this way can a harmonious design eventually be obtained for the complete structure. Why has only one of the competitors thought it worth while to provide for the ultimate harmonious completion of the hospital?" (Chambers, "Architects' Plans for New St. Luke's," p. 7). See also "St. Luke's, Old and New," *New-York Daily Tribune,* January 19, 1896, p. 21.

62. A plan of the Luxembourg Palace appears in Rosalys Coope, *Salomon de Brosse* (London: A. Zwemmer, 1972), fig. 137.

63. Coope, *Salomon de Brosse,* pp. 121–24. In addition to his firsthand knowledge of the Luxembourg Palace, Flagg may also have known the building through engravings in Alphonse de Gisors, *Le Palais du Luxembourg* (Paris: type de Plou frères, 1847), a work which he owned.

64. The reception room and Gisors's chapel in the Luxembourg Palace are illustrated in André Rousay, *Le Palais du Luxembourg* (Paris: Librairie Hachette, 1962), pls. 39, 31 respectively. The vestibule and chapel of St. Luke's are illustrated in Hoffman, "A Model Hospital," pp. 491, 494.

65. Chambers, "Architects' Plans for New St. Luke's," p. 7.

66. For a discussion of the germ theory of disease and its relationship to the public health movement in the United States during the second half of the nineteenth century, see Howard D. Kramer, "The Germ Theory and the Early Public Health Program in the United States," *Bulletin of the History of Medicine* XXII (May–June 1948), pp. 233–47.

67. I would like to thank Robert U. Massey, M.D., and Richard C. Tilton for sharing their knowledge of germ theory and nineteenth-century notions of ventilation. The origin and development of the pavilion plan are chronicled in John D. Thompson's and Grace Goldin's chapter "The Pavilion Hospital: A Designed Plan," from their book *The Hospital: A Social and Architectural History* (New Haven: Yale University Press, 1975), pp. 118–69. Helen Rosenau also deals with the early manifestations of the pavilion hospital in *Social Purpose in Architecture: Paris and London Compared, 1760–1800* (London: Studio Vista, 1970), pp. 52–76.

68. A modern pavilion plan was designed by an architect named Rowehead for the Royal Naval Hospital at Stonehouse near Plymouth, England (1764–65). Florence Nightingale was especially instrumental in persuading British hospital planners to adopt the most celebrated of the pavilion plans, M.P. Gauthier's Hôpital Lariboisière, Paris (1839–54). Two examples are Herbert Hospital, Woolich, England (1859–64), and St. Thomas's Hospital, London (1871), see Thompson and Goldin, *The Hospital: A Social and Architectural History,* pp. 142–65. See also Nikolaus Pevsner, *A History of Building Types* (Princeton, N.J.: Princeton University Press, 1976), pp. 151–56.

69. Thompson and Goldin, *The Hospital: A Social and Architectural History,* p. 189.

70. Edmund A. Parkes, *A Manual of Practical Hygiene,* 7th ed. (London: J. & A. Churchill, 1887), p. 217, as quoted in Ernest Flagg, "The Planning of Hospitals," *Brickbuilder* XII (May 1903), p. 90. Parkes preferred natural ventilation over artificial ventilation for its "powers of extraction," pp. 206–7. Flagg owned an edition of Parkes during his student years in Paris (EFP, AL, CU).

71. The New York Hospital design was the result of a collaboration between the architect George B. Post and Frederick A. Conkling, a precocious board member who believed in the germ theory of disease and the effectiveness of antiseptic cleansing and artificial ventilation to assure hospital safety. Moreover, in 1896 a progressive surgeon at New York Hospital, Lewis A. Stimson, performed the first operation in America that employed Lister's antiseptic methods. Eric Larrabee, *The Benevolent and Necessary Institution: The New York Hospital 1771–1971* (Garden City, N.Y.: Doubleday & Company, 1971), pp. 235–37, 242–43, 284. Such French writers on hospital plan-

ning as Casimir Tollet disapproved of its block plan because its lack of pavilions invited contagion. C. Tollet, *Les Hôpitaux modernes au XIXe siècle* (Paris, 1894), pp. 65–71. See also "The New York Hospital," *AABN* II (March 17, 1877), p. 85, and "Hospital Life in New York," *Harper's Magazine* LVII (July 1878), pp. 171–78.

72. Billings's plan of 1876 improved on an earlier one he had submitted in a competition of 1875 with four other entrants. For a discussion of Johns Hopkins Hospital, see Thompson and Goldin, *The Hospital: A Social and Architectural History,* pp. 181–87, fig. 183.

73. Flagg was specifically referring to this defect in Billings's plan for Johns Hopkins when he challenged "a hospital celebrated for the supposed excellence of its hygienic arrangement," see Flagg, "The Planning of Hospitals" (May 1903), p. 95.

74. Flagg, "Description of St. Luke's Hospital as it will be when completed," pp. 18, 26, 27. Flagg illustrated this device in his article, "The Planning of Hospitals," *Brickbuilder* XII (June 1903), p. 116.

75. The advantage of this new orientation was recognized by the editors of the *Brickbuilder* in their article, "Saint Luke's Hospital," V (February 1896), p. 20.

76. *Harper's Weekly* was among the journals that defended this position. "The order on which the pavilions [at St. Luke's] have been arranged is similar to that of the Johns Hopkins Hospital in Baltimore, which is undoubtedly the finest hospital in America today. The new St. Luke's, however, will be a notable improvement over the Baltimore institution, and will be, when completed, the finest hospital, without exception, in the world" ("St. Luke's New Hospital," p. 20).

77. The benefits of Morningside Heights were acknowledged in *The Thirty-Fourth Annual Report,* Board of Managers, St. Luke's Hospital, New York (year ending October 18, 1892), p. 7. "The new Hospital will have abundance of light and air, being on a plateau about one hundred feet above the level of the Harlem flats, with an unobstructed exposure to the south and east."

78. "At the time I designed St. Luke's Hospital porcelain lined bath tubs were just coming into use. None were made which did not stand on legs. It seemed to me that this was very bad especially for a hospital because it was difficult to clean under them and impossible to clean behind them . . . if they stood against a wall or partition. So I decided that I would omit the legs and have them built into the wall behind. I made a detail drawing showing how this should be done and applied to the J. L. Mott Company to have one made as a sample. They raised many objections and said it would be difficult to do and costly but they finally decided to try it. The difficulties were overcome and they were used for the first time in the private bath rooms of the hospital, i.e. for all bath rooms except those for the wards where the tubs stood free so that they could be reached on all sides. Tubs of this kind came quickly into use. The Mott Company called them Baronial style and when I built my house at Staten Island, they sent me one saying that it was their best type of tub and complementing me on its invention. Now hardly any other kind is used the world over. If I had taken out a patent on them I would have made a great deal"

(Ernest Flagg, "Inventions," unpublished essay [EFP, AL, CU]).

79. Flagg, "The Planning of Hospitals," (May 1903), p. 95.

80. Flagg, "The Planning of Hospitals," (June 1903), p. 113.

81. Two New York City hospitals, Arnold W. Brunner's Mount Sinai and McKim, Mead & White's Bellevue, perpetuated the pavilion plan during the twentieth century while permitting higher density through a skyscraper format. For plans and illustrations, see "New Mount Sinai Hospital, New York," *AABN* LXXXVII (April 22, 1905), and "New Bellevue Hospital, New York," *AABN* C (October 11, 1911).

82. Hoffman, "A Model Hospital," p. 492.

83. Flagg discusses the importance of fireplaces in "The Planning of Hospitals" (June 1903), p. 116.

84. Hoffman, "A Model Hospital," pp. 488–89.

85. Flagg, "The Planning of Hospitals" (May 1903), p. 92. See also C[asimir] Tollet, *Les Edifices Hospitaliers* (Paris, 1892), p. 151.

86. "Hospital Planning," *Brickbuilder* XII (June 1903), p. 111.

87. St. Margaret Memorial Hospital is located at 265 46th Street between Davison and Lawrence streets in the Lawrenceville section of Pittsburgh. A vigorous building program in the 1950s and 1960s radically altered the existing hospital. With the construction of a new facility in the early 1980s, St. Margaret's relocated. Flagg's building is currently undergoing adaptive reuse. For a summary of the building program, see "Years of Construction," *The Missile* [October 1973] (Seventy-fifth anniversary issue), pp. 34–43. From its completion in 1898 until October 1, 1910, when the hospital was officially opened and its first patients admitted, St. Margaret's lay dormant due to a lack of operating funds and other financial burdens resulting from the execution of the Shoenberger bequest. See also "Building a Hospital," *The Missile* [October 1973], pp. 14–17.

88. Last will and testament of John H. Shoenberger, Register of Wills, Allegheny County, Pennsylvania, Will Book 36, p. 504 (St. Margaret Memorial Hospital). See also "An Innovation in Philanthropy," *The Missile* [October 1973], pp. 4–12.

89. Last will and testament of John H. Shoenberger, p. 504 (St. Margaret Memorial Hospital).

90. In May 1894 the Building Committee contracted with Flagg, see "An Innovation in Philanthropy," p. 9.

91. "Pittsburg's New Hospital," *Philadelphia Press,* January 26, 1896, newspaper clipping (EFP, AL, CU).

92. S. Gill Wylie, *Hospitals: Their History, Organization, and Construction* (New York: Appleton, 1877), p. 202, as quoted in Thompson and Goldin, *The Hospital: A Social*

and Architectural History, p. 333, n. 59.

93. An elevation of St. Margaret's appears in "Works," p. 24, fig. 21.

94. The chapel vault originally was finished in plaster relief with varnished oak paneling below. When executed, the chapel departed from Flagg's conception of a white auditorium space. It was not until 1955 that hospital officials finally responded to Flagg's criticism that the chapel be painted white. See "Years of Construction," p. 37.

95. In addition to the administration building and chapel pavilion, separate pavilions housed the men's and women's wards, private patients, and nurses. The plan indicates an area for future expansion. "Works," p. 23, fig. 20.

96. "Works," p. 25, fig. 22.

97. While the Naval Hospital at Annapolis continues to serve the Naval Academy, the Naval Hospital in Washington, D.C., at 23rd and E streets is now the headquarters for The Bureau of Medicine and Surgery (BUMED).

98. "United States Naval Hospital, Washington, D.C." and "United States Naval Hospital, Annapolis, Md.," *Brickbuilder* XIII (May 1904), pls. 35–40.

99. The pavilion plan of Buckland's Hammond-Harwood House (1773–74) is a typical example of the Annapolis domestic type illustrated in William H. Pierson, Jr., *American Buildings and Their Architects, the Colonial and Neoclassical Styles,* vol. 1 (Garden City, N.Y.: Doubleday & Co., 1970), p. 151, figs. 109, 110. Flagg also designed a number of detached buildings for the Naval Hospital, Annapolis. Among them were the quarters for the commanding officer, a row of officers' houses, and a building to house the ambulance services. All were domestic in character.

100. See Pierre Chabat, *La Brique et la terre cuite* (Paris: A. Morel et Cie, 1881), Part II, p. 144, pl. 4. Flagg owned this publication (EFP, AL, CU).

101. Arthur J. Dillon, "The Proposed Tilden Trust Library," *Arch Rev I* (September 12, 1892), p. 71.

102. "The Lawrence Library, The Magnificent gift of Charles Farrar Lawrence to be dedicated June 15," *The Pepperell Advertiser,* June 15, 1901, unpaged [p. 3]. See also "Works," pp. 26–28, figs. 23, 24, 25.

103. This type of portal with emphasized corners derived from Italian Renaissance models, especially the garden entrance of Vignola's Palazzo Farnese at Caprarola (1559–73), was adopted by French architects in the nineteenth century.

104. Alan Burnham reproduced a photograph of Duncan's General Grant National Memorial in *New York Landmarks* (Middletown, Conn.: Wesleyan University Press, 1963), p. 167. See also David M. Kahn, "The Grant Monument," *JSAH* XLI (October 1982), pp. 212–31.

105. Arthur Pier, *Saint Paul's School, 1855–1934* (New York: Charles Scribner's Sons,

1934), pp. 256–57. See also August Heckscher, *St. Paul's* (New York: Charles Scribner's Sons, 1980), pp. 130–32 and "Works," pp. 103–4, figs. 100, 101.

106. For an illustration of Ledoux's Barrière de la Villette, Paris, see Allan Braham, *The Architecture of the French Enlightenment* (Berkeley and Los Angeles: University of California Press, 1980), p. 195, fig. 256.

107. The YMCA Building is located at the corner of Main and Fair streets. Baltard's Palais de Justice, Lyons, is illustrated in Hautecoeur, *L'architecture classique,* vol. 6, p. 158, fig. 121.

108. An example of this is the Levi Lincoln House, see Abbott Lowell Cummings, *Architecture in Early New England* (Sturbridge, Mass.: Old Sturbridge Village, 1958), unpaged.

109. Obituary "Alfred Corning Clark," *New York Times,* April 12, 1896, I, p. 5.

110. Walter R. Littell, *A History of Cooperstown* (Cooperstown, New York: Freeman's Journal Company, 1929), pp. 145–46.

111. By 1895 Flagg had submitted his cathedral designs and commenced negotiations. Two letters, Ernest Flagg to Dr. Douglass [The Reverend George W. Douglas], both dated May 6th, 1895 (Archives, Washington Cathedral). Flagg's two designs were widely published and exhibited in January 1896. They were also illustrated in two extensive articles: "Plans for the Great Cathedral," *New York Herald,* January 19, 1896, p. 2, and "The New Cathedral at Washington," *Harper's Weekly* XL (January 25, 1896), cover ill., p. 91.

112. A copy of the typewritten manuscript of this untitled essay (with corrections in Flagg's hand) was made available to me by the Clerk of the Works, Washington Cathedral. A notation on the manuscript identifies it: "Memorandum submitted by Flagg with his Cathedral Plan" (Archives, Washington Cathedral). No published source for the essay has been identified.

113. The editors of *American Architect,* who recognized Byzantine, Romanesque, and Gothic precedents, found Flagg's essay to contain "some very questionable assertions" and advocated leaving "the question of style an open one" ("The Style for a New Cathedral," *AABN* XLIX [August 17, 1895], p. 71).

114. The editors of *Architectural Review* (Boston) praised the practical benefits of Flagg's "Renaissance" scheme which had been widely published in the press in January 1896: "The gothic design has given way to the classic renaissance, which has been accepted, and, aside from all questions of sentiment, the latter will undoubtedly outlast the former in practical results" (Current Periodicals," *Arch Rev* IV, no. 1 [1896–97], p. 7). See also "The New Cathedral at Washington," p. 91.

115. "Plans for the Great Cathedral," p. 2.

116. See especially Jean-Camille Formigé's portals, *Palais des beaux-arts* and *Palais des arts*

libéraux. See Hautecoeur, *L'architecture classique,* vol. 7, p. 397, fig. 346.

117. Richard T. Feller and Marshall W. Fishwick, *For Thy Great Glory* (Culpeper, Va., Community Press, 1965), p. 15.

118. Ibid., pp. 16–17.

119. Flagg's Renaissance design would have been comparable in scale to Bodley's Gothic design (in collaboration with Henry Vaughan). The dimensions of Flagg's design — length, 272 feet; breadth, 200 feet; height of dome to cross, 280 feet — emphasized a centralized space while those of Bodley were modeled on English Gothic churches of the fourteenth century with their attenuated naves and decentralized plans: length, 476 feet; width, 132 feet; height, 130 feet, height of lantern tower, 258 feet. See "Plans for the Great Cathedral," p. 2; Feller and Fishwick, *For Thy Great Glory,* pp. 17–18.

120. Also known as the new Pearl Street Church and the Congregational Society Church, the Farmington Avenue Church (now Immanuel Congregational Church) is located at the corner of Farmington Avenue and Woodland Street. In 1914 when the Farmington Avenue Congregational Society joined with the Park Church, Immanuel Church was thereby incorporated. Stanley B. Weld, *The History of Immanuel Church 1824–1967* (Hartford: Immanuel Congregational Church, 1968), pp. 69–70. On August 5, 1897, Ernest Flagg was selected to be the architect. George M. Bartlett, who worked in Flagg's office, was associate architect, but the design was clearly Flagg's. See also "Works," p. 29, fig. 26.

121. Henry-Russell Hitchcock, *Architecture: Nineteenth and Twentieth Centuries* (Baltimore, Md.: Penguin Books, 1958), pp. 27, 89.

122. See Sarah Bradford Landau, "Mark Twain's House in Connecticut," *Architectural Review* (London) CLXIX (March 1981), pp. 162–66.

123. Published sources of the period consistently alluded to public criticism which Farmington Avenue Church received when first completed. See: "Will Open To-morrow," *Hartford Daily Courant,* September 9, 1899, p. 5; "Improvements in Church Architecture," *The Congregationalist,* November 16, 1899, p. 740; and *A Half-Century History of the Farmington Avenue Congregational Church* (Hartford: Farmington Avenue Church, 1901), p. 71. Arthur T. Sutcliffe chronicled local reaction to the church when he wrote in his diary, "the brick exterior is subject to much ridicule" (Arthur T. Sutcliffe Diary, March 30, 1902 [ATSP, AL, CU]). Church tradition maintains that when the structure was first erected, Mark Twain "christened" it the "Church of the Holy Oil Cloth" because of its yellow and green tile decoration. See Weld, *The History of Immanuel Church 1824–1967,* p. 63. This epithet may have been a variation of the one applied to Jacob Wray Mould's All Souls Unitarian Church, New York City (1853–55). Montgomery Schuyler reported that All Souls had been "stigmatized" as "The Church of the Homely Oilcloth." See his article, "A Great American Architect: Leopold Eidlitz," in Jordy and Coe, eds., *American Architecture and Other Writings,* vol. 1, pp. 152–53.

124. The Pearl Street Church was sold to the Connecticut Mutual Life Insurance Company on June 26, 1897. Subsequent to its demolition on August 26, 1899, the site became that of a new structure for Connecticut Mutual designed by Ernest Flagg. See *A Half-Century History of the Farmington Avenue Congregational Church,* pp. 61, 67.

125. These concerns were voiced by the chairman of the Building Committee at the Dedication Service on October 31, 1899. See *A Half-Century History of the Farmington Avenue Congregational Church,* p. 70.

126. *A Half-Century History of the Farmington Avenue Congregational Church,* p. 70.

127. "Improvements in Church Architecture," p. 740.

128. For illustrations of the Providence church, see "The Work of Messrs. Carrère & Hastings," *Arch Rec* XXVII (January 1910), pp. 12–13.

129. The date has been contested, but Hubert, Porcher and Volbach substantiate a seventh-century date for the baptistry. See J. Hubert, J. Porcher and W. F. Volbach, *L'Europe des invasions* (Paris: Gallimard, 1967), pp. 38–40.

130. See Ernest Flagg Diary, undated entry during the summer of 1890 (EFP, AL, CU). The entry reads: "One of the most interesting monuments of the past at Poitiers is the Temple St. Jean a small square building of the 5th or 6th centuries. In the 12th c three small apses were added and a construction at the West. I was disappointed. I had supposed, judging from Les Archives, were in a better state of preservation. The floor is ten or twelve feet below the level of the street. The building looks as if it had been partly made of Roman fragments. There is a very peculiar plan which might be used with success." See also A[natole] de Baudot and A. Perrault-Dabot, *Archives de la Commission des Monuments Historiques* (Paris: Henri Laurens [1899]; orig. pub. 1856–73), vol. 2, pl. 1.

131. While Flagg had consulted de Baudot's *Archives,* he may also have used Jules Gailhabaud's *Monuments anciens et modernes,* 4 vols. (Paris: Librairie de Firmin Didot Frères, Fils et Cie, 1865). The Baptistère Saint-Jean at Poitiers and S. Giorgio in Velabro are both illustrated in Gailhabaud, vol. 2 [unpaged], which Flagg owned.

132. An exterior view and a plan of the Commodore William Edgar House are illustrated in Vincent Scully, *The Shingle Style* (New Haven: Yale University Press, 1955), pls. 147, 148. A recent essay by Roderick Gradidge addresses the concept of architectural form in the work of Edwin Lutyens. See "Edwin Lutyens: the Last High Victorian," in Jane Fawcett, ed., *Seven Victorian Architects* (London: Thames and Hudson, 1976), pp. 122–36.

133. For a recent color illustration of the terra-cotta tile ornament of the Baptistère Saint-Jean, see Hubert, Porcher and Volbach, *L'Europe des invasions,* fig. 48.

134. In response to public opinion, the tile decoration of both pediments on the Farmington Avenue side were obscured with plaster and white paint early in this century, but have recently been restored. See Weld, *The History of Immanuel Church 1824–1967,* p. 63.

135. Ernest Flagg, "The Bonding of Brickwork," *Brickbuilder* VII (December 1898), pp. 259–61.

136. Flagg, "The Bonding of Brickwork," p. 261. Flagg maintained that these logical methods were also most economical. In his executed design, Flagg substituted brick for limestone quoins to produce a quieter, more integrated composition. Elevations and a section drawing of Flagg's first design for the Farmington Avenue Church appear in *Brickbuilder* VII (March 1898), pls. 21–24.

137. Flagg, "The Bonding of Brickwork," p. 260.

138. It was the effect that Flagg had sought for the chapel of St. Margaret Memorial Hospital, but one which had not been executed until 1955. The chapel windows were treated similarly with floral borders of red Bohemian glass surrounding clear glass. For an illustration of the interior, see "Works," p. 30, fig. 27.

139. Modifications of the church interior included moving the organ to accommodate a Tiffany glass mosaic. See Weld, *The History of Immanuel Church 1824–1967,* pp. 80–81, ill. p. 82.

140. Mrs. Ernest Flagg, interview with author, New York, May 11, 1973.

141. Two naval histories outline the significance of Mahan's thesis and his writings: E. B. Potter and Chester W. Nimitz, eds., *Sea Power* (Englewood Cliffs, N.J.: Prentice-Hall, 1960), pp. 341–45; Harold and Margaret Sprout, *The Rise of American Naval Power 1776–1918* (Princeton: Princeton University Press, 1946), pp. 202–22.

142. Potter and Nimitz, *Sea Power,* p. 343; Sprout and Sprout, *The Rise of American Naval Power 1776–1918,* pp. 227ff.

143. "The New Naval Academy," *Scientific American* LXXVIII (June 25, 1898), p. 405.

144. U.S. Congress, Senate, S. Doc. No. 288, 54th Cong., 1st Sess. 3357 (1896).

145. "Naval Academy Visitors," *New York Times,* May 10, 1895, p. 9.

146. "Report of the Board of Visitors," S. Doc. No. 288, 54th Cong., 1st Sess. 3357 (1896).

147. Flagg's plan accompanied the Matthews Board Report. S. Doc. No. 288, 54th Cong., 1st Sess. 3357 (1896).

148. "Thompson, Robert Means," *The National Cyclopedia of American Biography,* 1945, XXXIV, pp. 371–72. Park Benjamin, *The United States Naval Academy* (New York: Knickerbocker Press, 1900), pp. 336–38.

149. Benjamin, *The United States Naval Academy,* p. 409. Commander Richard Wainwright, "The New Naval Academy," *The World's Work* IV (July 1902), p. 2276.

150. S. Doc. No. 55, 55th Cong., 2nd Sess. 3592 (1898).

151. Ibid.

152. Ernest Flagg, "The Two Roosevelts," essay in unpublished manuscript "Observations" (Flagg Family Papers).

153. 29 Stat. 368 as reported in S. Doc. No. 213, 55th Cong., 2nd Sess. 3610 (1898).

154. S. Doc. No. 213, 55th Cong., 2nd Sess. 3610 (1898). S. Doc. No. 213 To Accompany S. Doc. No. 384, 56th Cong., 1st Sess. 3875 (1900).

155. Letter, E. K. Moore to The Superintendent, January 14, 1899, *Press Copies 4s Buildings & Grounds 1895–1910, Vol. 445, p. 292,* Records of the United States Naval Academy, Record Group 405, National Archives Building.

156. Prof. H. Marion, "The Naval Academy as it is," *Scientific American* LXXX (May 6, 1899), p. 283.

157. S. Doc. No. 384, 56th Cong., 1st Sess. 3875 (1900). See Exhibit No. 1, a map of the Naval Academy Grounds also indicating the annexed area.

158. P. H. Magruder, "The Colonial Government House of Maryland," *U.S. Naval Institute Proceedings* LXI (October 1935), pp. 1404–11. The colonial Government House of Maryland is not to be confused with the Governor's House (1743–45; completed 1789; now McDowell Hall at St. John's College at Annapolis). See Rodd L. Wheaton, "Annapolis Monument: The Governor's House," *JSAH* XXXIV (December 1975), pp. 307–8. For a plan showing Flagg's proposed buildings superimposed on the existing campus, see J. W. Bartlett, "The New Annapolis," *Munsey's Magazine* XXII (December 1899), p. 416.

159. Extant correspondence indicates that in November 1901, Comdr. Richard Wainwright, Superintendent of the Naval Academy, recommended changes to include "not rebuilding the old Library building," because, as Professor Dodge had indicated to Flagg earlier, it in part "obscures the end of the Armory." Flagg appears to have supported the decision in spite of his initial enthusiasm for retaining the older building. Letters, O. G. Dodge to Ernest Flagg, June 5, 1901, *Press Copies 4s Buildings & Grounds 1895–1910, Vol. 451, p. 398,* and November 4, 1901, *Press Copies 4s Buildings & Grounds 1895–1910, Vol. 454, p. 10,* RG 405, NA. "Uncle Sam's New $20,000,000 Naval Academy," *New York Times,* October 2, 1904, III, p. 4.

160. Kendall Banning, *Annapolis Today* (Annapolis: United States Naval Institute, 1963), p. 264.

161. Letter, John D. Long, Secretary of the Navy to Hon. Eugene Hale, Chairman of the Committee on Naval Affairs, United States Senate, January 8, 1898. To Accompany S. Doc. No. 55, 55th Cong., 2nd Sess. 3592 (1898), pp. 1–4. Act of May 4, 1898, Ch. 234, 30 Stat. p. 385. Ernest Flagg, "The New Naval Academy," *U.S. Naval Institute Proceedings* XXV (December 1899), pp. 872–73.

162. Contract dated May 28, 1898, *General File 5474,* Box 267, General Records of the Department of the Navy, Record Group 80, National Archives Building.

163. "National Capital Topics," *New York Times,* February 26, 1899, II, pp. 13. Many of

the then existing buildings appear in photographs of the Academy which accompany Commander Wainwright's article, "The New Naval Academy," pp. 2269–85.

164. H. Res. 408, 55th Cong., 3rd Sess. (1899); "National Capital Topics," *New York Times*, February 26, 1899, II, p. 13.

165. Act of June 7, 1900, Ch. 859, 31 Stat. pp. 696ff; H.R. No. 10450, 56th Cong., 1st Sess. (1900).

166. These events have been discussed in Chapter III.

167. Although a contract between Flagg and the Department of the Navy was not signed until September 22, 1900, Flagg was immediately informed that the matter of his future employment had been "practically settled" and that contracts would soon be forwarded to him. Letters, O. G. Dodge to Ernest Flagg, August 3, 1900, *Press Copies 4s Buildings & Grounds 1895–1910, Vol. 448, p. 357* and October 15, 1900, *Vol. 449, p. 194*, RG 405, NA.

168. Isherwood Hall along with Griffin and Melville halls, two more recently constructed buildings, were razed in 1982.

169. Most of these buildings were named subsequent to Flagg's article which copiously illustrated and described them, "New Buildings for The United States Naval Academy, Annapolis, Md.," *AABN* XCIV, Part I (July 1, 1908), pp. 1–8, pls. 1–18; Part II (July 8, 1908), pp. 9–13, pls. 19–32. Eleven brick Officers' Houses on Upshur and Rodger roads, designed by O. Von Nerta and built between 1891 and 1902, still survive. See "Endorsement," *Press Copies 4s Buildings & Grounds 1895–1910, Vol. 445, p. 260*, RG 405, NA. Two gate houses at Gate Number 3 (Main Gate; 1876 and 1881) and a small gabled house (c. 1868), which predate the Flagg campus, also survive. I wish to thank James W. Cheevers, Senior Curator, The Museum, United States Naval Academy, for this information.

170. The Naval Academy seal, designed by Park Benjamin and adopted by the navy in 1898, is described in Benjamin's definitive study *The United States Naval Academy*, p. 349. The national coat of arms was also placed on one side of each of the towers, see Letter, O. G. Dodge to Ernest Flagg, October 3, 1899, *Press Copies 4s Buildings & Grounds 1895–1910, Vol. 446, p. 400*, RG 405, NA.

171. Flagg, "New Buildings," Part 1, p. 7. See also "The U.S. Naval Academy Buildings," *Inland Architect and News Record* XLVII (May 1906), pp. 53–54.

172. Letter, James H. Sands, R. Adm. [Superintendent of the Naval Academy] to Charles J. Bonaparte, Secretary of the Navy, January 13, 1906, *General File 5474/413*, Box 267, RG 80, NA.

173. The Boullée project, B.N. Est., Ha 57, No. 29, is illustrated in *Visionary Architects: Boullée, Ledoux, Lequeu* (Houston: University of St. Thomas, October 19, 1967–January 3, 1968), p. 42.

174. *Croquis d'Architecture*, Intime Club, XXIII (December 1896), no. XII, f. 6.

175. See letter, G. E. Merrill [Clerk of the Works] to Ernest Flagg, July 24, 1901, *Press Copies 4s Buildings & Grounds 1895–1910, Vol. 452, p. 211,* RG 405, NA.

176. Two Ecole *projets* for railway stations, one by Jean-Camille Formigé of 1876 and another by Henri-Thomas-Edouard Eustache of 1891, as well as Victor Laloux's Gare de Tours (1895–98) and Gare du Quai d'Orsay, Paris (1898–1900) are reproduced in Drexler, ed., *Architecture of the Ecole des Beaux-Arts,* pp. 294–97, 301–3, 459–63.

177. *Les Diplômes d'architecte en France* (Paris: A. Guérinet, 189-?), pls. 148–51.

178. *Arch Rev* X (September 1903), pl. XLIII.

179. Banning, *Annapolis Today,* p. 294. For a plan of the Ecole Militaire, see Guadet, *Eléments et théorie de l'architecture* (Paris: Librairie de la Construction Moderne, 1929; orig. pub. 1901–4), vol. 4, fig. 1559.

180. Letters, O. G. Dodge to Ernest Flagg, November 2, 1900, November 9, 1900, November 13, 1900, and November 15, 1900, *Press Copies 4s Buildings & Grounds 1895–1910, Vol. 449, pp. 257–59, 296, 321, 327,* RG 405, NA. See Hughson Hawley perspective illustrated in *Arch Rev* VII (February 1900), pl. XIII.

181. The Caserne des Célestins was published in *AABN* LXIII (March 25, 1899), p. 95. The plate was copied from *La Construction Moderne.*

182. Letters, John C. Hollis [Ara Cushman Co., Auburn, Maine] to [Secretary of the Navy], October 31, 1898, *General File 5474/20,* and Hon. E. C. Burleigh to [Secretary of the Navy], December 10, 1898, *General File 5474/20,* Box 19, RG 80, NA.

183. Act of March 3, 1899, Ch. 421, 30 Stat. 1036. See also a summary of the appropriations and Flagg's commissions in the Petition he later filed against the government. See also contract with William S. White of Rockland, Maine, January 15, 1902, *General File 5474/332,* tray 122, Records of the Office of the Judge Advocate General (Navy), Record Group 125, National Archives Building.

184. Mrs. Ernest Flagg, interview with author, New York, May 11, 1973.

185. Guadet, *Eléments et théorie de l'architecture,* vol. 3, pp. 551, 553.

186. The Recreation Hall had been the intended location of the Mess Hall. But when the anticipated number of midshipmen increased from 500 to 900, it was relocated. See Flagg, "New Buildings," Part II, p. 12.

187. "Ecole des Beaux-Arts," *La Construction Moderne* III (March 17, 1888), pp. 267–68.

188. Hautecoeur reproduces Louis Bernier's Opéra-Comique in *L'architecture classique,* vol. 7, p. 437, fig. 378.

189. Originally the hall was to have been decorated in frescoes, but they were never executed, see Flagg, "New Buildings," Part II, p. 11, pl. 23. They are shown in Hughson Hawley's perspective of Memorial Hall, illustrated in *Arch Rev* VII (February 1900), pl. XIV. See also "Works," p. 89, fig. 85.

190. Peter Collins, *Concrete* (New York: Horizon Press, 1959), p. 71.

191. Letters, Henry Maurer & Son [tile manufacturer] to Charles A. Boutelle, February 28, 1899; Ernest Flagg to R. Adm. F. V. McNair [Superintendent of the Naval Academy], March 30, 1899; Chas. H. Allen [Acting Secretary of the Navy] to Charles A. Boutelle, April 4, 1899, *General File 5474/36*, RG 80, NA.

192. These buildings were named before 1908. Mahan, Sampson, Maury, and Isherwood are illustrated in Flagg's article "New Buildings," Parts I, II, pls. 7–14, fig. 11.

193. Act of March 3, 1903, Ch. 1010, 32 Stat. 1188.

194. For examples of clock towers, see French railroad stations including D. M. Toudoire's Gare de Lyon in Hautecoeur, *L'architecture classique*, vol. 7, p. 113, fig. 83, and E. Loviot's project for a Town Hall, *Encyclopédie d'Architecture* VI (1887–88), p. 48, pl. 1133. A sketch of the old academic building with its clock tower is illustrated in Lt. William F. Fullam, "The United States Naval Academy," *Overland Monthly* XXXI (May 1898), p. 396.

195. Flagg's design for the Chapel crypt is reproduced in "New Buildings," Part I, p. 4, fig. 7.

196. "Works," p. 90.

197. Flagg, "New Buildings," Part I, p. 6.

198. Samuel Eliot Morrison, *John Paul Jones* (Boston: Little, Brown and Company, 1959), pp. 407–9.

199. Letter, Ernest Flagg to Hon. George Von L. Meyer, Secretary of the Navy, March 8, 1911, *Entry 19, General File 12743/18*, RG 80, NA.

200. Ernest Flagg v. The United States, Petition No. 30838, The Court of Claims of the United States, *File 26549/36, 26549/47*, RG 80, NA.

201. Flagg had complained first in a letter of 1905 and later in an article of 1908. See letter, Ernest Flagg to C. H. Darling [Assistant Secretary of the Navy], April 19, 1905, *File 5435/14*, RG 80, NA. See also Flagg, "New Buildings," Part I, p. 6.

202. Flagg, "New Buildings," Part I, p. 6. For a chronology of the search, recovery, and transportation of the body of John Paul Jones to the United States, see *John Paul Jones Commemoration at Annapolis*, April 24, 1906 (Washington, D.C., 1907), pp. 183–84.

203. Ernest Flagg Diary, May 18, 1911 (EFP, AL, CU). Morrison, *John Paul Jones*, p. 409.

204. Wainwright, "The New Naval Academy," p. 2278.

205. Theo B. White, *Paul Philippe Cret* (Philadelphia: Art Alliance Press, 1973), p. 45, pl. 82. Banning, *Annapolis Today*, p. 222.

206. Letter, O. G. Dodge to Ernest Flagg, October 15, 1900, *Press Copies 4s Buildings &*

Grounds 1895–1910, Vol. 449, p. 194, RG 405, NA.

207. Flagg, "New Buildings," Part I, p. 5.

208. Ibid.

209. Ibid. The editors of *Inland Architect and News Record* deplored these forced economies, blaming Congress and the Naval Academy superintendent for inadequate appropriations. "The U.S. Naval Academy Buildings," pp. 53–54.

210. Flagg, "New Buildings," Part I, p. 5. See also Letters, Ernest Flagg to C. H. Darling, November 21, 1903, December 16, 1903; Chas. H. Darling to Ernest Flagg, December 18, 1903; Ernest Flagg to C. H. Darling, December 19, 1903; Ernest Flagg to Capt. W. H. Brownson [Superintendent of the Naval Academy], December 19, 1903; *General File 5474/261,* RG 80, NA.

211. Letters, O. G. Dodge to Ernest Flagg, September 10, 1902, *Press Copies 4s Buildings & Grounds 1895–1910, Vol. 457, p. 453,* and O. G. Dodge to The Trust Concrete Steel Co., June 20, 1906, and June 27, 1906, *Press Copies 4s Buildings & Grounds 1895– 1910, Vol. 488, pp. 242, 261,* RG 80, NA.

212. Day Allen Willey, "The New Concrete Chapel of The United States Naval Academy, Annapolis," *Scientific American* XCII (February 4, 1905), p. 101.

213. Dillon, "The Proposed Tilden Trust Library," p. 70.

214. Banning, *Annapolis Today,* p. 265.

215. Rear Adm. Alexander C. Husband, former Chief of the Bureau of Yards and Docks, U.S. Department of the Navy, interview with author, Old Saybrook, Connecticut, January 1974. See also "College Buildings," *Arch Rec* CXXXVII (June 1965), pp. 156–57. A master plan, completed in 1964 by John Carl Warnecke and Associates, called for additional facilities adjacent to Michelson and Chauvenet halls. Nimitz Library and Rickover Hall (engineering building) were completed in 1973 and 1975 respectively.

216. Montgomery Schuyler, "The Architecture of West Point," *Arch Rec* XIV (December 1903), pp. 462–92.

217. "Current Periodicals," *Arch Rev* IX (May 1902), p. 108.

218. *Architectural Annual,* Albert Kelsey, ed., 1900, p. 188.

219. For a discussion of the West Point competition, see Charles Moore, *Daniel H. Burnham: Architect, Planner of Cities* (Boston: Houghton Mifflin Company, 1921), vol. 2, pp. 189–96.

220. Ralph Adams Cram, *My Life in Architecture* (Boston: Little, Brown and Company, 1936), pp. 110–13.

221. Ernest Flagg v. The United States, No. 30838, 51 Court of Claims of the United States

511 (October 30, 1916). See also Arthur T. Sutcliffe Diary, October 30, 1916 (ATSP, AL, CU).

222. *The Pomfret Years: A Collection of Reminiscences in Commemoration of Pomfret School's 75th Anniversary* (Pomfret, Conn.: Pomfret School, 1970), unpaged. See entries in Arthur T. Sutcliffe Diary, especially August 9, 1907 (ATSP, AL, CU). A copy of a perspective rendering of an early scheme is extant, although Flagg's master plan no longer survives (Pomfret School Archives). Several of the Pomfret School buildings were published in *Brickbuilder* XVI (November 1907), pls. 173, 174 and *AABN* XCVI (November 17, 1909), p. 216.

223. McKim, Mead & White's Academic Building (1896–98) closed in the southern boundary of Jefferson's U-shaped campus at the University of Virginia. *A Monograph of the Works of McKim, Mead & White 1879–1915* (New York: Benjamin Blom, 1973), pls. 110–12.

224. By school tradition, the Chapel is alleged to be a copy of a Norman church in Pontefract, England (Yorkshire), for which the town of Pomfret was named (the altered spelling derived from its British pronunciation). While the Chapel revives Norman features, there is no evidence to suggest that it is a copy of one specific antecedent.

225. Ernest Flagg Diary, November 21, 1910 (EFP, AL, CU).

226. Whitney Darrow, *Princeton University Press* (Princeton, N.J.: Princeton University Press, 1951), p. 36. See *Letters from Charles Scribner, '75 to Whitney Darrow, '03 in the Early Days of Princeton University Press* (Princeton, N.J.: Princeton University Press, 1968). For a history of the Press, see Varnum Lansing Collins, *Early Princeton Printing* (Princeton, N.J.: Princeton University Press, 1911), pp. 44–45. See also "Princeton University Press, Erected through the Generosity of Charles Scribner, a New and Unique Adjunct to the University," *New York Times,* May 19, 1912, VIII, p. 7.

227. R. Phené Spiers, "The Plantin Museum, Antwerp," *Architectural Review* (London) II (January 1902), pp. 20–30.

228. Illustrations of the pressrooms of both the Plantin Museum and Princeton University Press appear in *Letters from Charles Scribner, '75 to Whitney Darrow, '03.*

229. Among the "Gothic" buildings of the Princeton campus are Cope & Stewardson's Blair Hall of 1897 and Stafford Little Hall of 1899; and Cram, Goodhue & Ferguson's Graduate College of 1911–13. See Constance M. Greiff, Mary W. Gibbons, and Elizabeth G. C. Menzies, *Princeton Architecture* (Princeton, N.J : Princeton University Press, 1967), pp. 164–65, figs. 174, 175, 184, 185.

230. Illustrations of the Bourne and Tilden tombs are included in the *Works,* pp. 102, 31–33, figs. 99 and 28–30, respectively. The New Britain Soldiers' and Sailors' Monument and the project for a Naval Arch, New York, also appear in the "Works," pp. 53, 4, figs. 50 and 1, respectively. A drawing of Flagg's Monument to William

Cullen Bryant accompanies a short article, "The Bryant Bust," in *Harper's Weekly* XXXVII (June 17, 1893), p. 582.

CHAPTER FIVE

1. Paul Cret, "The Ecole Des Beaux-Arts: What Its Architectural Teaching Means," *Arch Rec* XXIII (May 1908), p. 368.

2. "Blairsden" is illustrated in "The Work of Messrs. Carrère & Hastings" *Arch Rec* XXVII (January 1910), pp. 52, 53, 55, 56.

3. Ernest Flagg, "Influence of the French School on Architecture in the United States," *Arch Rec* IV (October–December 1894), pp. 210–28.

4. For an analysis of the West Side row house, see Sarah Bradford Landau, "The Row Houses of New York's West Side," *JSAH* XXXIV (March 1975), pp. 19–36.

5. Flagg, "Influence of the French School," pp. 213, 216, 217, 220.

6. Alvin F. Harlow, "Cutting, Robert Fulton," *DAB,* XXI, Supplement One (New York: Charles Scribner's Sons, 1944), pp. 216–17.

7. Sarah Bradford Landau has clarified the distinction between the American basement house and the true English basement plan in her article, "The Row Houses of New York's West Side," p. 28, n. 35.

8. "R. Fulton Cutting's New House," *New York Tribune Illustrated Supplement,* August 29, 1897, p. 3. See also *Architecture & Building* XXVIII (March 12, 1898); *Brickbuilder* VI (October 1897), p. 233, pls. 85–86; "Works," pp. 60–63, figs. 57–60.

9. Arthur T. Sutcliffe Diary, October 17, 1933 (ATSP, AL, CU).

10. "The Residence of O. G. Jennings, Esq., 7 East 72nd St., NYC," *Arch Rec* X (October 1900), pp. 213–24; *Architecture* II (August 15, 1900), p. 292; *Architects' and Builders' Magazine* II (January 1901), p. 181; "Works," pp. 54–59, figs. 51–56.

11. César Daly, *L'architecture privée au XIXe siècle,* 3 vols. (Paris: A. Morel, 1864).

12. The Arthur Scribner House was converted to a multiple dwelling in 1952. For an illustration of the Courtlandt F. Bishop Residence, see *AABN* LXXXIX (June 2, 1906), p. 188.

13. *Architecture* II (July 15, 1900), p. 252.

14. The corner site of the Clark House was only a small portion of the extensive West Side real estate holdings including The Dakota which Alfred Corning Clark inherited on the death of his father, Edward Clark, in 1884. When Alfred Corning Clark died in 1896, his widow and three sons inherited an estate purported to be worth $50 million. See "Alfred

Corning Clark," obituary, *New York Times,* April 12, 1896, I, p. 5.

15. For an illustration of 170 Queen's Gate, see Andrew Saint, *Richard Norman Shaw* (New Haven and London: Yale University Press, 1976), p. 244, ill. 184.

16. E. Viollet-le-Duc, *Lectures on Architecture,* vol. 2, Benjamin Bucknall, trans. (Boston: James R. Osgood and Co., 1881), pp. 277ff.

17. See Alan Colquhoun, "The Beaux-Arts Plan," *Architectural Design* XVII [1979], pp. 62–65, figs. 6, 7. The English use of the "butterfly" plan is the subject of several discussions. See Jill Franklin, "Edwardian Butterfly Houses," *Architectural Review* (London) CLVII (April 1975), pp. 220–25, and *The Gentleman's Country House and its plan, 1835–1914* (London: Routledge & Kegan Paul, 1981), pp. 232–37. See also Saint, *Richard Norman Shaw,* pp. 332–34. Plans of the Clark House are reproduced in "Works," p. 51, fig. 48. For other illustrations of the Clark House, see *AABN* LXX (December 22, 1900); LXXI (February 16, 1901); *Architects' and Builders' Magazine* II (August 1901), p. 392; "Works," pp. 50, 52, figs. 47, 49.

18. Montgomery Schuyler, "The Vanderbilt Houses," in William H. Jordy and Ralph Coe, eds., *American Architecture and Other Writings* (Cambridge, Mass.: Harvard University Press, 1961), vol. 2, pp. 493–99; Schuyler, "The Works of the Late Richard M. Hunt," in Jordy and Coe, eds., *American Architecture and Other Writings,* vol. 2, pp. 538–40. See also Paul R. Baker, *Richard Morris Hunt* (Cambridge, Mass.: MIT Press, 1980) pp. 340–45.

19. See Mardges Bacon, "Toward a National Style of Architecture: The Beaux-Arts Interpretation of the Colonial Revival," in Alan Axelrod, ed., *The Colonial Revival in America,* (New York: W. W. Norton & Co., 1985).

20. Montgomery Schuyler, "The New New York House," *Arch Rec* XIX (February 1906), p. 85.

21. "A New Type of City House," *Arch Rec* XXII (September 1907), pp. 177–94. This article reproduces photographs of the house showing its lunette windows. See also *AABN* LXXXIX (May 12, 1906), p. 164; *Brickbuilder* XVII (September 1908), p. 197.

22. David Gray, *Thomas Hastings* (Boston: Houghton Mifflin and Company, 1933), p. 6.

23. Mrs. Ernest Flagg, interview with author, New York, summer 1973.

24. "A New Type of City House," p. 177.

25. The Cutting, O. G. Jennings, Arthur Scribner, and Bishop houses all contained passenger elevators.

26. The dining room is illustrated in "A New Type of City House," p. 187, fig. 17.

27. Flagg's office manager, Arthur T. Sutcliffe, purchased many of these items, see Arthur T. Sutcliffe Diary, January 10, 1906 (ATSP, AL, CU).

28. Ernest Flagg Diary, March 6, 1908 (EFP, AL, CU); Arthur T. Sutcliffe Diary, August 14, 1919 (ATSP, AL, CU).

29. Mrs. Ernest Flagg, interview with author, New York, April 24, 1973.

30. "A New Type of City House," pp. 192–94.

31. The Jenks House is so similar to the Flagg House, that Flagg undoubtedly designed it, while Chambers may have secured the commission. Montgomery Schuyler illustrates, but does not fully identify, the Jenks House, in "New New York Houses," *Arch Rec* XXX (November 1911), pp. 450, 468.

32. Ernest Flagg Diary, November 14, 1908 (EFP, AL, CU).

33. Ibid., November 24, 1908.

34. Ibid., December 2, 1909.

35. Ibid., December 19, 1909.

36. George McKay Schieffelin, grandson of Charles Scribner (1854–1930), kindly provided me with this information.

37. The Shepard House (Lotos Club) is illustrated in Alan Burnham, ed., *New York Landmarks* (Middletown, Conn.: Wesleyan University Press, 1963), p. 191.

38. Wayne Andrews, *The Vanderbilt Legend* (New York: Harcourt, Brace and Company, 1941), p. 322.

39. Ernest Flagg Diary, March 5, 1909 (EFP, AL, CU).

40. Ibid., May 13, 1910.

41. Ibid., January 17, 1913. Plans and elevations (blueprints) of the two schemes are at the New-York Historical Society.

42. *Architecture and Building* XLVI (October 1914), p. 414.

43. Paul Thompson, *William Butterfield* (Cambridge, Mass.: MIT Press, 1971), p. 322, fig. 272.

44. For illustrations of these Shaw houses, see Saint, *Richard Norman Shaw*, pp. 177, 234, 235, ill. 140, 174, 175.

45. See "Works," pp. 64–66, figs. 61–63. Information pertaining to the Ginn House and stable was principally obtained from the "Assessor's Valuation," *Annual Reports of the Town Officers of Winchester, Mass.,* 1896, xv; 1898, p. 30; 1900, p. 33 (Winchester Historical Society). See also "Seven Stall Stables," *Arch Rev* IX (September 1902), p. 197.

46. Letter, Margaret Ginn Patterson (daughter of Edwin Ginn) to author, April 25, 1974.

47. Harry W. Desmond and Herbert Croly, *Stately Homes in America* (New York: D. Appleton and Company, 1903).

48. "Indian Neck Hall," *New York Herald,* September 9, 1900, V, p. 11.

49. "A Fine Residence," *Suffolk County News,* June 18, 1897, III, p. 2. I wish to thank Brother Roger Chingas, FSC, for making this newspaper article available to me and for sharing the results of his research on "Indian Neck Hall."

50. Liisa and Donald Sclare, *Beaux-Arts Estates* (New York: Viking Press, 1980), p. 209.

51. "Frederick G. Bourne To Surprise His Wife Builds a $400,000 Castle Instead of a Cottage," *New York Press,* August 6, 1905, III, p. 1.

52. Information regarding The Dakota was obtained from unidentified newspaper clippings, scrapbook, p. 7 (1895); p. 71 (January 12, 1904) (La Salle Military Academy).

53. The northeast elevation is illustrated in "Works," p. 68, fig. 65. See also *Brickbuilder* VI (May 1897), pls. 41, 42, and *Architecture and Building* XXVII (October 1897).

54. "Indian Neck Hall," *New York Herald,* September 9, 1900, V, p. 11. The original boathouse may have been moved. Letter, Brother Roger Chingas, FSC, to author, March 23, 1977.

55. I wish to thank Neil Levine for his observations on French *hôtel* planning. Jean Courtonne's Hôtel de Matignon, Paris (1722–24), demonstrates the use of a split axis by eighteenth-century French architects. See Wend Graf Kalnein and Michael Levey, *Art and Architecture of the Eighteenth Century in France* (Baltimore: Penguin Books, 1972), pp. 243–44, fig. 15. Robert Venturi discusses Edwin Lutyens's use of the split axis in his *Complexity and Contradiction in Architecture* (New York: Museum of Modern Art, 1966), pp. 30–31.

56. The drawing room is illustrated in "Works," p. 71, fig. 68.

57. Julian Cavalier, *American Castles* (South Brunswick, N.J., and New York: A. S. Barnes and Company, 1973), pp. 231–32; pp. 73–82.

58. Arthur T. Sutcliffe Diary, November 10, 1903 (ATSP, AL, CU).

59. Bourne was elected Vice-Commodore in 1902 and served as Commodore from 1903–5. Yearbook, New York Yacht Club, 1972, p. 271.

60. Arthur T. Sutcliffe Diary, May 12, 1905 (ATSP, AL, CU).

61. Mrs. Alexander D. Thayer (the former Marjorie Bourne), who inherited "The Towers," made the alterations. The northwest end of the squash court addition is inscribed "ADT 1928."

62. Sutcliffe recorded in his diary on August 17, 1904, "Am reading Woodstock by Scott. Mr. Flagg advised me to read this book because from it he got his ideas for the house we are building for Mr. Bourne" (ATSP, AL, CU).

63. Sir Walter Scott, *Woodstock* (London: Marcus Ward & Co., 1879), p. 421.

64. See plate VI of Viollet-le-Duc's *Histoire d'une maison* (Paris: J. Hetzel et Cie, [1873]).

65. Lawrence Weaver, *Houses and Gardens by E. L. Lutyens* (London: Country Life, 1914), pp. 127–39.

66. Scott, *Woodstock,* p. 68.

67. Ibid., p. 124.

68. "A Wealthy New Yorker's 'Castle of Mysteries,'" *New York Times,* September 10, 1905, III, p. 2.

69. Arthur T. Sutcliffe Diary, July 22, 1905 (ATSP, AL, CU).

70. Mrs. Ernest Flagg, interview with author, New York, October 30, 1974.

71. Arthur T. Sutcliffe Diary, June 10, 1905 (ATSP, AL, CU).

72. Mrs. Ernest Flagg, interview with author, New York, August 30, 1973. Deed, Thomas Dunn and Kate Hunter Dunn to Ernest Flagg, 9.5934 acres, December 27, 1897, Taxplot 891-plot 1, Liber 263, p. 139. "George Cromwell Dead at Age of 74," *New York Times,* September 18, 1934, p. 21. Charles W. Leng and William T. Davis, *Staten Island and Its People: A History 1609–1929* (New York: Lewis Historical Publishing Company, Inc., 1930), vol. 3, pp. 4–5.

73. The Vanderbilt Mausoleum is discussed and illustrated in Baker, *Richard Morris Hunt,* pp. 290–92, fig. 71.

74. "Memorandum of Events in the Life of Ernest Flagg," July 19, 1899 (EFP, AL, CU). For the Perine, Vanderbilt, and Lake-Tysen houses, see Leng and Davis, *Staten Island and Its People: A History 1609–1929,* vol. 1, opp. p. 118; vol. 2, frontispiece, opp. p. 912, opp. p. 914, pp. 917, 937, 965–66. See Shirley Zavin's observation on the Lake-Tysen House in Landmarks Preservation Commission, *Expanded Landmark Site of the Ernest Flagg House* (New York, 1983). See also Landmarks Preservation Commission, *Lake-Tysen House* (New York, 1969).

75. Harmon H. Goldstone and Martha Dalrymple, *History Preserved, A Guide to New York City Landmarks and Historic Districts* (New York: Simon & Schuster, 1974), pp. 501–2.

76. The main house, water tower, stables, and a plan of the main house are illustrated in the "Works," pp. 76–81, figs. 73–79. See *New Building Record* [Docket Book], Bureau of Buildings, Borough of Richmond, No. 1, #108, 112, 125, 243, 50. *New Building Record Alterations,* 1901, #454. See also *Robinson's 1898 Atlas,* pl. 27.

77. See *New Building Record* [Docket Book], No. 1, #251; No. 2, #483. *New Building Record Alterations,* 1904, #189. See also *E. Robinson Atlas,* 1907. Borough of Richmond Topographical Survey, New York, August 1909. An entry in Flagg's diary on September 14, 1909, lists these improvements. See also entry for September 7, 1909 (EFP, AL, CU).

78. Mrs. Ernest Flagg, interview with author, New York, August 30, 1973.

79. George W. & Walter S. Bromley, *1917 Atlas,* vol. 1, pl. 31. See Flagg's designs for the Flegg Ridge Estate in his *Small Houses: Their Economic Design and Construction* (New York: Charles Scribner's Sons, 1922).

CHAPTER SIX

1. For examples of this specialized typology, see the commercial buildings on the rue d'Uzès, Paris.

2. Pierre Chabat, *La Brique et la terre cuite* (Paris: A. Morel et Cie, 1881), p. 1.

3. E. Viollet-le-Duc, *Lectures on Architecture,* vol. 2, Benjamin Bucknall, trans. (Boston: James R. Osgood and Co., 1881) p. 121.

4. Ernest Flagg, "American Architecture as Opposed to Architecture in America," *Arch Rec* X (October 1900), p. 178.

5. Landmarks Preservation Commission, *Firehouse Engine Co. Thirty-Three Designation Report* (City of New York, 1968). *Annual Report of the Fire Department of the City of New York, Year Ending December 31, 1898* [1899], p. 35. *Report of the Fire Department of the City of New York For the Year Ending December 31, 1899* (New York, 1900), pp. 9, 10, 75. Firehouse Engine Co. 67 is illustrated in "Works," p. 49, fig. 46.

6. See Lowell M. Limpus, *History of the New York Fire Department* (New York: E. P. Dutton and Company, Inc., 1940).

7. Differences focus on brick color and size. Firehouse Engine Co. 67 employed light yellow brick and occupied a 25-foot lot. Firehouse Engine Co. 33 used red brick and occupied two lots with a 50-foot frontage. See "Works," p. 48, fig. 45.

8. Limpus, *History of the New York Fire Department,* pp. 291, 294ff.

9. The decade of the eighties was a fruitful period in the design, construction, and publication of such *pompiers* and *casernes.* See "Caserne de la Garde républicaine, rue Gracieuse, à Paris par M. A. Hermant, architecte," *Revue Générale de l'Architecture et des Travaux Publics* XLIV (1887), pp. 36–39, pls. 13–14; "Caserne des sapeurs-pompiers, boulevard de Port-Royal, par Julien Hénard," *Architecture* I (1888), p. 29; "Caserne Louviers, à Paris, M. J. Bouvard," *Encyclopédie d'architecture,* III. 4 (1885), pls. 1034–36, 1038, 1039, 1044, 1049, 1050.

10. Vincent Scully writes of Sullivan's National Farmers' Bank, Owatonna, Minnesota (1907–8): "The building both respects Main Street and ennobles it" (*American Architecture and Urbanism* [New York: Praeger Publishers, 1969], p. 127).

11. The *New York Herald* reported on October 13, 1893, that Charles Scribner's Sons had purchased the old Glenham Hotel, that they were to erect "a fine building to be used exclusively by themselves," and that Ernest Flagg was "now engaged on the plans."

Newspaper clipping (Charles Scribner's Sons Archives, Princeton University Library).

12. When the *New York Times* reported the removal of Charles Scribner's Sons from 743–745 Broadway to 153–157 Fifth Avenue, it summarized the previous moves: "The house of Scribner was removed there [743 and 745 Broadway] in January, 1875, following the march of the city up town, from 645 Broadway, from Grand Street, from 377 Broadway, at the corner of White Street, and from 145 Nassau Street, where it was founded in 1846" (May 25, 1894, p. 8). For a more comprehensive treatment of the history of the publishing house, see Charles Scribner, Jr., "A Family Tradition," *American Library Association Bulletin* (March 1957), pp. 189–94, and Roger Burlingame, *Of Making Many Books* (New York: Charles Scribner's Sons, 1946), pp. 73–78.

13. "The History of a Publishing House," *Scribner's Magazine* XVI (July–December 1894), p. 804. Charles Scribner (1854–1930) took control of the firm in 1879 following the death of his older brother, John Blair Scribner. See Scribner, "A Family Tradition," p. 191, and Burlingame, *Of Making Many Books,* pp. 78, 89; "Charles Scribner," obituary, *New York Times,* April 20, 1930, pp. 1, 25; R.C. [Royal Cortissoz], "Scribner, Charles," *DAB,* XVI, pp. 516–17. Following his graduation from Princeton, Arthur Hawley Scribner (1859–1932), Charles's younger brother, was associated with the firm from 1884. See Scribner, "A Family Tradition," p. 191. See also "Arthur Hawley Scribner," obituary, *New York Times,* July 4, 1932, p. 11.

14. "The History of a Publishing House," p. 804.

15. *The Independent* XLVI (May 31, 1894), pp. 22–23 (Charles Scribner's Sons Archives, Princeton University Library).

16. The influence of Viollet-le-Duc's publications on the work of Frank Furness has been the subject of investigation by James F. O'Gorman. See *The Architecture of Frank Furness* (Philadelphia: Museum of Art, 1973).

17. Flagg owned five volumes of Viollet-le-Duc's writings in 1890.

18. [Eugène-Emmanuel] Viollet-le-Duc, *Entretiens sur l'architecture,* vol. 2 (Paris: Vve A. Morel & Cie, 1872), lecture XIII, fig. 1, pls. XXIII, XXIV. Earlier than Flagg, Dankmar Adler and Louis Sullivan used this French compositional format with emphasized brick and stone corner piers for their Jewelers Building, Chicago (1881–82). See Carl W. Condit, *The Chicago School of Architecture* (Chicago and London: University of Chicago Press, 1964), p. 39, fig. 7.

19. Flagg and his brother-in-law discussed plans as early as January 10, 1911, when "Scribner called and talked about a new building on Fifth Avenue" (Ernest Flagg Diary, January 10, 1911 [EFP, AL, CU]).

20. I. N. Phelps Stokes documents conveyances of real estate after 1900 to support his contention that "Fifth Avenue between 23rd and 50th Streets, became more and more valuable as a site for fashionable retail shops." See *The Iconography of Manhattan Island 1498–1909* (New York: Robert H. Dodd, 1915), vol. 3, p. 819.

21. George McKay Schieffelin, interview with author, New York, January 24, 1978.

22. Specifications for the iron or steel structural system of each of the Scribner buildings were obtained from building permits. See Building Permit, Block 850, lot 4, December 6, 1893, and Revised Schedule, December 22, 1893, and Building Permit, Block 1284, lots 2 and 3, April 10, 1912, New York City Department of Buildings, Municipal Building, New York.

23. Henry-Russell Hitchcock, as quoted in Margaret Sheffield, "Renovation Brightens a Notable Interior," *New York Times,* April 7, 1974, VIII, pp. 1, 10.

24. When Charles Scribner's Sons was incorporated in 1904, Charles Scribner became president and Arthur H. Scribner, vice-president and treasurer. "Announcement," unpaged scrapbook (Charles Scribner's Sons Archives, Princeton University Library). Flagg chronicled his discussions with Charles and Arthur Scribner. See Ernest Flagg Diary, entries for March 10, 13, and 16, 1912 (EFP, AL, CU).

25. Ernest Flagg Diary, March 25 and 18, 1912, respectively (EFP, AL, CU). The need for generous display windows, according to George McKay Schieffelin, was the critical factor in the Scribners' decision to limit the number of entrances to the bookstore. Interview with author, September 29, 1977.

26. Ernest Flagg Diary, April 8, 1913 (EFP, AL, CU).

27. Ibid., June 5, 1912.

28. Viollet-le-Duc, *Lectures on Architecture,* vol. 2, Bucknall, trans., p. 124.

29. Ernest Flagg Diary, October 31, 1912 (EFP, AL, CU). Early photographs of the Scribner Building at 153–157 Fifth Avenue suggest that Flagg may have specified the use of gold paint on the foliated ornament of the iron grill. This metal and glass storefront with its marquee is no longer extant.

30. See list of contracts, loose manuscript page, "New Building 597–599 Fifth Avenue" (Charles Scribner's Sons Archives, Princeton University Library).

31. Recent renovations to the interior have removed the central aisle, replacing it with a circular information-cashier's desk for more centralized control. The concept is remarkably consistent with public library planning.

32. Ernest Flagg Diary, March 27, 1913 (EFP, AL, CU).

33. Ibid., November 11, 1912.

34. Ernest Flagg, "The Dangers of High Buildings," *The Cosmopolitan* XXI (May 1896), p. 76.

35. Ibid., p. 75.

36. Ibid., p. 76.

37. A transcript of the meeting was published in the *Proceedings of the Twenty-Eighth*

Annual Convention of the American Institute of Architects, October 15, 16, 17, 1894. A paper read by Thomas Hastings, "High Building and Good Architecture," was reprinted in *AABN* XLVI (November 17, 1894), pp. 67–68. See also "Limit to High Buildings," *New York Tribune,* December 30, 1894, p. 5, and C. H. Blackall, "The Endurance of Structural Metal Work," *Brickbuilder* III (November 1894), pp. 217–19. Flagg, who was not a member of the A.I.A., did not attend the meeting. Francisco Mujica also summarized early attitudes toward the skyscraper in chapter 5 of his *History of the Skyscraper* (Paris: Archaeology and Architecture Press, 1929), pp. 45–49.

38. Cervin Robinson's study, "Late Cast Iron in New York," discusses the Building Code of 1899 and its effects, *JSAH* XXX (May 1971), pp. 164–69.

39. Carl W. Condit, *American Building Art: The Nineteenth Century* (New York: Oxford University Press, 1960), p. 48.

40. Montgomery Schuyler, "The 'Sky-scraper' up to Date," *Arch Rec* VIII (January–March 1899), p. 231.

41. Ibid., p. 257.

42. Publicity for Sullivan's Bayard (Condict) Building appeared in *Architectural Annual 1900,* p. 215, where laudatory press comments were reprinted. Russell Sturgis saw the Bayard Building as a prototype in the evolution of metal architecture and "an example of rational building as Americans most commonly understand it" ("Good Things in Modern Architecture," *Arch Rec* VIII [July–September 1898], p. 101).

43. Flagg, "American Architecture as Opposed to Architecture in America," p. 178.

44. See "Memorandum of Events in the Life of Ernest Flagg," February 5, 1902: "Mr. Bourne asked me to make plans for building cor B'way and Spring [sic] St. Lot an L corner one" (EFP, AL, CU). See also Alan Burnham, "Forgotten Pioneering," *Architectural Forum* CVI (April 1957), pp. 116–21.

45. Montgomery Schuyler recognized the importance of Hunt's decorative use of iron in "The Works of the Late Richard M. Hunt." See Jordy and Coe, eds., *American Architecture and Other Writings* (Cambridge, Mass.: Harvard University Press, 1961), vol. 2, pp. 517–19.

46. In his diary Arthur Sutcliffe, then building superintendent of the Singer Loft, chronicled the excavating and shoring operation, which was also plagued by labor disputes. See entries from November 1902 to October 1903 (ATSP, AL, CU). For a sketch of the shoring-up procedure by Sutcliffe, see Mardges Bacon, "Ernest Flagg: Beaux-Arts Architect and Reformer" (Ph.D. diss., Brown University, 1978), fig. 144.

47. A discussion of the window wall appears in Keith W. Dills's "The Hallidie Building," *JSAH* XXX (December 1971), pp. 323–29.

48. Harry Desmond, "A Rational Skyscraper," *Arch Rec* XV (March 1904), p. 278.

49. In addition to Viollet-le-Duc's projects, a number of French structures used terra cotta in

a new and decidedly rational manner. Pierre Chabat illustrates such buildings in his anthology, *La Brique et la terre cuite.*

50. Anthony Blunt, *Philibert de l'Orme* (London: A. Zwemmer, 1958), pp. 118–19.

51. J[ulien] Guadet, *Eléments et théorie de l'architecture,* 4 vols. (Paris: Librairie de la Construction Moderne, 1929; orig. pub. 1901–4), vol. 1, p. 253, fig. 137.

52. "The New Singer Building," promotional brochure (Singer Manufacturing Company).

53. See Flagg, "Influence of the French School," p. 218. French critics of the Chicago fair included architects and engineers. See "A Frenchman on the World's Fair and America" (based on "Extracts from the report of the Marquis of Chasseloup-Laubat to the Société des Ingénieur [sic] Civils") *AABN* XXXIX (January 28, 1893), pp. 58–60; Jacques Hermant, "L'Architecture aux Etats-Unis," *L'Architecture* VII (October 20, 1894), pp. 341–46.

54. The Pan-American Exposition, held in Buffalo in 1901, chose to observe the Hispanic culture of North and South America with a "Spanish Renaissance" architectural theme. Appropriately, South American-born architect, John M. Carrère, was selected chief of design in June 1899 by the initial organizational body, the A.I.A. See Claude Bragdon, "Some Pan-American Impressions," *AABN* LXXII (May 11, 1901), pp. 43–44; Herbert Croly, "Some Novel Features of the Pan-American Exposition," *Arch Rec* XI (October 1901), pp. 590–614. By the summer of 1901, the Commission of Architects of the Louisiana Purchase Exposition had been selected along the lines of the D. H. Burnham organization in Chicago, with architectural teams from all regions of the United States represented. To interpret the French theme, the Commission selected as Chief of Design a Frenchman and *diplomé* of the Ecole des Beaux-Arts, Emmanuel-Louis Masqueray. Masqueray was responsible for the choice of two prominent New York architectural firms to represent the East at the Saint Louis fair: Carrère & Hastings and Cass Gilbert. See Franz Winkler [Montgomery Schuyler], "The Architecture of the Louisiana Purchase Exposition," *Arch Rec* XV (April 1904), pp. 336–60. The selection of architects for the Saint Louis fair was announced in *AABN* LXXIII (August 3, 1901), p. 33.

55. Viollet-le-Duc, *Lectures on Architecture,* vol. 2, Bucknall, trans., p. 331.

56. Arthur T. Sutcliffe Diary, April 21, 1904. For a detailed account of the construction, see entries October 22, 1902 to April 21, 1904 (ATSP, AL, CU).

57. Desmond, "A Rational Skyscraper," pp. 274–84. Montgomery Schuyler, "The Evolution of the Sky-scraper," *Scribner's Magazine* XLVI (September 1909), p. 268.

58. Desmond, "A Rational Skyscraper," pp. 277, 279.

59. Ibid., p. 279.

60. Ibid., pp. 276, 279.

61. "Current Periodicals," *Arch Rev* XI (April 1904), p. 147.

62. *Arch Rev* XVI (November 1909), p. 153.

63. According to George B. Ford, "In France the fire hazard is so small and buildings, commercial or otherwise, are in general so nearly fireproof that the thought of protecting structural steel seems never to have been considered" ("Rational Ironwork for Store and Loft Building," *AABN* XCIV [September 16, 1908], p. 89).

64. Arthur T. Sutcliffe Diary, September 29, 1904 (ATSP, AL, CU). I would like to thank Thomas Fisher for his help in analyzing the Singer Loft's structural system.

65. Desmond, "A Rational Skyscraper," p. 283.

66. Ernest Flagg, *Small Houses: Their Economic Design and Construction* (New York: Charles Scribner's Sons, 1922), p. 102.

67. Suppliers for the Singer Loft Building include an unidentified Indianapolis contractor for ornamental iron and Standard Terra Cotta Works of Perth Amboy, New Jersey.

68. Construction for the Automobile Club of America was begun on September 17, 1905, and completed April 5, 1907. Building Permit, Block 1026, lots 5, 5½, 6, 7, 8, 8½, 10, New York City Department of Buildings, Municipal Building, New York.

69. Dealers such as Smith & Mabley, Rochet-Schneider, Cadillac, Packard, and Baker-Lozier erected new structures in this automobile district near upper Broadway which encouraged a number of supporting services including Goodrich Tires. See Grace M. Mayer, *Once Upon a City* (New York: Macmillan Company, 1958), pp. 302–3. See also DeLeeuw's *Both Sides of Broadway* (New York: DeLeeuw Riehl Publishing Company, 1910), which documents the transition between the carriage trade and the newly emerging automobile district, see pp. 412ff.

70. "Auto Club's New Home Opened New Year's Day," *New York Times,* December 31, 1906, p. 5.

71. "Cornerstone is Laid for Auto Club," *New York Times,* March 22, 1906, p. 7.

72. Mrs. Ernest Flagg, interview with author, New York, summer 1973.

73. Harry W. Perry, "The New Home of the Automobile Club of America," *Scientific American* XCVI (April 21, 1907), p. 350.

74. "Motor Garages and Fire Protection," *AABN* XCII (July 6, 1907), pp. 4–5.

75. Perry, "The New Home of the Automobile Club of America," p. 349.

76. The Atlantic Terra Cotta Company supplied terra cotta for the Automobile Club of America, see *Brickbuilder* XVI (May 1907), p. 90. For a line drawing of the upper stories, see *AABN* XCI (May 4, 1907).

77. The polychromed decoration of the Automobile Club of America was described by Perry, "The New Home of the Automobile Club of America," p. 349.

78. Russell Sturgis, "Some Recent Warehouses," *Arch Rec* XXIII (May 1908), pp. 376–

77, 381–82, figs. 3, 4.

79. Peter Collins, *Concrete* (New York: Horizon Press, 1959), pp. 184–86; Edmond Uhry, "Garages d'automobiles," *L'Architecte* III (April 1908), pp. 27–30; "The Packard Garage, New York," *Architects' and Builders' Magazine* IX (December 1907), pp. 110–12. Perret's Garage-Ponthieu employed reinforced concrete, elevators, and a turntable, while Kahn's Packard Garage used reinforced concrete and elevators.

80. "A Garage of Reinforced Concrete," *Architects' and Builders' Magazine* VII (April 1906), pp. 296–301.

81. Flagg's own publications show that he was especially familiar with the writings of Auguste Choisy, the French engineer in charge of *ponts et chaussées*. See Ernest Flagg, "Stone Walls and Their Construction," *Country Life* XLII (May 1922), pp. 73–80.

82. The Hutton-Flagg designs are both discussed and illustrated in the Congressional Record. H.R. Doc. No. 578, 56th Cong., 1st Sess. 3995 (1900).

83. See illustrations of Léopold Hardy's *Palais de l'exposition,* Paris, of 1878 and Jean-Camille Formigé's *Palais des beaux-arts* and *Palais des arts libéraux,* Paris, of 1889 in Hautecoeur, *Histoire de l'architecture classique en France* (Paris: A. and J. Picard et Cie, 1957), vol. 7, pp. 385, 395–97.

84. Montgomery Schuyler, "Monumental Engineering," *Arch Rec* XI (October 1901), p. 620.

85. Ibid., p. 623.

86. Flagg landed in Liverpool on July 8, 1908, and toured England and France before returning via Liverpool on September 30, 1908. Ernest Flagg Diary, entries from July 8, 1908, to September 30, 1908 (EFP, AL, CU).

87. Ernest Flagg, "Stone Pavements in Two Cities," Letter to the Editor, *The Sun,* November 1, 1908, p. 8. Ernest Flagg, "Road Building and Maintenance," *The Century Magazine* LXXIX (November 1909), pp. 139–49. Flagg privately reprinted the *Century* article, *Roads and Pavements* (New York: De Vinne Press, 1910).

88. Ernest Flagg Diary, entries November 7, December 2, December 14, 1908; March 6, March 15, March 19, May 20, 1909 (EFP, AL, CU).

89. The Produce Exchange Bank Building survived less than two decades. When the Standard Oil Company wished to expand its headquarters at 26 Broadway, it demolished the Flagg structure and erected an addition in 1922 by Carrère & Hastings.

90. Brendan Gill chronicles the history of the building in *The U.S. Custom House on Bowling Green* (New York: New York Landmarks Conservancy, Inc., 1976).

91. "Produce Exchange Bank Building," *Record and Guide* LXXVI (November 4, 1905), p. 689. See also "The New York Produce Exchange Bank Building," *Architects' and Builders' Magazine* VII (October 1905), pp. 1–8.

92. Mardges Bacon, "The Hartford Federal Savings [First National] Bank Building," Historic Resources Inventory Form, National Register of Historic Places, 1979. Flagg's design was published in *Brickbuilder* VI (May 1897), pls. 45, 46.

93. William Jordy discusses this aspect of Sullivan's architecture in chapter II, "Functionalism as Fact and Symbol: Louis Sullivan's Commercial Buildings, Tombs, and Banks," of his *American Buildings and Their Architects, Progressive and Academic Ideals at the Turn of the Twentieth Century*, vol. 3 (Garden City, N.Y.: Doubleday & Company, 1972).

94. Ernest Flagg Diary, December 23, 1912 (EFP, AL, CU).

95. Ibid.

96. Arthur T. Sutcliffe Diary, December 23, 1912 (ATSP, AL, CU).

97. "The Gwynne Building," *Cincinnati Enquirer,* May 29, 1913, p. 11. No sooner was the Gwynne Building finished than the Procter & Gamble Company leased the entire building, the firm occupying the upper floors. In his diary Arthur Sutcliffe recorded the transaction on October 10, 1914 (ATSP, AL, CU). Procter & Gamble bought the Gwynne Building from the Vanderbilt estate in 1935. See "70-Days," *Moonbeams* (August 1956), pp. 4–7 (Procter & Gamble Co.). See also "The Gwynne Building" [building prospectus], The Frederick A. Schmidt Company, Managers and Rental Agents [1914].

98. Ernest Flagg Diary, January 8, 1913 (EFP, AL, CU).

99. Ibid., February 1, 1913. Earlier, in 1896, Alice Vanderbilt had attempted to develop the property (then approximately 41×162 feet) with an office and store building. "Mrs. Vanderbilt," *Cincinnati Enquirer,* January 1, 1896, p. 8.

100. A prospectus (circa 1890) of Norcross Brothers, contractors, illustrates the New York Insurance Company Building, Omaha (Corcoran Gallery of Art Archives).

101. "Specification for Exterior Mosaic Panels for Gwynne Building," September 11, 1913 (author's collection).

102. Conspicuously absent from Flagg's diary, which extends to 1914, is any discussion of his loft building at 645–651 Eleventh Avenue. There are, however, numerous comments on the progress of the Scribner and Gwynne buildings.

103. Arthur T. Sutcliffe, "Why the Model Fireproof Tenement Company," p. 5, unpublished manuscript (ATSP, AL, CU). No earlier use of flat-slab construction in New York has been identified.

104. Arthur T. Sutcliffe Diary, February 3 and March 13, 1913 (ATSP, AL, CU). See also building prospectus (ATSP, AL, CU).

105. Carl Condit describes the flat-slab system of construction, summarizes its advantages, and the history of its use in his *American Building Art: The Twentieth Century* (New York: Oxford University Press, 1961), pp. 166–70.

106. Ernest Flagg, "American Architecture of the Future," *New York American Souvenir Edition,* September 18, 1909, p. 4.

CHAPTER SEVEN

1. Construction on the Singer Tower began on September 19, 1906, and was "practically completed" for its opening on May 1, 1908. See O. F. [Otto Francis] Semsch, ed., *A History of the Singer Building Construction: Its Progress from Foundation to Flag Pole* (New York: Trow Press, 1908). See also *50th Anniversary, Singer Building* [1958] (The Singer Company), and "The Talk of the Town," *New Yorker* XLIII (September 9, 1967), p. 37.

2. Newspapers which chronicled the demolition in 1967 and 1968 widely publicized this record. See two articles by Joseph P. Fried, "End Near for Singer Building, A Forerunner of Skyscrapers," *New York Times,* August 22, 1967, p. 41, and "End of Skyscraper: Daring in '08, Obscure in '68," *New York Times,* March 27, 1968, p. 49.

3. "The Talk of the Town," p. 38.

4. The Singer Company sold the land and buildings two years before the United States Steel Corporation acquired them in 1964. By December 1967, the fifty-story office building was planned for the site. See Diana S. Waite, "Singer Tower," *New York Architecture* (HABS No. NY-5463) (National Park Survey, July 1969), pp. 87–88. See also Ada Louise Huxtable, "Sometimes We Do It Right," *New York Times,* March 31, 1968, II, p. 33.

5. President Bourne reported to the Board of Directors on April 16, 1890, that the Singer Company had taken title to property at 149, 151, and 153 Broadway. On September 23, 1896, the board decided to build a new home office on its present site, retaining Flagg as architect. This information from the *Singer Company Minutes, 1863–1905* was supplied to me by Robert Bruce Davies. I am very grateful to Professor Davies for sharing his research with me. The corner lot originally belonged to the Clark Estate. A sketch of the block (bordered by Broadway, Liberty, Church, and Cortlandt streets), identifying the Clark Estate on the corner of Broadway and Liberty Street, is contained in a letter, John M. Thompson & Co., Real Estate, to Frederick G. Bourne, Agent Clarke [sic] Estate, February 4, 1897 (Box 154, Correspondence, miscellaneous domestic and foreign, Singer Manufacturing Company Papers, State Historical Society of Wisconsin).

6. The building chronology is summarized in Semsch, ed., *A History of the Singer Building Construction,* p. 10.

7. Paul Baker illustrates the Tribune Building in his monograph, *Richard Morris Hunt* (Cambridge, Mass.: MIT Press, 1980), p. 221, fig. 43.

8. See "The New Singer Building," *New York Times,* January 10, 1897, p. 7, and "The Singer Building," *Record and Guide* LXII (July 23, 1898), p. 117.

9. Similar to the "modern French" style of the Singer Building of 1896, is Flagg's design for the Connecticut Mutual Life Insurance Company Building, Hartford, of 1900–1902 (demolished). Occupying the former site of the Pearl Street Church, this building was designed with George M. Bartlett, a member of the Flagg office, as associate architect. See *Brickbuilder* X (February 1901), pl. 9. See also "Works," p. 37, fig. 34. As the Connecticut Mutual structure neared completion, Sutcliffe recorded that Flagg "does not take a great amount of interest in the building" (Arthur T. Sutcliffe Diary, February 19, 1902 [ATSP, AL, CU]).

10. *The Singer Building* [1898], pamphlet (The Singer Company). See also "The New Singer Building," *New York Times,* January 10, 1897, p. 7.

11. *The Singer Building* [1898], pamphlet (The Singer Company).

12. Flagg, "The Dangers of High Buildings," *The Cosmopolitan* XXI (May 1896), p. 76.

13. Ibid., p. 77.

14. Ibid., pp. 72–73.

15. Schuyler, "The 'Sky-scraper' up to Date," *Arch Rec* VIII (January–March 1899), p. 253. Schuyler borrowed his observation from a statement that had appeared the previous year in *Record and Guide,* see "The Singer Building," p. 119. See also the favorable editorial comment in *AABN* LII (May 16, 1896), p. 61.

16. "Office Buildings Under Way," *Record and Guide* LXII (December 3, 1898), p. 828.

17. See Robert Bruce Davies, *Peacefully Working to Conquer the World: Singer Sewing Machines in Foreign Markets, 1854–1920* (New York: Arno Press, 1976), pp. 114–15.

18. A rendering of Flagg's design was published in "Works," p. 35, fig. 32. Extant letterpress copies of correspondence confirm that Siuzor was associated with the Leningrad Singer Building at least as early as 1902. Letter from W. F. Dixon, January 21 [1903]: "Enclosing copy of letter from Count Suzor of Dec. 20th last [1902]" (Box 188, vol. 114, Singer Manufacturing Company Papers, State Historical Society of Wisconsin). There are extensive references to Siuzor as architect and to the progress of the Nevskii Singer Building (Box 188, vols. 114, 115, 118, Singer Manufacturing Company Papers, State Historical Society of Wisconsin). See also *Architectural Monuments of Leningrad* (Leningrad: Leningrad Stroyizdat, 1975), pp. 166–67; M. Yogansen and V. Lissovski, *Leningrad* (Leningrad: Iskusstvo, 1982), pp. 292–94.

19. A photograph of *Dom Knigi* appears in William Craft Brumfield's *Gold in Azure* (Boston: Godine, 1983), p. 332, fig. 429.

20. Letter, Korn (vice-president, Bund der Architekten der Deutschen Demokratischen Republik) to author, April 2, 1975. Letterpress copies of correspondence among Singer executives indicate that Flagg's design for the Berlin Singer Building was carefully respected. Letter from [W. S.] Church, February 14, 1906 (Box 188, vol. 117, Singer Manufacturing Company Papers, State Historical Society of Wisconsin). No photograph

of the Berlin Singer Building has been located.

21. "Memorandum of Events in the Life of Ernest Flagg," May 9, 1902 (EFP, AL, CU).

22. Arthur T. Sutcliffe Diary, February 26, 1903 (ATSP, AL, CU).

23. Francisco Mujica, *History of the Skyscraper* (Paris: Archaeology and Architecture Press, 1929), p. 58.

24. M. G., "Famous Sewing Machine is now a Centenarian," *Glasgow Evening Times,* June 18, 1951, newspaper clipping (The Singer Company).

25. "The Erection of the 612-Foot Singer Building," *Scientific American* XCVII (September 7, 1907), p. 168.

26. Yet, unlike the Singer Tower, the structure of the Eiffel Tower is, according to Carl W. Condit, "a curved, tapering spire, [which] reduces the surface area exposed to the wind near the top and converts bending and shearing forces into compression at the base" (Condit, "The Wind Bracing of Buildings," *Scientific American* CCXXX [February 1974], p. 97).

27. Montgomery Schuyler, "The Towers of Manhattan," *Arch Rec* XXXIII (February 1913), p. 104.

28. See H. W. Desmond, "A Beaux-Arts Skyscraper — The Blair Building, New York City," *Arch Rec* XIV (December 1903), pp. 436–43.

29. Schuyler, "The Towers of Manhattan," p. 104. A discussion of the Woolworth Tower's structural bracing appears in Carl W. Condit, *American Building* (Chicago: University of Chicago Press, 1968), pp. 186–87, fig. 67. See also Semsch, ed., *A History of the Singer Building Construction,* which excerpts an analysis of the Singer Tower's wind-bracing from *Engineering Record* of May 18, 1907, and illustrates the progress of the construction, pp. 22–26. A comparable discussion of wind-bracing for the Woolworth Building was written by S. F. Holtzman of the Gunvald Aus Company, Consulting Engineers; see his "Design of the Woolworth Building," *Engineering Record* LXVIII (July 5, 1913), pp. 22–24. The Metropolitan Life Insurance Company Tower employed riveted plate girders, knee braces, and gussets; see John L. Hall, "Description of the Structural Steel Framework for the Tower of the Metropolitan Life Insurance Building, New York City," *AABN* XCVI (October 6, 1909), pp. 130–33.

30. Semsch, ed., *A History of the Singer Building Construction,* pp. 52–55, 68. For other descriptions of the Singer lobby, see "The New Singer Building," *New York Times,* January 10, 1897, p. 7, and "Singer Tower," *New York Architecture* (HABS No. NY-5463), pp. 94–96.

31. Howard Frederick Koeper, "The Gothic Skyscraper: A History of the Woolworth Building and Its Antecedents" (Ph.D. diss., Harvard University, 1969), pp. 89–95.

32. Schuyler, "The Evolution of the Sky-Scraper," *Scribner's Magazine* XLVI (September 1909), p. 271.

33. See Arthur T. Sutcliffe Diary, November 19, 1908 (ATSP, AL, CU).

34. See Koeper, "The Gothic Skyscraper," p. 84.

35. Names of the leading members of the Flagg office in 1908 appear in Semsch, ed., *A History of the Singer Building Construction,* [p. 6]. See also "Where Our Architects Work," *Arch Rec* X (January 1901), pp. 238–44.

36. Semsch's *A History of the Singer Building Construction,* which chronicled all phases of the Singer's foundation and construction, described this "Time System of Work," p. 30. *Scientific American* also reported the various problems of organization including the positioning of the derrick, the work of the riveting gangs, and the problems of storage, see "The Erection of the 612-Foot Singer Building," pp. 168–69.

37. Semsch, ed., *A History of the Singer Building Construction,* p. 32.

38. Davies, *Peacefully Working to Conquer the World,* pp. 108–13.

39. "The Largest Single Office Building in the World," *Scientific American* XCVII (November 23, 1907), p. 378.

40. "The Increasing Marvels of Lower Manhattan," *New York Times,* October 6, 1907, V, p. 3.

41. For a summary of the Singer Company's acquisition of land parcels at the corner of Broadway and Liberty Street, see Waite, "Singer Tower," *New York Architecture,* pp. 87–88. A contemporaneous analysis of urban land values is contained in Richard M. Hurd, *Principles of City Land Values* (New York: Record and Guide, 1903). A map indicating land valuation in the Manhattan business section appears on page 158.

42. Ernest Flagg, "The Limitation of Height and Area of Buildings in New York," *AABN* XCIII (April 15, 1908), p. 126.

43. Ibid.

44. Montgomery Schuyler, "To Curb the Skyscraper," *Arch Rec* XXIV (October 1908), p. 301.

45. Flagg, "The Limitation of Height and Area of Buildings in New York," p. 126.

46. See also "Tower Skyscrapers Planned for Future," *New York Times,* May 30, 1908, p. 16, and "Height Limitations," *New York Architect* II (October 1908), unpaged.

47. David Knickerbacker Boyd described and diagrammed both schemes in his article, "The Skyscraper and the Street," *AABN* XCIV (November 18, 1908), pp. 161–67.

48. Schuyler, "To Curb the Skyscraper," p. 302.

49. *Report of the Heights of Buildings Commission to the Committee on the Height, Size and Arrangement of Buildings of the Board of Estimate and Apportionment of the City of New York,* December 23, 1913, pp. 61–63. See also "Statement by Mr. David Knickerbacker Boyd, Architect, Philadelphia, June 27, 1913," pp. 188–90, and "Statement by

Mr. Ernest Flagg, Representing the New York Chapter of the American Institute of Architects, May 29, 1913," pp. 223–28.

50. *Minutes of the meeting of the Heights of Buildings Commission,* May 26, 1913, p. 4 (Box A-2507, Municipal Archives, New York City). Those Commission members who supported "aesthetic considerations" included C. Grant LaFarge, the New York architect, Burt L. Fenner, and Lawson Purdy. Ibid.

51. Ernest Flagg, "The Plan of New York, and How to Improve it," *Scribner's Magazine* XXXVI (August 1904), pp. 253–56; "A New Plan for Manhattan," *Record and Guide* LXXV (August 20, 1904), p. 390; *AABN* LXXXVII (May 20, 1905), p. 156. Flagg's plan for Manhattan of 1904 followed several proposals, including a scheme for Bryant Park and a Naval Arch at the Battery to serve as an entrance gate to New York City, which sought to introduce civic monuments and formal planning (see Chapter IV). See "The Architect's Portfolio, *Arch Rec* XIV (August 1903), p. 145; and *AABN* LXXII (May 11, 1901), p. 42.

52. Among the many articles in New York newspapers that announced the Metropolitan Life Insurance Company Tower as the new record skyscraper is one appearing in the *New York Tribune;* see "New York Will Soon Have the Highest Structure but One Ever Raised by Man," January 20, 1907, II, p. 1.

53. L. L. Redding, "Mr. Woolworth's Story," *World's Work* XXV (April 1913), p. 663, as quoted in Koeper, "The Gothic Skyscraper," pp. 80–81.

54. "Tallest Skyscraper to Stand in Broadway," *New York Times,* February 22, 1906, p. 1.

55. "Comparison of Victoria Falls with Niagara Falls and with the Sky Line of New York. Only the Singer Building's Tower Rises Above the Crest," *Scientific American* XCVI (June 29, 1907), cover [p. 525].

56. "Graphic Representation of the Enormous Energy Expended in Manufactures in the United States," *Scientific American* XCVII (October 19, 1907), cover [p. 269]. "A Giant Industry — The Meats We Eat," *Scientific American* XCVII (August 24, 1907), cover [p. 129].

57. William Jordy first made this observation.

58. Barr Ferree, "The Art of the High Building," *Arch Rec* XV (May 1904), pp. 460–63.

59. Semsch, ed., *A History of the Singer Building Construction,* p. 105.

60. "Tower 1,000 Feet High," *New York Times,* July 19, 1908, p. 1

61. Ernest Flagg Diary, June 5 and 8, 1911 (EFP, AL, CU). No drawings of either skyscraper project exist, nor has any visual documentation of them been located.

62. Flagg's drawing, which no longer survives, is reproduced in Semsch, ed., *A History of the Singer Building Construction,* p. 9.

63. Flagg, "The Limitation of Height and Area of Buildings in New York," p. 126.

64. See Donald Hoffmann, "The Setback Skyscraper City of 1891: An Unknown Essay by Louis H. Sullivan," *JSAH* XXIX (May 1970), pp. 181–87. See also Thomas S. Hines, *Burnham of Chicago* (New York: Oxford University Press, 1974), pp. 312–45.

65. Consult Moses King, ed., *King's Views of New York 1908–1909,* (New York, 1908) [p. 1]. Both the Flagg and Pettit views of 1908 figure in Cervin Robinson's article, "Wie wird man ein erfolgreicher Visionär?" Metropolis 2, *Archithese* XVIII (1976), pp. 5–12.

66. Ernest Flagg, "The City of the Future," *Scientific American* CXXXVII, Part 1 (September 1927), p. 238.

67. Ibid., p. 239.

68. Thomas Adams, *The Regional Plan of New York and its Environs,* vol. 2, *The Building of the City* (New York: Regional Plan of New York and its Environs, 1931), pp. 302–21.

69. Flagg, "The City of the Future," *Scientific American* CXXXVII, Part II (October 1927), p. 335.

70. Ibid., p. 336.

71. Similar cast-iron bridges were designed in the late nineteenth century for the elevated railroad in Paris. See for example, Paul Haag, "Le Chemin de fer Métropolitain," *La Construction Moderne* I (March 13, 1886), pp. 263–64.

72. Harvey W. Corbett, "Zoning and the Envelope of the Building," *Pencil Points* IV (April 1923), pp. 15–18. Hugh Ferriss, *The Metropolis of Tomorrow* (New York: Ives Washburn, 1929), pp. 72–81.

CHAPTER EIGHT

1. For the purpose of clarification, a tenement or tenement house refers to a building. A living unit within a tenement is called an apartment. I. N. Phelps Stokes, "Appendix: Historical Summary," in James P. Ford, *Slums and Housing* (Cambridge, Mass.: Harvard University Press, 1936), vol. 2, p. 871.

2. "Irrational Tenement House Planning," *Record and Guide* LIV (July 7, 1894), p. 2.

3. Sarah Bradford Landau, *Edward T. and William A. Potter: American Victorian Architects* (New York: Garland Publishing, 1979), pp. 390–409. David P. Handlin, *The American Home* (Boston: Little, Brown and Company, 1979), pp. 207–10. Among Potter's writings, see "A Study of Some New York Tenement-House Problems," *The Charities Review* I (January 1892), pp. 128–40. In 1879 George B. Post designed a plan for a colony of tenements in collaboration with a civil engineer, George W. Dresser. See Stokes, "Appendix: Notes on Plans," in Ford, *Slums and Housing,* vol. 2, p. 881, pl. 4. Vaux and Radford designed a group of "improved" tenements on First Avenue between 71st and 72nd streets (1879–81) which Stokes considered "the forerunner of

the modern model tenement, introduced by Mr. Flagg sixteen years later." See Stokes, "Appendix: Notes on Plans," in Ford, *Slums and Housing,* vol. 2, p. 882, pl. 5H.

4. Paul R. Baker, *Richard Morris Hunt* (Cambridge, Mass.: MIT Press, 1980), pp. 262, 509, n. 24.

5. Leland Roth discusses these row houses in his essay, "McKim, Mead & White Reappraised," which accompanies the new edition of the 1915 study, *A Monograph of the Works of McKim, Mead & White 1879–1915* (New York: Benjamin Blom, 1973), pp. 25–26. See also building prospectus, *The King Model Houses,* 1891 (Avery Library, Columbia University).

6. Stokes records that he "first attended the atelier of Godfroy [Jules-Alexis Godefroy] and Frenet [Jacques-Eugène Freynet], but soon transferred to the atelier and office combined of Henri Duray, a distinguished practitioner, who specialized in apartment-house work, which interested me as being closely akin to my chosen field of tenement-house design." Stokes failed his entrance exams and was never admitted to the Ecole des Beaux-Arts. I. N. Phelps Stokes, *Random Recollections of a Happy Life,* rev. ed. (New York, 1941), pp. 92, 98–99. Roy Lubove's article, "I. N. Phelps Stokes: Tenement Architect, Economist, Planner," *JSAH* XXIII (May 1964), documents and analyzes Stokes's contributions, pp. 75–87. In later years, Stokes recalled, "I believe I was the first architect, with the exception of Mr. Ernest Flagg, to take up the study of the housing of the working classes" (I. N. Phelps Stokes to Edward D. Duffield, President, Prudential Life Insurance Co., May 20, 1929. I. N. Phelps Stokes Letterbooks, XXII [New-York Historical Society]). I would like to thank Professor Lubove for kindly providing me with this reference.

7. Ernest Flagg, "Tenements," p. 1, essay from unpublished manuscript "Observations" (EFP, AL, CU).

8. Flagg, "Tenements," p. 6 (EFP, AL, CU).

9. Flagg consistently maintained that the vigorous legislation of the 1930s had outpriced housing rents "which the ordinary tenement dweller could pay." Letter, Ernest Flagg to I. N. Phelps Stokes, June 18, 1935, published by Stokes, "Appendix: Notes on Plans," in Ford, *Slums and Housing,* vol. 2, p. 884.

10. For a history of the tenement house movement in New York City before 1879, see Roy Lubove, *The Progressives and the Slums* (Pittsburgh: University of Pittsburgh Press, 1962), pp. 1–28; Stokes, "Appendix: Historical Summary" and "Appendix: Notes on Plans," in Ford, *Slums and Housing,* vol. 2, pp. 867–72, 877–80, pls. 1–3; Lawrence Veiller, "Tenement House Reform in New York City, 1834–1900," in Robert W. De Forest and Lawrence Veiller, eds., *The Tenement House Problem* (New York: Macmillan Co., 1903), vol. 1, pp. 71–99.

11. Lubove, *The Progressives and the Slums,* p. 8. Elgin R. L. Gould, "Financial Aspects of Recent Tenement House Operations in New York," in De Forest and Veiller, eds., *The Tenement House Problem,* vol. 1, p. 362.

12. Joseph D. McGoldrick, *Building Regulation in New York City* (New York: Commonwealth Fund, 1944), p. 66. See also De Forest and Veiller, eds., *The Tenement House Problem,* vol. 2, Appendix VI, pp. 272–73, 275–76.

13. Lubove, *The Progressives and the Slums,* p. 31. De Forest and Veiller, eds., *The Tenement House Problem,* vol. 2, Appendix II, p. 117.

14. Discussions of Ware's plan and modifications to it appear in Stokes "Appendix: Historical Summary," in Ford, *Slums and Housing,* vol. 2, pp. 872, 880–81, pl. 3C, D, E, F, G; Lubove, *The Progressives and the Slums,* pp. 29–32; Anthony Jackson, *A Place Called Home* (Cambridge, Mass.: MIT Press, 1976), pp. 63–65.

15. Ernest Flagg, "The New York Tenement-House Evil and Its Cure," *Scribner's Magazine* XVI (July 1894), p. 108.

16. Although both plans had 5,600 square feet of rentable room space, Flagg's had 3,060 square feet for light and air as opposed to 2,060 square feet in the dumb-bell plan. Flagg, "Tenement-House Evil," p. 112.

17. Flagg, "Tenement-House Evil," pp. 114, 115, 117.

18. Flagg, "Tenements," p. 5 (EFP, AL, CU).

19. Ibid., p. 2.

20. Flagg, "Tenement-House Evil," p. 117.

21. Stokes, "Appendix: Notes on Plans," in Ford, *Slums and Housing,* vol. 2, p. 883.

22. The Tenement House Law of 1867 defined a tenement house as a "residence of more than three families living independently of another, and doing their cooking upon the premises, or by more than two families on a floor, so living and cooking, but have a common right in the halls, stairways, water closets or privies, or some of them" (*New York State Laws,* Ninetieth Session, 1867, Chap. 908, Sec. 17, as quoted in Lubove, *The Progressives and the Slums,* p. 26).

23. The Tenement House Act of 1901 confirmed the 1867 definition of a tenement house. See De Forest and Veiller, eds., *The Tenement House Problem,* vol. 2, Appendix V, pp. 167–68. In Russell Sturgis's *A Dictionary of Architecture and Building,* George Hill defined a tenement house as "a building occupied by more than one family and usually having suites of rooms, a public stairway, dumb-waiter, and toilet room common to two or more families on each floor, each suite consisting of a living room, with one or more bedrooms opening therefrom . . ." (Sturgis, ed., *A Dictionary of Architecture and Building* [New York: Macmillan Company, 1902], vol. 3, p. 777).

24. Ernest Flagg, "The Planning of Apartment Houses and Tenements," *Arch Rev* X (August 1903), p. 87.

25. Flagg, "Tenement-House Evil," p. 116.

26. Flagg, "The Planning of Apartment Houses and Tenements," pp. 87–88.

27. See Emile Muller and Emile Cacheux, *Les habitations ouvrières en tous pays; situation en 1878* (Paris: J. Dejey & Cie, 1879), atlas, pls. 27, 28; see also Emile Cacheux, *Etat des habitations ouvrières à la fin du XIXe siècle; étude suivie du compte rendu des documents relatifs aux petits logements qui ont figuré à l'Exposition universelle de 1889* (Paris: Baudry & Cie, 1891), pl. 14. The *Société Philanthropique* sponsored a series of model tenements, among them a split-level housing complex at 15 bis rue d'Hautpoul. See Charles Lucas, *Etude sur les habitations à bon marché en France et à l'étranger* (Paris: Librairie de la Construction Moderne [1899]), pp. 64–68, figs. 10, 11. Another philanthropic organization, the *Société des Habitations économiques de Paris,* subsidized housing for middle-class railroad workers. The multiple dwelling at 112 rue du Château-des-Rentiers, Paris, for example, employed a hollowed-square plan with corner staircases. See also Lucas, *Etude sur les habitations à bon marché,* pp. 68–74, figs. 12–15.

28. Roger-H. Guerrand, *Les Origines du logement social en France* (Paris: Editions Ouvrières, 1967), pp. 159–67. Among the recent publications to appear on Guise, see Leo Balmer, Stefan Erni, and Ursula con Gunten, "Guise: L'unione cooperativa di capitale e lavoro/Cooperation between Capital and Labour," *Lotus 12,* pp. 58–71. *Jean-Baptiste André Godin, 1817–1888: le familistère de Guise ou les equivalents de la richesse* (Brussels: Archives d'architecture moderne, 1980).

29. "Apartment Houses I," *AABN* XXIX (September 27, 1890), pp. 194–95; "Apartment Houses II," *AABN* XXX (November 15, 1890), pp. 97–101. Andrew Alpern, *Apartments for the Affluent* (New York: McGraw-Hill Book Company, 1975), p. 1; Robert A. M. Stern, "With Rhetoric: The New York Apartment House," *VIA* IV (1980), pp. 79–88.

30. Anon., "Parisian 'Flats,'" *Appletons' Journal of Literature, Science and Art* VI (November 18, 1871), p. 562; Charles H. Israels, "New York Apartment Houses," *Arch Rec* XI (July 1901), p. 477; Schuyler, "The Works of the Late Richard M. Hunt," in Jordy and Coe, eds., *American Architecture and Other Writings* (Cambridge, Mass.: Harvard University Press, 1961), vol. 2, pp. 519–20; Stokes, "Appendix: Notes on Plans," in Ford, *Slums and Housing,* vol. 2, pp. 879–80, pl. 2D; Alan Burnham, "The New York Architecture of Richard Morris Hunt," *JSAH* XI (May 1952), p. 11; Baker, *Richard Morris Hunt,* pp. 204–8; Stern, "With Rhetoric," p. 80.

31. Montgomery Schuyler, "The Works of the Late Richard M. Hunt," in Jordy and Coe, eds., *American Architecture and Other Writings,* vol. 2, pp. 507–8; Burnham, "The New York Architecture of Richard Morris Hunt," p. 11.

32. The Vancorlear Apartment house is illustrated in *AABN* VII (January 24, 1880), p. 28, pl. 213. "Apartment Houses IV," *AABN* XXXI (January 17, 1891), pp. 37–39. See also "The Dakota Apartment House," *AABN* XX (July 24, 1886); "The Dakota Apartment House," *Sanitary Engineer* II (1885), p. 271; *Central Park West — West 73rd – 74th Street Historic District Designation Report,* Landmarks Preservation Commission, New York, 1977; Stern, "With Rhetoric," pp. 87–88; Diana S. Waite, "The Dakota," *New York Architecture* (HABS No. NY-5467), pp. 55–67.

33. Hubert, Pirsson and Hoddick, "New York Flats and French Flats," *Arch Rec* II (July 1892), pp. 55–64. This project is discussed by Handlin, *The American Home,* p. 226, and Stern, "With Rhetoric," p. 88.

34. For a plan of the Model Houses in Streatham Street, see Nikolaus Pevsner, "Early Working Class Housing," *Architectural Review* (London) XCIII (1943) reprinted in Pevsner, *Studies in Art, Architecture and Design* (New York: Walker and Company, 1968), vol. 2, pp. 18, 30–31.

35. John Nelson Tarn, *Five Per Cent Philanthropy* (London: Cambridge University Press, 1973), pp. 44–51.

36. Stokes, "Appendix: Notes on Plans," in Ford, *Slums and Housing,* p. 880, pl. 3A, B, p. 883, pl. 6C.

37. See Howard D. Kramer, "The Germ Theory and the Early Public Health Program in the United States," *Bulletin of the History of Medicine* XXII (May–June 1948), p. 245.

38. See Flagg, "Tenement-House Evil," pp. 108–17. See also Potter, "A Study of Some New York Tenement-House Problems," pp. 128–40; Landau, *Edward T. and William A. Potter: American Victorian Architects,* pp. 400–409; Handlin, *The American Home,* pp. 207–10.

39. Alfredo Melani, "Lettre d'Italie à 'La Construction Moderne,'" *La Construction Moderne* IX (July 21, 1894), pp. 493–95. Lucas, *Etude sur les habitations à bon marché,* pp. 150–56, figs. 47–49.

40. See "Brasserie J.-A. Pripp et Cie" in Charles Lucas, *Les habitations à bon marché en France et à l'étranger,* new edition by Will Darvillé (Paris: Librairie de la Construction Moderne [1912]), pp. 526–27, fig. 365. A light-court plan for a tenement house in Berlin appears in T. M. Clark, "Apartment-Houses," *AABN* XCI (January 5, 1907), p. 11, fig. 26.

41. Flagg, "Tenements," p. 2 (EFP, AL, CU).

42. "Health and Profit," *New York Times,* November 29, 1896, p. 13. Tenement House Committee of 1894, *Report,* No. 37 (Albany, 1895); and Lubove, *The Progressives and the Slums,* pp. 88–94.

43. The City and Suburban Homes Company was incorporated on July 6, 1896. *First Annual Report of the City & Suburban Homes Company,* New York, 1897. I wish to thank Cynthia Gould Wilcox for making City and Suburban Homes Company annual reports (1897–1921) available to me. See also "Health and Profit," *New York Times,* November 29, 1896, p. 13.

44. Veiller, "Tenement House Reform in New York City, 1834–1900," in De Forest and Veiller, eds., *The Tenement House Problem,* vol. 1, p. 108.

45. An excerpt from the City and Suburban Homes Company prospectus was published in "Health and Profit," *New York Times,* November 29, 1896, p. 13.

46. "Dr. Gould Killed by a Horse's Kick," obituary, *New York Times,* August 19, 1915, p. 9. H.S.W. [Helen Sumner Woodbury], "Elgin Ralston Lovell Gould," *DAB,* VII (New York: Charles Scribner's Sons, 1931), pp. 449–50. See also Lubove, *The Progressives and the Slums,* pp. 102–5.

47. E.R.L. Gould, *The Housing of the Working People,* Eighth Special Report of the Commissioner of Labor (Washington: Government Printing Office, 1895).

48. "Profitable Philanthropy in the Housing of the Working Classes," *Scientific American* LXXV (December 12, 1896), p. 422.

49. "Health and Profit," *New York Times,* November 29, 1896, p. 13.

50. In addition to Gould, the jury consisted of W. H. Folsom of the Improved Dwellings' Association, and A. W. Longfellow, an architect trained at the Ecole des Beaux-Arts who had experience in tenement house planning in Boston. See "Health and Profit," *New York Times,* November 29, 1896, p. 13.

51. See Ernest Flagg, "The New York Tenement-House Evil and Its Cure," in *The Poor in Great Cities* (New York: Charles Scribner's Sons, 1895), fig. 5, plan B. This is a revised version of Flagg's *Scribner's* article of 1894.

52. The program for the competition of 1896 stated that "no courts enclosed on all sides shall contain less than 900 square feet and should be as nearly square as possible; and no court enclosed on three sides shall be less than one-quarter as wide as it is deep from the open end." The program also required that "no wells or light shafts shall be used." See Stokes, "Appendix: Architectural Competitions," in Ford, *Slums and Housing,* vol. 2, p. 912.

53. Stokes, "Appendix: Notes on Plans," in Ford, *Slums and Housing,* vol. 2, p. 884.

54. "Model Tenement Houses," *New York Daily Tribune,* November 28, 1896, p. 7, and "Model Apartment Houses," *Architecture and Building* XXVI (January 2, 1897), p. 8.

55. Flagg, "Tenements," p. 6 (EFP, AL, CU).

56. Ibid., p. 7.

57. Norval White and Elliot Willensky, *AIA Guide to New York City,* rev. ed. (New York: Macmillan Publishing Co., 1978), pp. 174, 180–81.

58. *First Annual Report of the City & Suburban Homes Company,* New York, 1897.

59. *Central Park West — West 73rd – 74th Street Historic District Designation Report.* For the development of the New York row house in the vicinity of the elevated station at 72nd Street and for the holdings of the Clark Estate, see Sarah Bradford Landau, "The Row Houses of New York's West Side," *JSAH* XXXIV (March 1975), pp. 20–21.

60. *First Annual Report of the City & Suburban Homes Company,* New York, 1897 and *Second Annual Report, City & Suburban Homes Company,* New York, 1898.

61. "Better Homes for the Poor," *New York World,* November 29, 1896. I am grateful to Cynthia Gould Wilcox for making this newspaper clipping available to me. See also "Health and Profit," *New York Times,* November 29, 1896, p. 13, and *First Annual Report of the City & Suburban Homes Company,* New York, 1897.

62. For a comprehensive study of Scientific Management during the Progressive Era in America, see Samuel Haber, *Efficiency and Uplift* (Chicago: University of Chicago Press, 1964).

63. Veiller, "Tenement House Reform in New York City, 1834–1900," in De Forest and Veiller, eds., *The Tenement House Problem,* vol. 1, p. 108.

64. Stokes, "Appendix: Historical Summary," in Ford, *Slums and Housing,* vol. 2, p. 870.

65. "Health and Profit," *New York Times,* November 29, 1896, p. 13.

66. Ibid.

67. The structural features as well as the amenities are discussed in the *Second Annual Report, City & Suburban Homes Company,* New York, 1898. See also Veiller, "Tenement House Reform in New York City, 1834–1900," in De Forest and Veiller, eds., *The Tenement House Problem,* vol. 1, pp. 108–9.

68. "Health and Profit," *New York Times,* November 29, 1896, p. 13.

69. Stokes, "Appendix: Historical Summary," in Ford, *Slums and Housing,* vol. 2, p. 871.

70. For this comparison, see Veiller, "Tenement House Reform in New York City, 1834–1900," De Forest and Veiller, eds., *The Tenement House Problem,* vol. 1, p. 109. Professor Lubove examines the matter of rents in *The Progressives and the Slums,* pp. 108–9, n. 48.

71. Gould's use of the Octavia Hill method of rent collection has been the subject of recent study. See Lubove, *The Progressives and the Slums,* pp. 105–10, and Eugenie Ladner Birch and Deborah S. Gardner, "The Seven-Percent Solution: A Review of Philanthropic Housing, 1870–1910," *Journal of Urban History* VII (August 1981), p. 424. Tarn reviews Octavia Hill's method in his *Five Per Cent Philanthropy,* pp. 72–73.

72. See *Annual Reports, City & Suburban Homes Company,* New York, 1898, 1899, 1900, 1901, and 1902.

73. Veiller, "Tenement House Reform in New York City, 1834–1900," in De Forest and Veiller, eds., *The Tenement House Problem,* vol. 1, p. 109.

74. *Third Annual Report, City & Suburban Homes Company,* New York, 1899.

75. See *Annual Reports, City & Suburban Homes Company,* New York, 1898, 1899, 1900, 1901, and 1902. In his first annual report, Gould stated the company's goal: "to offer to capital what is believed to be a safe and permanent five per cent investment." See *First Annual Report, City & Suburban Homes Company,* New York, 1897.

76. Tarn discusses and illustrates a number of model tenement houses built by the George

Peabody Estate. See especially the Peabody Estate, Peabody Avenue, Pimlico, 1876–78, in Tarn, *Five Per Cent Philanthropy,* p. 50, pl. 4.7.

77. Flagg, "The Planning of Apartment Houses and Tenements," p. 86.

78. Flagg, "Tenements," p. 7 (EFP, AL, CU).

79. A large complex of thirteen tenement houses, Ware's earliest buildings of the First Avenue Estate at 401–423 East 64th Street (1900) contained 869 apartments. Stokes, "Appendix: Notes on Plans," in Ford, *Slums and Housing,* vol. 2, p. 903. See also *Annual Reports, City & Suburban Homes Company,* New York, 1899 and 1900.

80. Flagg, "Tenements," pp. 3, 6. Arthur T. Sutcliffe, "Why the Model Fireproof Tenement Company" (unpublished history of the company [1959]), pp. 1–2 (ATSP, AL, CU).

81. See "Model Tenements Planned," *New York Tribune,* March 3, 1899, p. 3; Sutcliffe, "Why the Model Fireproof Tenement Company," pp. 1–2 (ATSP, AL, CU). See also [Ernest Flagg] Prospectus of the Model Fireproof Tenement Co. [1909], pp. 1–16 (ATSP, AL, CU).

82. The New York Fireproof Tenement Association's first model tenements were located at 567–569 Tenth Avenue, 505–515 West 41st Street, and 500–512 West 42nd Street (1899–1901). See Ernest Flagg, "The Best Method of Tenement Construction," *Charities and The Commons* XVII (October 1906), p. 80. A plan and elevation appear in "Works," pp. 38–39, figs. 35, 36.

83. Flagg, "Tenements," p. 7 (EFP, AL, CU).

84. *Second Annual Report, City and Suburban Homes Company,* New York, 1898. [Flagg] *Prospectus of the Model Fireproof Tenement Co.,* p. 8 (ATSP, AL, CU).

85. [Flagg] *Prospectus of the Model Fireproof Tenement Co.,* p. 2 (ATSP, AL, CU).

86. A plan of the tenements at 506–516 West 47th Street appears in Stokes, "Appendix: Notes on Plans," in Ford, *Slums and Housing,* vol. 2, pp. 884, 902, pl. 29E. Four additional model tenements in New York designed by Flagg also employed fireproof construction: D. O. Mills Tenements, 183–185 Sullivan Street (1897–98); Bishop Tenements, 58–62 Hester Street (1901); Monroe Street Tenements (1902); De Forest Fireproof Tenements, a seven-story building at 203–205 East 27th Street (1906–7). See List of Works; [Flagg] *Prospectus of the Model Fireproof Tenement Co.,* p. 10 (ATSP, AL, CU); Stokes, "Appendix: Notes on Plans," in Ford, *Slums and Housing,* vol. 2, p. 903.

87. [Flagg] *Prospectus of the Model Fireproof Tenement Co.,* pp. 4–7 (ATSP, AL, CU).

88. In 1925 the Model Fireproof Tenement Company issued a 10 percent dividend and a 2 percent extra dividend. For reports of the earnings and dividends during these years, see Sutcliffe, "Why the Model Fireproof Tenement Company," pp. 4–14 (ATSP, AL, CU).

89. Sutcliffe, "Why the Model Fireproof Tenement Company," p. 7 (ATSP, AL, CU). See also [Flagg] *Prospectus of the Model Fireproof Tenement Co.,* p. 1 (ATSP, AL, CU).

90. "Appraisal, Charlesbank Homes, 333–343 Charles Street," by Carleton Hunneman [Hunneman and Company, Inc.], February 29, 1960 (Charlesbank Homes).

91. See Ernest Flagg Diary, October 11, 1909 (EFP, AL, CU).

92. "Charter of Charlesbank Homes," July 12, 1911 (Charlesbank Homes).

93. Conditions at the time of its appraisal in 1958 showed that the building was "largely occupied" ("Appraisal, Charlesbank Homes," by Carleton Hunneman). Herbert J. Gans has recorded the dramatic events leading up to the wholesale destruction and redevelopment of the West End in his sociological study, *The Urban Villagers* (New York: Free Press, 1962).

94. De Forest and Veiller, eds., *The Tenement House Problem,* vol. 2, Appendix I, pp. 95–96; Ford, *Slums and Housing,* vol. 1, p. 216.

95. Veiller, "Tenement House Reform in New York City, 1834–1900," in De Forest and Veiller, eds., *The Tenement House Problem,* vol. 1, pp. 109–16.

96. Flagg, "Tenements," p. 3 (EFP, AL, CU).

97. Lawrence Veiller, *Housing Reform* (New York: Charities Publication Committee, 1910), pp. 63–70.

98. Flagg, "Tenements," p. 5 (EFP, AL, CU).

99. Lubove, *The Progressives and the Slums,* p. 126; De Forest and Veiller, eds., *The Tenement House Problem,* vol. 2, Appendix I, p. 99.

100. For a history of the proceedings of the Tenement House Commission of 1900, see De Forest and Veiller, eds., *The Tenement House Problem,* vol. 2, Appendix I, pp. 93–100. Lubove discusses the work of the commission in *The Progressives and the Slums,* pp. 117–49.

101. The Flagg and Stokes plans based on 50-foot-wide lots are discussed and reproduced in Stokes, "Appendix: Historical Summary" and "Appendix: Notes on Plans" in Ford, *Slums and Housing,* vol. 2, pp. 870, 887, pls. 10D, 10E; Lubove, "I. N. Phelps Stokes," pp. 79–80.

102. The Tenement House Act [Law] of 1901 is contained in De Forest and Veiller, eds., *The Tenement House Problem,* vol. 2, Appendix V, pp. 167–99. Ford summarizes these provisions in his *Slums and Housing,* vol. 1, pp. 217–20.

103. Alfred Medioli has identified two new-law building patterns: one an inverted "T" plan, the other a light-court plan based on a 50-foot-wide lot. See "Housing Form and Rehabilitation in New York City," in Richard Plunz, ed., *Housing Form and Public Policy in the United States* (New York: Praeger, 1980), pp. 146–51, figs. 43, 44, 47, 48, 49, 51.

104. See especially First Avenue Estate, 401–423 East 64th Street (1899–1900) and 402–416 East 65th Street (1168–1200 First Avenue) of 1906. See also 501–539 East 78th Street, 502–542 East 79th Street (1470–1496 Avenue A) of 1901–13; 415–419 East 73rd Street (1907); 429 East 64th Street, 430 East 65th Street (1193–1207 Avenue A) of 1915. Stokes, "Appendix: Notes on Plans," in Ford, *Slums and Housing,* vol. 2, p. 903. See also *Annual Reports, City & Suburban Homes Company,* New York, 1899–1916.

105. The Tuskegee tenement and Phipps House model tenement are discussed and illustrated in Ford, *Slums and Housing,* vol. 2, pp. 680, 740–43, 889, figs. 121, 137, pls. 11B, 12C. Lubove, "I. N. Phelps Stokes," pp. 81–82.

106. Henry Atterbury Smith, "Exterior Stairs," *AABN* XCVII (February 23, 1910), pp. 93–94, 96. Henry L. Shively, M.D., "Hygienic and Economic Features of the East River Homes Foundation," *The New York Architect* V (November–December 1911), pp. 197–204. See also Stern, "With Rhetoric," pp. 84–85, 106 and n. 38, figs. 15–18.

107. The Apthorp and McKim, Mead & White's courtyard apartment house at 277 Park Avenue are discussed and illustrated in Stern, "With Rhetoric," pp. 90–91, figs. 29–33. For illustrations of Warren & Wetmore's apartment house at 270 Park Avenue, see Werner Hegemann and Elbert Peets, *Civic Art* (New York: Paul Wenzel & Maurice Krakow, 1922), pp. 194–95, figs. 832–34.

108. Medioli, "Housing Form and Rehabilitation in New York City," in Plunz, ed., *Housing Form,* p. 148.

109. [Flagg] *Prospectus of the Model Fireproof Tenement Co.,* p. 3. Flagg published an earlier version of a light-court plan for a 50-foot-wide lot in his 1903 article, "The Planning of Apartments and Tenements," p. 85, fig. 2.

110. Stokes, "Appendix: Historical Summary," in Ford, *Slums and Housing,* p. 871.

111. Stokes's 1901 plan is discussed and illustrated in De Forest and Veiller, eds., *The Tenement House Problem,* vol. 2, pp. 58–60. See also Stokes, "Appendix: Notes on Plans," in Ford, *Slums and Housing,* pp. 887–88, pl. 11A; Lubove, "I. N. Phelps Stokes," pp. 80–81.

112. For a discussion and illustrations of the Dunbar Apartments, see Ford, *Slums and Housing,* vol. 2, pp. 743–44, 893, fig. 138, pl. 18B.

113. Richard Plunz reproduces Thomas's plan of the Homewood Garden Apartments in Plunz, ed., *Housing Form,* pp. 160–61, fig. 9. John Taylor Boyd, Jr., "Garden Apartments in Cities," *Arch Rec* XLVIII (July 1920), pp. 52, 64–65. The garden apartment is the subject of two recent studies: Richard Plunz, "Institutionalization of Housing Form in New York City, 1920–1950," in Plunz, ed., *Housing Form,* pp. 158–68; Stern, "With Rhetoric," pp. 92–100.

114. "Mills, Darius Ogden," *The National Cyclopaedia of American Biography,* XVIII (New

York: James T. White & Co., 1922), pp. 133–34. A third hotel, Mills House No. 3 at 161 West 36th Street (1906–7), was designed by architects Copeland & Dole. I wish to thank Alan Burnham for providing me with this information. A Greek Revival "terrace," De Pauw Row, once occupied the Bleecker Street site of Mills House No. 1. Talbot Hamlin, *Greek Revival Architecture in America* (New York: Dover Publications, 1964; orig. pub. 1944), p. 131. The conversion of Mills House No. 1 in 1974–75 is discussed in Steven Greenhouse's article, "Down-at-Heels Hotel Gets a Natty New Identity," *New York Times,* September 28, 1975, VIII, pp. 1, 12.

115. John Lloyd Thomas, "Workingmen's Hotels," *Municipal Affairs* III (March 1899), pp. 85–86. John Lloyd Thomas was the day manager of Mills House No. 1. For a comparison with Rowton House, see pp. 83–84 of Thomas's article. See also [A. Shaw], "Model Lodging Houses for New York," *Review of Reviews* XV (January 1897), p. 59.

116. Elevations of Mills House No. 1 were published in *Arch Rev* VI (January 1899), pls. VI, VII, VIII.

117. "Works," p. 42.

118. "About the World," *Scribner's Magazine* XX (July 1896), pp. 129–30; [Shaw], "Model Lodging Houses for New York," pp. 59–61; *AABN* LVII (August 21, 1897), p. 61; "Mills House No. 1," *New York Times,* October 28, 1897, p. 4; "First Mills Hotel Opened," *New York Times,* November 2, 1897, p. 16; "An Interesting Sociological Experiment," *Scientific American* LXXVII (November 6, 1897), p. 291; Rev. T. Alexander Hyde, "A Paying Philanthropy: The Mills Hotel," *The Arena* XX (July 1898), pp. 76–86; E. Idell Zeisloft, *The New Metropolis* (New York: D. Appleton & Co., 1899), pp. 244–45; Thomas, "Workingmen's Hotels," pp. 72–94; Jacob B. Riis, *The Battle with the Slum* (New York: Macmillan Co., 1902), pp. 154–67; Ford, *Slums and Housing,* vol. 2, p. 754, fig. 140.

119. Alan Horlick discusses the efforts of the YMCA and other institutions to regulate the conduct of young men in his *Country Boys and Merchant Princes: The Social Control of Young Men in New York* (Lewisburg, Pa.: Bucknell University Press, 1975), pp. 226–66. See also C. Howard Hopkins, *History of the Y.M.C.A. in North America* (New York: Association Press, 1951), pp. 151–61.

120. Parish & Schroeder's Naval Branch YMCA Building at 159–167 Sands Street, Brooklyn (1901–2), followed Flagg's example with bedroom cubicles banking the perimeter of its covered court and outside walls. Irving K. Pond, "Buildings of the Young Men's Christian Association, II," *Brickbuilder* XV (March 1906), pp. 57–58. *Yearbook of the Young Men's Christian Associations of North America,* 1902, pp. 66, 71.

121. Thomas, "Workingmen's Hotels," p. 89.

122. "Mills House No. 1," *New York Times,* October 28, 1897, p. 4.

123. "First Mills Hotel Opened," *New York Times,* November 2, 1897, p. 16.

124. Hyde, "A Paying Philanthropy: The Mills Hotel," p. 80.

125. Riis, *The Battle with the Slum,* p. 159.

126. Ibid., p. 161; Ford, *Slums and Housing,* vol. 1, p. 346.

127. [Shaw], "Model Lodging Houses for New York," p. 59.

128. Hyde, "A Paying Philanthropy: The Mills Hotel," p. 84. See also Riis, *The Battle with the Slum,* p. 167.

129. Riis, *The Battle with the Slum,* p. 162.

130. Sutcliffe, "Why the Model Fireproof Tenement Company," p. 17 (ATSP, AL, CU). Flagg, "Tenements," p. 8 (EFP, AL, CU).

131. Sutcliffe recorded Flagg's unsuccessful attempts to obtain either public or private financing. See "Why the Model Fireproof Tenement Company," pp. 18–24 (ATSP, AL, CU).

132. Flagg Court occupied the site of the Schlegel estate. See "Finds New Way to Build Suites," *The Sun,* September 24, 1932, newspaper clipping (ATSP, AL, CU); *World Telegram,* circa 1936, newspaper clipping, scrapbook (EFP, AL, CU). Descriptions of Flagg Court are contained in several building prospectuses: *"Flagg Court" Ridge Boulevard,* January 17, 1933; *Flagg Court,* a one-page promotional brochure (ATSP, AL, CU); *Addition to Flagg Court,* circa 1937 (author's collection). Units 6 and 8 were never constructed, see *"Flagg Court" Ridge Boulevard,* p. 32.

133. *Addition to Flagg Court,* p. 3 (author's collection). "Apartment Houses at Bay Ridge, Brooklyn, N.Y.," *Architectural Forum* LXVI (May 1937), p. 414.

134. "Chicago Buyer Gets Flagg Court," *New York Times,* April 7, 1948, p. 44. In 1935, the estimated cost of Flagg Court's construction was $400,000. See "$400,000 Apartment Planned in Brooklyn," *New York Times,* May 18, 1935, p. 31.

135. Ernest Flagg was the architect of Unit A. "Portfolio of Apartment Houses," *Arch Rec* LXXI (March 1932), pp. 167–69.

136. Ford, *Slums and Housing,* vol. 2, pp. 705, 896–97, fig. 128, pl. 24C. Plunz, "Institutionalization of Housing Form," in Plunz, ed., *Housing Form,* pp. 175–76, fig. 51. Grosvenor House is illustrated in A.S.G. Butler, *The Architecture of Sir Edwin Lutyens* (New York: Charles Scribner's Sons, 1950), vol. 3, p. 35, fig. 89. I am grateful to Richard Chafee for drawing to my attention the similarities between Flagg Court and Lutyens's work.

137. The Towers is discussed and illustrated in Stern, "With Rhetoric," pp. 94–95, figs. 44, 45.

138. For illustrations of these motifs in Lutyens's New Delhi buildings, see Robert Grant Irving, *Indian Summer* (New Haven: Yale University Press, 1981), p. 267, fig. 183 (arcaded veranda, Hyderabad House); pp. 216, 217, 222, figs. 122, 123, 129, 130

(Mughal Garden, Viceroy's House); pp. 164–65, 181, figs. 58, 76 (*chattris,* Viceroy's House); p. 281, figs. 192, 193 (*chattris,* Secretariats).

139. *Addition to Flagg Court,* pp. 11, 14 (author's collection).

140. Ibid., p. 6.

141. According to one building prospectus, Flagg Court was "restricted to gentiles and the most scrupulous care taken in the selection of tenants" (*Addition to Flagg Court,* p. 11 [author's collection]). *Flagg Court* (ATSP, AL, CU).

142. Ernest Flagg, "Flagg Court," unpublished essay, August 6, 1934 (EFP, AL, CU).

143. Equipment, utilities, and amenities are described in *"Flagg Court" Ridge Boulevard* (ASTP, AL, CU).

144. Lubove, "I. N. Phelps Stokes," p. 82.

145. Flagg, "Tenements," p. 3 (EFP, AL, CU).

146. Veiller, "Tenement House Reform in New York City, 1834–1900," in De Forest and Veiller, eds., *The Tenement House Problem,* vol. 1, p. 109.

CHAPTER NINE

1. The Flagg office functioned until the architect's death in 1947. However, at the completion of the Flagg Court housing project in 1937, only a few office employees remained. Arthur Sutcliffe, who attended to the management of the Model Fireproof Tenement Company, was among them. See List of Patents.

2. Flagg, "Heaven and Hell," in "Observations" (EFP, AL, CU).

3. Ernest Flagg, "New Light on Greek Art," the first of two parts, *JRIBA* XXXII (December 6, 1924), p. 57. "New Light on Greek Art" was the text for a paper which Flagg presented at the Institute of France at a session of the Academy of Fine Arts on June 27, 1924. It was also reprinted in *JAIA* XIII (January 1925), pp. 1–4.

4. Flagg, *Small Houses: Their Economic Design and Construction* (New York: Charles Scribner's Sons, 1922), p. 6; Ernest Flagg, "The Module System in Architectural Design," *Architecture* XLII (July 1920), p. 206.

5. A list of Flagg's nine articles on Greek design for *Architecture* from 1920 to 1931, along with Flagg's other publications and unpublished manuscripts that discuss his theory of the module and its application to design and construction, appear in Selected Writings by Ernest Flagg.

6. Flagg, "New Light on Greek Art," *JRIBA,* p. 59.

7. Flagg, "Vitruvius and His Module," p. 63. See J[ulien] Guadet, *Eléments et théorie de*

l'architecture (Paris: Librairie de la Construction Moderne, 1929; orig. pub. 1901–4), vol. 1, p. 97.

8. In his writings Flagg relied on the research of Victor Laloux, Maxime Collignon, Francis Cranmer Penrose, A. J. and Lucien Magne, Auguste Choisy, and J. I. Hittorf. See Victor A. F. Laloux, *Restauration d'Olympie* (Paris: Maison Quantin, 1889); Maxime Collignon, *Le Parthénon* (Paris: Librairie Hachette, 1914); Francis Cranmer Penrose, *An investigation of the principles of Athenian architecture* (London: W. Nicol, 1851). See Flagg, *Small Houses,* p. 6 and his "New Light on Greek Art," *JRIBA,* p. 58. Flagg said that he relied upon archaeologists' data rather than on firsthand calculations of Greek temples, so that no one could accuse him of changing the figures to suit his theory. Albert Homer Swanke, telephone interview with author, November 24, 1982.

9. "New Light on Greek Art," *JRIBA,* pp. 58–59; *The Parthenon Naos* (New York: Charles Scribner's Sons, 1928).

10. When Flagg met with the members of the Academy, according to René de Blonay, then a young Swiss architect working in the Flagg office who served as interpreter, the French academicians were vehemently opposed to Flagg's theory. "When Flagg gave his talk before the French Academy, one gentleman afterwards got up and said, 'it's all very well, but we believe in Vitruvius and nothing will convince us otherwise.' I wanted to get up and speak extemporaneously in Flagg's defense, but Flagg would not let me. Flagg probably didn't understand what he [the French academician] said and I never told him" (René de Blonay, interview with author, Katonah, New York, November 7, 1973).

11. See Jay Hambidge, *Dynamic Symmetry: The Greek Vase* (New Haven: Yale University Press, 1920), *The Parthenon and Other Greek Temples* (New Haven: Yale University Press, 1924), and *The Elements of Dynamic Symmetry* (New Haven: Yale University Press, 1926).

12. David P. Handlin, *The American Home* (Boston: Little, Brown and Company, 1979), p. 207. John Sergeant, *Frank Lloyd Wright's Usonian Houses* (New York: Whitney Library of Design, 1976).

13. The full extent of Flagg's nationwide impact on interwar housing is currently undetermined. Flagg's small houses have been the object of a recent study: Daniel Levy, "Ernest Flagg and His Impact on Stone House Construction, 1920–1954" (Ph.D. diss., University of Maryland, 1979).

14. Flagg, *Small Houses,* p. 3.

15. Flagg credited Durand's *"Précis d'Architecture"*; see Flagg, *Small Houses,* p. 8.

16. Guadet, *Eléments et théorie de l'architecture,* vol. 1, pp. 52–53.

17. See Peter Collins, "The Origins of Graph Paper as an Influence on Architectural Design," *JSAH* XXI (December 1962), pp. 159–62; Letters to the Editor, *JSAH* XXII (May 1963), p. 107.

18. According to a published report, Flagg's offer, made in a letter of December 14, 1946, to Trygve Lie, Secretary General of the United Nations, was received too late for consideration. "Staten Island Site Suggested to U.N.," *New York Times,* December 15, 1946, I, p. 5.

19. Ernest Flagg Diary, March 22, 1908 (EFP, AL, CU).

20. Ibid., June 7, 1908; November 29, 1908; December 2 and 19, 1908; and October 21, 1910.

21. Ibid., February 6, 1911. Arthur T. Sutcliffe Diary, May 12, 1913 (ATSP, AL, CU).

22. Arthur T. Sutcliffe Diary, October 6, 1917 (ATSP, AL, CU).

23. Dates for the small houses were obtained from the Flagg and Sutcliffe diaries, as well as from docket books for the Borough of Richmond, atlases, maps, and a few surviving building permits, plans, and other building records on file with the Buildings Department, Borough of Richmond, Borough Hall, Staten Island. I wish to thank Shirley Zavin of the New York City Landmarks Preservation Commission for her assistance with these building records.

24. See perspectives (with people drawn by his daughter, Betsy), plans, and photographs of the small houses in the proposed Flegg Ridge Estate in Flagg, *Small Houses,* pl. 1, p. 2 (South Gate House); pl. 4, p. 13 [Hickling Hollow]; pl. 16, pp. 48–50 ("House-on-the-Wall"); pl. 17, pp. 20, 53 [Tower House]; pl. 43, pp. 124–26 (Gate House); pl. 50, pp. 145–46 ("Bowcot").

25. *New Building Record* [docket book], 1923, #1456. Shirley Zavin kindly provided me with this information.

26. Daniel A. Levy, "Bow-cot and the Honeymoon Cottage," *Fine Homebuilding* (October–November 1981), pp. 28–35.

27. The extent of Flagg's building on Staten Island is recorded in the docket books. See *New Building Record* [docket book], No. 1, #457 (1906–7); No. 3, #1105 (1916–18); No. 4, #708 (1917–18); #528 and #1328 (1918–22); #a1163 (1920–22); #1375 (1921); #1620 (1921–22); #135 (1923–24); #1456 (1923–24); #1233 (1924–25).

28. Flagg, *Small Houses,* p. ix.

29. Ibid., p. 15.

30. See Part L, "Symmetry, Order, and Balance," ibid., pp. 144, 146.

31. See Part XX, "Proportion," ibid., pp. 60, 62.

32. Letter, Ernest Flagg to Charles L. Borie, February 23, 1937 (EFP, AL, CU).

33. Flagg, *Small Houses,* p. ix.

34. Ibid., p. 18.

35. For discussions of the early use of concrete construction in England and America, see Peter Collins, *Concrete* (London: Faber and Faber, 1959), pp. 36ff., and Carl W. Condit, *American Building Art: The Nineteenth Century* (New York: Oxford University Press, 1960), pp. 223ff.

36. Flagg, "Stone Walls and Their Construction," *Country Life* XLII (May 1922), p. 78, fig. 22. Auguste Choisy, *L'Art de bâtir chez les Romains* (Paris: Ducher et Cie, 1873), p. 23, fig. 5. During his student years in Paris, Flagg acquired a copy of Choisy.

37. Flagg, "Stone Walls and Their Construction," p. 78. William L. MacDonald, *The Architecture of the Roman Empire: An Introductory Study* (New Haven: Yale University Press, 1965), p. 147, and John B. Ward-Perkins, *Roman Architecture* (New York: Harry N. Abrams, 1977), pp. 152–53. Levy discusses Roman masonry and concrete construction as well as Choisy's interpretation of them in his "Ernest Flagg and His Impact on Stone House Construction, 1920–1954," pp. 19–51.

38. Flagg, "Stone Walls and Their Construction," p. 78. Flagg obtained his first patent for formwork in 1916. U.S. Patent No. 1,176,532, Support for Cement Material, March 21, 1916. For subsequent patents for formwork, see List of Patents.

39. The Flagg method of construction is explained in "Stone Walls and Their Construction," pp. 78, 80, and Part VI, "Mosaic Rubble," of *Small Houses*, pp. 18–21.

40. Flagg's patent for "Skylight Construction" (1926) is contained in the List of Patents. See "The Lighting of Temples," folder pertaining to unpublished manuscript, "The Recovery of Art" (EFP, AL, CU).

41. An explanation of the ridge-dormer is contained in Part III, "Ridge-Dormers," *Small Houses*, pp. 9–11.

42. See Part IX, "Partitions," ibid., pp. 28–30.

43. Ernest Flagg, "Standard Details of Construction" in *New Garden Homes* (Philadelphia: Ladies Home Journal [1928]). See List of Patents.

44. John H. White, Jr., *The American Railroad Passenger Car* (Baltimore and London: Johns Hopkins University Press, 1978), p. 441. Henry-Russell Hitchcock, *The Architecture of H. H. Richardson and His Times* (Cambridge, Mass.: MIT Press, 1966), p. 258, fig. 96. James F. O'Gorman, *H. H. Richardson and His Office* (Cambridge, Mass.: Harvard College Library, 1974), pp. 182–83, cat. nos. 33a, 33b. Jeffrey Karl Ochsner, *H. H. Richardson, Complete Architectural Works* (Cambridge, Mass.: MIT Press, 1983), p. 367, cat. no. 128.

45. Ernest Flagg, *The Flagg Car*, prospectus, circa 1928 (ATSP, AL, CU). From 1916 to 1934 Flagg obtained six U.S. patents for sleeping cars; in 1924 and 1925 he obtained five foreign patents for sleeping cars. See Patents. Arthur T. Sutcliffe Diary, entries for June 11, September 16, November 24, and November 28, 1924; February 15 and April 28, 1928; June 30 and July 7, 1930; February 9, March 2, and March 4, 1938 (ATSP, AL, CU).

46. John White documents the Pullman Company's declining years in *The American Railroad Passenger Car,* pp. 263–66.

47. See Part XVIII, "Foundations and Cellars," in *Small Houses,* pp. 54, 56. Wright also eliminated conventional dormers; see his "Prairie Architecture," in Edgar Kaufmann, Jr., and Ben Raeburn, eds., Frank Lloyd Wright: *Writings and Buildings* (Cleveland: World Publishing Company, 1960), p. 41.

48. See entries in the Ernest Flagg Diary, July 19 to September 29, 1908. The trip included tours of Gloucestershire and Oxfordshire where Flagg drove through the Cotswold Hills and also recorded visits to Norman churches. The tour of Normandy and Brittany was made from August 10 to August 22, 1908 (EFP, AL, CU).

49. Flagg, *Small Houses,* pp. 13, 14, 122, 123, pls. 4, 42. Ernest Flagg Diary, July 30, 1908 (EFP, AL, CU).

50. René de Blonay, interview with author, South Salem, New York, June 30, 1973.

51. The church was commissioned as part of the Huguenot-Walloon Tercentenary celebration. The Bayard and de Forest (Shepherd) families, both church donors and Flagg patrons, were undoubtedly responsible for retaining Flagg as architect. Charles W. Leng and William T. Davis, *Staten Island and Its People: A History, 1609–1929* (New York: Lewis Historical Publishing Company, Inc., 1930), vol. 1, pp. 441–42. *New York City Guide* (New York: Random House, 1939), p. 613.

52. Instructions to that effect were inserted in each copy of *Small Houses.*

53. House Nos. 12, 18, 22, and 31 are among the grandest. Flagg, *Small Houses,* pp. 38, 55, 67, 93.

54. See Part VII, "Planning," ibid., pp. 22, 24.

55. The Gate House also contained two servants' rooms and a servants' hall; "House-on-the-Wall" and the Tower House had rooms for two house servants and a chauffeur. Flagg, *Small Houses,* pp. 48, 53, 125, pls. 16, 17, 43.

56. Mrs. John Melcher, interview with author, New York, April 24, 1973.

57. René de Blonay, interview with author, South Salem, New York, June 30, 1973.

58. Arthur Cort Holden, interview with author, New York, January 24, 1978.

59. René de Blonay, interview with author, South Salem, New York, June 30, 1973.

60. See Ernest Flagg, "The New McCall House, Step By Step," *McCall's Magazine* (October 1924), scrapbook (EFP, AL, CU). See also Arthur T. Sutcliffe Diary, November 18, 1924 (ATSP, AL, CU).

61. Leigh French, Jr., an architect specializing in housing, supported Flagg's "candid and rational methods" in his article "The Small House and Candor in Designing," *Architectural Forum* XLIV (March 1926), pp. 175–84.

62. Flagg, *Small Houses,* pp. ix, x. See also Flagg, "Waste in Building," in "Observations" (EFP, AL, CU). Harold Cary, *Build a Home — Save a Third* (New York: Reynolds Publishing Company, Inc., [1924]).

63. Harold Cary, "More Help for Home Builders," *Collier's* LXXI (May 5, 1923), p. 6. See also Harold Cary, "More House for Less Money, the Work of Ernest Flagg," *Scientific American* CXXVIII (March 1923), pp. 158–59; Flagg admitted that Cary "naturally made many mistakes and said a great deal that was not true, though he supposed it was . . ." (Flagg, "Waste in Building," in "Observations" [EFP, AL, CU]).

64. Harold Cary, "Collier's House is Done! Cost $10,767," *Collier's* LXXIII (May 17, 1924), pp. 14, 35. For a discussion of the first Collier's House, see Levy, "Ernest Flagg and His Impact on Stone House Construction, 1920–1954," pp. 91–100.

65. Harold Cary, "Counting the Costs on the Small House," *Collier's* LXXV (June 6, 1925), pp. 23, 39–40. For a discussion of the second Collier's House and a bibliography of *Collier's* articles on both houses, see Levy, "Ernest Flagg and His Impact on Stone House Construction, 1920–1954," pp. 100–103, 182.

66. In 1923 Harriet Sisson Gillespie claimed that "Ernest Flagg's Method of Small-House Construction Cut Costs in Halves"; see "A New Modus of House Building," *House Beautiful* LIV (September 1923), p. 218. During the late twenties and thirties several writers published evidence to prove that houses employing Flagg's methods were more expensive than Cary and others claimed: Margaret Hatfield, "How We Built Our $18,000 House for $28,500," *House Beautiful* LXIV (September 1928), pp. 272–73, 300–302, 304; Gerald Lynton Kaufman, "What is the Cost of an $18,000 House?" *House Beautiful* LXV (January 1929), pp. 52–53; Marjorie Reid Rodes, "Stone at Low Cost," *House Beautiful* LXXVIII (October 1935), pp. 74–75, 82.

67. For a study of Frazier Forman Peters's work in the 1930s, see Levy, "Ernest Flagg and His Impact on Stone Construction, 1920–1954," pp. 103–16.

68. Frazier Forman Peters, *Houses of Stone* (Westport, Conn.: 1933).

69. See Peters's second book, *Without Benefit of Architect* (New York: G. P. Putnam's Sons, 1937).

70. Frazier Forman Peters, *Pour Yourself a House: Low-Cost Building With Concrete and Stone* (New York: Whittlesey House, 1949), p. 8. Peters's late career is discussed in Levy, "Ernest Flagg and His Impact on Stone House Construction, 1920–1954," pp. 118–22.

71. The most significant interpreter of Flagg's methods both during and after the Second World War was Paul Corey. His books include *Buy an Acre: America's Second Front* (New York: Dial Press, 1944); *Build a Home* (New York: Dial Press, 1946); and *Homemade Homes* (New York: William Sloan Associates, 1950). See also Levy, "Ernest Flagg and His Impact on Stone House Construction, 1920–1954," pp. 122–24.

72. Arthur T. Sutcliffe Diary, May 16, 1924; July 19 and 26, 1924; November 24 and 28,

1924; December 23, 1924 (ATSP, AL, CU). Research is currently under way on several colonies of small houses based on Flagg's designs, including one built by Arnold F. Meyer and Company in Milwaukee. See Richard W. E. Perrin, "Up From Eclecticism: The Latter-Day Architecture of Ernest Flagg," *Wisconsin Academy Review* XV (March 1976), pp. 18–21. I wish to thank Virginia A. Palmer for providing me with a copy of this article.

73. Flagg, "Waste in Building," in "Observations" (EFP, AL, CU). The number of undocumented "Flagg" houses continues to expand.

74. Helen and Scott Nearing, *Living the Good Life* (New York: Schocken Books, 1970; orig. pub. 1954), p. 57.

75. See Chapter 3, "We Build a Stone House," *Living the Good Life,* pp. 47–81.

76. Letter, Scott Nearing to author, October 16, 1973.

77. Ibid.

78. Ken Kern, Steve Magers, and Lou Penfield, *Owner Builder Guide: Stone Masonry* (Oakhurst, Calif.: Owner Builder Publications, 1976), pp. 136–41.

79. Mark Alvarez (Assistant Editor, *Fine Homebuilding*) to author, September 16, 1982.

80. Letter, William Gray Purcell to Wayne Andrews, February 18, 1950 (New-York Historical Society, New York City). I wish to thank Wayne Andrews for drawing my attention to this correspondence.

81. Photographs of the Bradford, Todd and Arnold houses are included in the Andrews correspondence (New-York Historical Society, New York City).

82. Letter, William Gray Purcell to Wayne Andrews, February 18, 1950 (New-York Historical Society, New York City). David Gebhard discusses several of these houses, although he does not mention Purcell's interest in Flagg's small stone houses. "William Gray Purcell and George Grant Elmslie and the Early Progressive Movement in American Architecture from 1900 to 1920" (Ph.D. diss., University of Minnesota, 1957), p. 277.

83. Letter, William Gray Purcell to Mary Mix, November 3, 1945 (New-York Historical Society, New York City).

84. Contracts were awarded initially for 500 units, then for 650 units. See Arthur T. Sutcliffe Diary, April 27 and June 6, 1918 (ATSP, AL, CU).

85. Sam Bass Warner, *Urban Wilderness* (New York: Harper & Row, 1972), p. 223. For a survey of the Emergency Fleet Corporation and the U.S. Housing Corporation activities during the First World War, see Miles L. Colean, *Housing for Defense* (New York: Twentieth Century Fund, 1940), pp. 9–26.

86. Warner, *Urban Wilderness,* p. 222.

87. Memo, E. R. Will to F. L. Ackerman, May 15 [1918], *Records of the U.S. Shipping*

Board — Passenger, Transportation and Housing Division, Project File 9 – I (Chester, Pa., Sun Village), Record Group 32, National Archives (hereinafter cited as *Records, U.S. Shipping Board*).

88. Ernest Flagg, "Housing of the Workingmen," *Architecture* XXXVIII (October 1918), p. 269. A perspective drawing and rendering of an apartment group are contained in *United States shipping board emergency fleet corporation: Types of housing for shipbuilders* [Philadelphia], 1919. See especially Sunnyside Gardens (Clarence Stein and Henry Wright, planners; Frederick L. Ackerman, architect), Queens, New York, of 1924. Garden City planners accommodated Sunnyside to an existing street grid. "The Anglo-American Suburb," Robert A. M. Stern and John Montague Massengale, eds., *Architectural Design* LI (October – November 1981), p. 46. Richard Plunz, "Institutionalization of Housing Form in New York City, 1920 – 1950," in Richard Plunz, ed., *Housing Form and Public Policy in the United States* (New York: Praeger, 1980), pp. 165 – 67.

89. Flagg, *Small Houses,* pp. 61, 106, pls. 20, 36.

90. See "Districts 3 & 10, Chester" [itemization of building materials], May 11, 1918, *Records, U.S. Shipping Board.*

91. Arthur T. Sutcliffe Diary, June 29, July 17, and August 2, 1918 (ATSP, AL, CU).

92. Ibid., August 2 and September 3, 1918.

93. Colean records: "On December 12, 1918 Congress directed that work cease on all projects which were less than 75 per cent completed" (*Housing for Defense,* p. 24).

94. Memo, W. S. Church, Supervisor of Plans, Construction Branch, to J. B. Fisher, Chief, Property Bureau, February 21, 1919, *Records, U.S. Shipping Board.*

95. John Summerson, *The Classical Language of Architecture* (London: Methuen & Co., 1966), p. 45.

96. Flagg's belief in a common access to good design paralleled a notion among intellectuals during the First World War about a common access to culture. See May, *The End of American Innocence* (Chicago: Quadrangle Books, 1964), p. 329.

97. Arthur T. Sutcliffe Diary, April 10, 1947 (ATSP, AL, CU).

98. Although the quotation from Leo Marx refers specifically to William Ralph Emerson's admiration for the inventor and the advance of science, it can be applied to an increasingly prevalent attitude throughout the late nineteenth century. Leo Marx, *The Machine in the Garden* (London, Oxford, New York: Oxford University Press, 1964), p. 230.

99. Siegfried Giedion, *Mechanization Takes Command* (New York: Oxford University Press, 1948), pp. 41 – 44.

100. René de Blonay, interview with author, Katonah, New York, November 7, 1973.

Index

402